CARLING
POB
QUIZ
BOOK

CARLING POB QUIZ BOOK

Compiled by Paul Drew

Cartoons by Peter Coupe

ARCTURUS

Published by
Arcturus Publishing Limited
1-7 Shand Street
London SE1 2ES

For Bookmart Limited
Desford Road
Enderby
Leicester LE9 5AD

This edition published 2000

Printed and bound by WS Bookwell in Finland

The views and opinions of the writer are not necessarily
those of Bass Brewers Limited

Compiled by Paul Drew

© Arcturus Publishing Limited

ISBN 1 - 84193 - 009 - 1

FOREWORD

Poet laureate Alfred Tennyson penned the immortal line "Knowledge comes, but wisdom lingers". While the second part of that quotation is certainly true, the first is open to debate. Sometimes knowledge misses the bus, arriving only after you've handed the quiz sheet over the counter. Sometimes it gets stuck outside the station, before emerging from a tunnel in the middle of the night to reveal that it was indeed Sean Connery that played James Bond in *Goldfinger*, not Charlie Drake, which you wrote down and forgot to cross out. Knowledge comes of course, but invariably to others.

This book is intended to redress the balance, as well as to give pleasure and to inform. You might want to use it as material for a pub quiz you've arranged yourself or else you can ingest the information these pages impart to impress your mates down the local. The questions herein may just give you the edge when push comes to shove. When the eight beer vouchers or million quid are handed out at the end of the evening, you'll be glad of your wise purchase. This book may be your best short-term investment for long-term gain.

Enjoy the quizzes!

PAUL DREW

GENERAL KNOWLEDGE

ENTERTAINMENT

SPORT

POP MUSIC

ART AND LITERATURE

GEOGRAPHY

WORDS

SCIENCE

PEOPLE

HISTORY

GENERAL KNOWLEDGE

1. The heavy woollen cloth with a thick nap called duffel is named after a town in which European country?

2. Who is the author of the play *The Quare Fellow*?

3. What is the name of the Sunday preceding Ash Wednesday?

4. Who wrote the novel *The Ipcress File*?

5. What is the motto of the British Royal Air Force?

6. In which continent is the mountain system of the Andes?

7. What is the name of the Mediterranean coastal region between Cannes in France and La Spezia in Italy?

8. What was the name of *Lady Chatterley's Lover*?

9. Who was 1989 Wimbledon men's singles tennis champion?

10. What was the name of the French underground movement that fought against the Germans in World War II?

11. Who wrote the 1980 novel *Princess Daisy*?

12. Where would an Edwardian woman have worn a toque?

13. Which singer starred in the 1957 film *Jailhouse Rock*?

14. Who won a Best Actor Oscar for the film *The Godfather*?

15. Which British philosopher's books include *Principles of Mathematics*?

ANSWERS 1. Belgium **2.** Brendan Behan **3.** Quinquagesima **4.** Len Deighton **5.** 'Per ardua ad astra' **6.** South America **7.** The Riviera **8.** Oliver Mellors **9.** Boris Becker **10.** The Maquis **11.** Judith Krantz **12.** On the head - it was a small brimless hat **13.** Elvis Presley **14.** Marlon Brando **15.** Bertrand Russell.

ENTERTAINMENT

1. Who plays detective Philo Vance in the 1940 film *Calling Philo Vance*?

2. Director Jack Fisk's wife took the lead in the 1981 film *Raggedy Man*. Who is she?

3. Which child actor played the lead in the 1950 film *Kim*?

4. Who is the stepfather of Cenerentola in Rossini's opera *La Cenerentola*?

5. Who directed the 1981 film *Raiders of the Lost Ark*?

6. Who played Hector in the 2000 BBC TV drama *Monarch of the Glen*?

7. Which former *Coronation Street* actress played Dolly in *Dinnerladies*?

8. Who played Dr. Chase Meridian in the film *Batman Forever*?

9. Who plays Gale Weathers in the film *Scream 3*?

10. Who directed the 1948 film *Call Northside 777*?

11. Who directed the 1981 film *Southern Comfort*?

12. Who does Deena Payne play in *Emmerdale*?

13. In which U.S. state is the 1980 film *Heaven's Gate* set?

14. Who plays the lead in the 1981 film *An Unsuitable Job for a Woman*?

15. Who plays Albert Einstein in the 1994 film *I.Q.*?

ANSWERS 1. James Stephenson **2.** Sissy Spacek **3.** Dean Stockwell **4.** Don Magnifico **5.** Steven Spielberg **6.** Richard Briers **7.** Thelma Barlow **8.** Nicole Kidman **9.** Courtenay Cox **10.** Henry Hathaway **11.** Walter Hill **12.** Viv Windsor **13.** Wyoming **14.** Pippa Guard **15.** Walter Matthau.

SPORT

1. By what score did Uruguay beat Argentina in the 1930 World Cup Final in football?

2. On which horse did Tony McCoy win his 200th race of the 1999/00 season?

3. Who was men's 100m breaststroke swimming world champion in 1998?

4. Who in 1977 became the youngest player to appear in a Ryder Cup?

5. Who is the Olympic silver medal-winning father of runner Inger Miller?

6. How much did Steve Davis win for taking the 1988 World Matchplay title in snooker?

7. At what sport has Peter Knowles been a No. 1 in England?

8. Who won the 1965 golf World Cup?

9. What nationality is runner Gabriela Szabo?

10. With which sport are Elgin Baylor and Hakeem Olajuwan associated?

11. Where were the 1973 World Student Games held?

12. Diminuendo and Melodist dead-heated in which 1988 Irish Classic?

13. Where were the 1991 Pan-American Games held?

14. At what sport were François Brandt and Roelof Klein Olympic champions in 1900?

15. Who won the women's London Marathon in 2000?

ANSWERS 1. 4-2 **2.** Mr. Cool **3.** Frédéric Deburghgraeve **4.** Nick Faldo **5.** Lennox Miller **6.** £100,000 **7.** Badminton **8.** South Africa **9.** Romanian **10.** Basketball **11.** Moscow **12.** Irish Oaks **13.** Havana **14.** Rowing **15.** Tegla Loroupe.

POP

1. Mark Morris and Scott Morris are members of which 1990's group?

2. Which punk group released the 1980 record *The Black Album*?

3. In which year did PJ And Duncan have a Top 10 single with *Let's Get Ready To Rhumble*?

4. Which female singer had a 1999 Top 10 single with *I Try*?

5. Which rap group released the 1996 album *Temples of Boom*?

6. Which female singer had a 1994 No. 1 single with *Saturday Night*?

7. Which group recorded the 1983 mini-album *10-4-60*?

8. On which label was the Manic Street Preachers's number one single, *The Masses Against the Classes*?

9. Who recorded the 1999 dance hit *Madagascar*?

10. Who recorded the 1999 album *I See a Darkness*?

11. Who recorded the 1999 album *Maybe You've Been Brainwashed Too*?

12. Which artist directed Blur's video for the single *Country House*?

13. Who recorded the 1999 album *Sleepless*?

14. Who recorded the 2000 Top 10 single *U Know What's Up*?

15. In which year did Ian Dury and the Blockheads have a Top 10 hit with *Reasons To Be Cheerful, Pt. 3*?

ANSWERS 1. The Bluetones **2.** The Damned **3.** 1994 **4.** Macy Gray **5.** Cypress Hill **6.** Whigfield **7.** The Long Ryders **8.** Epic **9.** Art of Trance **10.** Bonnie 'Prince' Billy **11.** New Radicals **12.** Damien Hirst **13.** Kate Rusby **14.** Donell Jones **15.** 1979

ART

1. Dora Greenfield appears in which 1958 novel by Iris Murdoch?

2. In which French city was sculptor Jean Arp, a.k.a. Hans Arp, born?

3. Miss Spoelmann features in which 1909 novel by Thomas Mann?

4. Which English abstract sculptor's work includes 1962's *Early One Morning*?

5. Who wrote the 1913 novel *Chance*?

6. Which Spanish surrealist artist's works include 1931's *The Persistence Of Memory*?

7. Which pulp writer penned the stories *After Dark My Sweet* and *Savage Night*?

8. In which French city was illustrator Paul Gustave Doré born?

9. Who wrote the 1998 novel *Riven Rock*?

10. Which art movement did John Everett Millais and William Holman Hunt form with poet Dante Gabriel Rossetti?

11. In which city did Italian artist Antonio Canova die?

12. Who wrote the 1998 novel *Mr. Rinyo-Clacton's Offer*?

13. Who penned the 2000 novel *The Brethren*?

14. In which novel by Jane Austen do Mr and Mrs. Allen appear?

15. Who wrote the novel *Marrying The Mistress*, which was published early in 2000?

GENERAL KNOWLEDGE

1. Which actor's television roles included *The Six Million Dollar Man*?

2. In which market place was German 'wild boy' Kaspar Hauser found in 1928?

3. Which Russian statesman's original surname was Ulyanov?

4. In which year did country singer Patsy Cline die in an air crash?

5. What is the name given to the volume of water that would cover an area of 1 acre to a depth of 1 foot?

6. What is the name given to the chisel-edged tooth at the front of the mouth?

7. In which U.S. city was Barnett Newman, Abstract Impressionist painter and founder of the "Subject of the Artist' school of 1948 born?

8. Who is suitor of Bianca in the play *The Taming of the Shrew*?

9. Giacomo Balla, Italian artist, was one of the founders of which art movement?

10. Who wrote the novel *Oscar and Lucinda*?

11. In which year did sculptor Sir Jacob Epstein die?

12. What is the name given to the books *The Military Orchid*, *The Goose Cathedral* and *A Mine of Serpents* by author Jocelyn Brooke?

13. Which city is capital of Northern Ireland?

14. Who was a Best Actor Oscar nominee for the film *The Hasty Heart*?

15. On which Hawaiian island is the town of Wahiawa?

ANSWERS 1. Lee Majors **2.** Nuremberg **3.** Lenin **4.** 1963 **5.** An acre-foot **6.** Incisor **7.** New York **8.** Lucentio **9.** Futurism **10.** Peter Carey **11.** 1959 **12.** The Orchid Trilogy **13.** Belfast **14.** Richard Todd **15.** Oahu

ENTERTAINMENT

1. Which actress stars as a singer-songwriter in the 1994 film *Camilla*?

2. The stage musical *Cats* closes on Broadway in June, 2000. How many performances of the show will have been given by the end of its run?

3. Who directed the 1996 film *Sleepers*?

4. Which boxer plays himself in the film *Black and White,* during which he beats up Robert Downey Jr.?

5. Which actress stalks Clint Eastwood in the 1971 film *Play Misty For Me*?

6. In which town was the film *The Blair Witch Project* shot?

7. Which sculptor does Gérard Depardieu play in the 1988 film *Camille Claudel*?

8. Who played Egg in *This Life* on television?

9. Who is God of Thunder in Wagner's opera *Das Rheingold*?

10. Who plays an oil heiress in the 1929 film *Untamed*?

11. Whose television roles include Zoë in *Coronation Street* and Rachel in *Bad Girls*?

12. In which country is the 1957 film *Campbell's Kingdom* set?

13. Which actress plays Rita in the BBC TV drama *Playing The Field*?

14. Who directed the 1972 film *The Railway Children*?

15. How many million dollars did Ben Affleck earn for making the film *Forces Of Nature*?

SPORT

1. Who was the 1953-5 world 500cc motorcycling champion?

2. What nationality is judo player Eva Bisseni?

3. Who scored Manchester United's two goals in their 1979 F.A. Cup Final defeat?

4. Who scored both goals in Liverpool's 2-1 win at Wimbledon in April, 2000?

5. How long did Don Ritchie take to run 100 miles on 15th October, 1977?

6. Which country have been men's volleyball world champions the most times?

7. What country did cyclist Nikolay Makarov represent?

8. For which British basketball club does Jason Kimbrough play?

9. Which country won the 1975 women's world championships in hockey?

10. In which year did French tennis player André Gobert die?

11. Who was the 1997 FIA Formula 3000 champion?

12. After Western Province, which team have won the Currie Cup in South African rugby union the most times?

13. Which French woman won the 2000 Paris Open singles tennis title?

14. Where were the 1990 Asian Games held?

15. Which Briton was WBC flyweight boxing champion in 1983?

ANSWERS 1. Geoff Duke **2.** French **3.** McQueen & McIlroy **4.** Emile Heskey **5.** 11 hours 30 minutes 51 seconds **6.** USSR **7.** USSR **8.** London Leopards **9.** England **10.** 1951 **11.** Ricardo Zonta **12.** Northern Transvaal **13.** Nathalie Tauziat **14.** Beijing **15.** Charlie Magri.

POP

1. Which guitarist recorded the 1965 Capitol album *Summer Surf*?

2. Who recorded the 1999 album *Carboot Soul*?

3. Which group's debut album was 1986's *Heaven's End*?

4. Who recorded the 1999 album *Suicaine Gratifaction*?

5. On which label did Sting record the album *Brand New Day*?

6. Which U.S. group recorded the 1999 album *Black Foliage*?

7. Which Scottish group's debut L.P. was 1989's *C86*?

8. Who recorded the 1999 album *The Amateur View*?

9. Which group recorded 1994 Top 10 single *Steam*?

10. Which track from Los Lobos' E.P. *...And A Time To Dance* won a Grammy?

11. Who recorded the 1999 album *Niun Niggung*?

12. Who recorded 1999's *Utopia Parkway*?

13. On which Bon Jovi studio album does the song *Bad Medicine* feature?

14. Who recorded the 1999 album *60 Second Wipeout*?

15. Who recorded the 2000 Top 10 single *More Than I Needed To Know*?

ANSWERS 1. Dick Dale **2.** Nightmares in Wax **3.** Loop **4.** Paul Westerberg **5.** A & M **6.** Olivia Tremor Control **7.** BMX Bandits **8.** To Rococo Rot **9.** East 17 **10.** Anselma **11.** Mouse on Mars **12.** Fountains of Wayne **13.** New Jersey **14.** Atari Teenage Riot **15.** Scooch.

GEOGRAPHY

1. On which river is the town of Chepstow?

2. The island of Unst is in which island group?

3. Which Staffordshire village is famous for its Horn dance in September?

4. Barkhan, transverse, star and seif are examples of what?

5. In which Asian country is the village of Dien Bien Phu?

6. On which island of Japan is the city of Gifu?

7. Which northern city houses Lister Park and Cartwright Hall?

8. Is New Zealand's Sutherland Falls on South Island or North Island?

9. On which river does the Cornish cathedral town Truro stand?

10. In which English county is Daventry?

11. Which city in China was capital of the Manchu dynasty from 1644-1912?

12. Of what is Graubünden the largest in Switzerland?

13. Which African republic was formerly known as the Territory of the Afars and the Issas?

14. In which county of Northern Ireland is the district of Moyle?

15. In which county is the village of Grasmere?

ANSWERS 1. Wye 2. Shetlands 3. Abbots Bromley 4. Sand dunes 5. Vietnam 6. Honshu 7. Bradford 8. South Island 9. River Truro 10. Northamptonshire 11. Shenyang 12. Canton 13. Djibouti 14. County Antrim 15. Cumbria.

GENERAL KNOWLEDGE

1. Who was the U.S. author of poetry collection *I Shall Not Be Moved*?

2. Who authored the novel *Redgauntlet* which was published in 1824?

3. Which town in S. England is the administrative centre of the Isle of Wight?

4. Which Los Angeles-born singer-songwriter's albums include *Little Criminals*?

5. Who wrote the 1882 play *An Enemy of the People*?

6. Which theatre on Bankside in Southwark, London, was erected in 1599?

7. Who is the author of the novel *The House of the Spirits*?

8. Which British architect is noted for his planning of New Delhi, India?

9. Who was Soviet president from 1985-8?

10. In which African country is the city of Umtata?

11. For which 1957 film did Joanne Woodward win a Best Actress Oscar?

12. Who authored 1835 novel *The Yemassee*?

13. What is the capital of the state of Penang in Peninsular Malaysia?

14. Who was the 1970 world matchplay golf champion?

15. Which order of mammals includes the anteaters and sloths?

ANSWERS 1. Maya Angelou **2.** Sir Walter Scott **3.** Newport **4.** Randy Newman **5.** Henrik Ibsen **6.** The Globe **7.** Isabel Allende **8.** Edwin Luyens **9.** Andrei Gromyko **10.** South Africa **11.** The Three Faces of Eve **12.** William Gillmore Simms **13.** George Town **14.** Jack Nicklaus **15.** Edentata.

ENTERTAINMENT

1. Which musician scored the 1981 film *Ragtime*?

2. Which actor's films include *Wilde* and *eXistenZ*?

3. Who does Leah Bracknell play in *Emmerdale*?

4. Who played Batman in the film *Batman And Robin*?

5. Actor Jack Davenport is the son of which theatrical couple?

6. Who directed the 1988 road movie *Ariel*?

7. Who starred as Caligari in the 1962 film *The Cabinet Of Caligari*?

8. Who plays Jimmy Corkhill in the soap *Brookside*?

9. Who scripted the 1990 film *The Handmaid's Tale*?

10. Who conducted the score to the 1951 film *The Tales Of Hoffmann*?

11. The 1945 murder mystery film *Lady on a Train* is based on a story by which author?

12. Who directed the film *Sleepless In Seattle*?

13. Who plays a young pope in the 1986 film *Saving Grace*?

14. Which English football team did Reg support in the 1990s sitcom *The Boys from the Bush*?

15. In which year did *Tiswas* finish on television?

SPORT

1. For which Test cricket side does Sadagopan Ramesh play?

2. Who did the U.S.A. beat in the 1996 ice hockey World Cup Final?

3. What nationality is skater Irina Slutskaya?

4. Which was voted outstanding college American Football team in 1971 by United Press?

5. Who was the 1964 U.S. men's singles tennis champion?

6. Which rider was individual dressage champion at the 1928 Olympics?

7. Which four teams played in Pool 2 of the 1999/00 Heineken Cup in rugby union?

8. Who was the 1968 Olympic women's 400m freestyle swimming champion?

9. Which golfer won the 1946 U.S. Open?

10. What nationality is golfer Jarmo Sandelin?

11. What nationality is Nordic skier Matti Raivo?

12. Who was captain of the 1999 European Ryder Cup team?

13. How many runs did Don Bradman make for Australia in the 1930 five match series against England?

14. Who finished third in the 1999 German F1 Grand Prix?

15. By what score did San Francisco Giants lose the 1989 World Series in baseball?

ANSWERS 1. India **2.** Canada **3.** Russian **4.** Nebraska **5.** Roy Emerson **6.** Carl von Langen **7.** Bath, Padova, Swansea, Toulouse **8.** Debbie Meyer **9.** Lloyd Mangrum **10.** Swedish **11.** Finnish **12.** Mark James **13.** 974 **14.** Heinz-Harald Frentzen **15.** 4-0.

POP

1. Who recorded the 1999 album *Da Real World*?

2. Which solo artist had a 1980 Top 10 single with *Carrie*?

3. Which U.S. singer recorded the 1995 album *Vibrator*?

4. Which country group recorded the 1999 album *End Time*?

5. On which label did Nine Inch Nails record the album *The Fragile*?

6. Which artist recorded the 1999 album *Juxtapose*?

7. Who featured on Tamperer's hit single *Hammer To The Heart* in 2000?

8. Which singer recorded the song *Work, Rest, Play, Reggae* in 1977?

9. Who recorded the 1994 Top 10 single *She's Got That Vibe*?

10. The BBC banned the record *'Til The Following Night* in the 1960s. Who recorded it?

11. Who had a Top 10 hit in 2000 with *Don't Wanna Let You Go*?

12. Which female artist recorded the country album *Forget About It*?

13. Which U.S. singer had a 1987 Top 30 single with *Sexy Girl*?

14. Which rap group recorded the 1990 single *Brooklyn-Queens*?

15. Which song by Odyssey is covered by Tindersticks on the album *Simple Pleasure*?

HISTORY

1. Who instigated the Third Servile War in 73 B.C.?

2. In which year was the Treaty of Adrianople, which ended war between Russia and Turkey, signed?

3. In which battle did General Albert S. Johnston die in 1862?

4. Which king of Denmark introduced Christianity into the country in 960?

5. In which year did Sir Alec Douglas-Home die?

6. Which future prime minister was President of the Board of Trade from 1921-22?

7. In which year was John F. Kennedy elected U.S. president?

8. Which Spanish prime minister was murdered by ETA in 1973?

9. The Clayton-Bulwer Treaty signed in 1850 concerned the construction of what?

10. In which year was Patrice Lumumba, first prime minister of the Republic of the Congo, assassinated?

11. Who was the father of Carolingian ruler Charles Martel?

12. In which year was the Good Friday Agreement signed in Ireland?

13. In which year was General Pinochet made commander-in-chief of the Chilean Army?

14. In which year did Scottish theologian John Duns Scotus die?

15. In which year did Edward Gierek become First Secretary of the Communist Party in Poland?

GENERAL KNOWLEDGE

1. Who directed the 1935 film *Captain Blood* starring Errol Flynn?

2. What is the German name for the Polish port Gdansk?

3. Who became the first Aboriginal member of the Australian parliament in 1971?

4. Who wrote the 1922 novel *Huntingtower*?

5. Who directed the 1972 film *The Mechanic* starring Charles Bronson?

6. Who was the French composer of the 1884 opera *Manon*?

7. Who was Secretary-General of the Commonwealth from 1975-89?

8. Which novel by Iain Banks features the character Uncle Rory?

9. In which year was the siege at the mission in San Antonio, Texas, called the Alamo?

10. Which country was formerly known as Siam?

11. Who authored the farce *The Magistrate* and play *Two Hundred A Year*?

12. What was the name of Lord Howard of Effingham's flaghip against the Spanish Armada?

13. In which year was Newgate, the famous London prison, demolished?

14. Who was the son of Chingachgook in the novel *The Last of the Mohicans*?

15. What is the name given to the leader of congregational prayer in a mosque?

ENTERTAINMENT

1. What is Carole Lombard's profession in the 1935 film *Hands Across The Table*?

2. Who voiced Thomas O'Malley Cat in the Disney film *The Aristocats*?

3. Who directed the 1943 musical *Cabin in the Sky*?

4. Who played Bill Haydon in the 1979 BBC TV drama *Tinker Tailor Soldier Spy*?

5. Which sitcom featured the characters Lady Patience Hardacre and Henri Lecoq?

6. Who plays a Broadway priest getting mixed up with a chorus girl in the 1959 film *Say One For Me*?

7. In which year is the 1990 film *Total Recall* set?

8. Who played Bert in the sitcom *Till Death Us Do Part*?

9. Who plays Johnny Depp's uncle in the 1993 film *Arizona Dream*?

10. Who played 1996's *The Cable Guy* on screen?

11. Who directed the 1992 film *The Hand that Rocks the Cradle*?

12. What was Lady Penelope's surname in *Thunderbirds*?

13. In which year did the panel game *Through the Keyhole* first appear on television?

14. What is Linda Darnell's profession in the 1951 film *The Lady Pays Off*?

15. Which Hollywood actress appeared as Angie Tyler in the 1980s sitcom *Three Up, Two Down*?

SPORT

1. In tennis, who beat Andre Agassi in the final of the 1999 ATP Mercedes Benz Cup?

2. Who rode Oh So Wonderful to victory in the 1998 Juddmonte Diamond Stakes at York?

3. Which golfer won the European Masters in September, 1999?

4. Sisi Dolman was 1988-91 world women's powerlifting champion. In what weight division?

5. Which female golfer won the Donegal Irish Open in September, 1999?

6. Sanbon shobu and Ippon shobu are types of championship in which sport?

7. Which snooker player won the 1999 Champions Cup in Croydon?

8. Which football player transferred from PSV Eindhoven to Barcelona in July, 1996 for £13.2m?

9. Who won the 125cc San Marino Grand Prix in motorcycling in 1999?

10. Which women's field event did Ilke Wyludda win at the 1994 European Championships?

11. At what sport does Jens Voit compete?

12. In which year was the women's World Cup in cricket first held?

13. What nationality is golfer Marc Farry?

14. Gymnast Junichi Shimizu was 1978 world champion at horse vault. Which country did he represent?

15. Who lost to Ted Hankey in the 2000 Embassy World Darts Championship by 6-0?

ANSWERS 1. Pete Sampras **2.** Pat Eddery **3.** Lee Westwood **4.** 52kg **5.** Sandrine Mendiburu **6.** Karate **7.** Stephen Hendry **8.** Ronaldo **9.** Marco Melandri **10.** Discus **11.** Cycling **12.** 1973 **13.** French **14.** Japan **15.** Ronnie Baxter.

POP

1. Which group recorded the 1971 album *Teenage Head*?

2. In which year did Then Jericho have a Top 20 hit with *Big Area*?

3. In which year did singer Laura Nyro die?

4. Which group's singles included 1991's *Tingle* and *Sensitize*?

5. What is Morrissey's full name?

6. Which actress-model recorded 1999 single *Oh Yeah*?

7. In which city were the group Flaming Lips formed in 1983?

8. In which year did Mega City Four release the album *Sebastopol Road*?

9. The lead singer of Mother Love Bone died in 1990. What was his name?

10. Which group reformed in 1993 to play at Bill Clinton's inauguration party?

11. Which studio album by Motörhead features songs *Jailbait* and *The Hammer*?

12. From which city were vocal group The Orioles?

13. What is guitarist Bram Tchaikovsky's real name?

14. Who was the original lead singer in the group which became Mott The Hoople?

15. Which group recorded the 1999 single *Once Around the Block*?

WORDS

1. What is a redowa – a breed of beef cattle or Bohemian folk dance?

2. What type of creature is a douc?

3. What is a tourbillion?

4. In which sport would the term pebbling be used?

5. What in heraldry is an orle?

6. What type of creature is a motmot?

7. What would you do with lebkuchen - eat them or wear them?

8. What might you do with a regal?

9. If you are patriclinous do you show your father or mother's characteristics?

10. What is the name given to the science or philosophy of law?

11. What in Britain is drabbet?

12. What would you do in South Africa with jerepigo?

13. How many wheels does a jaunty car have?

14. What on a bird is a remex?

15. Which dance derives its name from the Portuguese phrase 'snapping of a whip'?

ANSWERS 1. Folk dance **2.** Monkey **3.** Whirlwind **4.** Curling **5.** A border around a shield **6.** A bird **7.** Eat them **8.** Play it - it's a musical instrument **9.** Father's **10.** Jurisprudence **11.** A type of linen **12.** Drink it **13.** Two **14.** A large feather **15.** Lambada.

GENERAL KNOWLEDGE

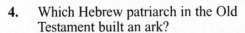

1. In which year was Soviet-born Icelandic pianist Vladimir Ashkanazy born?

2. In which African country is the city of Germiston which houses the world's largest gold refinery?

3. Who was the author of the 1934 novel *Fer-de-Lance*?

4. Which Hebrew patriarch in the Old Testament built an ark?

5. Which annual plant is also called ladies' fingers?

6. In which Shakespeare play does the clown Launcelot Gobbo appear?

7. For which 1950 film by Billy Wilder were both William Holden and Gloria Swanson Oscar-nominated?

8. What is the brightest star in the constellation Lyra?

9. What is a coelacanth?

10. In which U.S. state is the resort town of Aspen, which is noted for its skiing?

11. What is the name of the hill on which the city of Jerusalem stands?

12. What in heraldry is the name given to the colour red?

13. Which actor's television credits include the title role in *Father Dowling Investigates*?

14. Who directed the 1943 film *The Outlaw* starring Jane Russell?

15. What is the name of the wild mountain sheep of N. Africa, also called an aoudad?

ENTERTAINMENT

1. The 1983 film *Tales Of Ordinary Madness* is based on stories by which author?

2. Which actor played Dr. John Rennie in *Emergency - Ward 10*?

3. Which actor narrated the 1998 film *Armageddon*?

4. Who is the actress mother of Emma Thompson?

5. What was Eileen Pollock's character's name in the sitcom *Bread*?

6. In which year did *This Is Your Life* first appear on British television?

7. Who played Sydney Carton in the 1958 film *A Tale of Two Cities*?

8. Who played Michael Steadman in the television drama *thirtysomething*?

9. Who starred in, and directed, the 1986 film *Armour Of God*?

10. Who plays a barkeeper in Peru in the 1980 film *Caboblanco*?

11. Who played author Agatha Christie in the 1979 film *Agatha*?

12. On which children's show did Ant and Dec first work together?

13. Which actress plays a dizzy millionairess in the 1942 comedy *The Palm Beach Story*?

14. What is John Cusack's profession in the film *Being John Malkovich*?

15. Who was the female cast member in the ITV sketch show *Do Not Adjust Your Set*?

SPORT

1. Who won the 1958 Moroccan Grand Prix in F1?

2. Which golfer was the 1996 Sports Illustrated Sportsman of the Year?

3. Which country won rugby union's 1993 World Cup Sevens?

4. What nationality is swimmer Michael Klim?

5. At what weight was Virgil Hill a WBA world champion from 1987-91?

6. What nationality is golfer Elisabeth Esterl?

7. Which horse won the 1998 Hennessy Cognac Gold Cup at Leopardstown?

8. Who was the 1988 Olympic men's tennis champion?

9. In which year was automatic timing first used in athletics at the Olympic Games?

10. Who was the 1911 Wimbledon women's singles tennis champion?

11. Laura Badea was the 1996 Olympic women's individual foil champion in fencing. Which country did she represent?

12. Golfer Lee Westwood withdrew from the Los Angeles Open in 2000. Why?

13. Who was the 1992 Olympic women's 400m individual medley swimming champion?

14. Which 48 year old won the 1968 U.S. PGA golf title?

15. Who replaced Danny Wilson as the boss of Sheffield Wednesday in 2000?

ANSWERS 1. Stirling Moss **2.** Tiger Woods **3.** England **4.** Australian **5.** Light-heavyweight **6.** German **7.** Dorans Pride **8.** Miloslav Mecir **9.** 1932 **10.** Dorothea Lambert **11.** Romania **12.** He had flu **13.** Krisztina Egerszegi **14.** Julius Boros **15.** Peter Shreeves.

POP

1. Which group recorded the 1998 single *A Pessimist Is Never Disappointed*?

2. What was Thin Lizzy's second Top 10 single?

3. With which group was Barry Mooncult the dancer?

4. Which singer formerly ran the Yardbirds' fan club?

5. Which group had a 1981 hit single with *Platinum Pop*?

6. In which year did punk band Flux Of Pink Indians form?

7. Which female artist recorded country album *Sittin' On Top Of The World*?

8. In which year did Rufus Thomas have a hit single with *Do The Funky Chicken*?

9. Which guitarist recorded the solo album *Return To Metalopolis*?

10. Which group did Dave Pearce and Rachel Brook form in 1992?

11. Who recorded the album *Talking Book*?

12. Who recorded 1999's *The Slim Shady LP*?

13. Which female singer was born Love Michelle Harrison?

14. Who had a 1990 Top 10 single with *Happenin' All Over Again*?

15. Which group's debut album was 1995's *Olympian*?

SCIENCE

1. Which English physiologist originated the terms 'synapse' and 'neuron'?

2. What nationality was biologist Ernest Mayr?

3. In which German town is scientist Georgius Agricola buried?

4. Iapetus is a moon of which planet?

5. Approximately how many miles in diameter is Uranus's moon Portia?

6. In which county was botanist William Withering born?

7. Is fluorine lighter of heavier than air?

8. In computer science, what is pixel short for?

9. Which bird was cosmonaut Valentina Tereshkova's call sign on her Vostok VI space mission?

10. What is the symbol of the element Nobelium?

11. In which year was the first atomic bomb detonated?

12. In which year did nuclear physicist Eugene Paul Wigner die?

13. In which year was Nereid, a moon of neptune, discovered?

14. What are the two main types of computers in use today?

15. In which century did U.S. scientist Benjamin Franklin live?

ANSWERS 1. Charles Scott Sherrington 2. German 3. Zeitz 4. Saturn 5. 66 miles 6. Somerset 7. Heavier 8. Picture element 9. Seagull 10. No 11. 1945 12. 1995 13. 1949 14. Analogue and digital 15. 18th Century.

GENERAL KNOWLEDGE

1. Which comic actor played the title role in the film *Wayne's World*?

2. What is the capital of Azerbaijan?

3. Who was the 1976 Olympic men's downhill skiing champion?

4. Who wrote the 1974 novel *Shardik*?

5. What was the setting of the 1948 film *The Snake Pit* starring Olivia de Havilland?

6. Who was world middleweight boxing champion from 1941-7?

7. What is the capital of Jordan?

8. In which year did U.S. aviator Amelia Earhart disappear?

9. Who wrote the 1939 novel *Finnegans Wake*?

10. Which bone in the ear is also called the *incus*?

11. In which radio drama does the character Captain Cat appear?

12. Which book did Ebenezer Cobham Brewer famously publish in 1870?

13. What was the Roman name for Ireland?

14. Who wrote the 1957 novel *Gidget*?

15. In which year was Dutch abstract expressionist painter Karel Appel born?

ENTERTAINMENT

1. Who directed the 1985 film *Agnes Of God*?

2. Which comic actor played Clarence Darrow in a one-man show tour of Britain in 2000?

3. What was the name of Peter Perfect's car in the cartoon show *Wacky Races*?

4. Which contestant won *Stars In Their Eyes* in 1995?

5. Who does Joshua Jacks play in *Dawson's Creek*?

6. Which comedy duo star in the 1942 film *A-Haunting We Will Go*?

7. Who played Lawrence Bingham in the 1971 sitcom *Doctor at Large*?

8. Who played George Maple in the 1970s sitcom *Don't Forget to Write*?

9. Which *Top of the Pops* presenter also hosted the fashion show *She's Gotta Have It* in 2000?

10. Who directed the 1977 biopic *Valentino*?

11. What is Tobey Maguire's character name in the film *The Cider House Rules*?

12. Who plays Agent Scully in *The X-Files*?

13. Who played actress Coral Atkins in the ITV drama *Seeing Red* in 2000?

14. Which Italian actress starred in the 1953 film *Aida*?

15. Which actor from the film *L.A. Confidential* starred in the 1992 film *Romper Stomper*?

SPORT

1. In what sport would you encounter the terms ballet, moguls and aerials?

2. Who did Toulouse play in the quarter-finals of the Heineken Cup in rugby union in 2000?

3. Which wicket-keeper made 22 dismissals for Sri Lanka in the 1985 three match series against India?

4. How many Tests did Ian Botham play for England at cricket?

5. In baseball, who hit the most home runs in the 1949 season?

6. In which year did Jesper Parnevik first play in the Ryder Cup?

7. Which jockey rode Embassy to victory in the 1997 Cheveley Park Stakes?

8. Which tennis player won the ATP Hamlet Cup in August, 1999?

9. In which year was real tennis included in the Olympic Games?

10. How many golds did China get in the 1999 World Athletics Championships?

11. In which year were the first World Championships in korfball?

12. Where were the 1959 Pan-American Games held?

13. Who were 1980/1 First Division champions in football in England?

14. At what sport was Vadim Krasnochapka world champion in 1988?

15. Who was the 1996 U.S. PGA golf champion?

ANSWERS 1. Freestyle skiing **2.** Montferrand **3.** Amal Silva **4.** 102 **5.** Ralph Kiner **6.** 1997 **7.** Kieron Fallon **8.** Magnus Norman **9.** 1908 **10.** One **11.** 1978 **12.** Chicago **13.** Aston Villa **14.** Trampolining **15.** Mark Brooks.

POP

1. On which label did the Fire Engines release the 1981 single *Candyskin*?

2. Under what name does Richard Melville Hall record?

3. By what name was guiatrist Eddie Jones known?

4. Chris Stamey and Peter Holsapple were members of which 1980's U.S. group?

5. Which singer's albums include 1969's *Joy Of A Toy*?

6. Who replaced John Towe as drummer of Generation X?

7. Who played drums on Bryan Ferry's *The Price Of Love* E.P.?

8. Who recorded the 1984 album *Raining Pleasure*?

9. On which label did Adam Faith release the 1959 single *What Do You Want*?

10. On which label was *The Silent Sun* single by Genesis released?

11. In which year did The Dooleys have a Top 10 single with *Chosen Few*?

12. On which label did The Fall record the single *The Man Whose Head Expanded*?

13. Which performer recorded the song *Hitler's Liver* for the E.P. *A Factory Sampler*?

14. Which rock group released the 1973 album *In a Glass House*?

15. Which saxophone player fronted group Essential Logic?

PEOPLE

1. Camille Donatacci is the third wife of which comedy actor?

2. Which U.S. singer was involved in a fracas at Heathrow Airport in September, 1999?

3. Which actor did Courteney Cox marry in 1999?

4. How old was Clint Eastwood when son Morgan was born in 1996?

5. What age was Lolo Ferrari, a star of television show *Eurotrash*, when she died in 2000?

6. How many wives did American religious leader Brigham Young have?

7. In which year did U.S. outlaw Belle Starr die?

8. Which French writer authored novel *Clochemerle*?

9. What was the middle name of comedian Tommy Handley?

10. Who was the father of Alexander the Great?

11. In which year was the actress Claire Bloom born?

12. How many children did Cleopatra VII have by Antony?

13. In which country was fashion designer Oscar de la Renta born?

14. In which country was conductor Karl Böhm born?

15. With which group is Shane Lynch a singer?

GENERAL KNOWLEDGE

1. In which year did British field marshal Douglas Haig die?

2. Who was the German composer of 1717's *Water Music*?

3. Who wrote the 1600 play *Hamlet*?

4. What is the 20th letter in the Greek alphabet?

5. In which year did German Green Party activist Petera Kelly die?

6. In which European country is the market town of Eger?

7. What was the Indian Mutiny of 1857-8 also known as?

8. Which European freshwater fish is also called a pope?

9. Who was Roman emperor from 54-68 A.D.?

10. What is the name given to either of the two large flat triangular bones on each side of the back part of the shoulder?

11. Who was the author of *The Canterbury Tales*?

12. What is the name given to the liquorice-flavoured seeds of the anise plant?

13. Which sport is played by the Toronto Blue Jays and Boston Red Sox?

14. Who wrote the 1986 novel *The Bridge*?

15. The 1989 Ken Russell film *The Lair of the White Worm* was based on a tale by which writer?

ANSWERS 1. 1928 **2.** George Frederick Handel **3.** Shakespeare **4.** Upsilon **5.** 1992 **6.** Hungary **7.** The Sepoy Rebellion (or Sepoy Mutiny) **8.** Ruffe **9.** Nero **10.** Scapula **11.** Geoffrey Chaucer **12.** Aniseed **13.** Baseball **14.** Iain Banks **15.** Bram Stoker.

ENTERTAINMENT

1. Which comedy actress appeared as Kate Bancroft in the 1992 sitcom *Don't Tell Father*?

2. The 1997 biopic *Private Parts* is about which disc jockey?

3. Which actor plays Deborah Foreman's father in the 1983 film *Valley Girl*?

4. Who composed the 1844 opera *Ernani*?

5. Who plays the title role in the 2000 film *Ordinary Decent Criminal*?

6. What nationality is counter-tenor Paul Esswood?

7. What is William B. Davis's character name in the television show *The X-Files*?

8. Who is the star of the 1961 film *Yojimbo*?

9. Who composed the 1854 opera *The Northern Star*?

10. In which country is the 1969 film *Valley of Gwangi* set?

11. Who plays a con-man in the 1945 film *Yolanda and the Thief*?

12. Which comic duo play *Randall and Hopkirk (Deceased)* in the BBC TV comedy drama series remake?

13. Which cast member of *Friends* plays *The Pallbearer* in the 1996 film?

14. What nationality is bass baritone Simon Estes?

15. Who choreographed the 1957 film *The Pajama Game*?

SPORT

1. Which man set a world record of 26:38.08 for the 10,000m on 23th August, 1996?

2. In which year was the Grand Caledonian Curling Club formed in Edinburgh?

3. In which year did Lew Hoad & Ken Rosewall win the Wimbledon men's doubles tennis title for the 2nd time?

4. What nationality is rhythmic sportive gymnast Bianka Panova?

5. In which year did French tennis player Jean Cochet die?

6. Which New Zealander won the 1973 Swedish Grand Prix in F1?

7. Who was the 1994 Commonwealth men's 200m champion?

8. Which university has won the rugby union varsity match most times - Oxford or Cambridge?

9. What sport do Stephen Cooper and Rick Brebant play for Britain?

10. In which year did cricketer Christopher Batt make his county debut for Middlesex?

11. Which Briton became world undisputed welterweight boxing champion in 1986?

12. Which Irish jockey won the 1991 Breeders' Cup Sprint?

13. Who beat Biarritz in the 1999/00 European Shield quarter-finals in rugby union?

14. What nationality is Olympic archer Darrell Pace?

15. At what sport were Judy Wills and Nancy Smith world champions in 1967?

POP

1. Which group derives its name from the Russian word for milk?

2. Which songwriting team penned the Elgins' *Heaven Must Have Sent You*?

3. In which U.S. city did the Gigolo Aunts form in 1992?

4. On which label did Massive Attack record the album *Blue Lines*?

5. Who recorded the 1979 song *Back to Nature* on Mute Records?

6. Who produced the 1961 single by the Paris Sisters entitled *I Love How You Love Me*?

7. Which group recorded the 1979 single *Playing Golf With My Flesh Crawling*?

8. What was the B-side of Generation X single, *Ready Steady Go*?

9. Who wrote the song *He's A Rebel*?

10. Who was the drummer in The Pixies?

11. In which year did Manchester group The Chameleons form?

12. Which group had a hit in 1963 with *My Boyfriend's Back*?

13. Who recorded the 1991 album *New River Head*?

14. What age was Esther Phillips when she died?

15. Who recorded the 1988 album *The Tender Pervert*?

ANSWERS 1. Moloko **2.** Holland-Dozier-Holland **3.** Boston **4.** Wild Bunch **5.** Fad Gadget **6.** Phil Spector **7.** The Family Fodder **8.** NoNoNo **9.** Gene Pitney **10.** David Lovering **11.** 1981 **12.** The Angels **13.** The Bevis Frond **14.** 48 **15.** Momus.

ART

1. Which Italian painter was known as 'Lo Spagnuolo'?

2. What is the concluding part of Evelyn Waugh's *Sword of Honour* trilogy?

3. In which year did painter Frans Hals die?

4. What was Charles Dickens's first novel?

5. What is Helen Fielding's sequel to *Bridget Jones' Diary*?

6. In which year did Colette's book *Chéri* first appear?

7. Which Swiss painter taught at the Bauhaus from 1920-31?

8. Who is associated with the *Rougon-Macquart* novels?

9. Which Welsh portrait painter's sitters in the 1930's included Dylan Thomas and Tallulah Bankhead?

10. Who authored *A High Wind In Jamaica*?

11. How did French artist Antoine-Jean Gros die?

12. Which Spanish painter's works included 1814's *Third Of May, 1808*?

13. In Graham Greene's *Doctor Fischer Of Geneva*, how did the doctor make his millions?

14. Which Russian-born sculptor's last major work was a fountain for St. Thomas's Hospital in London?

15. Who wrote the 1969 novel *Ada*?

GENERAL KNOWLEDGE

1. Who was the female lead in the 1964 film *Woman Of Straw*?

2. Of which U.S. state is Augusta the capital?

3. Who wrote the novel *Salar the Salmon*?

4. Lake Champlain in the northeastern U.S. lies between which two mountain ranges?

5. Who composed the music for the ballet *Appalachian Spring*?

6. Which bone of the body is also called the *innominate bone*?

7. Which town in central Scotland is the administrative centre of Clackmannanshire?

8. Who was the French designer of the modern two-piece swimsuit?

9. Who was a Best Actor Oscar winner for the film *Goodbye, Mr. Chips*?

10. Who was the 1981 world rallying champion?

11. Off which U.S. state does the island of Nantucket, a former centre of the whaling industry, lie?

12. To which genus does the climbing plant the hop belong?

13. Which city and spa in Germany was the northern capital of Charlemagne's empire?

14. Who is the author of the Booker prize-winning novel *In a Free State*?

15. Which island in N.E. Indonesia is the largest of the Moluccas?

ENTERTAINMENT

1. On what novel is the 1962 film *Adorable Julia* based?

2. Which film director's daughter-in-law scripted the 1981 film *Tattoo*?

3. In which year did Lucille Ball marry Desi Arnaz?

4. Which comedian starred in the 1983 film *Easy Money*?

5. What nationality is mezzo-soprano Grace Bumbry?

6. Who is the female presenter of late-night weekend show *Something for the Weekend*?

7. The 1964 film *Advance to the Rear* is set during which war?

8. Who composed the 1942 opera *Capriccio*?

9. Who directed and starred in the 1988 film spoof *I'm Gonna Git You Sucka*?

10. Who played Lyn Turtle in 1980's drama series *A Very Peculiar Practice*?

11. Who is the female star of the 1987 film *Adventures in Babysitting*?

12. Who did Peter Vaughan play in a 1962 television adaptation of *Oliver Twist*?

13. Who co-directed and starred in the 1944 film *Tawny Pipit*?

14. Who directed the 1927 film *Easy Virtue*?

15. What does VHS stand for?

SPORT

1. Who is England rugby union coach?

2. What major contribution did Gabriel Hanot, soccer editor of newspaper L'Equipe, make in 1955?

3. What nationality is canoe racer Nikolai Boukhalov?

4. At what Olympic sport have Hubert Hammerer and Gary Anderson been champions?

5. Which country won the 1958 Eisenhower Trophy in golf?

6. In which year was the Squash Rackets Association formed?

7. Which club won the 1948 rugby league Challenge Cup Final?

8. How many times did Mike Procter take five wickets in an innings in his First-Class career?

9. Whose cap for the England rugby union team in March, 2000 against Italy was his 81st?

10. Raymond Ceulemans of Belgium was a 1983 world champion. At which ball game?

11. In the 1st Test between West Indies and Zimbabwe in March, 2000, which over of the Zimbabwe innings saw their first run?

12. How many wins did jockey Fred Archer have in 1878?

13. Who was captain of Scotland's 1990 rugby union grand slam side?

14. In which year was netball invented?

15. For which country did former England rugby union player Martin Donnelly play cricket?

POP

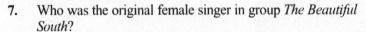

1. Which member of The Housemartins was also known as D.J. Ox?

2. Which ex-member of the group Kraftwerk penned the autobiography *Ich War Ein Roboter*?

3. Which Leicester group recorded the 1989 album *Shakespeare, Alabama*?

4. Which duo recorded the 2000 Top 10 single *Movin' Too Fast*?

5. Which U.S. female singer fronted 1970's rock band Blue Angel?

6. On which label was Wet Wet Wet's 1994 No. 1 single *Love Is All Around*?

7. Who was the original female singer in group *The Beautiful South*?

8. Which male vocalist had a 1967 Top 40 single with the song *Sam*?

9. What band was Robert Plant singing with immediately prior to joining Led Zeppelin?

10. Who recorded the 1999 Top 10 hit *Straight from the Heart*?

11. Which female duo had a 1989 hit with *Lolly lolly*?

12. In which year did Kool and the Gang have a Top 10 single with *Ladies Night*?

13. Whose Top 20 hits in 1993 included *Sunflower* and *Wildwood*?

14. Whose singles include *MTV Makes Me Want To Smoke Crack*?

15. Which group had a hit in 1992 with *The Queen Of Outer Space*?

ANSWERS 1. Norman Cook **2.** Wolfgang Flür **3.** Diesel Park West **4.** Artful Dodger and Romina Johnson **5.** Cyndi Lauper **6.** Precious **7.** Brianna Corrigan **8.** Keith West **9.** Hobbstweedle **10.** Doolally **11.** Wendy and Lisa **12.** 1979 **13.** Paul Weller **14.** Beck **15.** Wedding Present.

GEOGRAPHY

1. Which town in British Columbia is the S.E. terminus of the Alaska Highway?

2. In which county is the market town of Sutton-in-Ashfield?

3. What did British Honduras become in 1973?

4. Which island group in the Caribbean is named after St. Ursula?

5. On which river does Dodge City, Kansas stand?

6. What is the highest peak of the Cairngorms?

7. Is the town of Windermere on the west bank or east bank of Lake Windermere?

8. On which island is the port of Surabaya?

9. The Dead Sea lies between which two countries?

10. What is the chief city of West Bengal, India?

11. Which is longer – the River Severn or River Tyne?

12. Between which two African rivers is the region of Senegambia?

13. Which is greater in area – Cornwall or Dorset?

14. On which river is the Illinois city of Rockford situated?

15. In which Asian country is Lake Sevan?

GENERAL KNOWLEDGE

1. Who was a Best Actress Oscar nominee for the 1961 film *The Hustler*?

2. Carthaginian general Hasdrubal was the brother of which famous historical character?

3. Who wrote the book *Cakes And Ale*?

4. Who directed the 1974 film *Bring Me The Head Of Alfredo Garcia*?

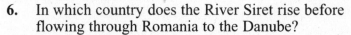

5. Who composed the 1733 oratorio *Athalia*?

6. In which country does the River Siret rise before flowing through Romania to the Danube?

7. Who authored the 1976 novel *The Family Arsenal*?

8. Which inland port in Argentina is the second largest city in the country?

9. Who composed the ballet *Agon*, first performed in 1957?

10. The 1951 film *Ten Tall Men* starring Burt Lancaster is about which organization?

11. What was the name of the character played by Ursula Andress in the Bond film *Casino Royale*?

12. In which year was the Verdi opera *Aida* first performed?

13. What was the former name, until 1930, of the Turkish city Ankara?

14. In which African country do the Ibibio people live?

15. Who was the lover of Leander in Greek mythology?

ANSWERS 1. Piper Laurie **2.** Hannibal **3.** W. Somerset Maugham **4.** Sam Peckinpah **5.** Handel **6.** Ukraine **7.** Paul Theroux **8.** Rosario **9.** Stravinsky **10.** The Foreign Legion **11.** Vespa Lynd **12.** 1871 **13.** Angora **14.** Nigeria **15.** Hero.

ENTERTAINMENT

1. In which year was Welsh tenor Stuart Burrows born?

2. What is Roddy McDowall's profession in the 1967 Disney film *The Adventures of Bullwhip Griffin*?

3. Who played Al Capone in the television show *The Untouchables*?

4. Which model is female presenter of Channel Five's *Fort Boyard*?

5. Which creature does the eating in Tobe Hooper's film *Eaten Alive*?

6. Who composed the 1836 opera *The Night Bell*?

7. In which city was the 1994 film *Immortal Beloved*, about the composer Beethoven, filmed?

8. What was Reg Varney's character name in the sitcom *On the Buses*?

9. Which stand-up comedian starred in the 1990 film *The Adventures of Ford Fairlane*?

10. Who played Major Mohn in the television drama series *Colditz*?

11. Which Oscar-winning song was the theme song of the 1965 film *The Sandpiper*?

12. What was Georgina Moon's character name in sitcom *Up Pompeii*?

13. What was the name of the Glaswegian crook in the 1996 sitcom *Bad Boys*?

14. In which opera do the characters Canio and Nedda appear?

15. Who played Laurence Kirbridge in the television drama *Upstairs Downstairs*?

ANSWERS 1. 1933 **2.** Butler **3.** Neville Brand **4.** Melinda Messenger **5.** A crocodile **6.** Donizetti **7.** Prague **8.** Stan Butler **9.** Andrew Dice Clay **10.** Anthony Valentine **11.** The Shadow of Your Smile **12.** Erotica **13.** Fraser Hood **14.** I Pagliacci **15.** Ian Ogilvy.

SPORT

1. What nationality is former moto-cross world champion Alessandro Chiodi?

2. What sport do Manchester Giants and London Towers play?

3. What was the attendance at the 1886 Scottish F.A. Cup Final?

4. Who partnered Anne Smith to victory in the 1982 French Open tennis women's doubles title?

5. Who won the 1995 New York women's marathon?

6. With which sport are Julia King and Kertsen Kielgass associated?

7. How many times did cyclist Eddy Merckx win the Milan-San Remo race?

8. At which sport was Clas Thunberg an Olympic champion in 1924 & 1928?

9. In which year did Gladiateur win the Epsom Derby?

10. Which women's event did Sarka Kasparkova win at the 1997 world championships in athletics?

11. Who lost 13-0 to New Zealand in a 1981 football World Cup qualifying game?

12. Where were the 1967 World Student Games held?

13. Who was the 1973 women's 400m freestyle swimming world champion?

14. Which country won the 1997 Alfred Dunhill Cup in golf?

15. Where were the 1999 Pan-American Games held?

ANSWERS 1. Italian 2. Basketball 3. 7,000 4. Martina Navratilova 5. Tegla Loroupe 6. Swimming 7. Seven 8. Speed skating 9. 1865 10. Triple jump 11. Fiji 12. Tokyo 13. Heather Greenwood 14. South Africa 15. Winnipeg.

POP

1. Which group had a 1999 Top 10 single with *Every Day I Love You*?

2. Which orchestra featured on Marti Webb's 1986 hit *Always There*?

3. Which 1950s singer released the 1989 album *Yo Frankie*?

4. Which group had a 1993 hit single with *Glastonbury Song*?

5. In which year did Jimmy Nail chart with the single *Crocodile Shoes*?

6. With whom did Mark Knopfler record the 1990 album of guitar duets *Neck and Neck*?

7. Which group recorded the 1999 Top 10 hit *Boom, Boom, Boom, Boom !!!*?

8. Which label did Leftfield sign for in 1992?

9. Which female singer had a 1993 hit with *Careless Whisper*?

10. Who had a 1999 Top 10 single with *Back In My Life*?

11. Which group had a 1990 hit with *Papa Was A Rolling Stone*?

12. On which label did Will Smith record the album *Willennium*?

13. In which year was Dionne Warwick born?

14. In which year did Sheryl Crow have a Top 10 single with *All I Wanna Do*?

15. In which year did Madness have a hit single with *One Step Beyond*?

ANSWERS 1. Boyzone **2.** Simon May Orchestra **3.** Dion **4.** The Waterboys **5.** 1994 **6.** Chet Atkins **7.** Vengaboys **8.** Hard Hands **9.** Sarah Washington **10.** Alice Deejay **11.** Was (Not Was) **12.** Columbia **13.** 1940 **14.** 1994 **15.** 1979.

HISTORY

1. Which Israeli prime minister was born in Brest Litovsk in 1913?

2. In which year did Julio Maria Sanguinetti first take office as Uruguayan president?

3. In which city was Lambert Simnel crowned on Whit Sunday in 1487?

4. In which year did Malta become independent?

5. Who became prime minister of New Zealand in 1990?

6. In which year did Minister of Defence Hafez al-Assad seize control of the Syrian government?

7. Marcus Junius Brutus, an assassin of Julius Caesar, was nephew of which Roman philosopher?

8. Who was shadow Chancellor of the Exchequer from 1955-61?

9. What age was Konrad Adenauer when he resigned as West German Chancellor in 1963?

10. In which year did Daniel Arap Moi become president of Kenya?

11. In which ship did John Cabot set sail from Bristol in May 1497?

12. Who succeeded Anthony Crosland in 1977 as Foreign Secretary?

13. Who was appointed Youth Leader of the Reich in June 1933?

14. The War of the Pacific from 1879-83 was between Chile and which two countries?

15. From 1880-81, James Longstreet was U.S. minister to which country?

ANSWERS 1. Menachem Begin **2.** 1985 **3.** Dublin **4.** 1961 **5.** James Bolger **6.** 1970 **7.** Cato the Younger **8.** Harold Wilson **9.** 87 **10.** 1978 **11.** The Matthew **12.** David Owen **13.** Baldur von Schirach **14.** Peru & Bolivia **15.** Turkey.

GENERAL KNOWLEDGE

1. What is the name of the writing paper measuring 13 and a half inches by 17 inches, named after the watermark which was formerly used on it?

2. Which opera by Ponchielli contains the ballet *Dance Of The Hours*?

3. What was the name of the actor who played Grandpa in the television series *The Waltons*?

4. Which comic book character's alter ego is Dr. Banner?

5. Who was the director of the 1980 comedy film *The Blues Brothers*?

6. What was the food of the gods in classical mythology?

7. Who wrote the 1979 novel *Office Life*?

8. Who wrote the 1889 operetta *The Gondoliers*?

9. In which novel by Charles Dickens does the character Uriah Heep appear?

10. What is the name of the British unit of measurement equal to one eighth of a fluid ounce?

11. In which U.S. state is Mount Elbert, the highest peak in the Rocky Mountains?

12. Which English conductor founded the Promenade Concerts in London?

13. Which American actor was known as *The Great Profile*?

14. Who wrote the 1976 science fiction novel *Children Of Dune*?

15. What is a fly agaric?

ENTERTAINMENT

1. Who played the title role in the 1993 film *The Adventures Of Huck Finn*?

2. What was Robert Vaughn's character called in the television series *The Protectors*?

3. What nationality is opera singer Sally Burgess?

4. Which English comedian starred in the 1960 film *Sands Of The Desert*?

5. Which comedian played the manager of *Ballyskillen Opera House* in a 1981 sitcom?

6. Who directed the 1954 film *The Dam Busters*?

7. What was Michael Caine's character name in the 1967 movie *Billion Dollar Brain*?

8. Which actress plays Jack Palance's girlfriend in the 1955 film *I Died a Thousand Times*?

9. Who directed the 1999 film *The Hurricane*?

10. Which actor's son plays the kidnapped child in the 1996 film *Ransom*?

11. What pseudonym did Ronnie Barker use to write the 1988 sitcom *Clarence*?

12. In which year did American music-hall artist Josephine Baker die?

13. Who plays demonic child Damien in the 1978 film *Damien – Omen II*?

14. In which year did U.S. actress Tallulah Bankhead die?

15. Which actress played the lead in the children's show *Clarissa Explains It All*?

SPORT

1. With which ball game are Karen Corr and Tessa Davidson associated?

2. Which horse won the 1972 Irish 1000 Guineas?

3. Which wicket-keeper made five dismissals for India against Zimbabwe in the 1983 cricket World Cup?

4. Who won the 1987 European Champion Clubs' Cup in football?

5. With which sport are Wilt Chamberlain and Scottie Pippen associated?

6. In which year was the first limited-overs international played in cricket?

7. What nationality is boxer Erik Morales?

8. Three Troikas won the 1979 Prix de l'Arc de Triomphe. Which other French classic did it win that year?

9. Which country were men's coxless fours Olympic rowing champions from 1924-32?

10. What country does boxer Dodie Penalosa represent?

11. Who was 1956 world 500cc motor cycling champion?

12. Which Olympic event did the Osborne Swimming Club, Manchester win in 1900?

13. In which month was the 1903 F.A. Cup Final between Bury and Derby County played?

14. What sport do Andrew Baggaley and Juan Yong Yun play?

15. How long did Petrus Silkinas take to run 1,000 miles in March, 1998?

ANSWERS 1. Snooker **2.** Pidget **3.** Syed Kirmani **4.** FC Porto **5.** Basketball **6.** 1971 **7.** Mexican **8.** Poule d'Essai des Pouliches **9.** Great Britain **10.** Philippines **11.** John Surtees **12.** Water polo **13.** April **14.** Table tennis **15.** 11days, 13 hours

POP

1. Which jazz band backed Bob Wallis on his 1961 hit *I'm Shy Mary Ellen I'm Shy*?

2. In which city did the Legendary Pink Dots form in 1980?

3. In which year did the Walker Brothers have a Top 10 single with *My Ship Is Coming In*?

4. In which year did Blondie have a Top 10 single with *Dreaming*?

5. Which Suzanne Vega song did The Lemonheads cover on the album *Lick*?

6. Who recorded the 1978 single *Murder of Liddle Towers*?

7. What is the real name of Guns n' Roses guitarist Izzy Stradlin?

8. Which female singer's albums include *Welcome To The Cruise?*

9. Who did Barry Jenkins replace as drummer in The Animals?

10. Which solo singer had a 1999 Top 10 single with *(You Drive Me) Crazy*?

11. In which year did Duran Duran have the hit single *Wild Boys*?

12. Which band covered the song *God Save The Queen* by the Sex Pistols on the 1985 mini-LP *Armed And Dangerous*?

13. Which German singer recorded the 1982 album *Nun Sex Monk Rock*?

14. Which group recorded the song *How Does A Duck Know?* on the album *God Shuffled His Feet*?

15. In which year was Blur's single *End of a Century* released?

ANSWERS 1. Storyville Jazz Band **2.** London **3.** 1965 **4.** 1979 **5.** Luka **6.** Angelic Upstarts **7.** Jeff Isabelle **8.** Judie Tzuke **9.** John Steel **10.** Britney Spears **11.** 1984 **12.** Anthrax **13.** Nina Hagen **14.** Crash Test Dummies **15.** 1994.

WORDS

1. If you torrefy something, what do you do to it?

2. What drink would you make from hyson?

3. What is the Latin phrase for a list of characters in a play?

4. What does the prefix hyper- mean?

5. The word harass comes from the Old French verb 'harer', meaning what?

6. How many lines of verse are in a tercet?

7. What does the French word goût mean?

8. How many people sing in a terzetto?

9. If you were vulturine, what creature would you resemble?

10. What is another name for a water tortoise?

11. What in Scotland is an orraman?

12. What does the adjective vorticose mean?

13. If something is volitant, what is it capable of?

14. How many faces does a pebble called a dreikanter have?

15. Huckle is a rare word for which part of the body?

ANSWERS 1. Dry it by roasting it 2. Tea 3. dramatis personae 4. Over, above or in excess 5. To set a dog on 6. Three 7. Taste or good taste 8. Three 9. A vulture 10. Terrapin 11. Oddjobman 12. Whirling or rotating quickly 13. Flying 14. Three 15. The haunch or hip.

GENERAL KNOWLEDGE

1. What is a bobwhite?

2. Which chesspiece can only move diagonally?

3. Which pop singer was born Marvin Lee Aday?

4. Which German was composer of choral work *A German Requiem*?

5. Who wrote the 1960 book *Born Free*?

6. Which U.S. president was known as Ike?

7. Who wrote the 1939 novel *Happy Valley*?

8. The 1951 film *The Magic Box* was about the life of which film pioneer?

9. Which former England Test cricket captain was India's representative at the League of Nations?

10. Who was the director of the 1964 film *The Pink Panther*?

11. Which 18th century politician was caricatured in the novel *The Adventures of Peregrine Pickle* by Tobias Smollett as Scragg?

12. Which theatre in the Waterloo Road, London, was managed by Lilian Baylis from 1912?

13. Who wrote the play *The Corn Is Green*?

14. Who penned the 1984 novel *The Angels Weep*?

15. Which England Test cricket captain was known as 'The Champion'?

ANSWERS 1. A North American quail **2.** Bishop **3.** Meat Loaf **4.** Johannes Brahms **5.** Joy Adamson **6.** Dwight D. Eisenhower **7.** Patrick White **8.** William Friese-Greene **9.** C.B. Fry **10.** Blake Edwards **11.** George Lyttelton **12.** Old Vic **13.** Emlyn Williams **14.** Wilbur Smith **15.** W.G. Grace.

ENTERTAINMENT

1. In which year did the R.S.C. move to the Barbican Theatre in London?

2. What was the name of Frank Spencer's wife in the sitcom *Some Mothers Do 'Ave 'Em*?

3. The 1962 film *Damn the Defiant!* is set during which series of wars?

4. What was the middle name of showman Phineas T. Barnum?

5. Which U.S. actress appeared as Madame Trentoni in the play *Captain Jinks Of The Horse Marines* in New York in 1901?

6. Who directed the 1943 film musical *I Dood It*?

7. Who composed the 1838 opera *Benvenuto Cellini*?

8. Gillian Pieface was a former stage name of which alternative comedian?

9. What nationality was soprano Erna Berger who died in 1990?

10. Who played Jerry Leadbetter in the sitcom *The Good Life*?

11. Actor Matthew James Almond is the son of which actress?

12. What was Sharon's surname in the sitcom *The Fenn Street Gang*?

13. The 1969 Disney film *Rascal* centres around a boy and his pet. What pet?

14. Who played Jack Mowbray in the 1980s sitcom *Ffizz*?

15. Who wrote and appeared in the 1972 sitcom *A Class By Himself*?

ANSWERS 1. 1982 **2.** Betty **3.** Napoleonic Wars **4.** Taylor **5.** Ethel Barrymore **6.** Vincente Minnelli **7.** Berlioz **8.** Julian Clary **9.** German **10.** Paul Eddington **11.** Genevieve Bujold **12.** Eversleigh **13.** A raccoon **14.** Richard Griffiths **15.** Richard Stilgoe.

SPORT

1. Which New Zealand golfer won the 2000 Australian Masters in Melbourne?

2. Which country were team pursuit champions at the 1990 world championships in cycling?

3. Where were the 1970 World Student games held?

4. In which year was the Le Mans 24-hour race inaugurated?

5. Which women's team won the FIH World Cup in hockey in 1994 & 1998?

6. Where were the 1994 Asian Games held?

7. In which year did the Curtis Cup finish in a draw for the first time?

8. What was the name of the winning craft in the 1885 America's Cup?

9. What nationality is boxer Jorge Paez?

10. Which Japanese boxer was a 1996 WBA light-flyweight boxing champion?

11. In which year did tennis player Pancho Gonzales die?

12. In which year was the National Hockey League founded in Montreal?

13. Who won the 1974 Tournament Players' Championship in golf?

14. Who scored 18 points in the 1985 Super Bowl for the San Francisco 49ers?

15. Who was the 1997 U.S. Open women's singles tennis champion?

ANSWERS 1. Michael Campbell **2.** U.S.S.R. **3.** Turin **4.** 1923 **5.** Australia **6.** Hiroshima **7.** 1936 **8.** Puritan **9.** Mexican **10.** Keiji Yamaguchi **11.** 1995 **12.** 1917 **13.** Jack Nicklaus **14.** Roger Craig **15.** Martina Hingis.

POP

1. Which author guests on the 1983 Hawkwind album *Zones*?

2. What was the B-side of the Cream single *Wrapping Paper*?

3. Who recorded the 1995 hit single *No More I Love Yous*?

4. Which singer-songwriter recorded the 1978 L.P. *The Future Now*?

5. Animal, P.J., Magoo and Winston comprised which punk group?

6. Which Irish group had a hit single in 1998 with *That's Why We Lose Control*?

7. Who is the leader of the group *My Life Story*?

8. What did the Cranberries change their name from in 1990?

9. Which Rolling Stones studio album features the song *Fool To Cry*?

10. Nasty Suicide was guitarist in which Finnish punk band?

11. Which U.S. rap group had a 1994 hit single with *Tap The Bottle*?

12. Dan Crouch and Adrian Stephens record under what name?

13. Which guitarist co-wrote the song *Split Decision* with Steve Winwood?

14. Who recorded the 1993 album *Surfing on Sine Waves*?

15. Which U.S. group's singles include *They Cleaned My Cut With a Wire Brush*?

ANSWERS 1. Michael Moorcock **2.** Cat's Squirrel **3.** Annie Lennox **4.** Peter Hammill **5.** Anti-Nowhere League **6.** Young Offenders **7.** Jake Shillingford **8.** The Cranberry-Saw-Us **9.** Black and Blue **10.** Hanoi Rocks **11.** Young Black Teenagers **12.** Bell **13.** Joe Walsh **14.** Aphex Twin **15.** Happy Flowers.

SCIENCE

1. Approximately how many miles in diameter is Uranus's moon Cordelia?

2. What is seismology?

3. In which year did Max Planck die?

4. What nationality is astronaut Wubbo Ockels?

5. In computing, what did the initials of military computer ENIAC represent?

6. What nationality was psychologist Jean Piaget?

7. In which year did electronic digital computer Colossus first become operational?

8. What period of time is defined as 9,192,631,770 periods of the radiation corresponding to the transition between the two hyperfine levels of the ground state of caesium-133?

9. In which year was British physicist Sir James Chadwick knighted?

10. In which year was Saturn's moon Hyperion discovered?

11. In which U.S. state is the Woods Hole Oceanographic Institution?

12. What is the approximate temperature of the surface of Neptune in degrees Celsius?

13. In which year did botanist Andrea Cesalpino die?

14. In which European capital was biochemist Max F. Perutz born?

15. Which Yorkshire-born biologist named the field of genetics?

GENERAL KNOWLEDGE

1. Who wrote the 1966 poetry volume entitled *Pleasures of the Flesh*?

2. Which Estonian composer's symphonies include *If Bach had kept bees*?

3. Which Indian tennis player appeared in the 1983 James Bond film *Octopussy*?

4. Which American actor born in 1908 voiced the cartoon characters Daffy Duck and Porky Pig?

5. Which drama critic born in 1877 wrote the nine-part autobiography *Ego*?

6. Who penned the 1945 novel *Loving*?

7. Who was director of the 1993 film *The Joy Luck Club*?

8. Which earthy mineral, also called sepiolite, is used to make tobacco pipes?

9. What is the basic S.I. unit of electric current?

10. What is the meltemi?

11. In which year did singer-actor Bing Crosby die?

12. Who was a Best Supporting Actress Oscar winner for the film *The English Patient*?

13. Who wrote the 1981 novel *Bliss*?

14. Which communicable disease is also called scarlatina?

15. Who wrote the 1950 novel *The Third Man*?

ENTERTAINMENT

1. Who played Eddie Catflap in the sitcom *Filthy, Rich and Catflap*?

2. Who starred as *The Climber* in a 1983 sitcom?

3. Which comedian played Jumbo in the 1960s sitcom *Fire Crackers*?

4. Who is television's *The Naked Chef*?

5. What is the name of 'entertainer' John Shuttleworth's wife?

6. Which of television's *Two Fat Ladies* died in 1999?

7. Who composed the 1956 one-act opera *Ruth*?

8. Who plays D.C. Rawton in *The Bill*?

9. Who directed the 1999 film *The Insider*?

10. Which of the Barrymore acting dynasty played Rasputin in the 1932 film *Rasputin and the Empress*?

11. Who plays a drunken helicopter pilot in the 1983 film *Dance of the Dwarfs*?

12. Who directed the 1957 film *The Undead*?

13. On whose bestseller is the 1993 film *Needful Things* based?

14. Who scored the 1962 film *A Walk on the Wild Side*?

15. For which magazine did Jane Lucas, played by Maureen Lipman, write a problem page in the sitcom *Agony*?

ANSWERS 1. Adrian Edmondson **2.** Robin Nedwell **3.** Joe Baker **4.** Jamie Oliver **5.** Mary **6.** Jennifer Paterson **7.** Sir Lennox Berkeley **8.** Libby Davison **9.** Michael Mann **10.** Lionel Barrymore **11.** Peter Fonda **12.** Roger Corman **13.** Stephen King **14.** Elmer Bernstein **15.** Person.

SPORT

1. In which fencing event was Laura Flessel the 1996 Olympic champion?

2. Who scored Ireland's winning try in their 1988 victory over Scotland in the Five Nations?

3. Who was the 1996 Olympic women's springboard diving champion?

4. Which American golfer won the 1979 World Matchplay championship?

5. In which year did Sergio Garcia first play in the Ryder Cup?

6. With what winter sport would you associate Fabrice Becker and Nikki Stone?

7. Which team won the Wadworth 6X National Village Cricket Championship Final in 1999?

8. At which ground did cricketer Victor Richardson of Australia take five field catches against South Africa in March, 1936?

9. Who did Wasps play in the quarter-finals of the Heineken Cup in 2000 in rugby union?

10. Who did the Baseball Writers' Association make Most Valuable Player of the Year in the National League in 1958?

11. How many Tests did cricketer Derek Pringle play for England?

12. Which horse won the 1981 Dewhurst Stakes?

13. What is the nickname of cricketer Mark Broadhurst?

14. Of what sport have Penny Fellows and Charlotte Cornwallis been British Open Champions?

15. How many golds did the U.S. win in the 1999 World Athletics Championships?

ANSWERS 1. Épée **2.** Michael Bradley **3.** Fu Mongxia **4.** Bill Rogers **5.** 1999 **6.** Freestyle skiing **7.** Linton Park **8.** Durban **9.** Northampton **10.** Ernest Banks **11.** 30 **12.** Wind and Wuthering **13.** Broady **14.** Real tennis **15.** Eleven.

POP

1. On which studio album by Creedence Clearwater Revival does the song *Bad Moon Rising* appear?

2. Who recorded the 1999 dance single *Destination Sunshine*?

3. Which singer released the soundtrack album *Pola X* in 2000?

4. Which group recorded the 1990 double album *i*?

5. Which male singer's Top 20 hits include *Tomb of Memories* and *Now I Know What Made Otis Blue*?

6. From which country do group Don Air originate?

7. Which solo artist recorded the 1984 hit single *Never Ending Story*?

8. Who composed the soundtrack to the Bond film *Thunderball*?

9. What was Jimmy Young's follow-up to his two No. 1 hits in 1955?

10. Yes had a U.S. No. 1 single with *Owner Of A Lonely Heart*. What was the song's highest chart placing in the U.K.?

11. What name does Conrad Lambert record under?

12. Who had a 2000 Top 10 hit with *Move Your Body*?

13. On which 1971 studio album by King Crimson does the song *Sailor's Tale* appear?

14. Which solo artist had a 1984 Top 10 single with *Self Control*?

15. Which member of Pink Fairies died in 1994?

ANSWERS 1. Green River **2.** Balearic Bill **3.** Scott Walker **4.** A.R. Kane **5.** Paul Young **6.** Germany **7.** Limahl **8.** John Barry **9.** Someone on Your Mind **10.** 28 **11.** Merz **12.** Eiffel 65 **13.** Islands **14.** Laura Branigan **15.** Mick Wayne.

PEOPLE

1. Which philosopher was also known as Doctor Angelicus?

2. In which country was holiday camp proprietor Sir Billy Butlin born?

3. Which film star gets beaten up in a 2000 Italian television advertisment for jewellers Damiani?

4. Who became president of Switzerland in 1987?

5. In which American city was choreographer Louis Falco born in 1942?

6. Which actor was dropped by director Sean Penn from the movie *The Pledge* as sidekick to Jack Nicholson?

7. In which year did fashion designer Pierre Balman die?

8. Of which country was Bülent Ecevit prime minister from 1978-9?

9. Which famous outlaw was born in Beaver, Utah in 1866?

10. Who won the Best Actor award at the 1999 Elle Style Awards?

11. What is the real name of band member 'H' of the group Steps?

12. Which actor's wife, Nerine Kidd, drowned in 1999?

13. Which Boston school did Jacob Abbott found in 1829?

14. Who shared the 1976 Nobel peace prize with Mairead Corrigan?

15. Jesse Wood is the son of which rock star?

GENERAL KNOWLEDGE

1. In which European country is the industrial city of Bytom?

2. Which bone of the human skeleton is also called the thighbone?

3. On which river is the German industrial city Cologne?

4. Which bowed stringed instrument is the alto of the violin family?

5. What is the derived S.I. unit of electrical resistance?

6. Which Ireland rugby union international was captain of the 1974 Lions tour of South Africa?

7. Who is wife of Antipholus of Ephesus in the play *The Comedy Of Errors*?

8. Who is the American author of the novel *The Wapshot Chronicle*?

9. What is the second sign of the zodiac?

10. Who was the director of the 1988 film *Tequila Sunrise*?

11. Who scripted the 1965 film *What's New, Pussycat?*?

12. Who was a Best Supporting Actress Oscar winner for film *Sayonara*?

13. Who wrote the 1937 book *Of Mice And Men*?

14. Which republic occupies the western part of the island of Hispaniola?

15. Who was the 1952 Wimbledon men's singles tennis champion?

ANSWERS 1. Poland **2.** Femur **3.** Rhine **4.** Viola **5.** Ohm **6.** Willie John McBride **7.** Adriana **8.** John Cheever **9.** Taurus **10.** Robert Towne **11.** Woody Allen **12.** Miyoshi Umeki **13.** John Steinbeck **14.** Haiti **15.** Frank Sedgman.

ENTERTAINMENT

1. Who played Raquel in *Coronation Street*?

2. Who does Christopher Chittell play in soap *Emmerdale*?

3. Who is the lover of *Manon* in an opera by Massenet?

4. Who voices Jessie in the film *Toy Story 2*?

5. Who plays a Houston dance instructor in the 1998 film *Dance With Me*?

6. Who won Best Actress in a Drama at the 2000 Golden Globes?

7. Who directed the 1987 film *Wall Street*?

8. What does Esther Williams play in the 1949 film *Neptune's Daughter*?

9. Who played Ann Fourmile in the sitcom *George and Mildred*?

10. What was Richard Gere's character name in 1990 film *Pretty Woman*?

11. Which actor played Boris in the 1959 sitcom *Gert and Daisy*?

12. Which writing team created the 1992 sitcom *Get Back*?

13. Which actor plays the lead in the 1944 cowboy film *Nevada*?

14. What is the nickname of Peter Langford in the comedy group The Barron Knights?

15. In which country is the 1949 Alfred Hitchcock film *Under Capricorn* set?

SPORT

1. Which sport does the UIPM govern?

2. Who broke his right tibia in a collision with Steve Waugh on the second day of Australia's first Test against Sri Lanka, in September, 1999?

3. Who beat Newport County 13-0 in football's Division Two in October, 1946?

4. In cricket, who scored 108 for Gloucestershire vs. Northants in the 1st innings of their 1999 county championship game?

5. Which man set a world record of 8.95 for the long jump on 30th August, 1991?

6. Which athlete was the 1966 Sports Illustrated Sportsman of the Year?

7. In which year was the Royal Montreal Curling Club formed?

8. In which year did cricketer Nathan Batson make his county debut for Warwickshire?

9. SC Magdeburg were winners of the European Cup in 1981. In which sport?

10. In which year was runner Donovan Bailey born?

11. Which Frenchman won the 1971 U.S. Grand Prix in F1?

12. In which year did tennis star Jean Borotra die?

13. In which year did Cumbria win their first English County Championship in rugby union?

14. In which year was runner Leroy Burrell born?

15. In which year did Terry Marsh become IBF super-lightweight boxing world champion?

ANSWERS 1. Modern Pentathlon **2.** Jason Gillespie **3.** Newcastle United **4.** Robert Cunliffe **5.** Mike Powell **6.** Jim Ryun **7.** 1807 **8.** 1998 **9.** Handball **10.** 1967 **11.** Francois Cevert **12.** 1994 **13.** 1997 **14.** 1967 **15.** 1987.

POP

1. In which state of the U.S. was singer Joan Osborne born?

2. Which member of the Foo Fighters left in 1999?

3. Who recorded the 1982 live album *Talk Of The Devil*?

4. Which U.S. group recorded the 1992 L.P. *Happy Hour*?

5. In which year did group Ozric Tentacles form?

6. Which jazz artist recorded the L.P. *Sketches of Spain*?

7. Which guitarist wrote the soundtrack to the film *Death Wish 2*?

8. What is the title of the 1999 album by *Rage Against The Machine*?

9. The string section of which orchestra played on the single *Thank You* by the Pale Fountains?

10. Who recorded the 1990 album *Cowboys From Hell*?

11. Which member of the Kinks wrote the autobiographical book *X-Ray*?

12. Who produced the 1976 album *Howlin' Wind* by Graham Parker and the Rumour?

13. Which group recorded the 1975 album *Chocolate City*?

14. In which year did the Style Council have a Top 10 single with *Shout To The Top*?

15. What animal features on the cover of the Gallon Drunk single *The Last Gasp (Safety)*?

ART

1. In which year did painter Otto Dix die?

2. *Our House In The Last World* was the first novel by which Pulitzer Prize-winning author?

3. Which French painter's works include 1906's *The Three Umbrellas*?

4. Which U.S.-born Dadaist published the 1963 autobiography *Self Portrait*?

5. In which year was Jane Austen's *Pride And Prejudice* first published?

6. Who wrote the 1999 autobiography *'Tis*?

7. Which French painter's works include *The Belfry Of Douai* and *Bridge Of Narni*?

8. Who wrote the novel *Atlantis Found*?

9. In which city was painter Jacques-Louis David born?

10. Who wrote the novel *Clayhanger*?

11. What did artist Max Ernst begin studying at the University of Bonn in 1909?

12. Whose stories include *The Legend of Sleepy Hollow*?

13. Which French artist born in 1881 painted 1954's *The Great Parade*?

14. Who wrote the 1956 novel *A Walk on the Wild Side*?

15. In which year was artist Bridget Riley made a Companion of Honour?

GENERAL KNOWLEDGE

1. Which husband and wife team created the television puppet series *Thunderbirds*?

2. Who was the Tanzanian president from 1964 to 1985?

3. Who wrote the 1930 novel *Rogue Herries*?

4. On which sea is the port of Odessa in the Ukraine?

5. Who is the female lead in the 1990 film *White Palace*?

6. In which year did Amy Johnson, British aviator, die?

7. Who was the author of the play *She Stoops To Conquer*?

8. Which actor directed and starred in the 1983 film *Sudden Impact*?

9. Who was Roman goddess of the hunt and the moon?

10. Which pop singer was born Reginald Dwight in 1947?

11. Which golfer captained the 1957 British P.G.A. Ryder Cup winning team?

12. Which British comedian starred in the 1937 film *Oh, Mr. Porter !*?

13. Gap is the capital of which department of S.E. France?

14. Christiania is the former name of which European capital city?

15. Who is the author of the 1978 novel *The Bad Sister*?

ENTERTAINMENT

1. Who replaced Robert Lindsay as Jakie Smith in the sitcom *Get Some In!*?

2. In which opera does the maid Despina appear?

3. Who co-produced and starred in the 1999 film *Never Been Kissed*?

4. Who wrote 1970's children's sitcom *The Ghosts Of Motley Hall*?

5. In which year was U.S. comedian Alan King born?

6. Who played The Skipper in the U.S. sitcom *Gilligan's Island*?

7. Who is Tony Soprano's psychiatrist in *The Sopranos*?

8. Who voices Hamm in the film *Toy Story 2*?

9. Which comedian plays a sadistic gangster in the 1960 British film *Never Let Go*?

10. Which actor plays thug Muerte in the 1993 film *Undercover Blues*?

11. Which former *Coronation Street* actress played Stella in 1990's sitcom *The Gingerbread Girl*?

12. Which comedy actor played Richard Gander in the 1972 sitcom *Alcock and Gander*?

13. What was Tracey Ullman's character name in the sitcom *Girls on Top*?

14. Who composed the 1899 opera *The Devil And Kate*?

15. Which footballer appeared as Sacha Distel in a 1999 *Stars In Their Eyes* celebrity special?

ANSWERS 1. Karl Howman **2.** Cosi fan tutte **3.** Drew Barrymore **4.** Richard Carpenter **5.** 1927 **6.** Alan Hale Jr. **7.** Dr. Jennifer Melfi **8.** John Katzenberger **9.** Peter Sellers **10.** Stanley Tucci **11.** Tracey Bennett **12.** Richard O'Sullivan **13.** Candice Valentine **14.** Dvorak **15.** David Ginola.

SPORT

1. Who was women's individual world trampolining champion from 1964-8?

2. Which jockey was leading money-winner in the U.S. in 1951?

3. In cricket, who scored 259 n.o. for Glamorgan vs. Notts in the 1st innings of their 1999 county championship game?

4. Who were men's team winners in archery at the 1996 Olympic Games?

5. Which U.S. pair won the 1957 Wimbledon men's doubles tennis title?

6. Who rode Emily Little to victory in the 1952 Badminton Horse Trials in Three-Day Eventing?

7. What nationality is rugby union player Agustin Pichot?

8. Who was the 1968 Olympic men's highboard platform diving champion?

9. What nationality was golfer Bobby Locke?

10. For which Minor Counties side has Surrey cricketer J.N. Batty played?

11. Bjarte-Engen Vik was a 1998 Olympic champion. At what sport?

12. Who did Yevgeny Kafelnikov beat in the semi-finals of the 2000 Australian Open tennis singles championship?

13. How many tons did David Gower make in his 117 Tests from 1978-92?

14. What is cricketer David Boon's middle name?

15. Which team lost the 1932 World Series in baseball?

ANSWERS 1. Judy Wills 2. Bill Shoemaker 3. Steve James 4. U.S.A. 5. Gardnar Mulloy & Budge Patty 6. Mark Darley 7. Argentinian 8. Klaus Dibiasi 9. South African 10. Oxfordshire 11. Nordic skiing 12. Magnus Norman 13. 18 14. Clarence 15. Chicago Cubs.

POP

1. Which was the only album by The International Submarine Band?

2. What is the title of Salaryman's 1999 album?

3. How old was Gram Parsons when he died?

4. Which Welsh folk singer's albums include 1970s *Outlander*?

5. Which studio album by Pavement features the single *Rattled By The Rush*?

6. Which group backed Graham Parker on the 1996 album *Live From New York*?

7. In which country did Robert Palmer spend much of his childhood?

8. Masters, Naismith, Cooper – which 1980s band?

9. Stewart, Sager, Underwood, Smith – which post-punk group?

10. Who had a hit single in 1980 with *DK 50-80*?

11. Who had a 1983 hit single with *Big Log*?

12. Which band did Randy Rhoads play in before joining Ozzy Osborne?

13. Singer Mimi Farina is sister of which singer?

14. What age was Clyde McPhatter when he died?

15. Who had a 1984 Top 10 single with *I'm Gonna Tear Your Playhouse Down*?

ANSWERS 1. Safe at Home **2.** Karoshi **3.** 26 **4.** Meic Stevens **5.** Wowee Zowee **6.** The Episodes **7.** Malta **8.** Pale Saints **9.** The Pop Group **10.** John Otway and Wild Willy Barrett **11.** Robert Plant **12.** Quiet Riot **13.** Joan Baez **14.** 39 **15.** Paul Young.

GEOGRAPHY

1. What is an inselberg?

2. Between the mouths of which two rivers does Aberdeen lie?

3. Of which country was Roskilde the capital until 1443?

4. What is the name given to a flat-topped plateau with steep edges?

5. Corinium was the Roman name of which market town?

6. On which river does the Iraqi city of Mosul stand?

7. In which Australian state is the fertile area of Gippsland?

8. Metz is the capital of which department of France?

9. What is the fishing village of Brighthelmston now known as?

10. In which U.S. state is Shenandoah National Park?

11. Which country lies immediately south of Kenya?

12. Into which sea does the River Dnieper flow?

13. Which river enters the North Sea at Berwick?

14. In which country is El Alamein?

15. Which country lies immediately south of Belarus?

GENERAL KNOWLEDGE

1. Liz Edgar is the sister of which Cardiff-born show jumper?

2. What is the brightest star in the constellation Cygnus?

3. Who wrote the 1961 novel *The Old Men at the Zoo*?

4. Which city in S.E. France was seat of the papacy from 1309-77?

5. What is the capital of the United Arab Emirates?

6. Who wrote the 1664 play *Tartuffe*?

7. Who was Chancellor of the Exchequer from 1993-7?

8. Who wrote the 1911 story collection *In a German Pension*?

9. In Greek mythology, which king of Thessaly was married to Alcestis?

10. Ungava is a sparsely inhabited region of which country?

11. In which constellation is the group of stars known as The Plough?

12. Who was the wife of King Ahab in the Old Testament?

13. Who was the author of the 1939 novel *The Grapes of Wrath*?

14. In which century did English composer and organist Thomas Tallis live?

15. Which actress' film roles include Diana in 1987's *White Mischief*?

ENTERTAINMENT

1. In the 1955 biopic *I'll Cry Tomorrow* who plays singer Lillian Roth?

2. Who played Major Otto Hecht in the 1979 film *Escape to Athena*?

3. Who plays a female cat-burglar in the 1993 film *The Real McCoy*?

4. Which British actress plays Marla Singer in the 1999 film *Fight Club*?

5. The 1936 Alfred Hitchcock film *Sabotage* was based on which novel by Joseph Conrad?

6. Who directed the video for Björk's single *It's Oh So Quiet*?

7. Who directed the 1975 film *The Day Of The Locust*?

8. Which Walt Disney film was recreated as a stage musical in London in 1999?

9. The 1953 film *Sabre Jet* has which war as its backdrop?

10. Who played Tina in the television drama *Casualty*?

11. Which wrestler starred in the 1991 film *Suburban Commando*?

12. Who played the title role in the 1955 film *Davy Crockett, King of the Wild Frontier*?

13. Who is the documentary maker in the spoof television series *People Like Us*?

14. Which comedian stars in the 1923 silent comedy *Safety Last*?

15. Which duo created, wrote, and performed in the 1999 sitcom *Spaced*?

SPORT

1. By what score did France beat Wales in the 2000 Six Nations tournament in rugby union?

2. Who rode the horse St. Jovite to victory in the 1992 King George VI & Queen Elizabeth Diamond Stakes?

3. Which medal did England win in the women's European Cup at hockey in 1999?

4. In what weight division was Göran Henrysson world champion at powerlifting from 1983-5?

5. How many golds did Ukraine win in the 1999 World Athletics Championships?

6. Which country were the 1997 winners of the women's World Cup in judo?

7. Which golfer won the 2000 Buick International golf tournament at Torrey Pines, California?

8. Which Italian club won the 1969 World Club Championship in football?

9. Which male squash player won the U.S. Open in November, 1999?

10. Who was men's high jump champion at the 1994 European Championships?

11. Which chess player won the FIDE world championship in August, 1999?

12. Which South African cricket competition was superseded by the Castle Cup in 1990?

13. Who took 5 for 12 for Leicestershire against Sussex at Leicester in 1996?

14. Jos Lux was 1907 parallel bars champion at the world championships in gymnastics. Which country did he represent?

15. For which rugby union club side does Jason Keyter play?

ANSWERS 1. 36-3 **2.** Stephen Craine **3.** Bronze **4.** 60 kg **5.** One **6.** Cuba **7.** Phil Mickelson **8.** A.C. Milan **9.** Simon Parke **10.** Steinar Hoen **11.** Alexander Khalifman **12.** Currie Cup **13.** Matthew Brimson **14.** France **15.** Harlequins.

POP

1. Who recorded a solo album in 1991 entitled *Fireball Zone*?

2. In which year did Kirsty MacColl have a Top 10 single with *A New England*?

3. Which singer-songwriter recorded the 1993 album *Perfectly Good Guitar*?

4. Who released the 2000 album *Waterfall Cities*?

5. Who had a 1999 Top 10 single with *Get Get Down*?

6. Which duo's songs include *Bloodsport For All* and *The Only Living Boy In New Cross*?

7. In which year did Phil Collins have a Top 10 single with *Another Day in Paradise*?

8. Which Irish singer recorded the 2000 album *Black River Falls*?

9. Which group recorded the 1994 album *Gideon Gaye*?

10. Which group recorded the 2000 album *Every Six Seconds*?

11. Which country artists albums include *Roses In The Snow* and *Angel Band*?

12. In which year was Johnny Cash discharged from the U.S.A.F.?

13. Who records under the name Juryman?

14. Which former member of Gong recorded the 1975 album *Fish Rising*?

15. Who produced the Wannadies album *Yeah*?

ANSWERS 1. Ric Ocasek **2.** 1985 **3.** John Hiatt **4.** Ozric Tentacles **5.** Paul Johnson **6.** Carter the Unstoppable Sex Machine **7.** 1989 **8.** Cathal Coughlan **9.** The High Llamas **10.** Group Dogdhill **11.** Emmylou Harris **12.** 1954 **13.** Ian Simmonds **14.** Steve Hillage **15.** Ric Ocasek.

HISTORY

1. Which American naval commander defeated the British in the Battle of Lake Erie in 1813?

2. Who was Solicitor-General from 1964-67?

3. In which year was the Secret Treaty of Dover signed?

4. What was the real name of 'Papa Doc', dictator of Haiti from 1957-71?

5. What was the name of the 1917 declaration by Great Britain in favour of a Jewish national home in Palestine?

6. In which year did spy Guy Burgess die?

7. Which pope crowned Otto I of Germany Holy Roman Emperor in 962?

8. What governmental post did Geoffrey Howe have from 1970-72?

9. In which year was the Achille Lauro cruise ship hijacked by the PLF?

10. Where is William Ewart Gladstone buried?

11. In which army did Guy Fawkes enlist in 1593?

12. Who was consecrated the first black African Methodist Bishop of Rhodesia in 1968?

13. In which year did the first shipment of British convicts sail to Australia?

14. Who was commander of the R.A.F. during the Battle of Britain?

15. Who was the father of Charles the Bold, the last Duke of Burgundy?

ANSWERS 1. Oliver Hazard Perry **2.** Sir Dingle Foot **3.** 1670 **4.** François Duvalier **5.** The Balfour Declaration **6.** 1963 **7.** Pope John XII **8.** Solicitor-General **9.** 1985 **10.** Westminster Abbey **11.** Spanish **12.** Abel Muzorewa **13.** 1787 **14.** Sir Hugh Dowding **15.** Philip the Good.

GENERAL KNOWLEDGE

1. What was the name of the songwriting brother of George Gershwin?

2. What is the standard monetary unit of Finland?

3. Which comedian wrote the novel *Stark*?

4. What is another name for the mountain K2?

5. What canine mammal is also called a prairie wolf?

6. Who wrote the 1931 stage production *Cavalcade*?

7. Who penned the 1881 children's book *Heidi*?

8. Which actress starred in the films *The Railway Children* and *Walkabout*?

9. Which river in Africa forms part of the border between the Democratic Republic of the Congo and Angola?

10. The constellation Volans lies between which two other constellations?

11. Who was director of the 1977 film *Eraserhead*?

12. Which singer-actress played *Evita* in the 1996 film?

13. In which year did country singer Jim Reeves die in an airplane crash?

14. Who was producer and director of the 1960 film *The Fall of the House of Usher*?

15. Which pair of aviators made the first non-stop flight across the Atlantic?

ANSWERS 1. Ira Gershwin **2.** Markka **3.** Ben Elton **4.** Godwin Austen (or Dapsang) **5.** Coyote **6.** Noël Coward **7.** Johanna Spyri **8.** Jenny Agutter **9.** Kasai **10.** Carina and Hydrus **11.** David Lynch **12.** Madonna **13.** 1964 **14.** Roger Corman **15.** John W. Alcock and A.W. Brown.

ENTERTAINMENT

1. Who played Mr. Salt in the 1971 film *Willy Wonka And The Chocolate Factory*?

2. Which comedy duo starred in the 1951 film *Sailor Beware*?

3. Who directed the 1994 film *Disclosure*?

4. What was the occupation of the *Cowboys* in a 1980's sitcom?

5. Who played Mick Travis in the 1968 film *If...*?

6. Who played Brian Quigley in television's *Ballykissangel*?

7. Who plays Dr. Jekyll in the 1996 film *Mary Reilly*?

8. Who plays Mr. Murdstone in the 1935 film *David Copperfield*?

9. Who directed the 1997 film *Career Girls*?

10. Who directed the 1994 film *I'll Do Anything*?

11. Who stars in the 2000 BBC TV drama series *Dirty Work*?

12. What was the name of comedian Leslie Crowther's actor father?

13. Who played Beth Jordache in *Brookside* on television?

14. What was Jodie Foster's character name in the film *Bugsy Malone*?

15. Which biblical character did Orson Welles play in the 1960 film *David And Goliath*?

SPORT

1. In which year did the Mexican Grand Prix gain world championships status in F1?

2. Which athlete was the 1982 B.B.C. Sports Personality of the Year?

3. How many rugby union international caps did Michel Crauste win for France from 1957-66?

4. In which year was the Central Council of Physical Recreation founded?

5. Who was world heavyweight boxing champion from 1926-30?

6. Who did Brazil play in the quarter-finals of the 2000 Davis Cup?

7. Which horse won the 1960 Hennessy Gold Cup?

8. Which woman won the 1971 WTA Tour Championships singles tennis title?

9. Who was the 1972 Olympic men's 800m champion?

10. Who was the 1952 Wimbledon men's singles tennis champion?

11. Which rider won the 1992 King George V Gold Cup on Midnight Madness at the Royal International Horse Show?

12. What nationality is boxer Lou Savarese?

13. Who was the 1968 Olympic men's 100m backstroke swimming champion?

14. In which month is the Sam Maguire Cup played for in Gaelic Football?

15. What nationality is F1 driver Pedro Diniz?

ANSWERS 1. 1963 2. Daley Thompson 3. 63 4. 1935 5. Gene Tunney 6. Slovakia 7. Knucklecracker 8. Billie Jean King 9. David Wottle 10. Frank Sedgman 11. Michael Whitaker 12. American 13. Roland Matthes 14. September 15. Brazilian.

POP

1. What was the title of Erasure's debut album in 1985?

2. Which female singer recorded the 2000 album *Tropical Brainstorm*?

3. Which singer-songwriter recorded the 1981 album *Black Snake Diamond Role*?

4. On which label did Ocean Colour Scene record the album *One From The Modern*?

5. Which Bob Dylan song was covered by Nick Cave and the Bad Seeds on the L.P. *The First Born Is Dead*?

6. Which female singer recorded the soundtrack to the 1999 movie *Magnolia*?

7. In which year did Hole bass player Kristen Pfaff die of an overdose?

8. Who recorded the 2000 L.P. *Welcome To The Palindrome*?

9. From which West Yorkshire city do the group Orange Can hail?

10. Which Manchester group recorded the 1983 album *Script Of The Bridge*?

11. Which songwriter's albums include *Born Again* and *12 Songs*?

12. Who wrote Buddy Holly's hit *It Doesn't Matter Anymore*?

13. On which label is Embrace's *Drawn From Memory*?

14. On which label did the Fall record the single *Fiery Jack*?

15. Which two of her own songs does Joni Mitchell sing on the 2000 standards album *Both Sides Now*?

ANSWERS 1. Wonderland **2.** Kirsty MacColl **3.** Robyn Hitchcock **4.** Island **5.** Wanted Man **6.** Aimee Mann **7.** 1994 **8.** Osymyso **9.** Leeds **10.** The Chameleons **11.** Randy Newman **12.** Paul Anka **13.** Hut **14.** Step Forward **15.** 'Both Sides Now' and 'A Case of You'.

WORDS

1. What in New Zealand is a ricker - a bird, a fish, or a tree?

2. What is otalgia better known as?

3. What in Brazil is a maxixe?

4. A sakai is an aborigine of which country?

5. The word lumbricoid refers to which creature?

6. What in North America is a buttonball – a turkey or a tree?

7. What in a plant does a lactifer contain?

8. What in South Africa is a tolly?

9. Why wouldn't you want to be in a larnax?

10. What is the derogatory Japanese term for an office worker?

11. In the U.S. what is the phrase used to denote the highest designation for above-average achievement in exams?

12. What type of bird is a kokako in New Zealand?

13. From which language does the word *shawl* meaning an item of clothing come?

14. What in the game of bowls is the kitty?

15. What type of creature is a suslik?

ANSWERS 1. Tree **2.** Earache **3.** A dance **4.** Malaysia **5.** Worm **6.** A tree **7.** Latex **8.** A casturated calf **9.** It's a coffin **10.** Salaryman **11.** Summa cum laude **12.** A crow **13.** Persian **14.** The jack **15.** Squirrel.

GENERAL KNOWLEDGE

1. Who was a Best Supporting Actor Oscar nominee for the film *Anne Of The Thousand Days*?

2. In which year did Sonja Henie, Norwegian figure-skater and Hollywood star die?

3. Which unpleasant character in the novel *Great Expectations* marries Estella?

4. Which town in Umbria, Italy, was birthplace of St. Francis?

5. In which African country is the port of Agadir, which was virtually destroyed by an earthquake in 1960?

6. Which lawyer chaired the commission that investigated the murder of president Kennedy?

7. The River Douro in S.W. Europe forms part of the border between which two countries?

8. Which England cricketer was the first bowler to take 300 Test wickets?

9. Which fruit in Greek mythology induced forgetfulness in those who ate it?

10. Who wrote the 1867 poem *Dover Beach*?

11. In which year was Kent-born fashion designer Katharine Hamnett born?

12. Which order of insects includes the bees and wasps?

13. Which blackish mineral is the principal source of radium and uranium?

14. In which year was Will Carling, former England rugby union captain, born?

15. In which novel by Charles Dickens does the character Smike appear?

ANSWERS 1. Anthony Quayle 2. 1969 3. Bentley Drummle 4. Assisi 5. Morocco 6. Earl Warren 7. Portugal and Spain 8. Fred Trueman 9. Lotus 10. Matthew Arnold 11. 1948 12. Hymenoptera 13. Pitchblende 14. 1965 15. Nicholas Nickleby.

ENTERTAINMENT

1. Who directed the 1997 film *Face/Off*?

2. Who wrote the sitcom *In Sickness And In Health*?

3. Who plays Rachel in the ITV drama *Cold Feet*?

4. Which television show won Best Drama Series at the 1999 Emmy Awards?

5. Who plays the wife of the President of the U.S. in the 1993 comedy *Dave*?

6. Which historical figure is played by Christopher Plummer in the 1977 film *The Day That Shook The World*?

7. In which Mozart opera is the aria *Dalla sua pace*?

8. Who directed and starred in the 1988 film *A New Life* with Ann-Margret?

9. Which comedian died during the making of the 1994 film *Wagon's East*?

10. Who created the 1970's sitcom *...And Mother Makes Three*?

11. Who plays Daffy in the film *The Beach*, based on the novel by Alex Garland?

12. Which comedy actor played Uriah Heep in a 1999 BBC TV adaptation of *David Copperfield*?

13. Who directed the 1999 film *Wonderland*?

14. Who plays Jim in the comedy series *The Royle Family*?

15. Who played Mrs. Nick Leeson in the film *Rogue Trader*?

SPORT

1. With what sport are Britt Laforgue and Patricia Emonet associated?

2. What nationality is tennis player Nicolas Lapentti?

3. With which sport are Stephen Train and Andrew Train associated?

4. In which year was the former England Test batsman Maurice Leyland born?

5. Tonny Olsen-Ahm and Aase Jacobsen were women's doubles winners at badminton at the 1952 All-England Championships. Which country did they represent?

6. What nationality is boxer Acelino Freitas?

7. Which peer owned horses that won 20 Classic races?

8. Who beat David Telesco on points in January 2000 to retain his three world light-heavyweight boxing titles?

9. How many a side play in a polo game?

10. What is the nickname of darts player Ted Hankey?

11. Which country were men's world team champions in short-track speed skating in 1992, 1994 & 1997?

12. What sport is played by Rowan Brassey and Richard Corsie?

13. Which Spanish team won the 1985 U.E.F.A. Cup?

14. Which four teams played in Pool 1 of the 1999/00 Heineken Cup in rugby union?

15. How many Commonwealth Games gold medals did Debbie Flintoff win from 1982-90?

POP

1. What is Eithne Ni Bhraonain's more familiar name?

2. Who recorded the 1999 album *Nexus ...?*

3. Which group recorded the 1979 single *Tell That Girl To Shut Up?*

4. Which group recorded the 1967 album *The 5000 Spirits Or The Layers Of The Onion?*

5. In which year was the L.P. *Blank Generation* by Richard Hell and the Volvoids first released?

6. Martin Duffy played keyboards for the Charlatans at Knebworth in 1996. With which group does he normally play?

7. Who had a 2000 Top 10 hit with *Won't Take It Lying Down?*

8. In which city were the Alice in Chains formed?

9. Who had a 1999 Top 10 single with *Don't Stop?*

10. Eddie Cochran died whilst being driven to which airport?

11. In which year did Shakespears Sister have a Top 10 single with *You're History?*

12. In which year was blues singer Elmore James born?

13. Who did David Bowie marry in 1970?

14. Which group recorded the 1999 single *New York City Boy?*

15. On what label was Kevin Rowland's solo album *The Wanderer* released?

ANSWERS 1. Enya **2.** Another Level **3.** Holly and the Italians **4.** The Incredible String Band **5.** 1977 **6.** Primal Scream **7.** Honeyz **8.** Seattle **9.** ATB **10.** Heathrow **11.** 1989 **12.** 1918 **13.** Angie Barrett **14.** Pet Shop Boys **15.** Fontana.

SCIENCE

1. Approximately how many miles in diameter is Uranus' satellite Belinda?

2. At which Cambridge college did Alfred North Whitehead teach mathematics from 1885-1911?

3. In which year was Sir William Maddock Bayliss awarded the Copley Medal?

4. What in computing does CD-ROM stand for?

5. Which American spacecraft obtained the first views of Mars in 1964?

6. In which year was the Royal Institution in London founded?

7. Who discovered Mimas, a moon of Saturn, in 1789?

8. For which scientist was the chair of physical chemistry created at the Sorbonne in 1910?

9. Approximately how much of the Martian atmosphere is carbon dioxide?

10. In which year did Nomo Taguchi coin the term 'nanotechnology'?

11. What is the atomic number of the element Californium?

12. On what continent was the meteorite known as ALH84001 discovered in 1984?

13. In which year was Sir Roger Penrose knighted for services to science?

14. In which year was the space probe Cassini launched by NASA?

15. Which Nobel prize winner was head of the Department of Physics at the University of Chicago from 1892-1929?

GENERAL KNOWLEDGE

1. Which golf course hosted the 1989 British Open tournament?

2. Who was the 1968 Olympic men's 400m hurdles champion?

3. Who directed the 1979 film *Mad Max* starring Mel Gibson?

4. What is the name of the poisonous Mediterranean plant, *Hyoscyamus niger,* which yields the drug hyoscyamine?

5. Who authored the 1937 novel *The Citadel*?

6. Which Dutch tennis player was the 1973 French men's doubles champion with John Newcombe?

7. Which Scottish psychiatrist's books include *The Divided Self*?

8. Which colourless acid found in sour milk is used in the preservative E270?

9. In which European country is the town of Ascoli Piceno?

10. Who was Best Actress Oscar winner for the film *Coquette*?

11. Which South African Zulu organization was founded by Chief Buthelezi in 1975?

12. Which Off-Broadway play of 1971 reworked the Gospel according to St. Matthew?

13. Who was author of the play *The Government Inspector*?

14. Which tennis player was runner-up in the 1993 U.S. Open ladies singles championship?

15. Which Italian poet is famous for his epic *Orlando Furioso*?

ENTERTAINMENT

1. Who hosts the comedy quiz show *They Think It's All Over*?

2. In which opera do Manrico and Leonora appear?

3. Who scored the 1951 film *The Day The Earth Stood Still*?

4. What is comedian Roy Chubby Brown's real name?

5. In which year did comedy show *Who Do You Do?* first appear on television?

6. Who was the star of the 1965 comedy show *... And So To Ted*?

7. What is Gene Kelly's character name in the film *Singin' In The Rain*?

8. *Friends* actress Lisa Kudrow has a degree in what subject?

9. Who played poet Pablo Neruda in the film *Il Postino*?

10. Which comedian is behind Channel Four's *Trigger Happy TV*?

11. The 1999 film drama *RKO 281* was about the making of which film?

12. Who plays vet Nick in the sitcom *Beast*?

13. Who directed the 1993 film *Dazed And Confused*?

14. Who plays Mr. Digby in the sitcom *The Grimleys*?

15. Who played Joseph K in the 1962 film *The Trial*?

ANSWERS 1. Nick Hancock 2. Il Trovatore 3. Bernard Herrmann 4. Royston Vasey 5. 1972 6. Ted Rogers 7. Don Lockwood 8. Biology 9. Philippe Noiret 10. Dom Joly 11. Citizen Kane 12. Alexander Armstrong 13. Richard Linklater 14. Brian Conley 15. Anthony Perkins.

SPORT

1. Which golfer won the Alfred Dunhill Championship in Johannesburg in January, 2000?

2. In which year did Leicestershire first take part in the cricket county championship?

3. In cricket, who scored 101 for Leicestershire vs. New Zealand XI in the 2nd innings of their 1999 game?

4. Zoltan Magyar was 1976 & 1980 Olympic men's pommel horse winner. Which country did he represent?

5. What nationality is skier Kjetil Andre Aamodt?

6. Which New Zealander won the 1967 German Grand Prix in F1?

7. Who won gold in the three-metre springboard for Britain in the 1999 European Championships?

8. In which year did a penalty kick in rugby union become worth three points?

9. In cricket, who scored 112 for Gloucestershire against Yorkshire in the 1999 Super Cup Final?

10. Who won the Professional Bowlers' Association's Tournament of Champions in ten-pin bowling in 1988?

11. Which county does motor racing driver Jenson Button hail from?

12. Which horse won the Champion Hurdle at Cheltenham from 1949-51?

13. What nationality is boxer Wilson Palacios?

14. Who was Olympic men's discus champion from 1904-8?

15. How many nations contested the women's events at the 1993 Taekwondo world championships?

POP

1. In which year did the band The James Gang form?

2. Which two musicians played piano and organ on the album *Aftermath* by the Rolling Stones?

3. Which former member of Pulp now plays with the group Venini?

4. Which singer gigged in 1999 under the name *The Priory Of Brion*?

5. Johnny Ha-Ha was drummer with which London-based Goth band?

6. D'Arcy Wretzky left which band in 1999?

7. Who had a 2000 Top 10 single with *Ooh Stick You*?

8. Which female singer formed the band Mice in 1995?

9. Which member of Crosby, Stills, Nash and Young broke both legs in a boating accident in 1999?

10. Oasis guitarist Jem was formerly in which band?

11. Taka Hirose is bass player with which group?

12. Which song by the Beatles did Joe Cocker cover on the 1989 album *Night Calls*?

13. Which railway station features on the cover of Oasis' single *Some Might Say*?

14. Which duo's compilation hits album *Tales From New York* charted in 2000?

15. Jon Brookes and Tony Rogers are members of which group?

THE CARLING PUB QUIZ BOOK

PEOPLE

1. Hockey player Pavel Bure is an ex-fiancé of which tennis star?

2. In which year did writer J.M. Barrie die?

3. Cynric was the son of which Saxon leader?

4. Spice Girl Mel B's sister acts in soap *Emmerdale*. What is her name?

5. In which city was publisher Sir Allen Lane born?

6. Richard Neville is a member of which boy band?

7. Which television cook was born Phyllis Primrose-Pechey?

8. Which member of the Foot family was M.P. for Ipswich from 1957-70?

9. In which country was astronomer Thomas Gold born in 1920?

10. In which year did comedian Tommy Cooper die?

11. Which airline did Sir Hudson Fysh begin in 1920?

12. With which group is Faye Tozer a singer?

13. Who became New York's first black mayor in 1989?

14. Which actress had been actor Frank Langella's girlfriend for five years until the couple split in 2000?

15. Who became Secretary-General of the United Nations in 1992?

ANSWERS 1. Anna Kournikova **2.** 1937 **3.** Cerdic **4.** Danielle Brown **5.** Bristol **6.** Five **7.** Fanny Cradock **8.** Dingle **9.** Austria **10.** 1984 **11.** QANTAS **12.** Steps **13.** David Dinkins **14.** Whoopi Goldberg **15.** Boutros Boutros Ghali.

GENERAL KNOWLEDGE

1. Which singer-actress starred in the title role of the 1953 film *Calamity Jane*?

2. What is the name of the strait in the Caribbean between Cuba and N.W. Haiti?

3. *Lutra lutra* is the Latin name of which freshwater carnivorous mammal?

4. Which 1968 film featured the song *The Windmills of Your Mind*?

5. Which England Test bowler took 7 for 50 against Pakistan at Birmingham in 1978?

6. Who wrote the 1949 novel *A Town Like Alice*?

7. Which actor played a crippled attorney in the film *The Lady from Shanghai*?

8. What is the name of the rabbit in the film *Bambi*?

9. Who was a Best Actress Oscar nominee for the film *The Goodbye Girl*?

10. What is the site on the Zambezi River in Mozambique of the largest dam in southern Africa?

11. Which Union general in the American Civil War defeated the Confederates at Gettysburg in 1863?

12. What is the name of the dog in the strip cartoon *Peanuts*?

13. Who is author of the novel *From Doon with Death*?

14. In which year did Australian operatic soprano Dame Nellie Melba die?

15. Which African leader was also known as Ras Tafari Makonnen?

ENTERTAINMENT

1. Who played Nannie Slagg in the 2000 BBC TV production of *Gormenghast*?

2. Who plays DI Frost in *A Touch Of Frost*?

3. Who plays Mrs. Bradley in *The Mrs. Bradley Mysteries* on BBC TV?

4. Who does John Cleese play in the 1981 film *Time Bandits*?

5. Which actress in *Friends* had Telly Savalas as a godfather?

6. Who played Bob in the 1969 film *Bob and Carol and Ted and Alice*?

7. Who plays a circus manager in the 1941 film *The Wagons Roll at Night*?

8. Which two actors hosted the panel game *Whodunit* on television?

9. Who plays Norma in the comedy series *The Royle Family*?

10. Which country singer plays a safecracker in the 1998 film *The Newton Boys*?

11. Which character does Moroni Olsen play in the 1935 film *Annie Oakley*?

12. Who played Supt. Yelland in the BBC TV drama *Spender*?

13. Who played Forrest Junior in the film *Forrest Gump*?

14. Who played Det. Supt. Inman in the television show *Special Branch*?

15. Who directed the 1998 film *Another Day in Paradise*?

ANSWERS 1. June Brown **2.** David Jason **3.** Diana Rigg **4.** Robin Hood **5.** Jennifer Aniston **6.** Robert Culp **7.** Humphrey Bogart **8.** Edward Woodward and Jon Pertwee **9.** Liz Smith **10.** Dwight Yoakam **11.** Buffalo Bill **12.** Paul Greenwood **13.** Haley Joel Osment **14.** Fulton Mackay **15.** Larry Clark.

SPORT

1. Ernst Linder was the 1924 Olympic individual dressage champion. Which country did he represent?

2. Who, in 1997, became the youngest qualifier in the history of the Australian Open tennis tournament?

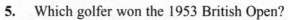

3. What nationality is nordic skier Bjørn Dæhlie?

4. Who was the 1964 Olympic women's 400m freestyle swimming champion?

5. Which golfer won the 1953 British Open?

6. Who owns the basketball team Magic M7?

7. Which swimmer's nickname is Thorpedo?

8. How many innings did Sunil Gavaskar take to make 10,000 Test runs?

9. Where were the 1979 World Student Games held?

10. Which team beat Oakland Athletics to win the 1988 World Series in baseball?

11. Who knocked Walney Central out of the 2000 rugby league Silk Cut Challenge Cup?

12. Which jockey rode Opera House to victory in the 1993 King George VI & Queen Elizabeth Diamond Stakes?

13. Where were the 1987 Pan-American Games held?

14. In which weight division was Mike Bridges a powerlifting world champion from 1981-3?

15. For which rugby union club side does Dave Lougheed play?

ANSWERS 1. Sweden **2.** Lleyton Hewitt **3.** Norwegian **4.** Virginia Duenkel **5.** Ben Hogan **6.** Magic Johnson **7.** Ian Thorpe **8.** 212 **9.** Mexico City **10.** Los Angeles Dodgers **11.** Lancashire Lynx **12.** Michael Roberts **13.** Indianapolis **14.** 82.5 kg **15.** Leicester.

POP

1. Who recorded the 1971 album *Time Of The Last Persecution*?

2. Who recorded the 1994 album *Return of the Space Cowboy*?

3. Which disc jockey runs the record label Perfecto?

4. Olly Peacock is drummer with which group?

5. What was the first record that singer Joe Cocker bought?

6. Who had a 1999 Top 10 single with *Never Let You Down*?

7. Which group recorded the 1974 album *Psychomodo*?

8. In which year was John and Yoko's *Wedding Album* released?

9. The Fifth Dimension hit No. 1 in the U.S. charts in 1969 with which Laura Nyro song?

10. Which group recorded the 1990 album *Ritual De Lo Habitual*?

11. Which group had their name emblazoned on Cardiff City shirts in 1999 to celebrate the club's centenary?

12. Which group recorded the 1973 album *Mekanïk Destructïw Kommandoh*?

13. Which female singer had a 1989 Top 10 single with *Wouldn't Change a Thing*?

14. Who was the drummer on the 1978 album *Crossing the Red Sea with the Adverts*?

15. Who had a No. 1 single in 2000 with *Rise*?

ANSWERS 1. Billy Fay **2.** Jamiroquai **3.** Paul Oakenfold **4.** Gomez **5.** Long Tall Sally by Little Richard **6.** Honeyz **7.** Cockney Rebel **8.** 1969 **9.** Wedding Bell Blues **10.** Jane's Addiction **11.** Super Furry Animals **12.** Magma **13.** Kylie Minogue **14.** Laurie Driver **15.** Gabrielle.

ART

1. *The Beckoning Lady* and *The China Governess* are crime novels by which writer?

2. Which art movement did André Derain become a member of in 1905?

3. Which characters, in addition to the narrator, make up the *Three Men in a Boat*?

4. What is Jenny Colgan's debut novel?

5. In which century did Dutch artist Pieter de Hooch live?

6. Whose novels include 1955's *That Uncertain Feeling*?

7. In which city was artist Henry Fuseli born in 1741?

8. Who wrote the 1812 novel *The Absentee*?

9. In which year did Cubist artist Georges Braque enlist in the French army?

10. Who wrote the 1974 book *Centennial*?

11. Who does Ivanhoe return from the Holy Wars to claim as his bride in a novel by Walter Scott?

12. In which year did Auguste Rodin complete the sculpture *The Burghers of Calais*?

13. Quebec Bagnet and Woolwich Bagnet appear in which novel by Charles Dickens?

14. Which French artist's works include 1878's *Street Pavers In The Rue Mosnier*?

15. Nurse Catherine Barkley appears in which 1929 novel?

GENERAL KNOWLEDGE

1. Which Irish writer was the author of the play *The Plough and the Stars*?

2. In which year did Italian composer and violinist Niccolo Paganini die?

3. Which nobleman ranks below an earl and above a baron in the British Isles?

4. What is the informal name for the automatic pilot in an aircraft?

5. Who was the author of the play *Waiting For Godot*?

6. What is the name of the wolf-boy in Rudyard Kipling's *The Jungle Book*?

7. Who was the author of the 1932 novel *The Thin Man*?

8. Who was first president of Chile from 1817-23?

9. Who was the 1980 Olympic men's 100m breaststroke swimming champion?

10. In which year was the Russian daily newspaper *Izvestia* founded?

11. At which horse racecourse is the Irish Derby run?

12. Which island in the Caribbean is largest of the Virgin Islands of the U.S.?

13. Who wrote the 1953 novel *The Kraken Wakes*?

14. Who is owner of Doubting Castle in the book *The Pilgrim's Progress*?

15. Who composed the one-act opera *Aleko*?

ANSWERS 1. Sean O'Casey **2.** 1840 **3.** Viscount **4.** George **5.** Samuel Beckett **6.** Mowgli **7.** Dashiell Hammett **8.** Bernardo O'Higgins **9.** Duncan Goodhew **10.** 1917 **11.** Curragh **12.** St. Croix **13.** John Wyndham **14.** Giant Despair **15.** Rachmaninov.

ENTERTAINMENT

1. Who starred as senator Norman Grant in the 1987 U.S. television series *Space*?

2. Who plays Swiss Toni in *The Fast Show*?

3. In which year was television presenter Dermot O'Leary born?

4. Who composed the 1954 opera *The Turn Of The Screw*?

5. What won Best Foreign-language film at the 2000 Oscars ?

6. Which actress plays Ling in the television comedy *Ally McBeal*?

7. Who plays Catwoman in the 1992 film *Batman Returns*?

8. Who composed the 1948 opera *Down In Te Valley*?

9. Who directed the 1991 film *Light Sleeper*?

10. Who is the male lead in the 1977 film *Another Man, Another Chance*?

11. Who directed the 1945 film *Vera Cruz*?

12. Which Hollywood actor was arrested in October, 1999 for resisting arrest at his home in Austin, Texas?

13. What is Kurt Russell's character name in the 1996 film *Escape From L.A.*?

14. Who plays Martha in the 1998 film *Martha – Meet Frank, Daniel and Laurence*?

15. Who won a Best Supporting Actress Oscar for her role in the 1936 film *Anthony Adverse*?

ANSWERS 1. James Garner **2.** Charlie Higson **3.** 1973 **4.** Benjamin Britten **5.** Pedro Almodovar's *All About My Mother* **6.** Lucy Liu **7.** Michelle Pfeiffer **8.** Kurt Weill **9.** Paul Schrader **10.** James Caan **11.** Robert Aldrich **12.** Matthew McConaughey **13.** Snake Plissken **14.** Monica Potter **15.** Gale Sondergaard.

SPORT

1. Which word did Funakoshi Gichin introduce into the world of sport in the 1920s?

2. Who scored two goals in Manchester United's 4-0 win over Sunderland in April, 2000?

3. Which side from Argentina lost the 1969 & 1970 World Club Championship Finals in football?

4. In which year did tennis player Vitas Gerulaitis die?

5. Who was women's 800m champion at the 1982 European Championships?

6. Who scored both goals in West Ham United's 2-1 win at Derby County in April, 2000?

7. Which South African wicket-keeper made 65 dismissals in the 1982/3 season?

8. Where were the 1966 Asian Games held?

9. Gymnast Osvaldo Palazzi was the 1911 world champion at pommel horse. Which country did he represent?

10. Which athlete was the 1974 BBC Sports Personality of the Year?

11. Who won the 1998 Monaco Grand Prix in Formula 1 driving a McLaren?

12. Where were the 1977 World Student Games held?

13. How many dropped goals did rugby union player Hugo Porta score for Argentina from 1972-90?

14. In which city is the headquarters of the Athletics Association of Wales?

15. Who was world professional undisputed heavyweight boxing champion from 1970-3?

THE CARLING PUB QUIZ BOOK

POP

1. Which veteran pop singer guested on Janet Jackson's 1984 album *Dream Street*?

2. Who had a 2000 Top 10 single with *Thank God I Found You*?

3. What were Pete Shelley and Howard Devoto of the Buzzocks studying at college in Bolton when they met?

4. Which group had a 1989 Top 10 single with *Sweet Surrender*?

5. Which U.S. record label do group Muse record on?

6. Which group recorded the 1999 album *The Ladder*?

7. Which Aerosmith studio album features the song *Dude (Looks Like A Lady)*?

8. To what did duo Oister change their name in 1974?

9. Which punk group recorded the 1999 album *Modern*?

10. Which song by Joy Division features the lyric "Dance, dance to the radio"?

11. Bobby Gillespie is lead singer with which group?

12. Which group recorded the album *The Wayward Bus*?

13. Which artist recorded the 1999 album *Mock Tudor*?

14. Which studio album by The Clash featured the song *Guns of Brixton*?

15. What was the opening track of John Fogerty's debut solo album?

ANSWERS 1. Cliff Richard **2.** Mariah Carey **3.** Electronics **4.** Wet Wet Wet **5.** Maverick Records **6.** Yes **7.** Permanent Vacation **8.** The Dwight Twilley Band **9.** Buzzocks **10.** Transmission **11.** Primal Scream **12.** The Magnetic Fields **13.** Richard Thompson **14.** London Calling **15.** Rocking All Over the World.

GEOGRAPHY

1. In which Northumberland village was Grace Darling born?

2. What is Rapa Nui better known as?

3. What is the central crossroads of old Oxford known as?

4. What is the name of the rocky island two miles off the coast of the Lleyn peninsula in Wales?

5. Roanoke Island is off the coast of which U.S. state?

6. What Strait links the Java Sea with the Indian Ocean?

7. Which Indian city houses Punjabi University?

8. Ruthin is the administrative centre of which Welsh county?

9. At which place does the Sussex Ouse flow into the English Channel?

10. On which sea is the port and resort of Sevastopol?

11. What is the name of the channel between Iceland and S.E. Greenland linking the Arctic and Atlantic Oceans?

12. In which U.S. state is the Sequoia National Park?

13. In which century did New York change its name from New Amsterdam?

14. Castlebay is the only town on which island of the Outer Hebrides?

15. In which ocean is the island of New Providence?

ANSWERS 1. Bamburgh **2.** Easter Island **3.** The Carfax **4.** Bardsey Island **5.** North Carolina **6.** Sunda Strait **7.** Patiala **8.** Denbighshire **9.** Newhaven **10.** Black Sea **11.** Denmark Strait **12.** California **13.** 17th **14.** Barra **15.** Atlantic.

GENERAL KNOWLEDGE

1. In which year did trombonist and bandleader Tommy Dorsey die?

2. Who wrote the 1815 novel *Guy Mannering*?

3. Grenoble is the capital of which department of France?

4. What is the eleventh letter in the Greek alphabet?

5. The 1975 film *A Bigger Splash* is about which artist?

6. Who was the leader of the Liberal Democrat party in Britain from 1988-99?

7. Which England Test batsman scored 123 against Pakistan at Lord's in 1987?

8. Which French actress starred in the 1968 film *Shalako*?

9. Which England Test batsman scored 113 against India at Bombay in 1972/3?

10. The Rio Negro forms part of the border between which two South American countries?

11. Who directed the 1950 film *The Asphalt Jungle*?

12. William Marshal was regent of England for which king?

13. Who was the second president of the U.S.A.?

14. Quentin Tarantino's film *Jackie Brown is* based on which book by Elmore Leonard?

15. In which year was minimalist sculptor Carl Andre born?

ANSWERS 1. 1956 **2.** Walter Scott **3.** Isère **4.** Lambda **5.** David Hockney **6.** Paddy Ashdown **7.** Bill Athey **8.** Brigitte Bardot **9.** Keith Fletcher **10.** Colombia and Venezuela **11.** John Huston **12.** Henry III **13.** John Adams **14.** Rum Punch **15.** 1935.

ENTERTAINMENT

1. Who is Sabrina's boyfriend in the television show *Sabrina, the Teenage Witch*?

2. What is entertainer Graham Norton's real name?

3. Who made the 1995 short film *The Hard Case*?

4. Who voices Woody in the film *Toy Story 2*?

5. Which actor is the star of the 1932 film *A Farewell to Arms*?

6. Which female singer stars in the 1999 film *Ride with the Devil*?

7. Which author hosts the radio show *A Prairie Home Companion* in the U.S.?

8. Which former *EastEnders* actress played Charlotte in the 1999 ITV show *Lucy Sullivan is Getting Married*?

9. Words of how many letters feature in the *Countdown* conundrum?

10. In which opera does the character Mrs. Peachum appear?

11. Who directed the 1970 film *Darling Lili*?

12. What nationality was opera singer Cornélie Falcon?

13. Who directed the 1979 film *The Driller Killer*?

14. Which *Coronation Street* actress played Frances in the 1990s BBC TV series *Spender*?

15. Who played gentleman thief *Raffles* in a 1940 film?

ANSWERS 1. Harvey **2.** Graham Walker **3.** Guy Ritchie **4.** Tom Hanks **5.** Gary Cooper **6.** Jewel **7.** Garrison Keillor **8.** Letitia Dean **9.** Nine **10.** The Threepenny Opera **11.** Blake Edwards **12.** French **13.** Abel Ferrara **14.** Denise Welch **15.** David Niven.

SPORT

1. Which two teams contested Super Bowl XXXIV?

2. Which horse won the 1957 King George VI Chase?

3. What nationality is tennis player Lindsay Davenport?

4. In what time did Michael Marsh win his 1992 Olympic 200m title?

5. Who was the 1951 Wimbledon men's singles tennis champion?

6. Who was the 1951 winner of the Badminton Horse Trials in Three-Day Eventing?

7. Which England swimmer won the 50m butterfly in the 2000 world short-course championships?

8. Which country were 1964 Olympic men's 4 x 200m freestyle relay swimming champions?

9. In which year was the United States Golf Association founded?

10. Darryl van der Velde coaches which rugby league side?

11. Thomas Wassberg was a 1980 Olympic champion. At which sport?

12. For which rugby league side does Martin Pearson play?

13. How many tons did Viv Richards score in his 121 Tests from 1974-91?

14. What nationality is tennis star Thomas Enqvist?

15. Which team lost the 1931 World Series in baseball?

ANSWERS 1. St. Louis Rams and Tennessee Titans **2.** Mandarin **3.** American **4.** 20.01 seconds **5.** Dick Savitt **6.** Hans Schwarzenbach **7.** Mark Foster **8.** U.S.A. **9.** 1894 **10.** Warrington **11.** Nordic skiing **12.** Halifax **13.** 24 **14.** Swedish **15.** Philadelphia Athletics.

THE CARLING PUB QUIZ BOOK

POP

1. Who had a 2000 Top 10 single with *The Great Beyond*?

2. Who wrote *The Beast In Me* on Johnny Cash's L.P. *American Recordings*?

3. Which pop star wrote the novel *Nalda Said*?

4. In which year did Martika have a Top 10 single with *Toy Soldiers*?

5. Which rock 'n' roller was born Brian Holden?

6. In which country was Death in Vegas' Richard Fearless born?

7. Which Barry White song did Greg Dulli of the Afghan Whigs cover, on the soundtrack of the film *Beautiful Girls*?

8. Which Kent-born artist recorded the 1999 album *Beyond Skin*?

9. The book *Forever the People* by Paolo Hewitt is about which pop group?

10. Who released the 1988 album of children's songs *Shake Sugaree*?

11. Who is the male lead singer with London group *Spearmint*?

12. Who recorded the 1986 album *Blah Blah Blah!*?

13. *Westway to the World* was a television documentary on which group?

14. Which male singer had a 1989 Top 10 single with *We Didn't Start the Fire*?

15. What was Joe Jackson's debut L.P. called?

ANSWERS 1. R.E.M. **2.** Nick Lowe **3.** Stuart David **4.** 1989 **5.** Vince Taylor **6.** Zambia **7.** Can't Get Enough Of Your Love, Babe **8.** Nitin Sawhney **9.** Oasis **10.** Taj Mahal **11.** Shirley Lee **12.** Iggy Pop **13.** The Clash **14.** Billy Joel **15.** Look Sharp.

HISTORY

1. Who was appointed governor of the Cape Colony in 1897?

2. In which year was the Hindenburg airship disaster?

3. In which year did Abel Tasman first visit the island now known as Tasmania?

4. What was the former name of Jordan from 1922-1949?

5. In which century was St. Dominic, founder of the Dominicans, born?

6. Who became president of Haiti in 1991?

7. In which month of 1666 was the Great Fire of London?

8. In which year after World War II did Princess Elizabeth get married?

9. Who led an army coup in Ghama in 1972?

10. Which future prime minister was speaker of the House of Commons from 1789-1801?

11. Which tax did John Hampden refuse to pay in 1637 precipitating the English Civil War?

12. Who was the father of Richard the Lionheart?

13. In which month of the year 1536 was Anne Boleyn beheaded?

14. Who in 1869 became marshal of Hays City, Kansas?

15. In which year did former Bulgarian communist leader Todor Zhivkov die?

ANSWERS 1. Alfred Milner **2.** 1937 **3.** 1642 **4.** Trans-Jordan **5.** 12th century **6.** Jean Bertrand Aristide **7.** September **8.** 1947 **9.** Colonel Acheampong **10.** Henry Addington, Viscount Sidmouth **11.** Ship money **12.** Henry II **13.** May **14.** Wild Bill Hickok **15.** 1998.

GENERAL KNOWLEDGE

1. In which American novel does the character George Shelby appear?

2. What is the capital of New York State?

3. Who wrote the 1974 novel *The Abbess of Crewe*?

4. Which industrial city in France was the medieval capital of Flanders?

5. In music, what symbol is placed after a note to increase its time value by a half?

6. For which 1997 film was Robert Duvall a Best Actor Oscar nominee?

7. What was the name of the first dog in space?

8. Which film director's works include 1968's *Barbarella*?

9. Which Brazilian footballer signed for Internazionale from Barcelona in 1997?

10. Who was the Muse of love poetry in Greek mythology?

11. Who was the 1942 U.S. P.G.A. golf champion?

12. Which English admiral was executed in 1757 after failing to relieve Minorca?

13. Which Australian bowler took 16 wickets against England on his Test debut in 1972?

14. Who was the 1960 Australian men's singles tennis champion?

15. In which ocean is the group of uninhabited volcanic islands called St. Kilda?

ANSWERS 1. Uncle Tom's Cabin 2. Albany 3. Muriel Spark 4. Lille 5. Dot 6. The Apostle 7. Laika 8. Roger Vadim 9. Ronaldo 10. Erato 11. Sam Snead 12. John Byng 13. Bob Massie 14. Rod Laver 15. Atlantic.

ENTERTAINMENT

1. Who plays the prosecuting attorney in the 1959 film *Anatomy of a Murder*?

2. Who played Kate in the 1929 film version of *The Taming of the Shrew*?

3. What is Lesley Joseph's character name in *Birds of a Feather*?

4. Under which city is there a time bomb buried in the 1973 film *And Millions Will Die*?

5. Who plays *Carrie* in the television show *Sex and the City*?

6. Who portrayed Clark Gable in the 1976 film *Gable and Lombard*?

7. Who directed the 1999 film *Dogma*?

8. Who plays the lead in the 1973 film *Galileo*?

9. What is the surname of talk show hostess *Leeza*?

10. Who plays The Shoveler in the 1999 comedy film *Mystery Men*?

11. Who directed the 1973 horror film *And Now the Screaming Starts*?

12. Who plays Nikki Shadwick in *Brookside*?

13. Which U.S. actress starred in the 1966 French film *The Game is Over*?

14. What creature is *Stuart Little* in the 1999 film?

15. Which former *Coronation Street* actress plays Jasmine in *Holby City*?

ANSWERS 1. George C. Scott **2.** Mary Pickford **3.** Dorien Green **4.** Hong Kong **5.** Sarah Jessica Parker **6.** James Brolin **7.** Kevin Smith **8.** Chaim Topol **9.** Gibbons **10.** William H. Macy **11.** Roy Ward Baker **12.** Suzanne Collins **13.** Jane Fonda **14.** Mouse **15.** Angela Griffin.

SPORT

1. Which horse won the 1999 Martell Grand National?

2. Who rode the 1994 July Cup-winning horse Owington?

3. Which male tennis player won the Champions Cup at Indian Wells in March, 2000?

4. In what weight division was Andrzej Stanaszek a powerlifting world champion from 1993-7?

5. What nationality is swimmer Jani Sievinen?

6. Britain's Diane Bell was 1986 & 1987 women's judo world champion. In which weight category?

7. Who won the 500cc motorcycling South African Grand Prix in March, 2000?

8. In football, how often has the Copa America been played since 1987?

9. For which rugby union club side does Danny Grewcock play?

10. In athletics, who was men's 200m champion at the 1978 European Championships?

11. For which side did cricketer Michael Bell make his county debut in 1992?

12. In which year was the Plunket Shield first contested in New Zeland cricket?

13. Which golfer won the 2000 Heineken Classic in Perth, Australia?

14. How many Olympic gold medals did gymnast Agnes Kaleti win from 1952-6?

15. What nationality is snooker player Kristian Helgason?

POP

1. On which label did The Buzzcocks release their L.P. *Another Music in a Different Kitchen*?

2. Who had a 2000 Top 10 single with *What a Girl Wants*?

3. In which U.S. city did the band H.P. Lovecraft form in 1967?

4. Who had a 1980 Top 10 single with *Do That to Me One More Time*?

5. Who did Richey James Edwards replace in the band The Manic Street Preachers?

6. Gram Parsons quit the Byrds before a proposed tour to which country?

7. What was the title of the 1986 album release by The Human League?

8. Which artist had a 1989 Top 10 single with *The Time Warp*?

9. The Gun Club's singer Jeffrey Lee Pierce was formerly president of which group's fan club?

10. In which year did Humble Pie release their eponymous L.P. *Humble Pie*?

11. In which year was the Velvet Underground's L.P. *Squeeze* released?

12. Which solo artist recorded the 1999 album *Twenty Four Seven*?

13. Which group recorded the 1994 album *Casa Babylon*?

14. Which former member of the group Talking Heads released the 1992 L.P. *Uh-Oh*?

15. Which duo had a 1993 hit single with *Next Time You Fall In Love*?

WORDS

1. What in East Africa is a jembe?

2. Which part of the body would a pauldron protect if you were wearing armour?

3. What would you have done with a jupon in the Middle Ages – worn it or eaten it?

   SPECIAL: FRIED JUPON AND CHIPS

4. Laverock is a dialect word for which bird?

5. What type of creature is a morwong - a bird or a fish?

6. What in ancient Greece was a rhyton?

7. In Scottish place names what does kyle mean?

8. What is the male of a cat called?

9. What would you do with a lassi – play it or drink it?

10. What is a perchery?

11. Which animals would shelter in a byre?

12. What does the Latin verb *secare* mean, from which we derive the name of the garden implement secateurs?

13. What in South Africa is one's oupa?

14. Why would you want to avoid a franc-tireur?

15. The wasting of the shoulder muscles called *sweeny*

ANSWERS 1. A hoe **2.** Shoulder **3.** Worn it **4.** Skylark **5.** Fish **6.** A horn-shaped drinking vessel **7.** Narrow strait or channel **8.** Tom **9.** Drink it **10.** A barn where hens can move unrestrictedly **11.** Cows **12.** To cut **13.** Grandmother **14.** It's a sniper **15.** Horse.

GENERAL KNOWLEDGE

1. Who is the author of the novel *Cold Comfort Farm*?

2. Who was the director of the 1985 film *Insignificance*?

3. Which river in S.W. Australia flows to the Indian Ocean below Perth?

4. Who was the third son of Adam in the Old Testament?

5. Who is the curate in Anne Brontë's novel *Agnes Grey*?

6. Who wrote the 1775 comedy play *The Rivals*?

7. What was the name of the Greek prime minister who died in 1996?

8. What is the name of the walkway around the base of the dome of St. Paul's Cathedral in London?

9. Who is the usurped Duke of Milan in Shakespeare's play *The Tempest*?

10. Who wrote the 1696 play *The Relapse*?

11. What is the name of the sacred river in Coleridge's poem *Kubla Khan*?

12. Who directed the 1985 comedy film *Clue* which was based on the board game *Cluedo*?

13. What is the name of the largest island in the Alexander Archipelago in S.E. Alaska?

14. Which river in Siberia flows from Lake Baikal to the Yenisei River?

15. Who wrote the 1895 novel *Effi Briest*?

ENTERTAINMENT

1. Which comedy duo starred in the 1930 film *Half Shot at Sunrise*?

2. Who plays the doctor in the 1963 film *Tammy and the Doctor*?

3. Who is the father of actress Angelina Jolie?

4. Who directed the 1945 film *And Then There Were None*?

5. Who starred as *Inspector Gadget* in the 1999 film?

6. Who directed the 1999 film *Sleepy Hollow*?

7. Who directed the 1929 film *Hallelujah*?

8. Who starred as Anna Leonowens in the 1999 film *Anna and the King*?

9. In which year in the future is the 1995 film *12 Monkeys* set?

10. Who plays the lead in the 1974 film *Andy Warhol's Dracula*?

11. In which year did *Tomorrow's World* begin on television?

12. Which actress plays an addicted gambler in the 1949 film *The Lady Gambles*?

13. Who played Marjery Frobisher in the sitcom *To the Manor Born*?

14. Who played conman Charles Jackson in the 1971 sitcom *Birds on the Wing*

15. What was Heather Locklear's character name in the television series *T.J. Hooker*?

SPORT

1. In which year was the Luxembourg Grand Prix in Formula 1 first held?

2. Which two countries contested the America's Cup in 2000?

3. How many international caps did Michael Lynagh win for Australia from 1984-95?

4. Who did Germany play in the quarter-finals of the 2000 Davis Cup?

5. In which year were the women's world indoor bowls championships first held?

6. Prior to meeting in the 2000 Australian Open tennis singles final, Agassi and Kafelnikov had met nine times in tournaments. Who was winning 5-4?

7. Which horse won the 1959 Hennessy Cognac Gold Cup?

8. Which German tennis player won the 1993 ATP Tour Championships Final?

9. Juan Carlos Zabala won the 1932 Olympic marathon. Which country was he representing?

10. What was the married name of tennis player Nancye Wynne?

11. György Bardos was individual world champion in 1978 & 1980 at what equestrian event?

12. How many golds did Finland win in the 1999 World Athletic Championships?

13. Who was the 1996 Olympic women's 100m breaststroke swimming champion?

14. Which golfer won the 1947 U.S. Open?

15. Where were the 1963 Pan-American Games held?

ANSWERS 1. 1997 **2.** Italy and New Zealand **3.** 72 **4.** Australia **5.** 1988 **6.** Agassi **7.** Kerstin **8.** Michael Stich **9.** Argentina **10.** Nancye Bolton **11.** Carriage driving **12.** One **13.** Penny Heyns **14.** Lew Worsham **15.** São Paulo.

POP

1. What was the title of Marillion's second album?

2. Which Scottish group had a 1980 hit single with *Motorbike Beat*?

3. Which U.S. group's third single was *Get Me To The World On Time* in 1967?

4. Who had a hit in 1968 with *Captain Of Your Ship*?

5. At which London college did John Cale study viola and cello?

6. What was Renee and Renato's chart follow-up to their smash hit *Save Your Love*?

7. Which singer-songwriter recorded the 1980 album *Grace And Danger*?

8. Which male singer had a 1966 hit single with *Mr. Zero*?

9. In which town was blues player John Mayall born?

10. Which solo female singer had a 1989 Top 10 single with *I Need Your Lovin'*?

11. In which year did Jim Reeves have a hit single with *Adios Amigo*?

12. Which U.S. group recorded the 1987 album *Warehouse: Songs and Stories*?

13. In which year was the singer Johnnie Ray born?

14. Who had a 1964 hit single with *Wild Side Of Life*?

15. Who had a 1989 Top 10 with the single *I'd Rather Jack*?

ANSWERS 1. Fugazi **2.** Revillos **3.** The Electric Prunes **4.** Reparata and the Delrons **5.** Goldsmith's **6.** Just One More Kiss **7.** John Martyn **8.** Keith Relf **9.** Macclesfield **10.** Alyson Williams **11.** 1962 **12.** Hüsker Dü **13.** 1927 **14.** Tommy Quickly **15.** The Reynolds Girls.

SCIENCE

1. What nationality was scientist Vannevar Bush?

2. In molecular biology what does PCR stand for?

3. In which century did scientist Robert Boyle live?

4. With which science was Scot Sir Charles Lyell associated?

5. What does BSE, also known as 'mad cow disease', stand for?

6. Which bacteriologist determined the cause of yellow fever?

7. In the hexadecimal system what letter represents the number 13?

8. What in physics is QED?

9. Approximately how many miles in diameter is Uranus's satellite Rosalind?

10. In which year was the British Association for the Advancement of Science founded?

11. Who was awarded the 1944 Nobel prize for Physics?

12. In which year was the element Barium first isolated?

13. Who wrote the 1892 book *The Grammar of Science*?

14. In the Periodic Table of Elements, how many Alkali metals are there?

15. Approximately how many miles in diameter is the Earth's moon?

ANSWERS 1. American **2.** Polymerase chain reaction **3.** 17th Century **4.** Geology **5.** Bovine Spongiform Encephalopathy **6.** Walter Reed **7.** D **8.** Quantum electrodynamics **9.** 33 miles **10.** 1831 **11.** Isidor Isaac Rabi **12.** 1808 **13.** Karl Pearson **14.** Six **15.** 2160 miles.

GENERAL KNOWLEDGE

1. Who was the author of the 1984 novel *Hotel du Lac*?

2. Who wrote the 1816 book *The Devil's Elixir*?

3. What is the name of the line of latitude about 23°N of the equator?

4. Which port was capital of the Belgian Congo until 1926?

5. Which city in S.W. Brazil is capital of Mato Grosso do Sul state?

6. In which South American country is the seaport of Antofagasta?

7. Who wrote the 1952 novel *The Old Man and the Sea*?

8. Which former lead singer and guitarist with the pop group T.Rex died in a car crash in 1977?

9. Who wrote the 1931 novel *The Good Earth*?

10. Which make of motor car won the 1935 Le Mans 24 Hour race?

11. Which city in S.E. Italy was the seat of Emperor Frederick II?

12. In which year did English prison reformer Elizabeth Fry die?

13. Who wrote the 1966 novel *The Jewel In The Crown*?

14. Who was the French painter of *Le Déjeuner sur l'herbe*?

15. Which actor played Hercule Poirot in the film *Death On The Nile*?

ENTERTAINMENT

1. *An Angel At My Table* was a 1990 biopic of which author?

2. In which year was Alan Titchmarsh born?

3. Which two actresses provide the love interest for Albert Finney in the 1960 film *Saturday Night And Sunday Morning*?

4. Who stars as jewel thief Miles Logan in the 1999 film *Blue Streak*?

5. What is Jamie Lee Curtis's character name in the 1998 film *Halloween H20*?

6. Who appears as Miss Marple in the 1966 film *The Alphabet Murders*?

7. Who plays disc jockey Super Soul in the 1971 film *Vanishing Point*?

8. Which girl group appear in the 2000 film *Honest*?

9. Which father and daughter acting team appear in the 1973 film *Paper Moon*?

10. How many million dollars was Demi Moore paid for the film *Striptease*?

11. Which comedienne directed the 1978 film *Rabbit Test* about the world's first pregnant man?

12. Who plays Clarrie in Radio Four's soap *The Archers*?

13. Who played Sgt. Morgan O'Rourke in the sitcom *F Troop*?

14. Which actress married director Louis Malle in 1980?

15. In which year did English actor-manager Sir Frank Robert Benson die?

ANSWERS 1. Janet Frame **2.** 1949 **3.** Rachel Roberts and Shirley Anne Field **4.** Martin Lawrence **5.** Laurie Strode **6.** Margaret Rutherford **7.** Cleavon Little **8.** All Saints **9.** Ryan and Tatum O'Neal **10.** $12m **11.** Joan Rivers **12.** Rosalind Adams **13.** Forrest Tucker **14.** Candice Bergen **15.** 1939.

SPORT

1. What nationality was champion Nordic skier Johan Gröttumsbraaten?

2. Who was the 1938 Commonwealth men's 3 mile champion?

3. Who took 16 wickets for India against the West Indies on his Test debut in 1988?

4. In cricket, who scored 104 for Lancashire vs. Derbyshire in the 2nd innings of their 1999 county championship game?

5. With which sport are Pinky Higgins and Moose Dropo associated?

6. What nationality is tennis player Xavier Malisse?

7. In which year was the Yorkshire Oaks horserace first run?

8. By what score did Keighley beat Cardiff in the 2000 rugby league Silk Cut Challenge Cup 3rd round?

9. What are the three separate lifts in powerlifting?

10. For which rugby union club side does Chad Eagle play?

11. Kata and Kumite are types of championship in which sport?

12. In cricket, who scored 127 n.o. for Essex vs. Kent in the 1st innings of their 1999 county championship game?

13. Who in June 1995 became the most expensive transfer between two English football clubs?

14. Who in 1999 became the fastest man in major league history in baseball to hit 500 home runs?

15. In athletics, in which year were the European Indoor Championships first held, in Dortmund?

POP

1. Which Jamaican group had a 1967 hit single with *Train Tour to Rainbow City*?

2. Who had a 1997 Top 20 single with *Earthbound*?

3. On which book was Camel's 1992 album *Dust And Dreams* based?

4. What was R.E.M.'s first U.K. chart single, in 1987?

5. On which label did Republica have a Top 10 single in 1997 with *Drop Dead Gorgeous*?

6. Which song by Radiohead features the lyric "Kicking squealing Gucci little piggy"?

7. Which New York-born singer's bands included Fast Eddie and the Electric Japs?

8. In which year did George Michael top the singles chart with *Careless Whisper*?

9. Who featured on Joey Negro's 2000 Top 10 single *Must Be The Music*?

10. In which year did Wham have a No. 1 single with *Freedom*?

11. In which year did singer Jacques Brel die?

12. Which album chart-topping band were once called Glass Onion?

13. Which artist recorded the live L.P. *17-11-70*?

14. Roy Loney was lead singer of which 1960s band?

15. In which year did King have a Top 10 hit with *Love And Pride*?

THE CARLING PUB QUIZ BOOK

PEOPLE

1. Which trumpet player was nicknamed 'Little Jazz'?

2. What was the nickname of Australian athlete Reginald Leslie Baker?

3. What was the nickname of Roman emperor Gaius Julius Caesar Germanicus?

4. In which year was Nelson Mandela freed after 25 years in prison?

5. What was the name by which American football coach Paul William Bryant was known?

6. In which year was actor Sir Derek Jacobi born?

7. In which country was King Edward IV of England born?

8. Which saint was appointed Archbishop of Canterbury in 960?

9. In which year was ballerina Dame Beryl Grey born?

10. Which model married millionaire Howard Marshall II in 1994?

11. In which year did composer Leonard Bernstein die?

12. Which actor was born Cyril Louis Goldbert?

13. In which country was financier Meyer Guggenheim born?

14. Who wrote the 1901 autobiography *Up From Slavery*?

15. What was the middle name of folk singer Woody Guthrie?

ANSWERS 1. Roy Eldridge **2.** Snowy **3.** Caligula **4.** 1990 **5.** Bear **6.** 1938 **7.** France **8.** St. Dunstan **9.** 1927 **10.** Anna Nicole Smith **11.** 1990 **12.** Peter Wyngarde **13.** Switzerland **14.** Booker T. Washington **15.** Wilson.

GENERAL KNOWLEDGE

1. What is the capital of St. Lucia?

2. What is the second brightest star in the constellation Gemini?

3. Which London-born boxer was world middleweight champion in 1961?

4. In which year did French painter Raoul Dufy die?

5. At the foot of which mountain is the Swiss village and resort of Zermatt?

6. Who was the 1980 world Formula 1 motor racing champion?

7. Which oil tanker was forced on to rocks on the Brittany coast of France in 1978?

8. Which Indian cricketer's 17 Test centuries included 164 n.o. against Australia in 1986-7?

9. On which river is the port of Bordeaux in S.W. France?

10. Who was leader of the conspiracy to assassinate Caesar in 44 B.C.?

11. Who was the author of the children's book *Charlie And The Chocolate Factory*?

12. Which Hebrew prophet of the Old Testament was swallowed by a great fish?

13. Who was the 1961 U.S. Open golf champion?

14. Who was the Greek author of the novel *Zorba the Greek*?

15. Who was the 1969 world matchplay golf champion?

ANSWERS 1. Castries **2.** Castor **3.** Terry Downes **4.** 1953 **5.** Matterhorn **6.** Allan Jones **7.** Amoco Cadiz **8.** D.B. Vengsarkar **9.** River Garonne **10.** Marcus Junius Brutus **11.** Roald Dahl **12.** Jonah **13.** Gene Littler **14.** Nikos Kazantzakis **15.** Bob Charles.

ENTERTAINMENT

1. Who played Friar Domingo in the 1982 BBC TV drama *Shogun*?

2. Who played Tessa Piggott alongside Adam Faith in television's *Love Hurts*?

3. Which comedian's daughter played Jenny Piccalo in *Happy Days*?

4. What is Eddie Constantine's character name in the 1965 film *Alphaville*?

5. For what radio station did detective *Shoestring* work?

6. Who wrote the sitcom *Fairly Secret Army*?

7. In which year was radio presenter Ned Sherrin born?

8. Who played Fran in the television comedy *Shelley*?

9. In which European capital was the 1984 film *Amadeus* filmed?

10. Who played Huw Evans in the sitcom *Doctor In The House*?

11. Who directed the 1994 film *Vanya on 42nd Street*?

12. In which opera does Fiordiligi appear?

13. Which music video veteran directed the 1988 film *Paperhouse*?

14. What is the nightly weekday Radio Four arts programme at 7.15 P.M. called?

15. What was Geoffrey Palmer's character name in *The Fall And Rise Of Reggie Perrin*?

SPORT

1. Who beat Perpignan in the 1999/00 European Shield quarter-finals in rugby union?

2. Which women's cricketer took 7-6 for England against Australia on 22nd February, 1958?

3. In which year did U.S. tennis player Maureen Connolly die?

4. Gymnast Karin Janz was the 1970 world champion at what exercise?

5. In which city is the headquarters of British Athletics?

6. Which Briton won the 1998 San Marino Grand Prix in Formula 1?

7. Which athlete was the 1972 BBC Sports Personality of the Year?

8. In which year were the Hong Kong Sevens first held in rugby union?

9. By what score did London Irish beat Ebbw Vale in a 1999/00 European Shield quarter-final in rugby union?

10. Victor Cordoba was WBA super-middleweight world champion from 1991-2. What country did he represent?

11. Who was the 1970 Commonwealth men's 3000m steeplechase champion?

12. Which two men shared the title of champion jockey in National Hunt racing in 1944/5?

13. Who was the 1991 winner of the Grand Slam Cup in tennis?

14. In which year were the world indoor archery championships first held?

15. Who was the 1909 Wimbledon women's singles tennis champion?

ANSWERS 1. Castres **2.** Mary Duggan **3.** 1969 **4.** Asymmetrical bars **5.** Birmingham **6.** David Coulthard **7.** Mary Peters **8.** 1976 **9.** 21-20 **10.** Panama **11.** Tony Manning **12.** Fred Rimmell and Frenchie Nicholson **13.** David Wheaton **14.** 1991 **15.** Dora Boothby.

POP

1. In which year did group Buffalo Springfield split?

2. The U2 song *The Ground Beneath Her Feet* features lyrics by which author?

3. Who duets with actress Susan Sarandon on the song *Croon Spoon* in the film *The Cradle Will Rock*?

4. Mark Brydon and Roisin Murphy comprise which dance duo?

5. Which female singer recorded the 1991 album *Pop Pop*?

6. Which singer's album has ninety words in it's full title, beginning with *When The Pawn...*?

7. Which female singer recorded single *How Long Do I Get* in 2000?

8. Who recorded the 1999 album *Midnite Vultures*?

9. In which year did Janis Joplin's group The Kozmic Blues Band debut on stage?

10. Which member of the Beatles was attacked with a knife in December, 1999?

11. On which label did The Fall record the single *Look, Know*?

12. Who recorded the album *Kontiki* in 1998?

13. Which Captain Beefheart song is covered by the Buzzcocks on the live L.P. *Time's Up*?

14. What is the real name of Charlie Harper of the U.K. Subs?

15. Which singer recorded the 2000 album *Infinite Possibilities*?

ART

1. Which artist worked for most of his life for the Pall Mall Property Company in Manchester?

2. What is Rupert Baxter's nickname in various works by P.G. Wodehouse?

3. Who was the founder of the Vienna Secession movement?

4. Who wrote the 1834 novel *Jacob Faithful*?

5. In which year did Berlin-born artist George Grosz become an American citizen?

6. Thurston Benson appears in which 1853 novel by Elizabeth Gaskell?

7. Which artist married Agnes Frey in Nuremberg in 1494?

8. Who is the author of *The Sacred And Profane Love Machine*?

9. Whose paintings include 1862's *Gentlemens' Race: Before The Start*?

10. Which novel by Charles Dickens features Dr. Manette?

11. Miss Temple is a school superintendent in which novel by Charlotte Brontë?

12. Where did artist Claude Monet move to in 1883?

13. In which French city was artist Odilon Redon born?

14. Whose paintings include 1893's *The Bridge At Moret-sur-Loing*?

15. Where in Yorkshire was sculptor Henry Moore born in 1898?

GENERAL KNOWLEDGE

1. Who was the Roman god of doorways?

2. Which U.S. photographer was born Emmanuel Rudnitsky?

3. Which journalist is noted for his invention of the rhyme form, the clerihew?

4. Who authored the 1977 novel *The Ice Age*?

5. Who was the Roman goddess of agriculture?

6. Who was the author of the 1973 play *Magnificence*?

7. Who was the author of the 1934 book *Shabby Tiger*?

8. Which American general compelled the surrender of the British at Saratoga in 1777?

9. Which horse won the 1977 & 1978 Prix de l'Arc de Triomphe?

10. Which former England Test cricket captain scored 148 against India at Bombay in 1972-3?

11. In which year was the astronaut Edwin Aldrin born?

12. Which Florentine sculptor painted the ceiling of the Sistine Chapel?

13. Which F.B.I. special agent headed the investigation of Al Capone's gangsterism in Chicago?

14. In which sea is the island of Cuba?

15. Who was the Scottish star of the 1988 film *The Presidio*?

ANSWERS 1. Janus 2. Man Ray 3. E.C. Bentley 4. Margaret Drabble 5. Ceres 6. Howard Brenton 7. Howard Spring 8. Horatio Gates 9. Alleged 10. Tony Greig 11. 1930 12. Michelangelo 13. Eliot Ness 14. Caribbean Sea 15. Sean Connery.

ENTERTAINMENT

1. In which 1942 opera does the character Flamand appear?

2. Which film did producer Bernie Brillstein describe as "Dallas with French Costumes"?

3. Who directed the 1945 film *The Bells Of St. Mary's*?

4. Who wrote and produced the 1965 television documentary-drama *The War Game*?

5. Showbiz writer Pia Lindstrom is the daughter of which actress?

6. Who played Master at Arms Heron in the BBC TV drama *Warship*?

7. Who plays Bert in the Radio Four soap *The Archers*?

8. Which actor plays a racing driver in the 1954 film *Race For Life*?

9. How many million dollars did Jim Carrey earn for the film *The Cable Guy*?

10. Who directed and starred in the 1962 film *Panic in Year Zero*?

11. Which comedian stars in the 1959 film *Alias Jesse James*?

12. Which wrestler starred in the 1996 film *SantaWith Muscles*?

13. Who played Tarzan in the 1947 film *Tarzan And The Huntress*?

14. Which actor and actress discover they drove their son to suicide in the 1949 film *Edward, My Son*?

15. Who produced the television shows *Flipper* and *Daktari*?

SPORT

1. Which rider won the 1992 Queen Elizabeth II Cup at the Royal International Horse Show?

2. Which golfer won the 2000 Bay View invitational?

3. Who was the 1984 Olympic men's 100m butterfly swimming champion?

4. At what sport have Klaus Holinghaus and Hans-Werner Grosse held world records?

5. For which rugby league team does Tony Mestrov play?

6. What nationality is skier Katja Seizinger?

7. How long did the 19th and deciding frame between Gary Wilkinson & Jason Ferguson take in their 2000 World Professional Snooker Championship qualifying game?

8. How many Test matches did Dilip Vengsarkar play for India from 1976-92?

9. By what score did Wales beat Italy in the 2000 Six Nations Tournament?

10. In which year was the European Badminton Union founded?

11. By what score were Scotland leading Ireland in their 2000 Six Nations match before Ireland replied with 44 points on the trot?

12. Who rode the 1988 Ascot Gold Cup winner Sadeem?

13. Which Swedish golfer won the 2000 Madeira Island Open?

14. In which year was the American Powerboat Association formed?

15. Which golfer won the 2000 Los Angeles Open?

POP

1. On what label is Boss Hog's album *Whiteout* released?

2. Which group recorded the 1988 album *The Frenz Experiment*?

3. From which group did guitarist Neal Schon join Journey?

4. Which group recorded the 1972 album *Farther Along*?

5. What is the title of Ian Brown's second solo album?

6. In which institution's car park did the drummer meet the other members of Joy Division for the first time?

7. Which group recorded the 1981 album *Sticky George*?

8. Which group's albums include *Sounds Of The Satellites*?

9. Which U.S. artist appears on Jackie Leven's album *Defending Ancient Springs*?

10. In which year did Culture Club have a Top 10 single with *The War Song*?

11. Which group recorded the album *Do the Collapse*?

12. Which studio album by The Communards contains the song *Never Can Say Goodbye*?

13. In which year did Ray Parker, Jr. have a Top 10 single with *Ghostbusters*?

14. Which country singer's debut album was 1969's *Gliding Bird*?

15. Who recorded the 1999 Top 10 single *Will 2K*?

ANSWERS 1. City Slang **2.** The Fall **3.** Santana **4.** The Byrds **5.** Golden Greats **6.** Strangeways Prison **7.** The Korgis **8.** Laika **9.** David Thomas **10.** 1984 **11.** Guided By Voices **12.** Red **13.** 1984 **14.** Emmylou Harris **15.** Will Smith.

GEOGRAPHY

1. The island of Gotland lies off the S.E. coast of which country?

2. In which country is the industrial city of Shakhtu?

3. Which U.S. city is built around the Vieux Carré?

4. In which Scottish city is the landmark of Calton Hill?

5. Semeru is the highest peak on which island?

6. On which river does Elgin stand?

7. In which county is Sunbury-on-Thames?

8. On which river is Winchester?

9. On what Mediterranean island is Syracuse?

10. Which Scottish castle is perched on a promontory opposite Bass Rock?

11. Damaraland is a plateau region of which African country?

12. Toxteth is part of which northern city?

13. In which Berkshire village was the Atomic Weapons Research Establishment set up after World War Two?

14. What is the name of the plain which extends from Tel Aviv to Haifa?

15. Marmolada is the highest peak of which European mountain range?

ANSWERS 1. Sweden **2.** Russia **3.** New Orleans **4.** Edinburgh **5.** Java **6.** River Lossie **7.** Surrey **8.** Itchen **9.** Sicily **10.** Tantallon Castle **11.** Namibia **12.** Liverpool **13.** Aldermaston **14.** Plain of Sharon **15.** Dolomites.

GENERAL KNOWLEDGE

1. Which ancient Egyptian fertility goddess is depicted as a woman with cow's horns?

2. What is the name of the central character in the novel *Billy Liar*?

3. Who directed the 1974 film *Chinatown* starring Jack Nicholson?

4. What is the capital of Afghanistan?

5. What is the name of the rod on which flax is wound preparatory to spinning?

6. What is oolong?

7. What is the name given to the four teeth situated between the incisors and the premolars?

8. What is the capital of Cyprus?

9. In which island group is the neolithic village of Skara Brae?

10. Which South Africa-born actress directed a 1987 production of *Othello* in Johannesburg?

11. In which African country is the university town of Ife?

12. How many times was South African rugby union player Frik Du Preez capped between 1960 and 1971?

13. Who authored the 1962 novel *One Flew Over the Cuckoo's Nest*?

14. Who was the 1972 U.S. Open men's singles tennis champion?

15. What was the Mississippi birthplace of singer Elvis Presley?

ANSWERS 1. Isis **2.** Billy Fisher **3.** Roman Polanski **4.** Kabul **5.** Distaff **6.** A kind of dark tea grown in China **7.** Canines **8.** Nicosia **9.** Orkney Islands **10.** Janet Suzman **11.** Nigeria **12.** 38 times **13.** Ken Kesey **14.** Ilie Nastase **15.** Tupelo.

ENTERTAINMENT

1. Who directed the 1938 French film *La Bête Humaine*?

2. Which tough-guy actor played Spats Columbo in the film *Some Like It Hot*?

3. What was the name of the dragon in 1960s puppet series *Torchy*?

4. Who plays the devil in the 1949 film *Alias Nick Beal*?

5. Which comedy actor played Miguel Garetta in the 1960s drama *Top Secret*?

6. Which member of the Monty Python team wrote the 1986 film *Labyrinth*?

7. What nationality was opera singer Rose Caron, who died in 1930?

8. Who played lawyer Sam Bowden in the 1962 film *Cape Fear*?

9. The 1935 baseball picture *Alibi Ike* is based on a story by which author?

10. Who is the actress daughter of Dame Lilian Braithwaite?

11. Who directed the 1995 film *La Cérémonie*?

12. Who authored the 1974 stage work *The Churchill Play*?

13. What song does Annie Lennox sing in the 1991 film *Edward II*?

14. Who does Sue Nicholls play in *Coronation Street*?

15. Who plays Mini-Me in the film *Austin Powers: The Spy Who Shagged Me*?

SPORT

1. Angelique Seriese was the 1988 Olympic judo champion in the Over 72 kg category. Which country was she representing?

2. What nationality is the golfer Paul McGinley?

3. Which German team won the 1997 U.E.F.A. Cup in football?

4. Which golfer was the 1990 British Amateur champion?

5. In athletics, which country won the first European Combined Events Cup for men, in 1973?

6. What sport do Annika and Charlotta Sorenstam play?

7. In cricket, in which year did South Australia first win the Sheffield Shield?

8. For which ice hockey team do Blair Scott and Alexei Lozhkin play?

9. In gymnsatics, who was the 1972 Olympic women's horse vault champion?

10. For which rugby union club side does Matt Dawson play?

11. Which Italian won the 1966 Italian Grand Prix in Formula 1?

12. At which sport does Laszlo Nemeth coach England?

13. Which country has won the Five Nations (now Six Nations) Triple Crown most times in rugby union?

14. Where do Newcastle rugby union side play their home matches?

15. Geoff Kelly and Bert Palm won the 1966 men's pairs bowls world outdoor championships in 1966. Which country did they represent?

ANSWERS 1. Holland **2.** Irish **3.** Schalke 04 **4.** Rolf Muntz **5.** Poland **6.** Golf **7.** 1894 **8.** Manchester Storm **9.** Karin Janz **10.** Northampton **11.** Lodovico Scarfiotti **12.** Basketball **13.** England **14.** Kingston Park **15.** Australia.

POP

1. What was the title of the 1999 studio album by James?

2. Who recorded the 2000 Top 10 single *Bye Bye Bye*?

3. Which guitarist recorded the 1972 album *Into The Purple Valley*?

4. Which underground station features on the cover of The Jam's single *Down in the Tube Station at Midnight*?

5. In which year was Bobby Gillespie's first gig with The Jesus and Mary Chain?

6. With which member of Blur did Michael Nyman write the soundtrack to the film *Ravenous*?

7. Which group recorded the 1999 album *You, My Baby & I*?

8. Which song did Robbie Williams sing with Tom Jones on the album *Reload*?

9. Which female singer recorded the 1999 album *Afterglow*?

10. What is the title of Bryan Ferry's 1999 covers album?

11. Which former Beatle recorded the 1974 album *Dark Horse*?

12. Which group recorded the 1999 album *Simple Faboo*?

13. Who produced The Incredible String Band's album *The Hangman's Beautiful Daughter*?

14. Which producer fronted the group *The Boxes*?

15. What is Tori Amos's real forename?

ANSWERS 1. Millionaires **2.** NSYNC **3.** Ry Cooder **4.** Bond Street **5.** 1984 **6.** Damon Albarn **7.** Alex Gopher **8.** Are You Gonna Go My Way **9.** Dot Allison **10.** As Time Goes By **11.** George Harrison **12.** The Gentle People **13.** Joe Boyd **14.** Clive Langer **15.** Ellen.

HISTORY

1. Which king of Sweden was known as 'the Lion of the North'?

2. In which year was the Malta Summit between Gorbachev and Bush?

3. Who was Minister of Industry in Cuba from 1961-5?

4. In which year did the ayatollah Ruhollah Khomeini die?

5. To which country did French statesman Jacques Necker retire following the French Revolution?

6. What job did Benjamin Disraeli do between the ages of 17 and 20?

7. In which year did the South African government lift the ban on the A.N.C.?

8. Of which country did Alberto Fujimori become president in 1990?

9. Monticello was the Virginia home of which U.S. president?

10. In which year was Joan of Arc burnt at the stake?

11. Who was Home Secretary under Gladstone from 1880-85?

12. In which English county was Charles Darwin born?

13. In which year was the Battle of Adwa between Italy and Ethiopia?

14. In which year was General Custer killed?

15. In which year did the Anti-Corn Law League form in Manchester?

GENERAL KNOWLEDGE

1. The island of Banaba is part of which independent republic in the W. Pacific?

2. Who was the male star of the 1963 Alfred Hitchcock film *The Birds*?

3. With which writer is the balsa wood raft Kon-Tiki associated?

4. When was the U.S. space station Skylab launched?

5. Which English scientist, born in 1766, gave the first accurate description of colour blindness?

6. In the Old Testament, who was mother of Joseph and wife of Jacob?

7. What was the name of the son of Agamemnon in Greek mythology who killed his mother?

8. Who was Muse of comedy and pastoral poetry in Greek mythology?

9. On which river is the Spanish city of Toledo, which is associated with sword manufacturing?

10. Who directed the 1969 film musical *Sweet Charity* starring Shirley MacLaine?

11. Which feminist writer was author of *The Female Eunuch*?

12. In which year was French marshal Michel Ney executed for treason?

13. Which port in S.W. England houses the Royal Naval College?

14. In which year did English stage and film actor Sir Felix Aylmer die?

15. Which small constellation is also called the *Little Bear*?

ENTERTAINMENT

1. Who played the Mock Turtle in the 1933 film *Alice in Wonderland*?

2. Who composed the 1844 opera *Caterina Cornaro*?

3. Actress Jean Harlow died during the making of which film?

4. Who directed the 1999 film *Magnolia*?

5. Who played Big Jim in the 1980s television series *Big Jim and the Figaro Club*?

6. Who is star of the 1999 film *End of Days*?

7. In which mountain range does the plane crash in the 1993 film *Alive*?

8. In which opera does the aria *Casta diva* appear?

9. Who plays *The Limey* in a 1999 film?

10. Which actress plays the title role in the 1974 film *Effi Briest*?

11. Who played Tarzan in the 1998 film *Tarzan and the Lost City*?

12. Who directed and starred in the 1999 film *The Muse*?

13. Who played Peter Smith-Kingsley in the film *The Talented Mr. Ripley*?

14. In which year was opera singer José Carreras born?

15. Who directed the 1999 film *EdTV*?

SPORT

1. Which Scottish golfer won the 2000 Algarve Portuguese Open?

2. Which horse won the 1997 Whitbread Gold Cup?

3. What was the World Team Cup in tennis formerly known as?

4. Who won the 1984 Olympic 3000m steeplechase title?

5. At what sport have José Marquez and Tan Arzu been world champions?

6. Robin Mason and Jonathan Mole won the Kinnaird Cup in 1998. At what sport?

7. Where were the 1971 Pan-American Games held?

8. Who was the 1973 men's 1500m freestyle swimming world champion?

9. Which U.S. pair won the 1993 World Cup in golf?

10. Who were the 1982 Commonwealth men's 4 x 100m relay champions in athletics?

11. Which snooker player won the 1998 Benson & Hedges Masters?

12. Who won the 1981 Lance Todd award in rugby league?

13. For which country does Sanath Jayasuriya play cricket?

14. Who was the 1994 Commonwealth men's pole vault champion?

15. Which basketball team have been NBA champions in the U.S. the most times?

ANSWERS 1. Gary Orr **2.** Harwell Lad **3.** Nations Cup **4.** Julius Korir **5.** Taekwondo **6.** Eton Fives **7.** Cali **8.** Steve Holland **9.** Fred Couples and Davis Love III **10.** Nigeria **11.** Mark Williams **12.** Mick Burke **13.** Sri Lanka **14.** Nick Winter **15.** Boston Celtics.

POP

1. Who is vocalist with the group Screaming Trees?

2. For which group did Jim Webb write the song *MacArthur Park*?

3. Who is the singer with U.S. group *Wheat*?

4. Who recorded the album *Cobra and Phases Group Play Voltage In The Milky Night*?

5. Which group recorded the 1999 Top 10 single *Turn*?

6. In which year did Noel Gallagher record the song *Setting Sun* with the Chemical Brothers?

7. Who recorded the 1993 L.P. *My Field Trip To Planet 9*?

8. Which female singer guests on *In Denial* by the Pet Shop Boys?

9. What is Bono's real name?

10. In which year did Ian Curtis of Joy Division die?

11. Which Phoenix rock star formed the group The Earwigs in the 1960s?

12. What was U2's debut single for Island?

13. On which label did Robbie Williams record the single *She's The One*?

14. Which group's albums include *Sonic Flower Groove*?

15. In which U.S. city was the singer Julianna Hatfield born?

ANSWERS 1. Mark Lanegan **2.** The Association **3.** Scott Levesque **4.** Stereolab **5.** Travis **6.** 1996 **7.** Justin Warfield **8.** Kylie Minogue **9.** Paul Hewson **10.** 1980 **11.** Alice Cooper **12.** 11 O'Clock Tick Tock **13.** Chrysalis **14.** Primal Scream **15.** Boston.

WORDS

1. What type of creature is a frogmouth?

2. What shape is an area known as a henge?

3. If you heft something what do you do?

4. What is *per cent* a shortened form of in Latin?

5. What in Scotland is a lum?

6. What would you do with frumenty - wear it or eat it?

7. What in the nautical word is partners?

8. What part of the body does the word osculate refer to?

9. What in India is a maund?

10. What is a pasquinade?

11. In which hobby would you encounter a tête-bêche?

12. Which four letter suffix of nouns can mean female, small or imitation?

13. What in Ireland is drisheen?

14. Laetrile is an extract from the stone of which fruit?

15. Flittermouse is a dialect name for which creature?

ANSWERS 1. A bird **2.** Circular **3.** Weigh it by lifting **4.** per centum **5.** Chimney **6.** Eat it, it's a porridge **7.** A wooden construction around an opening in a deck supporting a mast **8.** Mouth **9.** A unit of weight **10.** A lampoon or satire **11.** Philately (stamp collecting) **12.** -ette **13.** Pudding made of sheep's intestines **14.** Peach **15.** Bat.

GENERAL KNOWLEDGE

1. Who authored the children's novel *The Village by the Sea*?

2. At which battle is Lord Clifford killed in the play *Henry VI, Part III*?

3. Who directed the 1954 film *The Seven Samurai*?

4. What is the capital of Zimbabwe?

5. The 1997 film *The Rainmaker* starring Matt Damon is based on whose novel?

6. Which city and port in Finland was capital of the country until 1812?

7. What was the former name, until 1966, of Botswana?

8. Who authored the 1977 novel *Dreamland*?

9. In which U.S. city is O'Hare airport?

10. Which county of the Republic of Ireland on the Atlantic coast lies east of County Mayo?

11. Which American novelist authored the 1919 book *Jurgen*?

12. Who directed the 1995 film *The Crossing Guard* starring Jack Nicholson?

13. In which year did Prague-born poet Rainer Maria Rilke die?

14. Who is the American author of the novel *Giles Goat-Boy*?

15. Who authored the 1908 novel *The Blue Lagoon*?

ENTERTAINMENT

1. Which husband and wife team starred in the 1969 film *Can Hieronymus Merkin Ever Forget Mercy Humppe And Find True Happiness*?

2. Who was a Best Actress Oscar nominee for her role in the 1999 film *The End Of The Affair*?

3. The 1954 film *The Rainbow Jacket* is about which sport?

4. For which film was Jude Law a Best Supporting Actor Oscar nominee in 2000?

5. What type of creature is *K-9* in a 1989 film?

6. Which of the characters in *The Simpsons* was killed off in 2000?

7. Which actresses play elderly sisters in the 1989 film *An Unremarkable Life*?

8. Who composed the five-act opera *Don Carlos*?

9. Who plays Renée Radick in *Ally McBeal*?

10. Which film director narrated the 1982 film *Cannery Row*?

11. Who plays Miranda on the television show *Sex and the City*?

12. What was the 1992 film follow-up to *Honey I Shrunk the Kids*?

13. Which comedy team star in the 1940 film *Saps At Sea*?

14. Who plays Arthur Sullivan in the film *Topsy Turvy*?

15. Who was a Best Director Oscar nominee for his film *The Cider House Rules*?

ANSWERS 1. Anthony Newley and Joan Collins **2.** Julianne Moore **3.** Horse-racing **4.** The Talented Mr. Ripley **5.** Dog **6.** Maude Flanders **7.** Shelley Winters and Patricia Neal **8.** Verdi **9.** Lisa Nicole Carson **10.** John Huston **11.** Cynthia Nixon **12.** Honey I Blew Up the Kid **13.** Laurel and Hardy **14.** Allan Corduner **15.** Lalle Hallström.

SPORT

1. Where were the 1993 World Student games held?

2. In which year was the Irish Derby first run?

3. What nationality is women's weightlifter Monka Mincheva?

4. At what sport were Vaclav Kozak & Pavel Schmidt 1960 Olympic champions?

5. Who scored a hat-trick of tries for England against Italy in the 2000 Six Nations in rugby union?

6. Who was the 1979 world 50cc motorcycling champion?

7. In which year was the tug-of-war first included as an Olympic event?

8. By what score did Chelsea lose the 1915 F.A. Cup Final to Sheffield United?

9. What is the nickname of cricketer Graeme Archer?

10. Fanny Blankers-Koen set a world record for the high jump of 1.71m. In what year?

11. Who was the 1974 Argentine Grand Prix winner in Formula 1?

12. Maurice Perrin and Louis Chaillot won the 1932 Olympic men's 2000m tandem cycle race. For which country?

13. In which year did British tennis player Charlotte Cooper die?

14. With which sport are Robert G. Farrington and John Campbell associated?

15. Which horse won the 1981 Prix de Diane Hermès?

ANSWERS 1. Buffalo 2. 1866 3. Bulgarian 4. Rowing 5. Austin Healey 6. Eugenio Lazzarini 7. 1900 8. 3-0 9. Bunka 10. 1943 11. Denny Hulme 12. France 13. 1966 14. Harness racing 15. Madam Gay.

POP

1. Who wrote Badfinger's hit *Come And Get It*?

2. In which year did girl group L7 form?

3. Who had a 1981 hit single with *Europa And The Pirate Twins*?

4. What is the title of the second album from David Devant and his Spirit Wife?

5. Who is the bass player of Oasis?

6. Which Bob Dylan song features on Rod Stewart's studio album *Every Picture Tells A Story*?

7. Mark, Des and Jim Morris comprise which band?

8. Who replaced drummer John Timson in The La's?

9. On which label did Steps record *Love's Got A Hold On My Heart*?

10. Which Scottish folk singer recorded the 1968 album *A Gift from a Flower to a Garden*?

11. Who recorded the 2000 best-selling album *Supernatural*?

12. Which rap artist recorded the album *Chronic 2001*?

13. Which singer had a 1988 hit single with *Roll With It*?

14. Which punk singer featured on Timezone's single *World Destruction*?

15. Which U.S. female singer had a hit in 1984 with *Let's Hear It For The Boy*?

SCIENCE

1. Which banker and scientist was made Baron Avebury in 1900?

2. What is the second largest moon of Saturn?

3. What is the symbol of the element Praseodymium?

4. In which county was Michael Faraday born?

5. What percentage of the light that falls on it does the Moon reflect into space?

6. With what is the surface of Jupiter's moon Europa covered?

7. In which year was radio survey of the stars Project Ozma made?

8. Metis is a small moon of which planet?

9. What was the name of the small roving vehicle carried by the Mars Pathfinder spacecraft in 1997?

10. What is the second largest moon of Neptune?

11. What is the symbol of the element Seaborgium?

12. How did French scientist Antoine Lavoisier die?

13. Which is the second largest planet in the solar system?

14. What is the element ununbium also called?

15. In which year did physiologist Ivan Pavlov die?

GENERAL KNOWLEDGE

1. Who was president of Egypt from 1956-70?

2. Who won a Best Supporting Actor Oscar for his role in the 1985 film *Cocoon*?

3. Who wrote the 1983 musical *Blood Brothers*?

4. Which region of N.W. Italy includes the province of Genoa?

5. Which Canadian port is the capital of Prince Edward Island?

6. Who was the king of England from 946-955?

7. Which sea is also called Lake Tiberias?

8. Thimbu is the capital of which kingdom in central Asia?

9. In which year of the 1960s did the Abbey Theatre in Dublin reopen following a fire?

10. Who directed the 1980 film *Fame*?

11. Who wrote the 1967 play *A Day In The Death Of Joe Egg*?

12. Who authored the 1968 novel *Airport*?

13. Which comedy play by Ben Jonson is subtitled *The Fox*?

14. Which woman authored the novel *The Golden Notebook*?

15. The Dead Sea lies between which two countries?

ANSWERS 1. Gamal Abdel Nasser **2.** Don Ameche **3.** Willy Russell **4.** Liguria **5.** Charlottetown **6.** Eadred **7.** The Sea of Galilee **8.** Bhutan **9.** 1966 **10.** Alan Parker **11.** Peter Nichols **12.** Arthur Hailey **13.** Volpone **14.** Doris Lessing **15.** Israel and Jordan.

ENTERTAINMENT

1. Who plays the lead in the1944 film *The Canterville Ghost*?

2. Who plays Sidney Prescott in the film *Scream 3*?

3. Who was a Best Supporting Actress Oscar nominee for the film *Boy's Don't Cry* in 2000?

4. Who played Lois Lane in the 1978 film *Superman*?

5. Who has created computer games *The Sims* and *Sim City*?

6. Which Oscar-winning actress directed the 1995 film *Unstrung Heroes*?

7. Which comedian starred in the London West End play *Cooking with Elvis* in 2000?

8. In which city did Mozart's opera *Don Giovanni* premier in 1787?

9. Who performs the song *Ole Buttermilk Sky* in the 1946 film *Canyon Passage*?

10. Who was a Best Supporting Actor Oscar nominee in 2000 for *The Green MIle*?

11. Who is the host of the comedy quiz show *It's Only T.V.... But I Like It?*

12. Who presents television's words and numbers game *Countdown*?

13. Which former *Coronation Street* actress appears in the sitcom *The Peter Principle*?

14. Who played Philippa in the sitcom *Dinnerladies*?

15. What is the version of *Teletubbies* on the comedy show *Goodness Gracious Me*?

SPORT

1. Which team won the Constructor's Championship in Formula 1 in 1997?

2. In which year was the Ryder Cup a drawn result for the first time?

3. In which year was rugby union first played in Australia?

4. Who was the 1985 winner of the European Grand Prix in Formula 1?

5. Veeraphol Sahaprom was the 1995 WBA bantamweight boxing champion. Which country does he represent?

6. Which country won the 1953 golf World Cup?

7. How many people play in an ice hockey team?

8. Which cricketer took 7-51 for the West Indies against Australia at Leeds in the 1983 World Cup?

9. Which college American Football player won the 1967 Heisman Trophy?

10. How many times did John McEnroe win the Wimbledon men's singles tennis title?

11. At which Olympics was the fencing competition first held?

12. In which year did José-Maria Olazabal first play in the Ryder Cup?

13. Who was the 1912 Olympic women's highboard platform diving champion?

14. Which U.S. golfer won the 1955 U.S. PGA championship?

15. In which year was cricketer Alistair Brown born?

POP

1. Which U.S. group recorded the 1999 album *Issues*?

2. Which U.S. group's debut single in 1992 was *Everlast*?

3. Which U.K. group's Top 30 singles include *Just In Lust* and *Sick Of Drugs*?

4. Which Bruce Springsteen studio album features the single *Dancing In The Dark*?

5. Which group recorded the 1975 album *Northern Lights, Southern Cross*?

6. In which year did Robbie Williams have a hit single with *Old Before I Die*?

7. Which group recorded the 1999 album *SYR 4: Goodbye 20th Century*?

8. When Pat Simmons joined the group Pud in 1970, what did they change their name to?

9. Which U.S. vocalist had a 1975 hit single with *The Snake*?

10. Which group recorded the 1994 Kraftwerk cover album *Trans-Slovenia Express*?

11. Which group recorded the 1994 hit *9PM (Till I Come)*?

12. What was the first U.K. hit single for vocal group Wilson Phillips?

13. In which U.S. city were the group The Butterflies of Love formed?

14. Who was the lead singer and lyricist in The Band of Holy Joy?

15. In which year did the Electric Light Orchestra have a Top 10 single with *Don't Bring Me Down*?

ANSWERS 1. Korn **2.** LaBradford **3.** Wildhearts **4.** Born In The U.S.A. **5.** The Band **6.** 1997 **7.** Sonic Youth **8.** The Doobie Brothers **9.** Al Wilson **10.** Laibach **11.** ATB **12.** Hold On **13.** New Haven, Connecticut **14.** Johny Brown **15.** 1979.

PEOPLE

1. Which U.S. statesman was killed in 1804 in a duel with Aaron Burr?

2. How old was Jack Nicholson when his son Raymond was born in 1992?

3. Which film director did Madonna start dating in 1999?

4. Which member of the group All Saints was actor Jonny Lee Miller dating in early 2000?

5. Who did Louis Theroux profile in the 2000 television show *When Louis Met Jimmy*?

6. Which singer has written the autobiography *If Only...*?

7. As what was apache leader Goyathlay better known?

8. In which country was innovative teacher Rewi Alley born?

9. Who became editor of the Daily Telegraph in 1990?

10. Who was prime minister of the Republic of Ireland from 1954-7?

11. What was the middle name of film director Alfred Hitchcock?

12. What was the middle name of U.S. vice-president George Dallas?

13. In which country was Henry II, king of England, born?

14. In which year was train robber Ronnie Biggs born?

15. In which country was author Bessie Head born?

ANSWERS 1. Alexander Hamilton 2. 54 3. Guy Ritchie 4. Natalie Appleton 5. Jimmy Savile 6. Geri Halliwell 7. Geronimo 8. New Zealand 9. Max Hastings 10. John Costello 11. Joseph 12. Mifflin 13. France 14. 1929 15. South Africa.

GENERAL KNOWLEDGE

1. Who wrote the 1937 book *The Hobbit*?

2. Who directed the 1971 film *Gumshoe* starring Albert Finney?

3. Who directed the 1990 film *The Hot Spot* starring Don Johnson?

4. In which African country is the port of Beira?

5. Which Saudi Arabian politician was minister of petroleum and natural resources from 1962-86?

6. Who was president of Chile from 1970-73?

7. What is the name of the parrot in the novel *Treasure Island*?

8. Pula is the chief city of which peninsula in the N. Adriatic Sea?

9. Asmara is the capital of which small country in N.E. Africa?

10. Who wrote the 1936 play *The Boy David*?

11. Who composed the 1946 two-act opera *Street Scene*?

12. What was the name of the former Labour Party Chief Whip who died in 1998?

13. In which year was the Palestinian terrorist organization Al Fatah founded?

14. What is the tree called the white poplar also known as?

15. Halifax is the capital of which province of Canada?

ENTERTAINMENT

1. Who plays Samantha in the television show *Sex and the City*?

2. Which star of *Coronation Street* played the lead in the 1993 Ken Loach film *Raining Stones*?

3. For which film was Meryl Streep a 2000 Best Actress Oscar nominee?

4. What is the name of the farmer bridegroom of Amina in the opera *La Sonnambula* by Bellini?

5. Which 1962 film is based on John D. MacDonald's novel *The Executioners*?

6. Who stars as a heavyweight boxing champion in the 1936 film *Cain and Mabel*?

7. The 1969 film *A Talent for Loving* is based on whose novel?

8. What is Ian's profession in the sitcom *How Do You Want Me*?

9. Who plays a blind girl in the 1959 western *The Hanging Tree*?

10. Who did Blanche Yurka play in the 1935 film *A Tale of Two Cities*?

11. Who does Howard Keel play in the 1953 film *Calamity Jane*?

12. Who won Best Male award at the 1999 European MTV Awards?

13. Who plays opera singer Jenny Lind in the 1930 film *A Lady's Morals*?

14. Who played Jill Masterson in the Bond film *Goldfinger*?

15. Who plays a one-legged pirate in the 1973 film *Scalawag*?

SPORT

1. At which theatre in Sheffield is the World Professional Snooker championship held?

2. How many golds did Russia win in the 1999 World Athletics Championship?

3. Which England Test player took 49 wickets in the 1913/4 four match series against South Africa?

4. In which year did British tennis player Blanche Bingley die?

5. Who did the Baseball Writers' Association make Most Valuable Player of the Year in the American League in 1959?

6. Who did Munster play in the quarter-finals of the Heineken Cup in rugby union in 2000?

7. Over what distance is the Middle Park Stakes run at Newmarket?

8. How many Tests did Phil De Freitas play for England at cricket?

9. At what sport was Jim Shoulders a world champion from 1956-9?

10. In cricket, who scored 115 for Surrey vs. Sussex in the 2nd innings of their 1999 county championship game?

11. How many nations were in the International Korfball Federation in 1998?

12. In cricket, who scored 136 for Warwickshire vs. Glamorgan in the 1st innings of their 1999 county championship game?

13. Who were football's First Division champions in England in 1979/80?

14. What nationality is racing driver Nick Heidfeld?

15. Edwin Bloss set a world record for the triple jump on 16th September 1893. What distance was it?

POP

1. Who was the keyboard player with The Doors?

2. Who produced David Gilmour's solo album *David Gilmour*?

3. In which city were the group JJ72 formed?

4. In which year was former Pink Floyd front man Syd Barrett born?

5. Which group released the single *The Last Good Day of the Year*?

6. Which band recorded the title track of the Bond film *The World Is Not Enough*?

7. Who was the drummer on the Jethro Tull album *The Broadsword and the Beast*?

8. On which label did Stereophonics record the 1999 album *Performance and Cocktails*?

9. Who guests on Elastica's song *How He Wrote Elastica Man*?

10. On which label did Shelby Lynne record the album *I Am Shelby Lynne*?

11. Which Australian group's debut single was *Lee Remick/Karen*?

12. Who had a 1990 Top 10 single with *I Wish It Would Rain Down*?

13. Embrace's Danny McNamara was born on New Year's Eve of which year?

14. Which city were Scottish group The Poets from?

15. What was the debut album by the Go-Go's?

ART

1. Sir Thomas Booby appears in which novel by Henry Fielding?

2. Which artist was director of the French Academy in Rome from 1834-41?

3. In which city was painter George Stubbs born?

4. Who is the author of the thriller novel *Single & Single*?

5. Edward and Rose Driffield appear in which 1930 novel by W. Somerset Maugham?

6. Who authored the 2000 thriller novel *Day of Reckoning*?

7. Who painted the portrait *Charles V in an armchair*?

8. Who authored the detective novel *Arms and the Women*?

9. In which year did artist Paul Chagall die?

10. Who is the author of the thriller *Archangel*?

11. In which U.S. city was Andy Warhol born?

12. In which year did the artist Giotto die?

13. Who painted the 1488 work *Madonna with Saints*?

14. Which French artist's works include *St. Sebastian Tended by St. Irene*?

15. In which French city was the artist Tissot born in 1836?

GENERAL KNOWLEDGE

1. Who directed the 1996 film *Jack* starring Robin Williams?

2. Who did Chuck Connors play in television western drama *The Rifleman*?

3. Who was the 1998 winner of cycling's Tour de France?

4. What was *noyade* in France in the late 18th Century?

5. Who was the 1998 British Open golf champion?

6. In which famous novel does Catherine Earnshaw appear?

7. Ndjamena is the capital of which African country?

8. Which Old Testament prophet of the 9th Century B.C. denounced Ahab and Jezebel?

9. Who was a Best Supporting Actress Oscar nominee for the film *Nashville*?

10. What is the name of the rocky headland on an island at the extreme southern tip of South America?

11. In which year was fire-fighting specialist Paul 'Red' Adair born?

12. Which island in the Irish Sea lies between Cumbria and Northern Ireland?

13. What is the name given to the point after deuce in tennis?

14. Who is the male star of the 1998 Woody Allen film *Celebrity*?

15. In which country is the port and university city of Izmir?

ENTERTAINMENT

1. Who composed the 1915 musical comedy *Stop! Look! Listen!*?

2. Which former *Coronation Street* actor played prison warden Mr. Lithgow in the sitcom *The Bright Side*?

3. In which year did actress Sarah Bernhardt make her debut at the Comédie Française?

4. Who directed the 1978 film *California Suite*?

5. Who starred as the singer in the 1994 T.V. movie *Madonna: Innocence Lost*?

6. Which comedy team created the sitcom *The Brittas Empire*?

7. What ws the 1975 sequel to the film *True Grit*?

8. What is the job of Phil Silvers in the 1943 film comedy *A Lady Takes a Chance?*

9. Which skater played Bibi in the Bond film *For Your Eyes Only*?

10. Which sitcom featured Elmo's Wine Bar?

11. What toy is Arnold Scwarzenegger on a quest for in the film *Jingle All the Way*?

12. Who played Sherlock Holmes in the 1991 T.V. movie *Crucifer of Blood*?

13. Who plays the title role in the 1951 film *Calling Bulldog Drummond*?

14. Which actress, who died in 1999, voiced all the female characters in the cartoon show *South Park*?

15. Who directed the 1982 Gene Wilder comedy film *Hanky Panky*?

ANSWERS 1. Irving Berlin **2.** Geoffrey Hughes **3.** 1862 **4.** Herbert Ross **5.** Terumi Matthews **6.** Richard Fegen and Andrew Norriss **7.** Rooster Cogburn **8.** A bus tour guide **9.** Lynn-Holly Johnson **10.** Brush Strokes **11.** Turbo Man **12.** Charlton Heston **13.** Walter Pidgeon **14.** Mary Kay Bergman **15.** Sidney Poitier.

SPORT

1. For which U.S. ice hockey team does Pavel Bure play?

2. In which year were the croquet world championships first held?

3. In cricket, which Derbyshire debutant made a king pair in 1999?

4. Who was men's overall champion in the 1990 gymnastics World Cup?

5. In cricket, who scored 116 for Surrey vs. Middlesex in the 1st innings of their 1999 county championship game?

6. Who was runner-up in the 1965 Formula 1 world championships?

7. In which year was the World Cup in trampolining first held?

8. Who replaced John Player in the 1988/9 as sponsors of the RFU knock-out competition?

9. Which 1976 Olympic champion is godfather to runner Inger Miller?

10. Who took over from Jimmy Carter in 1955 as undisputed world lightweight boxing champion?

11. Which golfer was the 1971 Sports Illustrated Sportsman of the Year?

12. Which jockey won the 1979 Preakness Stakes?

13. In which year did the cricketer R.T. Bates make his debut for Nottinghamshire?

14. Lake Echternach was the venue for the 1981 world fly-fishing championships. In which country is it?

15. Which duo won the 1937 Wimbledon women's doubles tennis title?

ANSWERS 1. Florida Panthers **2.** 1989 **3.** James Pyemont **4.** Valeriy Belenky **5.** Adam Hollioake **6.** Graham Hill **7.** 1980 **8.** Pilkington **9.** Don Quarrie **10.** Wallace Bud Smith **11.** Lee Trevino **12.** Angel Cordero, Jr. **13.** 1993 **14.** Luxembourg **15.** Simone Mathieu & Billie Yorke.

POP

1. What is the B-side of Ian Dury's single *What a Waste*?

2. Which record producer made the album *I Hear a New World*?

3. Who replaced Billy Murcia on drums in The New York Dolls?

4. Which group recorded the 1999 single *Hooligan*?

5. In which city was Randy Newman born?

6. Gavin Goodman is singer with which Welsh group?

7. Which group recorded the 1981 single *Kick out the Tories*?

8. Which country artist recorded the 1999 album *A Place in the Sun*?

9. *Cocaine Socialism* was the B-side of which single by Pulp?

10. Which solo male artist recorded the 1999 album *Forever*?

11. Which group's albums include *Levelling the Land*?

12. Which band were Peter and Chris Coyne in before *The Godfathers*?

13. What singer was born Christa Päffgen in 1938?

14. From which group did Kevin Shields join Primal Scream?

15. On which label did the Nightingales E.P. *Use Your Loaf* appear?

GEOGRAPHY

1. Which river does the Clifton Suspension Bridge span?

2. Which of the Tropics runs through Taiwan?

3. The Glomma River in Norway, largest in Scandinavia, flows into which body of water?

4. In which Irish county does the River Shannon rise?

5. What is the second largest city in Austria?

6. Which country lies due north of Yemen?

7. Graben, oxbow and kettle are all types of what?

8. Into which bay does the Susquehanna River flow in the U.S.?

9. Nuku'alofa is capital of which Pacific kingdom?

10. In which European country is the town of Anzio?

11. Near which Devon resort is Kent's Cavern, an important prehistoric site?

12. On which Scottish island is Brodick Castle?

13. In which group of hills does the River Clyde rise?

14. What is a tombolo?

15. Darfur is a region of which African country?

ANSWERS 1. Avon 2. Tropic of Cancer 3. Skagerrak 4. Cavan 5. Graz 6. Saudi Arabia 7. Lakes 8. Chesapeake Bay 9. Tonga 10. Italy 11. Torquay 12. Arran 13. Lowther Hills 14. A narrow bar of sand or shingle linking an island with another island or the mainland 15. Sudan.

GENERAL KNOWLEDGE

1. Who composed the three-act opera *The Nose* which was first performed in 1930?

2. What is the name of the house in the novel *Gone with the Wind*?

3. Which late writer authored the 1988 book *Empire of the Senseless*?

4. What nationality was the 18th Century mathematician Leonhard Euler?

5. What is deuterium oxide also known as?

6. Who directed the 1979 film *Tess*?

7. Which film actor directed the 1981 work *Tarzan - the Ape Man* which starred his wife Bo?

8. Which 1986 film starred David Bowie as the *Goblin King*?

9. In which novel does character Adela Quested appear?

10. To which Greek poet is the *Odyssey* attributed?

11. Who authored the 1985 novel *The Good Terrorist*?

12. What is the state capital of Oregon in the U.S.?

13. Who authored the 1923 novel *Confessions of Zeno*?

14. Which American actress born in 1916 was a sister of Gypsy Rose Lee?

15. Which actor played the lead in the 1977 film *Eraserhead*?

ENTERTAINMENT

1. Who was director of the Phoenix Theatre in Leicester from 1973-7?

2. Which Hollywood actress played Wendy Killan in the 1980s sitcom *Buffalo Bill*?

3. What is Chris Morris's 2000 Channel Four version of the radio show *Blue Jam*?

4. Which horror actor plays a gunsmith in the 1971 film *Hannie Caulder*?

5. Who plays Patrick Bateman in the 2000 film *American Psycho*?

6. Which *Coronation Street* actress played Sarah Prentiss in the 1960s sitcom *Bulldog Breed*?

7. In which year did actor Colin Blakeley make his stage debut in England?

8. How old was comedian George Burns when he died in 1996?

9. What nationality is the theatre director Benno Besson?

10. Which comedy actress played Mary in the 1999 drama *The Flint Street Nativity*?

11. Which actress made her film debut in 1954's *The Angel Who Pawned Her Harp*?

12. Who plays Mick in the soap *Brookside*?

13. Which actor is credited as 'First Saxon' in the 1955 film *Lady Godiva*?

14. Who played the king in the 1946 film *Anna and the King of Siam*?

15. Which sharp shooter does Catherine O'Hara play in the 1995 film *Tall Tale*?

SPORT

1. What was the former name of the Professional Darts Council?

2. For which international Test cricket team do Franklin Rose and Reon King play?

3. In which year was the international surfing federation founded?

4. Who did Aberdeen beat 3-0 in the 1985/6 Scottish League Cup Final?

5. Fabien Pelous is French rugby union captain. For which club side does he play?

6. At what sport is Picabo Street an Olympic champion?

7. Who drove the fastest lap in the 2000 Australian Formula 1 Grand Prix?

8. With which sport would you associate Kay Bluhm and Torsten Gütsche?

9. At which sport was Marie Kettnerova world champion from 1933-5?

10. Henry Colden Harrison and Thomas Wills were the main initiators of which game?

11. What nationality is tennis player Roger Federer?

12. In which year did Lester Piggott win the Epsom Derby on The Minstrel?

13. Who did Doncaster beat in the 2000 Silk Cut Challenge Cup 3rd round in rugby league?

14. What nationality is women's short-track speed skater Kim Yoon-mi?

15. How many golds did France win in the 1999 World Athletics Championships?

ANSWERS 1. World Darts Council **2.** West Indies **3.** 1978 **4.** Hibernian **5.** Toulouse **6.** Skiing **7.** Rubens Barrichello **8.** Canoe racing **9.** Table tennis **10.** Australian Rules Football **11.** Swiss **12.** 1977 **13.** St. Gaudens **14.** South Korean **15.** One.

POP

1. Which Dutch group did Cesar Zuiderwijk join in 1969?

2. Which of his own compositions is on the B-side of Bryan Ferry's single *You Go To My Head*?

3. Cash, Days, Watson, La Brittain. The line-up of which punk group?

4. In which city was singer Goldie born?

5. On which label did the Dooleys record the single *Wanted*?

6. Who produced the Marillion album *Clutching at Straws*?

7. Who released the 1988 album *Miss America*?

8. What nationality was Gong's Daevid Allen?

9. In which year did B.A. Robertson have a Top 10 single with *Bang Bang*?

10. Who drew the cartoon on the front cover of the Who album *The Who by Numbers*?

11. Which group recorded the 1999 album *Pickled Eggs and Sherbet*?

12. Who had a 1999 No. 1 single with *Keep on Movin'*?

13. Which group recorded the 1991 live album *Alive Alive O*?

14. Who had a 1990 No. 1 single with *Nothing Compares 2U*?

15. Which group recorded the 1999 album *Strange Weather Lately*?

HISTORY

1. In which city did the Indian Mutiny break out in 1857?

2. How old was Queen Victoria when she ascended the throne in 1837?

3. In which month of 1965 did Winston Churchill die?

4. In which year did British forces under Francis Younghusband reach Lhasa?

5. What was Bertie Ahern's career before entering politics?

6. In which month of 1815 was the Battle of Waterloo?

7. In which year was the R101 airship disaster?

8. Which governmental post did Neville Chamberlain take up in 1922?

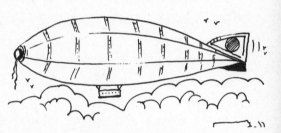

9. In which year did Japan take control of Port Arthur in China?

10. The Gunpowder Plot was a conspiracy to kill which King of England?

11. In which year of the 1930s was the Crystal Palace destroyed by fire?

12. In which year was the Treaty of European Union, also known as the Maastricht Treaty, signed?

13. In which year did General Gordon arrive in Khartoum?

14. In which year did navigator Juan Sebastian del Cano die?

15. In which year of the early 20th century was there a major earthquake in San Francisco?

ANSWERS 1. Meerut **2.** 18 **3.** January **4.** 1904 **5.** Accountancy **6.** June **7.** 1930 **8.** Postmaster-general **9.** 1905 **10.** James I **11.** 1936 **12.** 1992 **13.** 1884 **14.** 1526 **15.** 1906.

GENERAL KNOWLEDGE

1. Which 19th century British poet coined the term 'sprung rhythm'?

2. Lake Tahoe in the Sierra Nevada Mountains lies between which two states?

3. What is the colour of the ball in snooker worth five points?

4. Who authored the play *Baal* which was first performed in 1923?

5. What is the name given to the adult male of a red deer?

6. Who was 1975-8 U.S. Open women's singles tennis champion?

7. What is the standard monetary unit of Nicaragua?

8. In which year did French film pioneer Charles Pathé die?

9. Who authored the 1891 novel *New Grub Street*?

10. What was the name of the Indian religious leader who founded Sikhism?

11. Which is southernmost of the Great Lakes of North America?

12. Which officer of Pharaoh in the Old Testament bought Joseph as a slave?

13. Who is narrator of the novel *Moby-Dick*?

14. Which U.K. rower won four Olympic gold medals from 1984-96?

15. Who captured the ancient city of Numantia in N. Spain in 133 B.C.?

ANSWERS 1. Gerard Manley Hopkins **2.** California and Nevada **3.** Blue **4.** Bertolt Brecht **5.** Stag **6.** Chris Evert **7.** Cordoba **8.** 1957 **9.** George Gissing **10.** Nanak **11.** Erie **12.** Potiphar **13.** Ishmael **14.** Steve Redgrave **15.** Scipio the Younger.

ENTERTAINMENT

1. Who directed the 1950 film *Halls of Montezuma*?

2. In which year in the future is the 1993 film *Demolition Man* set?

3. What is Donald Sutherland's profession in the 1973 film *Lady Ice*?

4. Who created the sitcom *Surgical Spirit*?

5. Who plays Greta Garbo's husband in the 1935 film *Anna Karenina*?

6. Who was the first host of television's *Sunday Night at the London Palladium*?

7. Who penned the comedy serial *A Bit of A Do*?

8. Which singer/actress played *Barmy Aunt Boomerang* in a children's television show?

9. Who played the butler, Beach, in the 1967 sitcom *Blandings Castle*?

10. Which actress read the diary extracts in the 1995 film *Anne Frank Remembered*?

11. Which U.S. television presenter was nicknamed 'The Great Stone Face'?

12. Which comedian co-wrote the sitcom *Blind Men* with creator Chris England?

13. Which actress played Terry Scott's mum in the sitcom *Son of the Bride*?

14. What was the 1940 sequel to the film *Anne of Green Gables*?

15. Who directed the 1961 Doris Day film *Lover Come Back*?

SPORT

1. Ivar Ballangrud was the 1936 world men's speed skating champion. What nationality was he?

2. Who finished second in the 1999 Belgian Grand Prix in Formula 1?

3. In football, which Portuguese team lost the 1984 European Cup-Winners' Cup Final?

4. Which cyclist was the 1965 BBC Sports Personality of the Year?

5. Who was the 1995 & 1997 women's 3000m champion at the world indoor athletics championship?

6. In cricket, who scored 100 for Kent vs. Gloucestershire in the 1st innings of their 1999 county championship game?

7. The first recorded inter-county cricket match was between Kent and Surrey. In which year?

8. In which year did American tennis player Wilmer Allison die?

9. Which golfer won the 1997 British Women's Open championship?

10. For which basketball club did Kenny Simms resign in August 1999?

11. At which circuit was the 1964 Austrian Grand Prix in Formula 1 held?

12. In which year was the Scottish Athletics Federation founded?

13. Who won the Henry Sunderland Trophy in 1981 whilst with Hull Kingston Rovers?

14. For which national hockey side do Rhona Simpson and Susan Gilmour play?

15. Guglielmo Scheibmeier and Andrea Zambelli were the 1954 two-man bob winners at the world bobsleigh championships. Which country did they represent?

POP

1. Who had a 1985 Top 10 single with *The Last Kiss*?

2. Which musician played Billy Shears in the film *Sgt. Pepper's Lonely Hearts Club Band*?

3. Which duo had a 1994 Top 10 single with *7 Seconds*?

4. Who recorded the 1978 single *The Hippy's Graveyard*?

5. Which Irish group's songs include *Fashion Crisis Hits New York*?

6. Who played Hammond organ in the 1980s group *The Prisoners*?

7. Who produced Jilted John's single *Jilted John*?

8. Which boy band had a 1994 Top 10 with *I'll Make Love To You*?

9. Which studio album by Frankie Goes to Hollywood included the single *Rage Hard*?

10. Who was the original singer in the group Menswe@r?

11. Who wrote Grace Jones' single *The Apple Stretching*?

12. Which group recorded the 1993 album *Boces*?

13. In which year did Atlantic buy Aretha Franklin's contract from CBS/Columbia?

14. Who had a 1979 Top 10 single with *When You're In Love With A Beautiful Woman*?

15. Which solo female singer had a 1999 Top 10 single with *Heartbreaker*?

ANSWERS 1. David Cassidy **2.** Peter Frampton **3.** Youssou N'Dour and Neneh Cherry **4.** Johnny G **5.** The Frank & Walters **6.** James Taylor **7.** Martin Zero **8.** Boyz II Men **9.** Liverpool **10.** Johnny Dean **11.** Melvin Van Peebles **12.** Mercury Rev **13.** 1966 **14.** Dr. Hook **15.** Mariah Carey.

WORDS

1. In law what is the name given to a person to whom a legacy is bequeathed?

2. What is a penna?

3. What does the Latin phrase *non licet* mean?

4. How many related works of drama would be in a tetralogy?

5. What is the name given to a person between 90 and 99 years of age?

6. What in South Africa is muti?

7. What does the word *tong* mean with regards Chinese secret societies?

8. From what is miso made?

9. What is a thornback - a type of fruit or type of fish?

10. What would you do with ninon - make a cocktail or make a dress?

11. The word lyonnaise describes food cooked or garnished with what vegetable?

12. The word esquire derives from the Latin word *scutum*, meaning what?

13. What type of creature is a junco?

14. If you were esurient would you be penniless or greedy?

15. Inkle is used for trimming fabric. Of what is it made?

ANSWERS 1. Legatee **2.** A large feather **3.** It is not allowed **4.** Four **5.** Nonagenarian **6.** Medicine **7.** Meeting-place **8.** Soya beans **9.** Fish **10.** A dress - it is a fabric **11.** Onion **12.** Shield **13.** Bird **14.** Greedy **15.** Linen.

GENERAL KNOWLEDGE

1. Who is the author of the third Gospel in the New Testament?

2. In which play by Shakespeare does Spaniard Don Adriano de Armado appear?

3. Who was Labour minister of health from 1945-51?

4. What was the name of the 1988 film about the Chicago White Sox throwing the 1919 World Series in baseball?

5. Which river flows out of Lake Malawi to the Zambesi?

6. Which male actor was star of the 1993 film *Little Buddha*?

7. Who was premier of France from 1946-7?

8. In which year did stage photographer Angus McBean die?

9. Who authored the 1929 book *A Farewell to Arms*?

10. Which port in Germany is at the confluence of the Rivers Rhine and Main?

11. In which year was French cubist painter Fernand Léger born?

12. Which Old Testament character was struck dead for lying in Acts 5?

13. What is the name given to a squirrel's nest?

14. In which year did Irish painter Francis Bacon die?

15. October 21st is the feast day of which saint and martyr?

ENTERTAINMENT

1. What was Karl Malden's character name in the cop show *The Streets of San Francisco*?

2. Which singer played Ophelia in the 1969 film *Hamlet*?

3. Who composed the opera *Cavelleria Rusticana*?

4. Who plays the female lead in the 1980 outer-space film *Saturn 3*?

5. In which year were the Chelsea Opera Group formed?

6. Who played Lady Maud Lynchwood in the 1985 televsion comedy serial *Blott on the Landscape*?

7. What is the name of Countess Almavira's page in the opera *The Marriage of Figaro*?

8. Who plays the lead as a native eskimo in the 1960 film *The Savage Innocents*?

9. What nationality is the opera singer Boris Christoff?

10. Who is the older - Stephen Fry or Hugh Laurie?

11. Who directed the 1974 film *The Tamarind Seed*?

12. Who played General Custer in the 1968 film *Custer of the West*?

13. Who composed the 1885 opera *Le Cid*?

14. Which *Doctor Who* actor played magician Koura in the film *The Golden Voyage of Sinbad*?

15. Who played Josef Lanner in the 1972 historical television drama *The Strauss Family*?

ANSWERS 1. Mike Stone **2.** Marianne Faithfull **3.** Mascagni **4.** Farrah Fawcett **5.** 1950 **6.** Geraldine James **7.** Cherubino **8.** Anthony Quinn **9.** Bulgarian **10.** Stephen Fry **11.** Blake Edwards **12.** Robert Shaw **13.** Massenet **14.** Tom Baker **15.** Derek Jacobi.

SPORT

1. How many runs did Graham Thorpe score in his six Tests against the West Indies in 1997/8?

2. Who rode the 1859 Grand National-winning horse Half Caste?

3. What sport does Raquel Carriedo play?

4. How many Olympic gold medals did athlete Shirley de la Hunty win from 1948-56?

5. Who was the 1975 Australian Open women's singles tennis champion?

6. In which year were France first crowned team sabre champions at the world fencing championships?

7. What nationality is boxer Andrew Golota?

8. Which swimming event did Charles de Vendeville win at the 1900 Olympics?

9. Which U.K. golfer won the 1998 Volvo PGA championship?

10. At which hole did Darren Clarke get a hole in one in the third round of the Smurfit European Open in 1999?

11. Which snooker player won the Rothmans Grand Prix in 1983?

12. By what score did England beat Canada at rugby union in August 1999?

13. How many Tests did Walter Hammond play for England at cricket?

14. In which year was athlete Marion Jones born?

POP

1. Which group was Andy Fraser playing bass with before joining Free?

2. Which Welsh singer recorded the single *The Young New Mexican Puppeteer* in 1972?

3. In which year did Big Star's Chris Bell die in a car smash?

4. Which Irish singer recorded the 1992 album *Adam 'n' Eve*?

5. Which member of the Replacements died in 1995?

6. Which punk group recorded the 1977 E.P. *An Ideal For Living*?

7. *The Heavenly Music Corporation* and *Swastika Girls* are the two tracks on which 1972 album?

8. What is the opening track on Metallica's 1984 album *Ride the Lightning*?

9. On which label did girl group Kleenex record the single *Ü* in 1979?

10. On what label was Klark Kent's single *Don't Care* released?

11. Who played violin on Robert Wyatt's 1974 cover of the song *I'm a Believer* by the Monkees?

12. What is the B-side of John Lennon's 1973 single *Mind Games*?

13. Which member of Soft Machine formed the group Gong?

14. In which year did the musician Phil Ochs kill himself?

15. Which female singer had a 1999 Top 10 single with *Not Over You Yet*?

SCIENCE

1. In which city did John Dalton die in 1844?

2. What is the symbol of the chemical element Meitnerium?

3. In computing, from what is the word FORTRAN derived?

4. In which country was scientist Ernest Rutherford born?

5. Which scientist was known as 'Darwin's Bulldog'?

6. In which European capital was physicist Ludwig Boltzmann born?

7. Approximately how many times heavier is an atom of carbon than an atom of hydrogen?

8. Which scientist received the first Atoms for Peace Award in 1957?

9. In which year did French physicist Paul Langevin die?

10. Which is the hottest and driest biome?

11. Which element makes up 88% of the atmosphere of Saturn?

12. In which country was astronomer Gerard Pieter Kuiper born?

13. Who was the first scientist to win two Nobel prizes in the same category?

14. What in computing does PC stand for?

15. In the Periodic Table of Elements, how many elements are in the Actinide series?

ANSWERS 1. Manchester **2.** Mt **3.** Formula Translator **4.** New Zealand **5.** Thomas Henry Huxley **6.** Vienna **7.** Twelve **8.** Niels Bohr **9.** 1946 **10.** Desert **11.** Hydrogen **12.** Netherlands **13.** John Bardeen **14.** Personal computer **15.** Fifteen.

GENERAL KNOWLEDGE

1. What, in Christianity, is the name given to the 40th day after Easter?

2. What is the collective noun for a flock of geese in flight?

3. In which country was British poet Hilaire Belloc born in 1870?

4. Which family of Italian painters founded a teaching academy in Bolgna in 1582?

5. Who was the male lead in the 1958 film western *The Big Country*?

6. What is the name of the python in the novel *The Jungle Book*?

7. In British folklore which giant is associated with the giant Magog?

8. Who created the literary detective Inspector Morse?

9. What is the name of the six-volume tale by Compton Mackenzie tracing the life of John Ogilvie?

10. Who authored the 1988 novel *Nice Work*?

11. Estragon is another name for which plant?

12. In which year was English astronomer Edmund Halley born?

13. With which song is American entertainer Thomas Rice associated?

14. Which U.S. composer is known for the musical *A Chorus Line*?

15. On which river is the Irish port of Coleraine?

ENTERTAINMENT

1. Which actor takes over responsibility for three children in the 1975 comedy film *The Apple Dumpling Gang*?

2. Who won Best Male artist at the 2000 Brit Awards?

3. Who plays Det. Chief Inspector Tom Barnaby in *Midsomer Murders*?

4. In which year did the television show *Songs of Praise* start on the BBC?

5. What nationality is soprano Lucrezia Bori?

6. Who played Colour Sgt. Ian Anderson in the ITV drama *Soldier, Soldier*?

7. Who plays Mandy Dingle on *Emmerdale*?

8. Who directed the 1988 film *Appointment with Death* starring Peter Ustinov as Hercule Poirot?

9. The 1998 horror film *The Last Broadcast* closely resembles which 1999 box-office smash?

10. Who plays Jane in the film *American Beauty*?

11. Who played the father in the 1971 film *The Railway Children*?

12. What herb was Les scared of on the comedy show *Vic Reeves' Big Night Out*?

13. What nationality is composer Pierre Boulez?

14. Which film director wrote the novel *The Comedy Writer*?

15. Who plays Jeannie in the 2000 BBC TV remake of *Randall and Hopkirk (Deceased)*?

SPORT

1. In cricket, who scored 123 for Yorkshire vs. Glamorgan in the 2nd innings of their 1999 county championship game?

2. Who rode Pampapaul to victory in the 1977 Irish 2000 Guineas?

3. How many golds did the Bahamas win in the 1999 World Athletics Championships?

4. In which year were the world figure skating championships in roller skating first held?

5. In which year did Darren Altree make his county cricket debut for Warwickshire?

6. Sébastien Deleigne was the 1977 men's world champion. At what sport?

7. In which year did the French tennis player 'Toto' Brugnon die?

8. At which ground was the 1890 English F.A. Cup Final played?

9. What nationality is runner Margaret Ngotho?

10. Helen Stephens set a women's 100m world record on 10th August, 1936. What time did she run?

11. What nationality is swimmer Martyn Zuidweg?

12. What was the célerifère, demonstrated in 1791, a forerunner of?

13. What nationality is golfer Alberto Croce?

14. Which team beat Afghanistan 86-2 in a handball match in August 1981?

15. What nationality is triathlete Dave Scott?

ANSWERS 1. Richard Blakey 2. Franco Dettori 3. One 4. 1947 5. 1996 6. Modern Pentathlon 7. 1978 8. Kennington Oval 9. Kenyan 10. 11.5 seconds 11. Dutch 12. The bicycle 13. Italian 14. U.S.S.R. 15. American.

POP

1. On which record label did The Birthday Party record the 1982 album *Junkyard*?

2. Which studio album by the Lightning Seeds features the single *The Life of Riley*?

3. Which song by the Dead Boys did Guns n' Roses cover on the 1993 album *The Spaghetti Incident*?

4. Who recorded the album *Synkronized*?

5. Who had a 1999 Christmas hit with *I Have A Dream/Seasons in the Sun*?

6. Which girl group had a 1979 hit with single *My Simple Heart*?

7. In which year was Björk born?

8. In which country was guitarist Arto Lindsay born?

9. Which U.S. group had a 1995 hit with *Milkman's Son*?

10. On which label was Typically Tropical's 1975 No. 1 *Barbados* recorded?

11. Which male artist was guest singer on Bonnie Tyler's 1985 song *Loving You's a Dirty Job But Somebody's Gotta Do It*?

12. Which former member of the Pixies recorded the 1994 album *Teenager of the Year*?

13. In which year did 2 Unlimited chart with the single *Workaholic*?

14. What was Twiggy's only Top 20 single?

15. Jello Biafra of the Dead Kennedy's ran for mayor of which U.S. city in 1979?

PEOPLE

1. What is the middle name of designer Terence Conran?

2. Who was founder of the Religious Society of Friends?

3. What was cartoonist Georges Rémi better known as?

4. Who is chairman of the radio comedy panel game *I'm Sorry, I Haven't a Clue*?

5. In which century did Swiss fabulist Ulrich Boner live?

6. Which folk singer was born James Miller in 1915?

7. In which year did cartoonist and designer Rowland Emmett die?

8. Which saint became bishop of Liège in 708?

9. Which actress is Michael Douglas planning to wed in 2000?

10. In which year was president Samuel Doe killed by rebels in Monrovia?

11. In which country was mathematician Pierre de Fermat born?

12. With which board game is Emanuel Lasker associated?

13. In which country was film director Alberto Cavalcanti born?

14. In which year did broadcaster Brian Johnston die?

15. In which country was choreographer Kurt Jooss born?

GENERAL KNOWLEDGE

1. Anchorage is the largest city in which U.S. state?

2. In which play by Shakespeare does the characer Iras appear?

3. Which cult television series featured Kyle MacLachan as Agent Dale Cooper?

4. In which year was dancer and choreographer Robert Cohan born?

5. Who wrote the 1969 novel *The Estate*?

6. What is the name given to the back part of a golf club head where it bends to join the shaft?

7. In which year did British conductor Sir Georg Solti die?

8. Who did actress Mary Tamm play in the television series *Doctor Who*?

9. Who were the male and female leads in the 1997 film *A Life Less Ordinary*?

10. Which river in eastern France joins the Rhône at Lyon?

11. Which actor played an assassin in the 1973 film *The Day of the Jackal*?

12. Which of The Marx Brothers was born Leonard Marx?

13. In which year did Italian composer Luigi Nono die?

14. Which comedian starred with Richard Burton in the 1981 film *Absolution*?

15. Who was the director of the 1945 film *Blithe Spirit*?

ANSWERS 1. Alaska **2.** Antony and Cleopatra **3.** Twin Peaks **4.** 1925 **5.** Isaac Bashevis Singer **6.** Heel **7.** 1997 **8.** Romana **9.** Ewan McGregor and Cameron Diaz **10.** Saône **11.** Edward Fox **12.** Chico **13.** 1990 **14.** Billy Connolly **15.** Sir David Lean.

ENTERTAINMENT

1. Which football club's hooligan element did Donal MacIntyre travel to Denmark with in the 1999 series *MacIntyre Undercover*?

2. Who won Best International Male at the 2000 Brit Awards?

3. Which French actress stars in the 1969 comedy film *The April Fools* with Jack Lemmon?

4. Who plays Dr. John Becker in the U.S. sitcom *Becker*?

5. What nationality was the soprano Julie Dorus-Gras?

6. Who played *The Last Musketeer* on television in the 2000 ITV drama?

7. Who created the role of Swallow in the opera *Peter Grimes*?

8. Which film won the Best Visual Effects Oscar in 2000?

9. Who played the title role in the 1999 television show *Lucy Sullivan is Getting Married*?

10. Who directed the 1968 film *Yellow Submarine*?

11. In which year did the BBC first broadcast opera on the radio?

12. In which country is the 1959 war film *Yesterday's Enemy* set?

13. Who plays cop Della Pesca in the 1999 biopic *The Hurricane*?

14. On whose novella is the 1998 film *Apt Pupil* based?

15. Who won Best Pop Act at the 2000 Brit Awards?

ANSWERS 1. Chelsea **2.** Beck **3.** Catherine Deneuve **4.** Ted Danson **5.** Belgian **6.** Robson Green **7.** Owen Brannigan **8.** The Matrix **9.** Sam Loggin **10.** George Dunning **11.** 1923 **12.** Burma **13.** Dan Hedaya **14.** Stephen King **15.** Five.

SPORT

1. How many Formula 1 Grand Prix wins did Carlos Reutemann have in his career from 1972-82?

2. Where were the 1951 Pan-American Games held?

3. In which year was the Scottish Club Championship in rugby union inaugurated?

4. In cricket, who scored 111 n.o. for Hampshire vs. Somerset in the 1st innings of their 1999 county championship game?

5. Which Frenchman was a 1928 undisputed featherweight boxing world champion?

6. Which veteran golfer won the Energis Senior Masters in August 1999?

7. Which horse won the Melbourne Cup in 1974 & 1975?

8. Who won the 2000 London men's marathon?

9. Which Canadian Football team won the Grey Cup in 1939 for the first time?

10. In which year did Gerald Patterson and Suzanne Lenglen win the Wimbledon mixed doubles tennis title?

11. Which team appeared in the 1992 and 1996 European Championship Finals in football?

12. What nationality is golfer Mathias Gronberg?

13. With which sport are Tamas Darnyi and Luca Sacchi associated?

14. In which year was the Eisenhower Trophy first competed for in golf?

15. Which horse was the dam of Istabraq?

ANSWERS 1. Twelve **2.** Buenos Aires **3.** 1974 **4.** Adrian Aymes **5.** Andre Routis **6.** Neil Coles **7.** Think Big **8.** Antonio Pinto **9.** Winnipeg Blue Bombers **10.** 1920 **11.** Germany **12.** Swedish **13.** Swimming **14.** 1958 **15.** Betty's Secret.

POP

1. Which group had a 1968 Top 10 single with Elenore?

2. In which year was *I Don't Like Mondays* a No. 1 single for the Boomtown Rats?

3. Which British rock band recorded the 1993 album *Jam*?

4. Which member of the Lightning Seeds produced the debut single in 1980 of the group Dead or Alive?

5. Which female singer had a 1993 Top 20 single with *Disco Inferno*?

6. On which label did The Troggs record the 1966 hit *I Can't Control Myself*?

7. Hawkes, West, Blakely and Munden make up which 1960s pop group?

8. Which guitarist played in the 1973 band Wood Brass & Steel?

9. Who had a hit in 1978 with *What's Your Name What's Your Number*?

10. Which band were originally known as Greasy Little Toes?

11. Which male singer had a 1960 hit with *Is a Blue Bird Blue*?

12. Which group feature D.J.s Towa Towa and Dmitry Brill?

13. Which rapper guested on 2Pac's 1998 hit *Runnin'*?

14. In which year was The Tymes' first U.K. Top 30 hit?

15. Which reggae group had a 1980 hit single with *The Way You Do the Things You Do*?

ART

1. Which painter's works include 1903's *Girl in a Straw Hat* and 1925's *The Table*?

2. In which century did French painter Jean-François Millet live?

3. Who wrote the novel *Enduring Love*?

4. In which year did artist Paul Cézanne die?

5. Who is the author of the murder mystery *The Drowning People*?

6. Who painted the 1850 work *Burial at Ornans*?

7. In which city was artist Sir Sidney Nolan born?

8. In which century did artist Honoré Daumier live?

9. Who painted 1829's *Ulysses Mocking Polyphemus*?

10. Simon Tappertit appears in which novel by Charles Dickens?

11. Who is the author of the thriller *Southern Cross*?

12. In which century did Italian sculptor Nicola Pisano live?

13. Which thriller writer authored *The White House Connection*?

14. In which country was artist Edvard Munch born?

15. Who is the author of the 2000 crime novel *Set in Darkness*?

GENERAL KNOWLEDGE

1. Who was the 1972 Olympic men's high jump bronze medal winner?

2. Who directed and starred in the 1973 film *High Plains Drifter*?

3. Who was the first Protestant Archbishop of Canterbury?

4. In which county is the ancient town of Winchelsea?

5. Which poet's volumes include *The Less Deceived*?

6. The throstle is a poetic name for which bird?

7. Who was a Best Actor Oscar nominee for his role in the 1951 film *Bright Victory*?

8. Who choreographed the one-act ballet *The Firebird* which was composed by Stravinsky?

9. Lake Iliamna is the largest lake in which U.S. state?

10. What is the acknowledgement in fencing that a scoring hit has been made?

11. Which channel of the Irish Sea separates the Welsh mainland from Anglesey?

12. What is the capital of South Korea?

13. Who wrote the 1975 novel *Blott on the Landscape*?

14. What is the name of the great plain of central South America between the Andes and the Paraguay River?

15. Debbie Harry is the lead singer of which pop group?

ANSWERS 1. Dwight Stones 2. Clint Eastwood 3. Thomas Cranmer 4. East Sussex 5. Philip Larkin 6. Thrush 7. Arthur Kennedy 8. Fokine 9. Alaska 10. Touché 11. Menai Strait 12. Seoul 13. Tom Sharpe 14. Gran Chaco 15. Blondie.

THE CARLING PUB QUIZ BOOK

ENTERTAINMENT

1. Which Perrier Award-winning comic starred in the 1999 sitcom *Small Potatoes*?

2. Who played Carolyn in the film *American Beauty*?

3. In which Mozart opera does the aria *Dove sono* appear?

4. Who played *Monsignor Renard* in the 2000 ITV drama series?

5. What illness does Glenn Ford contract in the 1966 film *Rage*?

6. Who plays a pursued murder witness in the 1990 film *Narrow Margin*?

7. The 1983 film *Under Fire* is set in which country?

8. Who played Morticia in the sitcom *The Addams Family* on television?

9. Who composed the 1882 opera *The Devil's Wall*?

10. Who directed the 1958 film *The Big Country*?

11. Who won a Best Supporting Actress for the 1944 film *National Velvet*?

12. Who won Best Actor in a Comedy/Musical at the 2000 Golden Globes?

13. Who did Gregory Peck play in the 1978 film *The Boys from Brazil*?

14. In which Verdi opera does Princess Eboli appear?

15. Who directed the 1994 film *Underneath*?

SPORT

1. With what sport are Sam Ermolenko and Joe Screen associated?

2. What nationality is judo player Heidi Rakels?

3. Which cricketer took four wickets in consecutive balls twice, in 1931-2 and 1934?

4. At which sport does Barry Dancer coach Great Britain?

5. Who was the 1979 U.K. professional billiards champion?

6. What nationality is cricketer Usman Afzaal?

7. Who was champion flat racing jockey from 1964-71?

8. Who was Yorkshire's Young Player of the Year in cricket in 1989?

9. Which club won the 1947 rugby league Challenge Cup?

10. Who beat Featherstone in rugby league's 2000 Silk Cut Challenge Cup 4th Round?

11. What nationality is former moto-cross world champion Eric Geboers?

12. What sport are Alez Zülle and Andrew Olano associated with?

13. Which club won the 1885 Scottish F.A. Cup Final?

14. For which ice hockey team do Todd Wetzel and Shawn Wansborough play?

15. Who won the 1994 New York women's marathon?

Loroupe.

Rhinos **11.** Belgian **12.** Cycling **13.** Renton **14.** London Knights **15.** Tegla
6. Pakistani **7.** Lester Piggott **8.** Richard Blakey **9.** Bradford Northern **10.** Leeds
ANSWERS 1. Speedway **2.** Belgian **3.** Bob Crisp **4.** Hockey **5.** Rex Williams

POP

1. Who was lead singer of the group Black Grape?

2. Which punk group had a 1980 hit single with *Party in Paris*?

3. With what song did the Ramones have a 1980 Top 10 hit?

4. Who had a 1999 Christmas hit with *Two in a Million/You're My Number One*?

5. In which year did the Crusaders have a Top 10 single with *Street Life*?

6. Which group recorded the 1999 single *I Wouldn't Believe Your Radio*?

7. Which member of R.E.M. produced the 1986 album *The Good Earth* by The Feelies?

8. Which U.S. singer fronted a band called Popcorn Blizzard?

9. Which group had a 1999 No. 1 single with *We're Going To Ibiza*?

10. Who had a Top 10 hit in February 2000 with *Sweet Love 2K*?

11. Which country artist recorded the album *Love Will Always Win*?

12. Which group released the 1983 mini-L.P. *The Splendour of Fear*?

13. Who features on Chicane's 2000 No. 1 single *Don't Give Up*?

14. Who recorded the 1994 Top 10 single *Oh Baby I ...*?

15. Which singer released the 1973 album *Heart Food*?

ANSWERS 1. Shaun Ryder **2.** UK Subs **3.** Baby I Love You **4.** S Club 7 **5.** 1979 **6.** Stereophonics **7.** Peter Buck **8.** Meat Loaf **9.** Vengaboys **10.** Fierce **11.** Faith Hill **12.** Felt **13.** Bryan Adams **14.** Eternal **15.** Judee Sill.

GEOGRAPHY

1. Which has the larger population, Amsterdam or Rotterdam?

2. Of which Irish county is Lifford the county town?

3. Which is the largest of the Aran Islands off the Irish coast?

4. The Gironde estuary in S.W. France is formed by the confluence of which two rivers?

5. On which river does the Northumberland town of Alnwick stand?

6. Which of the Tropics runs through Mexico?

7. In which county is Broadmoor hospital?

8. Which strait separates Mexico from Cuba?

9. In which country is the village of Roquefort, famed for its cheese?

10. Into which sea does the River Danube flow?

11. In which South American country is Porto Alegre?

12. Which three countries contain part of Lake Victoria?

13. Llangefni is the administrative headquarters of which Welsh council?

14. Which three countries contain part of Lake Malawi?

15. The town of Nakamura is on which Japanese island?

GENERAL KNOWLEDGE

1. Which western author's works include *Trail Boss*?

2. With which music hall performer would you associate the song *Any Old Iron*?

3. Which large wolf-like breed of dog is also called a German shepherd?

4. Who wrote the 1920 novel *This Side of Paradise*?

5. Which maiden in Greek mythology agreed to marry any man who could defeat her in a running race?

6. What is the name given to any one of the four officers who command the Yeomen of the Guard?

7. Elba is a mountainous island off the west coast of which country?

8. Who authored the 1971 play *Butley*?

9. In which year did English actor and clown Joseph Grimaldi die?

10. What was the 1998 venue of the winter Olympic Games?

11. Who was author of the classic novel *The Three Musketeers*?

12. Who was the author of novel *The Red Badge of Courage*?

13. Who wrote the 1976 play *American Buffalo*?

14. The 1989 film *Scandal* was about which political controversy?

15. Which novel by Nick Hornby features the characters Will and Marcus?

ENTERTAINMENT

1. What nationality is the opera singer Otto Edelmann?

2. Who played Loana in the 1966 film *One Million Years B.C.?*

3. Which musician scored the 1984 film *The Natural?*

4. Who played Jane Wellington-Bull in the 1959 sitcom *The Adventures of Wellington-Bull?*

5. Who played Det. Chief Supt. Jack Lambie in the television show *Strangers?*

6. Which actress stars in the sitcom *Gimme Gimme Gimme?*

7. In which year was television presenter Michaela Strachan born?

8. Who plays a cook in the 1992 film *Under Siege?*

9. Who plays twin brothers in the 1942 film *Nazi Agent?*

10. Which female doctor was a host on the television science show *Don't Ask Me?*

11. Who played the lead in the 1996 film *Sgt. Bilko?*

12. What was the name of Marina's pet seal in the puppet show *Stingray?*

13. Who hosts the comedy quiz show *Never Mind the Buzzcocks?*

14. Who directed the 1970 film *Ned Kelly?*

15. Which actor wrote the 1985 sitcom *Affairs of the Heart?*

SPORT

1. Who coached Surrey cricket club in the 1999 season?

2. Which Swiss cyclist won the 1992 Tour of Lombardy?

3. By how many runs did New Zealand beat England in the 1999 4th Test at the Oval?

4. In which year did Election win the Epsom Derby?

5. Which year saw Colin Montgomerie's first Ryder Cup appearance?

6. Who was the 1988 and 1989 world rally driving champion?

7. How many golds did Cuba win at the 1999 World Athletic Championships?

8. At what Olympic sport have Russell Mark and Vasiliy Borissov been champions?

9. Which cyclist was the 1989 Sports Illustrated Sportsman of the Year?

10. At what Olympic sport have Rolf Peterson and Mihaly Hesz been champions?

11. In cricket, who scored 153 for Yorkshire vs. Kent in the 1st innings of their 1999 county championship game?

12. Which female skater was the 1925 world figure skating champion?

13. By what score did Ireland beat France in Paris in the 2000 Six Nations rugby tournament?

14. Which two teams met in the 1946 play-off for the NFL championship in American Football?

15. Who partnered Anders Järryd to victory in the 1983 French Open men's doubles tennis title?

POP

1. In which year did Bryan Ferry audition to replace Greg Lake in King Crimson?

2. Which group recorded the 1983 single *The Cabaret*?

3. What was Tanita Tikaram's only Top 10 single?

4. With which Goth group was Carl McCoy vocalist?

5. What was the only hit single of female vocal group Thunderthighs?

6. Which brothers formed the group Meat Puppets in 1981?

7. Who was the drummer with the groups The Fire Engines and Win?

8. What was the only hit single of the group Three Good Reasons?

9. Which male singer's only hit single was 1963's *Alley Cat Song*?

10. Which female singer featured on the 1999 Top 10 single *What I Am* by Tin Tin Out?

11. Which group released 1991 album *Flyin' the Flannel*?

12. Bailey, Currie, Leeway. Which 1980s pop group?

13. Ferguson, Holiday, Pinkney. Which female vocal group?

14. Which group recorded the 1999 single *Fire in My Heart*?

15. Which group's Top 30 singles included 1991's *Love Walked In*?

HISTORY

1. In which year did the Japanese statesman Tokugawa Ieyasu die?

2. In which year did Erwin Rommel join the German Army?

3. In which year was the Battle of Worcester?

4. In which year did Catherine the Great of Russia die?

5. In which year was the Boston Port Act passed?

6. Gabriel Bethlen was king of which country from 1620-1?

7. Who became king and queen of England following the 'Glorious Revolution'?

8. In which year did William Hague become the leader of the Conservative Party?

9. Who in 1387 became Queen of Denmark, Norway and Sweden?

10. In which year was the Rye House Plot?

11. In which year was the ANZUS Pact signed between Australia, New Zealand and the U.S.?

12. In which year did Edward VI succeed to the throne?

13. In which year did James Cook first sight the east coast of Australia?

14. Who became chaplain to Henry VIII in 1541?

15. In which year did Paddy Ashdown become a member of the Liberal Party?

ANSWERS 1. 1616 2. 1910 3. 1651 4. 1796 5. 1774 6. Hungary 7. William and Mary 8. 1997 9. Margaret I 10. 1683 11. 1951 12. 1547 13. 1770 14. Nicholas Ridley 15. 1976.

GENERAL KNOWLEDGE

1.   What is the name of the marshy area of S.E. England which includes Dungeness?

2.   Who became Labour's Chancellor of the Exchequer in 1997?

3.   Which actor played Mr. Humphries in the sitcom *Are You Being Served ??*

4.   Who was the author of the play *The Glass Menagerie*?

5.   In which U.S. state was tennis player Pancho Gonzales born?

6.   Who wrote the novel *Tarzan of the Apes*?

7.   Who authored the 1962 novel *King Rat*?

8.   Who was the male star of the 1964 comedy film *A Shot in the Dark*?

9.   Who wrote the poem *Ode on a Grecian Urn*?

10. What is the smallest unit of weight in the avoirdupois system?

11. Who is the author of the novel *The Famished Road*?

12. Which name was adopted by comedian Julius Marx?

13. Who was the female star of the 1997 film *G.I. Jane*?

14. The name of which god of the Philistines in the Old Testament meant lord of flies?

15. What was the name given to the journey of about 6,000 miles undertaken by around 100,000 Chinese Communists between 1934-5?

ANSWERS 1. Romney Marsh **2.** Gordon Brown **3.** John Inman **4.** Tennessee Williams **5.** California **6.** Edgar Rice Burroughs **7.** James Clavell **8.** Peter Sellers **9.** John Keats **10.** Grain **11.** Ben Okri **12.** Groucho **13.** Demi Moore **14.** Beelzebub **15.** The Long March.

ENTERTAINMENT

1. Who produced the ITV game show *The Price is Right*?

2. Who directed the 1995 film *Strange Days*?

3. Who played David McCallum's boss Walter Carlson in the television show *The Invisible Man*?

4. Who plays a seedy private eye in the 1992 film *Under Suspicion*?

5. In which year did the comedy actress Joan Sanderson die?

6. Which sitcom arose from the 1962 *Comedy Playhouse* show *The Offer*?

7. Who plays Leanne Battersby in *Coronation Street*?

8. Who played Captain Dobey in *Starsky and Hutch*?

9. Who composed the 1957 opera *Dialogues of the Carmelites*?

10. Who composed the 1889 opera *Edgar*?

11. Who played the lead in the 1970 film *Captain Nemo and the Underwater City*?

12. Who is 'entertainer' John Shuttleworth's agent?

13. Who plays a truck driver and singer in the 1959 film *Daddy-o*?

14. Which comedy duo's revues included 1957's *At the Drop of a Hat*?

15. The 1997 film *The Ice Storm* is an adaptation of whose novel?

SPORT

1. What is the main difference between a Rugby Fives court and an Eton Fives court?

2. What game do Bracknell Bees and Sheffield Steelers play?

3. Who was the 1973 men's 200m breaststroke swimming world champion?

4. Which U.S. pair won the 1994 World Cup in golf?

5. What is the nickname of Test bowler Shoaib Akhtar?

6. Which snooker player won the 1997 Scottish Masters?

7. By what score did England win in Italy in the 2000 Six Nations tournament in rugby union?

8. For which country does cricketer Ian Healy keep wicket?

9. At what sport do Ian Schuback and David Gourlay compete?

10. In basketball, in which year were the Chicago Bulls first crowned NBA champions in the U.S.?

11. Which rugby league club released Brett Green in February 2000?

12. Who rode Alydaress to victory in the 1989 Irish Oaks?

13. At what sport do James Cracknell, Tim Foster and Ed Coode compete?

14. At what sport were Boris Dubrovsky and Oleg Tyurin Olympic champions in 1964?

15. What sport does Ahmed Barada play?

POP

1. What was Tiffany's only U.K. and U.S. No. 1?
2. Who joined Mott the Hoople on keyboards in 1973?
3. Who had a 1999 Top 10 single with their song *Mickey*
4. In which year did Johnny Tillotson have a U.K. No. 1 single with *Poetry in Motion*?
5. Which group recorded the 1989 single *Under the God*?
6. Which singer produced the 1971 album *Heavy on the Drum* by Medicine Head?
7. Which Joni Mitchell song is covered by Travis on the B-side of single *Why Does It Always Rain On Me*?
8. Which group recorded the 2000 album *Sleeve with Hearts*?
9. Which group recorded the 1993 album *Give a Monkey a Brain & He'll Swear He's the Centre of the Universe*?

10. The 1999 No. 1 single *Lift Me Up* was by which female singer?
11. Which U.S. author wrote the sleeve notes for Lotion's 1995 album *Nothing's Cool*?
12. Who recorded the 1999 dance hit *Rendez-Vu*?
13. Which U.S. rock 'n' roll singer recorded the 1961 hit *Quarter to Three*?
14. Who had a 1999 No. 1 single with *Genie in a Bottle*?
15. Which singer recorded the 1999 album *Staying Power*?

ANSWERS 1. I Think We're Alone Now **2.** Morgan Fisher **3.** Lolly **4.** 1960 **5.** Tin Machine **6.** Keith Relf **7.** The Urge For Going **8.** Broken Dog **9.** Fishbone **10.** Geri Halliwell **11.** Thomas Pynchon **12.** Basement Jaxx **13.** Gary 'US' Bonds **14.** Christina Aguilera **15.** Barry White.

WORDS

1. The word *ruse* meaning a misleading action comes from the French verb *ruser*, meaning what?

2. What is the name given to the art of stuffing and mounting animal skins?

3. Where in New Zealand would you find a koneke?

4. What is the name given to a parish priest in France?

5. What would you do with a kroon in Estonia - eat it or spend it?

6. From which natural phenomenon would a lapillus be thrown?

7. What in East Africa is a mzee?

8. What would you do with a sabayon - beat it or eat it?

9. What in the Caribbean would you do with mauby?

10. What is a gooney bird better known as?

11. What is neat's-foot oil used for?

12. What in the U.S. is a lister to a farmer?

13. For what is a sadiron used?

14. If something is ligneous, what does it resemble?

15. What in South Africa is kwela?

GENERAL KNOWLEDGE

1. Paramaribo is the capital of which republic in South America?

2. Who was the 11th president of the U.S.?

3. What was the legendary birthplace of Romulus and Remus?

4. Who was the author of the novel *Kim* published in 1901?

5. What is the brightest star in the constellation Virgo?

6. What place near Lewes in Sussex was the site of a famous scientific forgery of 1912?

7. What is the name of the city in S. France whose Roman antiquities include the Maison Carrée?

8. Who wrote the 1965 play *A Patriot For Me*?

9. In which year did Scottish explorer Mungo Park die?

10. In which African country is the Atlantic port of Tema?

11. Who was the 1997 world professional snooker champion?

12. Which diminutive pop singer had a 1977 No. 1 single with *When I Need You*?

13. What is the capital and chief port of Papua New Guinea?

14. Which golfer won the 1976 Volvo PGA Championship?

15. Who was the comedy partner of Lou Costello?

ENTERTAINMENT

1. Who played Russian diplomat Grischa Petrovitch in the 1960s sitcom *Foreign Affairs*?

2. Akira Kurosawa's film *Ran* is an adaptation of which Shakespeare play?

3. Which actor played patriarch Samuel Foster in the 1970s sitcom *The Fosters*?

4. What nationality was tenor Jussi Björling?

5. Who played *Captain Sindbad* in a 1963 film?

6. What was the name of Sir Arthur Bliss's 1949 opera?

7. Who starred as *The Clairvoyant* in a 1986 sitcom?

8. Who played Zorro in a 1958 television series?

9. In which city was Alfred Hitchcock's *I Confess* made?

10. What was the name of the ranger in the cartoon series *Yogi Bear*?

11. In which year did *Yes, Minister* first appear on television?

12. Which presenter of *Stars on Sunday* was known as 'The Bishop'?

13. Who played the two wives of Alec Guinness in the 1953 film *The Captain's Paradise*?

14. What is the name of the French housemaid in *The Wombles*?

15. Which politician did Eric Porter play in the 1981 television drama *Winston Churchill - The Wilderness Years*?

SPORT

1. Who was the 1953 & 1954 world 250 cc motorcycling champion?

2. Where were the 1963 World Student games held?

3. Who did Newcastle United beat 1-0 in the 1952 F.A. Cup Final?

4. At which sport did Inna Ryskal of the U.S.S.R. win four Olympic medals from 1964-76?

5. In which year did Iolanda Balas set a world record of 1.86m for the women's high jump?

6. Who was voted England's Player of the Series against the West Indies in cricket in 1995?

7. Which Japanese cyclist was men's world sprint champion from 1977-86?

8. Where were the 1951 Asian Games held?

9. Which two men's teams won every Olympic hockey gold from 1928-68?

10. In which year did tennis player Lew Hoad die?

11. How many races did Jochen Rindt win in the European Formula Two Championship?

12. Where were the 1975 Pan-American Games held?

13. In which country is the Ranfurly Shield contested in rugby union?

14. Who scored two goals for Aston Villa in their 4-2 win at Tottenham in April 2000?

15. Dado Marino was 1950-2 world boxing champion. At what weight?

POP

1. Which former member of The Cult formed a band called the Holy Barbarians?

2. Who had a 2000 Top 10 single with *Stand Tough*?

3. Which member of The Kinks wrote two tracks on Big Country's album *Driving to Damascus*?

4. Who wrote the song *The Band Played Waltzing Matilda* which features on the album *Rum Sodomy & the Lash* by The Pogues?

5. What is the title of Fun Lovin' Criminals' Barry White tribute single?

6. Who, under the pseudonym of Apollo C. Vermouth, produced the single *I'm the Urban Spaceman* by The Bonzo Dog Doo-Dah Band?

7. Which guitarist guested on Love's 1970 track *The Everlasting First*?

8. Which group recorded the live album *Music For Hangovers*?

9. Which group's singles include 2000's *The F-Word*?

10. *Are You Receiving Me* is the second album by which group?

11. From which city do duo Four Lauderdale hail?

12. Who featured on Eminem's 1999 hit single *Guilty Conscience*?

13. In which year did the Boo Radleys form?

14. Which U.S. country group's albums include *Odessa* and *Milk and Scissors*?

15. Who had a Top 10 single in 1999 with *2 Times*?

ANSWERS 1. Ian Astbury **2.** Point Break **3.** Ray Davies **4.** Eric Bogle **5.** Love Unlimited **6.** Paul McCartney **7.** Jimi Hendrix **8.** Cheap Trick **9.** Babybird **10.** Subcircus **11.** Bristol **12.** Dr. Dre **13.** 1988 **14.** The Handsome Family **15.** Ann Lee.

SCIENCE

1. In which year did Atari introduce the video game 'Pong'?

2. The largest of the seas on the Moon is the Mare Imbrium. What does it translate as?

3. What is the atomic number of Scandium?

4. In the hexadecimal system, what letter represents the number 15?

5. In which country was British biologist Sir Peter Brian Medawar born?

6. Approximately how many miles in diameter is Uranus's satellite Cressida?

7. In which year was the Royal Society founded?

8. What is the atomic number of Rutherfordium?

9. Which liquid's formula is C6H6?

10. What does a bolometer measure?

11. Which chemical element has the symbol V?

12. Approximately how many days does the moon Enceladus take to orbit Saturn?

13. In which year did Edison invent the kinetoscope?

14. Which chemical element has the symbol Ce?

15. Who was appointed director of the Kaiser Wilhelm Institute for Physics in Berlin in 1913?

GENERAL KNOWLEDGE

1. In which European capital city was cellist Yo-Yo Ma born in 1955?

2. Who wrote the 1947 play *A Streetcar Named Desire*?

3. In which year did German engineer and car manufacturer Gottlieb Daimler die?

4. Who was the author of the 1955 novel *The Angry Hills*?

5. Which is the smaller of the two satellites of Mars?

6. In which year was U.S. car manufacturer Ransom Eli Olds born?

7. Who authored the 1848 novel *Mary Barton*?

8. Who was the male star of the 1955 Alfred Hitchcock film *To Catch A Thief*?

9. Which river in Yugoslavia forms the boundary between Montenegro and Bosnia-Herzegovina?

10. Which German playwright wrote the 1964 work *Marat/Sade*?

11. Which U.S. chemist created, with Edwin McMillan, the element neptunium?

12. What is the name given to the scale of temperature in which 0° represents the melting point of ice?

13. Who was the author of autobiographical novel *A Death in the Family*?

14. Which actor's television roles include Thomas Magnum in *Magnum PI*?

15. Rothesay is a town on the east coast of which Scottish island?

ENTERTAINMENT

1. Who plays an amnesiac war veteran in the 1942 film *Random Harvest*?

2. Which U.S. president did Ralph Bellamy play in the television drama *The Winds of War*?

3. In which year did Nicholas Witchell join the BBC as a trainee?

4. Hugh Leonard appeared in the 1988 film adaptation of his play *Da*. What did he play?

5. Which child actress played Sue Peters in television's *Worzel Gummidge*?

6. What were the forenames of comedy team Clapham and Dwyer?

7. In which year was impressionist Mike Yarwood born?

8. Who played Ivy Teesdale in the sitcom *You Rang, M'lord?*?

9. Who directed the 1948 film *An Ideal Husband*?

10. Who played Jim Anderson in the U.S. sitcom *Father Knows Best*?

11. Who directed the 1952 western film *Rancho Notorious*?

12. Who played WPC Bayliss in the television drama *Z Cars*?

13. Who plays DC Lennox in police drama series *The Bill*?

14. Who created the 1974 television series *The Zoo Gang*?

15. Who composed the 1683 opera *Venus and Adonis*?

SPORT

1. Whose goal for Sheffield Wednesday beat Chelsea 1-0 in April 2000?

2. In which year were the women's world championships in ice hockey first held?

3. Where were the 1965 World Student Games held?

4. Who were voted outstanding college American Football team in 1986 by United Press?

5. Who was the 1965 U.S. men's singles tennis champion?

6. Who was the 1986 individual Three-Day Eventing champion at the world championships?

7. For which rugby league team does Simon Haughton play?

8. Who was the 1988 Olympic men's 100m butterfly swimming champion?

9. At what sport was George Lee of the U.K. an Open world champion in 1978?

10. What nationality is golfer Rachel Hetherington?

11. Nikolay Bayukov was a 1976 Olympic champion. At what sport?

12. What nationality is alpine skier Spela Pretnar?

13. How many times did Allan Border captain the Australian Test cricket team from 1984-94?

14. At what sport is Julia Mann England's No. 1?

15. Valeriy Maslov of the U.S.S.R. won eight gold medals from 1961-77 at the world championships of which team game?

ANSWERS 1. Wim Jonk **2.** 1990 **3.** Budapest **4.** Penn State **5.** Manuel Santana **6.** Virginia Leng **7.** Wigan Warriors **8.** Anthony Nesty **9.** Gliding **10.** Australian **11.** Nordic skiing **12.** Slovenian **13.** 93 **14.** Badminton **15.** Bandy.

POP

1. In which year was Culture Club's first Top of the Pops appearance on television?

2. Which studio album by Sly and the Family Stone features the song *Spaced Cowboy*?

3. Who recorded the 2000 album *2001*?

4. Who was the Swedish-American singer with Curved Air?

5. Which Temptations song did Love and Rockets cover as their first single?

6. Which member of The Band died in December 1999?

7. Which reggae artist was born Roy Reid in 1950?

8. Who replaced bassist Louis Steinberg in Booker T and the MGs?

9. Which group recorded the 1999 mini-album *Stranger Blues*?

10. Which reggae artist recorded the 1977 album *Police and Thieves*?

11. Which duo recorded the 1999 hit single *Feel Good*?

12. Which group recorded the 1982 album *Pornography*?

13. Which female singer recorded 1999 album *Electric Chair*?

14. Who had a hit single in 1980 with *And the Beat Goes On*?

15. Which Tammy Wynette song did Lyle Lovett cover on album *Lyle Lovett and his Large Band*?

ANSWERS 1. 1982 **2.** There's A Riot Goin' On **3.** Dr. Dre **4.** Sonja Kristina **5.** Ball of Confusion **6.** Rick Danko **7.** I-Roy **8.** Donald 'Duck' Dunn **9.** Dream City Film Club **10.** Junior Murvin **11.** Phats and Small **12.** The Cure **13.** Sandy Dillon **14.** The Whispers **15.** Stand By Your Man.

PEOPLE

1. Which conductor was married to cellist Jacqueline du Pré from 1967-87?

2. Whose plays include *The Norman Conquests* and *Joking Apart*?

3. In which city was footballer Denis Law born?

4. In which year was comedian Robin Williams born?

5. Which actor was born Horace John Waters?

6. Which female new Zealand aviator broke Amy Johnson's record for the solo flight from England to Australia in 1934?

7. In which country was statesman Kemal Jumblat born?

8. What nationality was traveller and viceroy Affonso d'Alburquerque?

9. What was the middle name of astronaut Alan Bean?

10. Which actor has written the autobiography *Parcel Arrived Safely: Tied With String*?

11. In which year was the German Nazi leader Joachim von Ribbentrop hanged?

12. In which country was neuropathologist Alois Alzheimer born?

13. What was the middle name of jazz musician Dexter Gordon?

14. What is the middle name of snooker player Alex Higgins?

15. Which 19th century politician was known as 'the apostle of free trade'?

GENERAL KNOWLEDGE

1. Which genus of trees and shrubs includes the holly?

2. What is the sixth letter in the Greek alphabet?

3. In which European country is the formerly important gold-mining town of Tomsk?

4. What is the state capital of Pennsylvania?

5. Who was the 1988 world professional darts champion?

6. What was the name of the imperial dynasty of China from 1279-1368?

7. In which year did William Bligh, former commander of the H.M.S. Bounty, die?

8. Who was the England cricket captain from 1993-8?

9. What is the colour of the ball worth six points in snooker?

10. Which Hebrew prophet led the Israelites out of Egypt into the Promised Land?

11. To which genus of trees does conifer the larch belong?

12. What is the capital of Botswana?

13. In which year did British contralto Kathleen Ferrier die?

14. Which bandleader, born in 1891, was known in his early days as 'the King of Jazz'?

15. Which 1970s television drama starred Julie Covington as singer Dee Rhoades?

ENTERTAINMENT

1. Who plays brain surgeon George Brent's wife in the 1939 film *Dark Victory*?

2. In which U.S. state was the television drama *Whirlybirds* set?

3. Who directed the 1991 film *New Jack City*?

4. Who directed the 1995 film *Waiting to Exhale*?

5. Which actress played the manager of an amateur rugby league side in the 1973 sitcom *All Our Saturdays*?

6. Who directed and starred in the 1996 film *Matilda*?

7. Who played Flay in the 2000 BBC TV production of *Gormenghast*?

8. During which war was the 1970 film *Darling Lili* set?

9. Who directed the 1971 film *The French Connection*?

10. What was Arthur Bostrom's character name in the sitcom *'Allo, 'Allo*?

11. Who composed the opera *Les Danaïdes*?

12. Who played Jim Phelps in the 1996 film *Mission: Impossible*?

13. Who plays Darby Snow in the 1993 film *The Pelican Brief*?

14. Who plays Dr. Fu Manchu in the 1931 film *Daughter of the Dragon*?

15. Who does Jim Carrey play in the 1994 film *The Mask*?

ANSWERS 1. Bette Davis **2.** California **3.** Mario Van Peebles **4.** Forest Whitaker **5.** Diana Dors **6.** Danny DeVito **7.** Christopher Lee **8.** World War I **9.** William Friedkin **10.** Crabtree **11.** Salieri **12.** Jon Voight **13.** Julia Roberts **14.** Warner Oland **15.** Stanley Ipkiss.

SPORT

1. Which golfer won the 2000 Qatar Masters?

2. Who rode the 1993 July Cup-winning horse Hamas?

3. For which rugby union club side does Mark Mapletoft play?

4. At what sport have Britain's Bob Spalding and Jonathan Jones been world champions?

5. How long did the 19 frame qualifying match between Garry Wilkinson and Jason Ferguson in the 2000 World Championships in snooker take to complete?

6. Who was the 1987-91 men's open world judo champion?

7. Which Ethiopian runner broke the world two mile record in February 2000?

8. The European Super Cup in football was first played in 1972. At the suggestion of which Dutch newspaper?

9. What nationality is hurdler Anier Garcia?

10. Who was the men's 100m winner at the 1982 European Championships?

11. Which female swimmer won the 50m, 100m and 200m breaststroke at the British Grand Prix in Leeds in February 2000?

12. Which Indian cricketer scored 1604 runs in the 1964/5 season?

13. Who won the 2000 Welsh Open snooker title?

14. How many Olympic gold medals did gymnast Vera Caslavska win from 1964-8?

15. What nationality is golfer Eric Carlberg?

ANSWERS 1. Rolf Muntz **2.** Willie Carson **3.** Saracens **4.** Powerboating **5.** 11 hours and 38 minutes **6.** Naoya Ogawa **7.** Hailu Mekkonen **8.** De Telegraaf **9.** Cuban **10.** Frank Emmelmann **11.** Heidi Earp **12.** Chandu Borde **13.** John Higgins **14.** Seven **15.** Swedish.

POP

1. Which guitarist's early groups included Nightshift and The Tridents?

2. Which couple released the 1968 album *Two Virgins*?

3. Which U.S. group recorded 1990's *Smooth Noodle Maps*?

4. Who had a No. 1 album in 1999 with *By Request*?

5. From which country did The Waikikis, who had a 1965 hit with *Hawaii Tattoo*, come?

6. Who had a 1999 Top 10 hit with *Re-Rewind the Crowd Say Bo Selecta*?

7. In which year did Visage have a Top 20 hit with *Night Train*?

8. Who had a 1989 No. 1 single with *You Got It (The Right Stuff)*?

9. What was Randy Vanwarmer's only U.K. hit single?

10. In which year did Frankie Vaughan have his last chart hit single with *Nevertheless*?

11. Which studio album by The Beloved features singles *The Sun Rising* and *Hello*?

12. Which institution did Annie Lennox quit in 1971 before sitting her final exams?

13. Which two 1950s hits for Malcolm Vaughan feature the word 'Roses'?

14. In which year did Soul II Soul have a Top 10 single with *Get A Life*?

15. Which group presented the 'Protected Passion Tour' in 1981?

ANSWERS 1. Jeff Beck **2.** John Lennon and Yoko Ono **3.** Devo **4.** Boyzone **5.** Belgium **6.** Artful Dodger **7.** 1982 **8.** New Kids on the Block **9.** Just When I Needed You Most **10.** 1968 **11.** Happiness **12.** Royal Academy of Music in London **13.** *St. Therese of the Roses* and *Chapel of the Roses* **14.** 1989 **15.** Dexy's Midnight Runners.

ART

1. Who authored the ghost story *The Romance of Certain Old Clothes*?

2. What was William Hogarth's father's occupation?

3. Who is the heroine of Edith Wharton's novel *The House of Mirth*?

4. In which city did Henri Matisse die in 1954?

5. Which political cartoonist created the satirical strip *If ...*?

6. Who authored the short story collection *The Illustrated Man*?

7. Which Cleveland artist drew the Superman comic-book originally?

8. In which year did Tolstoy begin to write *Anna Karenina*?

9. Which book won the 1987 Booker prize?

10. Which Edinburgh-born writer's short stories include *Alice Long's Dachshunds*?

11. Michael Angelo Titmarsh was a pseudonym of which author?

12. Who wrote the 1984 novel *Doctor Slaughter*?

13. Which Trinidad-born writer authored the 1975 novel *Guerrillas*?

14. In which month of 1824 did Lord George Byron die?

15. In which novel by Charles Dickens does the character Sir Mulberry Hawk appear?

GENERAL KNOWLEDGE

1. What is the derived SI unit of electric capacitance?

2. Who was the French composer of the ballet *Daphnis et Chloé*?

3. Which 1996 film directed by Roland Emmerich featured Bill Paxton as the U.S. President?

4. What is the other name used for cocuswood, which is used for inlaying?

5. Which Dublin-born actress's films included 1943's *Jane Eyre*?

6. What type of creature is an australorp?

7. What is the name given to the strap from the reins to the girth of a horse preventing it from carrying its head too high?

8. What is the real name of writer Barbara Vine, a.k.a. Ruth Rendell?

9. Which stand-up comic and actor starred in the 1986 film *The Golden Child*?

10. What is the former name of Kennedy airport, New York?

11. In which novel does Rawdon Crawley marry Becky Sharp?

12. What is the colour of the ball worth one point in snooker?

13. Which character in the film *Star Wars* was played by Mark Hammill?

14. Who were the mother and father of Galahad in Arthurian legend?

15. Who created the fictional district attorney Perry Mason?

ANSWERS 1. Farad **2. Maurice Ravel 3.** Independence Day **4.** Jamaican ebony (or West Indian ebony) **5.** Sara Allgood **6.** A heavy black breed of domestic fowl **7.** Martingale **8.** Ruth Barbara Grasemann **9.** Eddie Murphy **10.** Idlewild **11. Vanity Fair 12. Red 13.** Luke Skywalker **14.** Elaine and Lancelot **15.** Erle Stanley Gardner.

ENTERTAINMENT

1. Which comedienne played music hall singer Millie Goswick in the sitcom *The Fossett Saga*?

2. Who directed and starred in the 1971 film comedy *A New Leaf* with Walter Matthau?

3. Who starred as *Wild Bill* in a 1995 western film?

4. In which year was comedian Allan Sherman born?

5. Who plays a small town barber in the 1952 film *Wait ill the Sun Shines, Nellie*?

6. Which Oscar-winning actress played Pearl Slaghoople in the 1994 film *The Flintstones*?

7. Which author does Chris O'Donnell play in the 1997 film *In Love and War*?

8. Who played the title role in the 1951 western film *Sugarfoot*?

9. What nationality was soprano Suzanne Danco?

10. Who played Mr. Step in the 1997 film *Spice World*?

11. Who is the female star of the 2000 film *The Next Best Thing*?

12. Which English actor played photographer Brian in the 1996 film *The Truth About Cats and Dogs*?

13. In which year did *The Wheeltappers' and Shunters' Social Club* first appear on television?

14. Who directed and starred in the 1997 comedy film *Waiting for Guffman*?

15. The stories of which three historical figures is told in the 1954 film *Daughters of Destiny*?

ANSWERS 1. June Whitfield **2.** Elaine May **3.** Jeff Bridges **4.** 1924 **5.** David Wayne **6.** Elizabeth Taylor **7.** Ernest Hemingway **8.** Randolph Scott **9.** Belgian **10.** Michael Barrymore **11.** Madonna **12.** Ben Chaplin **13.** 1974 **14.** Christopher Guest **15.** Elizabeth I, Joan of Arc and Lysistrata.

SPORT

1. Which Briton won the 1967 Italian Grand Prix in Formula 1?

2. For which team did cricketer J.E. Benjamin make his county debut in 1988

3. By what score did England beat Wales at rugby union on 20th February 1998?

4. For which rugby league club does Richard Pachniuk play?

5. Who won the men's singles title in the 1986 and 1987 world indoor bowls championships?

6. Who did Russia play in the quarter-finals of the 2000 Davis Cup?

7. Which horse won the 1996 Whitbread Gold Cup?

8. Which tennis player won the 1992 ATP Tour Championship Final?

9. In what time did Allen Johnson win the 1996 Olympic 110m hurdles title?

10. What was the married name of tennis player Kerry Melville?

11. Edouard Artigas was the 1947 sabre world champion. Which country did he represent?

12. What is the nickname of cricketer Mark Wayne Alleyne?

13. How old was Hjalmar Johansson when he won the 1908 Olympic highboard diving title?

14. Which U.S. golfer won the 1988 Tournament Players' Championship?

15. What nationality is junior-middleweight boxer Paul Vaden?

POP

1. In which year did Suzanne Vega have a hit single with *Luka*?

2. On which label did The Levellers record the 1995 album *Zeitgeist*?

3. For what was Chuck Berry imprisoned in 1979?

4. On which label did Ricky Martin record his eponymous 1999 album?

5. Which U.K. vocal group had a 1963 hit single with *Do the Bird*?

6. Which French group had a 1989 hit single with *Lambada*?

7. What was the Verve's first chart single, in 1992?

8. Which group charted in 1989 with *Homely Girl*?

9. Which punk group had a 1978 Top 40 single with *Automatic Lover*?

10. Which Dutch rock group recorded the 1995 album *Lamprey*?

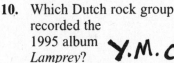
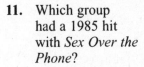

11. Which group had a 1985 hit with *Sex Over the Phone*?

12. Which duo charted in 1989 with the song *Don't Know Much*?

13. In which year did Gene Vincent have a U.K. Top 20 with *Blue Jean Bop*?

14. What telephone number forms the title of a song on the album *The B-52's* by The B-52's?

15. Which group released the 1994 album *Meanwhile Gardens*?

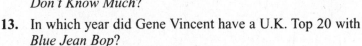

ANSWERS 1. 1987 **2.** China **3.** Tax Evasion **4.** Columbia **5.** Vernons Girls **6.** Kaoma **7.** She's a Superstar **8.** UB 40 **9.** The Vibrators **10.** Bettie Serveert **11.** Village People **12.** Linda Ronstadt and Aaron Neville **13.** 1956 **14.** 6060-842 **15.** Levitation.

GEOGRAPHY

1. Which is larger - El Salvador or Guatemala?

2. On which river does Bedford stand?

3. Which has the greater population - Norfolk or Suffolk?

4. In which ocean are the volcanic D'Entrecasteaux Islands?

5. In which country is Mount Sir Sandford in the Selkirk Mountains?

6. The port of Galata is a suburb of which city in Turkey?

7. Which country claimed Queen Maud Land, Antarctica, in 1939?

8. In which country is the most northerly point of South America?

9. The island of Quemoy, off the coast of China, lies in which strait?

10. Gatun Lake is part of which canal?

11. In which county is the carpet manufacturing town of Wilton?

12. On which sea coast is Scotland's St. Andrews?

13. Which river flows through the Sea of Galilee?

14. What is the name of the channel between the mainland of N. Scotland and the Orkney Islands?

15. St. Cloud is a suburb of which French city?

ANSWERS 1. Guatemala 2. Ouse 3. Norfolk 4. Pacific 5. Canada 6. Istanbul 7. Norway 8. Colombia 9. Formosa Strait 10. Panama Canal 11. Wiltshire 12. North Sea 13. River Jordan 14. Pentland Firth 15. Paris.

GENERAL KNOWLEDGE

1.   Between which two constellations in the southern hemisphere does the small constellation of Reticulum lie?

2.   Who authored the 1869 novel *Good Wives*?

3.   Who was the director and star of the 1995 film *Braveheart*?

4.   Who wrote the novel *Cry, the Beloved Country*?

5.   Who composed the one-act opera *Suor Angelica*?

6.   What is the capital of the Ukraine?

7.   Who is the author of the novel *Schindler's Ark*?

8.   What is teosinte?

9.   In which year did U.S. jazz pianist and composer Thelonious Monk die?

10. Which operetta by Gilbert and Sullivan is subtitled *Bunthorne's Bride*?

11. Of which republic in the Caribbean is Port-au-Prince the capital?

12. Who directed the 1998 film *Godzilla* starring Matthew Broderick?

13. Lake Taupo is the largest lake in which country?

14. Who was a Best Actor Oscar nominee for the 1948 film *Sitting Pretty*?

15. What was the debut novel by writer Nick Hornby?

ENTERTAINMENT

1. Who is the female star of the 2000 film *Stigmata*?

2. Who played Long John Silver in the 1996 film *Muppet Treasure Island*?

3. Which two actors co-star in the 2000 boxing film *Play it to the Bone*?

4. Who plays Grouty in the sitcom *Porridge*?

5. Which female novelist authored the television plays *Splinter of Ice* and *Poor Cherry*?

6. Who directed the 1987 film *Dark Tower* under the pseudonym Ken Barnett?

7. What is the character name of Derek Fowlds in the drama series *Heartbeat*?

8. Who directed the 1993 film *Shadowlands*?

9. Who is the female lead in the 1945 film *I Know Where I'm Going*?

10. Which comedian starred in the 1999 film *Big Daddy*?

11. Which actress does a striptease in the 1994 film *Prêt-à-Porter*?

12. Which stand-up comic's alter egos include Alan Parker: Urban Warrior?

13. Which comic magician starred in the 1952 BBC TV series *It's Magic*?

14. Which *Live and Kicking* presenter formerly worked on the Irish show *The Den*?

15. Who starred as Fagin in Alan Bleasdale's 1999 television adaptation of *Oliver Twist*?

ANSWERS 1. Patricia Arquette **2.** Tim Curry **3.** Woody Harrelson and Antonio Banderas **4.** Peter Vaughan **5.** Fay Weldon **6.** Freddie Francis **7.** Oscar Blaketon **8.** Richard Attenborough **9.** Wendy Hiller **10.** Adam Sandler **11.** Sophia Loren **12.** Simon Munnery **13.** Tommy Cooper **14.** Emma Ledden **15.** Robert Lindsay.

SPORT

1. Who won the 1980 British Open in snooker?

2. Who won the 1999 German Grand Prix in Formula 1?

3. Who took 7-37 for Pakistan against India in a Limited-Overs International on 25th October 1991?

4. What nationality is swimmer Pieter van den Hoogenband?

5. In which city is the U.S. governing body of basketball, the NBA, based?

6. By what score did Scotland beat Romania at rugby union in August 1999?

7. Which horse won the 1976 Irish 2000 Guineas?

8. In which year did Australian tennis player Norman Brookes die?

9. What sport is governed by the Fédération Internationale des Sociétés d'Aviron?

10. How many golds did Denmark win in the 1999 World Athletics Championships?

11. Irina Kiselyeva was 1986 and 1987 world champion at what sport?

12. What nationality is the former European triathlon champion Gregor Stam?

13. What was the attendance of the 1891 F.A. Cup Final?

14. What nationality is runner Derartu Tulu?

15. Jarmila Kratochvilova set a women's world record for 800m on 26th July 1983. What time did she run?

POP

1. In which year was Bobby Vinton's *Blue Velvet* a U.K. Top 10 single?

2. Who had a 1999 Top 10 hit with *Right Now*?

3. Who had a 1980 Top 10 single with *So Good To Be Back Home Again*?

4. Who had a 1979 top 10 single *Strut Your Funky Stuff*?

5. In which year did Bo Diddley tour Britain for the first time?

6. Which group's first single, in 1989, was *Retard Girl*?

7. Who had a 1999 Top 10 single with *The Launch*?

8. Who had a 1990 Top 10 single with *Tears on My Pillow*?

9. Which 1970s singer featured on the song *Walk Like A Panther* by the All Seeing I?

10. In which year did singer David McComb die?

11. What was the final single made by the original line-up of the group Gang of Four?

12. Which duo had a 1981 hit with *Wedding Bells*?

13. Which U.S. group recorded the album *Double Nickels on the Dime*?

14. Which 1960s model was the subject of a 1979 single by Glaxo Babies?

15. Aston, Aston, Rizzo, Stevenson, Gilvear. Which 1980s group?

HISTORY

1. How many days did Hannibal take to cross the Alps during the Second Punic War?

2. Which treaty, signed in 1648, established Switzerland as an independent state?

3. In which year did Athelstan, King of Wessex, die?

4. Who succeeded Charles IV as Holy Roman Emperor in 1378?

5. In which year was the Battle of Dunbar?

6. Who stood as Socialist Labour candidate at Newport East in May 1997?

7. Who was Chancellor of the Exchequer from 1964-67?

8. Where was Mary, Queen of Scots born in 1542?

9. In which year did Charles Howard, 1st Earl of Nottingham, die?

10. Who became dictator of Venezuela in July, 1811?

11. In which year was Pompeii destroyed by Vesuvius?

12. In which year did Anne of Cleves die?

13. Who replaced James A. Garfield as U.S. president in 1881?

14. In which year did the Praetorian Guard assassinate Emperor Pertinax?

15. Which U.S. battleship was blown up on February 15th, 1898 in Havana?

ANSWERS 1. Fifteen **2.** Peace of Westphalia **3.** 939 **4.** Wenceslas **5.** 1650 **6.** Arthur Scargill **7.** James Callaghan **8.** Linlithgow **9.** 1624 **10.** Francisco de Miranda **11.** 79 A.D. **12.** 1557 **13.** Chester A. Arthur **14.** 193 **15.** Maine.

GENERAL KNOWLEDGE

1. Who wrote the 1977 novel *Bloodline*?

2. Which Phrygian goddess of nature was often called the 'Mother of the Gods'?

3. Which comic actor played the title role in the film *Uncle Buck*?

4. Which unit of fluid measure is equal to one sixtieth of a drachm?

5. What, in New Zealand, is a tawa?

6. What is the symbol of the silvery-grey element Technetium?

7. In which year did French sculptor Auguste Rodin die?

8. Who wrote the 1943 novel *The Ship*?

9. What is the 17th letter in the Greek alphabet?

10. What, in Australia, is a tammar?

11. What is the name given to a young salmon that returns to fresh water after one winter in the sea?

12. Who is the author of the novel *In the Land of Israel*?

13. What is the name of the knife with a curved blade used by the Gurkhas?

14. Who was the 1939 U.S. Open golf champion?

15. Which actor played *Barton Fink* in a 1991 film?

ANSWERS 1. Sidney Sheldon **2.** Cybele **3.** John Candy **4.** Minim **5.** A tall timber tree **6.** Tc **7.** 1917 **8.** C.S. Forester **9.** Rho **10.** Small wallaby **11.** Grilse **12.** Amos Oz **13.** Kukri **14.** Byron Nelson **15.** John Turturro.

ENTERTAINMENT

1. Which singer played Renfield in the 1992 film *Bram Stoker's Dracula*?

2. Which comedian directed and starred in the 1960 film *Mr. Topaze*?

3. Who played playwright Eugene O'Neill in the 1981 film *Reds*?

4. Which 1989 British film was released in the U.S. in 1991 as *Dark Obsession*?

5. The 1993 film *Sommersby* is a remake of which earlier film?

6. Who plays Rigsby in the sitcom *Rising Damp*?

7. Who plays Frank Pierce in the 1999 film *Bringing Out the Dead*?

8. Who directed the 1946 film *The Dark Mirror*?

9. Who played Kramer in the sitcom *Seinfeld*?

10. Which comedy actor played Sgt. Sam Short in the 1970s sitcom *Coppers End*?

11. Which *Friends* actress appeared in the 1998 film *The Opposite of Sex*?

12. What was the name of David Hasselhoff's character in television series *Knight Rider*?

13. Who plays *Buffy the Vampire Slayer* on television?

14. Which Hollywood actress played Audrey Griswold in the 1989 film *National Lampoon's Christmas Vacation*?

15. Who directed the 1999 film *Runaway Bride*?

ANSWERS 1. Tom Waits **2.** Peter Sellers **3.** Jack Nicholson **4.** Diamond Skulls **5.** The Return of Martin Guerre **6.** Leonard Rossiter **7.** Nicolas Cage **8.** Robert Siodmak **9.** Michael Richards **10.** Bill Owen **11.** Lisa Kudrow **12.** Michael Knight **13.** Sarah Michelle Gellar **14.** Juliette Lewis **15.** Garry Marshall.

SPORT

1. In cricket, who scored 117 for Warwickshire vs. Durham in the 1st innings of their 1999 county championship game?

2. What nation did Olympic cyclist Arie van Vliet represent?

3. Who beat Stephen Hendry in the 1st round of the 2000 World Professional Snooker Championships?

4. In which year were trotting races first held in the Netherlands?

5. Which women's golfer won the Du Maurier Classic in August 1999?

6. How many Formula 1 Grand Prix wins did Alan Jones have in his career from 1975-86?

7. Which Spanish tennis player won the Estoril Open men's singles title in April 2000?

8. How many times in the 1940s did St. Mary's Hospital win the Middlesex Sevens competition in rugby union?

9. Which golfer won the MCI Heritage Classic in April 2000?

10. Lupe Pintor was WBC super-bantamweight world boxing champion from 1985-6. Which country did he represent?

11. What nationality is cyclist Paolo Bettini?

12. Who rode Pilsudski to victory in the 1997 Japan Cup in Tokyo?

13. Who sponsored the 1999/00 Basketball Championship in the U.K.?

14. Which Canadian Football team won the Grey Cup from 1978-82?

15. In which year did Randolph Lycett and Elizabeth Ryan win the Wimbledon mixed doubles tennis title for the second time?

POP

1. Which group's second single was called *Subhuman*?

2. What are the baby birds riding on the cover of Gallon Drunk's single *Some Fool's Mess*?

3. Who produced The Glitter Band's 1974 single *Goodbye My Love*?

4. Which girl group recorded the 1969 album *Philosophy of the World*?

5. Who wrote Gloria Gaynor's hit *Never Can Say Goodbye*?

6. After which songwriter was guitarist Jerry Garcia named?

7. In which year did Abba have a Top 10 single with *Gimme Gimme Gimme (A Man After Midnight)*?

8. What was the second single by Leeds group, The Mission?

9. Which studio album by the Gang of Four features *I Love a Man in a Uniform*?

10. Who sang lead vocal on the Moonglows song *Mama Loocie*?

11. What is the B-side of David Gamson's Rough Trade single *Sugar Sugar*?

12. Who is lead singer with the Scottish group The Blue Nile?

13. On which label did the Flying Lizards release the 1979 single *Money*?

14. Who was the singer with the band Gaye Bykers on Acid?

15. Who had a 1999 Top 10 single with *Bailamos*?

ANSWERS 1. Garbage **2.** A motorcycle **3.** Mike Leander **4.** The Shaggs **5.** Clifton Davis **6.** Jerome Kern **7.** 1979 **8.** Garden of Delight **9.** Song of the Free **10.** Marvin Gaye **11.** Honey Honey **12.** Paul Buchanan **13.** Virgin **14.** Mary Mary **15.** Enrique Inglesias.

WORDS

1. The Italian sweet tiramisu derives its name from which phrase?

2. What, on a bishop's mitre, are the infulae?

3. If you performed an escalade to attack a fort, what would you use?

4. What does the French phrase *amour-propre* mean?

5. In biology, what does the phrase ananthous mean?

6. What in Greece is a flokati?

7. If an artist were an animalier what would they specialize in painting?

8. What is the name given to the end of a hammer head opposite the striking face?

9. If you suffered from apnoea, what would you be unable to do?

10. Where would you find a nobiliary particle?

11. In fencing, what is an appel?

12. What type of creature is a jumping mouse - a bird or a rodent?

13. What is the French term for a secondary school?

14. What call in solo whist declares that a hand will win no tricks?

15. What in ancient Greece was a peltast?

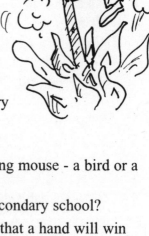

ANSWERS 1. Pull me up **2.** The ribbons hanging from the back **3.** Ladders **4.** Self-respect **5.** Having no flowers **6.** Rug **7.** Animals **8.** Peen **9.** Breathe **10.** In a title or surname **11.** A stamping of the foot as a warning **12.** Rodent **13.** A lycée **14.** Misère **15.** A lightly-armed foot soldier.

GENERAL KNOWLEDGE

1. Who authored the 1883 novel *Under Drake's Flag*?

2. Which 1996 film comedy starred Jack Nicholson as the U.S. president?

3. Who wrote the 1971 novel *The Onion Eaters*?

4. What is the name given to the national assembly of Spain?

5. Which Mexico-born film star played Rupert of Hentzau in 1922's *The Prisoner of Zenda*?

6. Who was the Best Supporting Actress Oscar winner for the film *In Old Chicago*?

7. Who wrote the 1973 novel *The Onion Field*?

8. In which BBC sitcom did Penelope Keith feature as Margo Leadbetter?

9. Tobermory is the chief town on which island in the Inner Hebrides?

10. In which year did Toronto-born jazz pianist and composer Gil Evans die?

11. Which number is represented by the letters XIV in Roman numerals?

12. What is the cgs unit of force?

13. Who was South African prime minister from 1939-48?

14. Which U.S. stand-up comedian and film actor appeared as a con man in the 1997 film *The Spanish Prisoner*?

15. The 1997 film *Starship Troopers* by Paul Verhoeven was based on a novel by which author?

ANSWERS 1. G.A. Henry **2.** Mars Attacks! **3.** J.P. Donleavy **4.** Cortes **5.** Ramon Novarro **6.** Alice Brady **7.** Joseph Wambaugh **8.** The Good Life **9.** Mull **10.** 1988 **11.** Fourteen **12.** Dyne **13.** Jan Smuts **14.** Steve Martin **15.** Robert A. Heinlein.

ENTERTAINMENT

1. Who directed the 1999 film *Felicia's Journey*?

2. What is Brian Aherne's profession in the 1935 film *I Live My Life*?

3. Who directed, and is one of the stars of, the 1994 film *Reality Bites*?

4. Which comedian's alter egos include Tommy Cockles?

5. Who plays television's *Columbo*?

6. Which landmark is featured in the finale of the 1942 Alfred Hitchcock film *Saboteur*?

7. Which former soap actress starred as Anna in the 1999 Broadway production of the play *Closer*?

8. Which *Fast Show* cast member played Annie in the 1987 sitcom *The Corner House*?

9. Who plays Jenny in the television drama series *Cold Feet*?

10. In the animated television series *Bob and Margaret*, what is Bob's profession?

11. Who played the title role in the 1930 film *Abraham Lincoln*?

12. What are the surnames of television's Ant and Dec?

13. What was the Elizabethan name for a prompter in the theatre?

14. Who played the title role in the 1940 film *The Earl of Chicago*?

15. In which country was the stage actress Agnes Booth born in 1846?

SPORT

1. Who scored Scotland's goal in their 1998 Group A football World Cup finals game against Norway?

2. Which former American football player is uncle of Leicester Riders' basketball star Purnell Perry?

3. Who was the 1975 women's 100m breaststroke swimming world champion?

4. Which U.S. golfer was the leading money winner in 1953 on the US tour?

5. For which rugby league team did Martin Offiah make his debut in February 2000?

6. In which year was the Amateur Softball Association of America formed?

7. In which year did Darren Clarke first take part in the Ryder Cup?

8. Which cricket team scored 1107 runs in their game with New South Wales in December 1926?

9. In cricket, who scored 150 for Worcestershire vs. Essex in the 2nd innings of their 1999 county championship game?

10. David Robinson was NBA's leading scorer in 1994. What was his average per game?

11. In which year was athlete Carl Lewis born?

12. Who rode Victory Note to victory in the 1998 Poule d'Essai des Poulains?

13. What is the nickname of cricketer Kim Barnett?

14. Which country were coxless four rowing champions in the 1997 world championships?

15. How many golds did Greece win in the 1999 World Athletics Championships?

ANSWERS 1. Craig Burley **2.** William 'The Refrigerator' Perry **3.** Hannelore Anke **4.** Lew Worsham **5.** Salford City Reds **6.** 1933 **7.** 1997 **8.** Victoria **9.** Graeme Hick **10.** 29.8 points **11.** 1961 **12.** John Reid **13.** Barn **14.** U.K. **15.** Two.

POP

1. On which label did Fun Boy Three record the single *The Lunatics Have Taken Over The Asylum*?

2. Who was the composer and lead vocalist with group Fischer Z?

3. Who recorded the 1992 album *The Happy Club*?

4. Which singer-songwriter released the 1979 single *All Sewn Up*?

5. Who recorded the 1977 album *Don Juan's Reckless Daughter*?

6. In which year did John Foxx have a hit single with *Underpass*?

7. Which John Lennon song did Generation X cover on the B-side of the single *King Rocker*?

8. Jerry Rosalie was the lead singer of which 1960s group?

9. What is the B-side of Gary Glitter's 1973 single *Hello! Hello! I'm Back Again*?

10. In which city did the Raspberries form in 1970?

11. Which band recorded the 1999 single *No Distance Left To Run*?

12. In which year did Kiss drummer Eric Carr die?

13. Which solo singer had a 1999 No. 1 with *When You Say Nothing At All*?

14. Which studio album by Queen features the song *We Will Rock You*?

15. Which solo artist had a 1984 Top 10 single with *Too Late For Goodbyes*?

SCIENCE

1. In which year did Charles Darwin graduate from Cambridge University?
2. Of what is thanatology the science?
3. In which century did scientist Daniel Bernoulli live?
4. Who won the 1905 Nobel prize for medicine?
5. Symbolic, connectionist and evolutionary are the three types of what?
6. In aeronautics, which organization is represented by the acronym ESA?
7. In which year did John Logie Baird first transmit pictures between London and Glasgow using telephone lines?
8. Who was named Professor of Chemistry at Lille University in 1854?
9. What is the approximate diameter in miles of Uranus's moon Miranda?
10. In which year did chemist Robert Wilhelm Bunsen die?
11. Thalassa is a small satellite of which planet?
12. In which English city was Nobel prize winner Sir Edward Victor Appleton born?
13. Who succeeded Sir Humphry Davy as Professor of Chemistry at the Royal Institution?
14. In which year did the comet Shoemaker-Levy 9 collide with Jupiter?
15. In which year did Hans Christian Oersted isolate aluminium?

GENERAL KNOWLEDGE

1. Who wrote the one-act play *Salomé*, which was produced in Paris in 1896?

2. What was the signature tune of violinist and bandleader Joe Loss?

3. Which creature of Australia and New Guinea is also called a spiny anteater?

4. What is the name given to the first period of the Mesozoic era during which reptiles flourished?

5. Who authored the 1879 novel *Daisy Miller*?

6. In which year did the long-running BBC current affairs TV programme *Panorama* begin?

7. Who wrote the 1973 play *Equus*?

8. In which year was BBC news reporter Kate Adie born?

9. Which Roman road runs from London to Wroxeter near Shrewsbury?

10. Which ancient Greek city was site of the most famous oracle of Apollo?

11. How many pennies was the English silver coin a groat worth?

12. Who were the two male leads in the 1997 film *Blood and Wine*?

13. Who was the designer of the British aircraft the Spitfire which was used in the Battle of Britain?

14. Who became president of Gabon in 1967?

15. What is the standard monetary unit of Botswana?

ANSWERS 1. Oscar Wilde **2.** In the Mood **3.** Echidna **4.** Triassic period **5.** Henry James **6.** 1953 **7.** Peter Shaffer **8.** 1945 **9.** Watling Street **10.** Delphi **11.** Four **12.** Jack Nicholson and Michael Caine **13.** Reginald Mitchell **14.** Omar Bongo **15.** Pula.

ENTERTAINMENT

1. Who is the female presenter of children's television show *SM: TV Live*?

2. In the 1953 film *Abbott and Costello meet Dr. Jekyll and Mr. Hyde*, who plays Dr. Jekyll?

3. Who appeared as Margaret Thatcher in the 1982 television comedy play *Anyone for Dennis*?

4. Who directed and starred in the 1999 film *Guest House Paradiso*?

5. Who played Mr. Murdstone in the 1999 BBC TV dramatisation of *David Copperfield*?

6. Who directed the 1964 film *The Earth Dies Screaming*?

7. Who is the male star of the 1999 film *The Straight Story*?

8. In which year did English actor-manager Arthur Bourchier die?

9. Which American comedian stars in the 1965 film *I'll Take Sweden*?

10. Who plays Dr. Arliss Loveless in the 1999 film *Wild Wild West*?

11. What is the name of the kidnapped dolphin in the film *Ace Ventura, Pet Detective*?

12. Who played the Sheriff of Nottingham in the 1991 film *Robin Hood, Prince of Thieves*?

13. What is the profession of Peter Sellers in the film *I Love You, Alice B. Toklas*?

14. Who plays bad guy Arjen Rudd in the 1989 film *Lethal Weapon*?

15. Who directed the 1963 film *Jason and the Argonauts*?

ANSWERS 1. Cat Deeley **2.** Boris Karloff **3.** Angela Thorne **4.** Adrian Edmondson **5.** Trevor Eve **6.** Terence Fisher **7.** Richard Farnsworth **8.** 1927 **9.** Bob Hope **10.** Kenneth Branagh **11.** Snowflake **12.** Alan Rickman **13.** Lawyer **14.** Joss Ackland **15.** Don Chaffey.

SPORT

1. How many Grand Prix wins did motorcyclist Giacomo Agostini achieve in total?

2. For which Test cricket side does bowler Nicky Boje play?

3. Who scored Arsenal's goal in their 1969 League Cup Final defeat?

4. In which year was runner Frank Fredericks born?

5. What nationality is athlete Ingrid Kristiansen?

6. How many Tests did cricketer Chris Lewis play for England?

7. What nationality was cyclist Georges Ronsse?

8. In which year was runner Maurice Greene born?

9. Which hockey team won the National Women's League in 1997 & 1998?

10. At what sport were Alfredo Mendoza and Willa McGuire world champions in 1955?

11. How many times did Jacky Ickx win the Le Mans 24-hour race?

12. In cricket, who scored 164 for Glamorgan vs. Nottinghamshire in the 1st innings of their 1999 county championship game?

13. In sailing, in which year did Italy first win the Admiral's Cup?

14. In which year did French tennis player Marcel Bernard die?

15. At which Olympic Games was boxing first included in the programme?

POP

1. Which group recorded the 1989 single *The 3rd Time We Opened the Capsule*?

2. What was the title of the first No. 1 single by Oasis in 2000?

3. Who produced Northside's album *Chicken Rhythms*?

4. Who recorded the album *Bleeker & MacDougal*?

5. In which year did The Justified Ancients of Mu Mu form?

6. Which singer-actress was married to actor Jack Webb?

7. Who played bass on Rainbow's album *Down to Earth*?

8. Which group claimed *Up in the Sky* by Oasis was too similar to their song *Apple Green*?

9. Which Slade studio album features the song *My Friend Stan*?

10. In which year did Gladys Knight & the Pips record *Letter Full of Tears*?

11. In which year did The Police have a No. 1 single with *Message in a Bottle*?

12. Who recorded the album *Vigil in a Wilderness of Mirrors*?

13. Which group recorded the 1991 album *Sugar Tax*?

14. Who recorded the 1999 No. 1 single *King of My Castle*?

15. Which Gerry Rafferty studio album includes the song *Get It Right Next Time*?

PEOPLE

1. What was the pseudonym of author John Griffith Chaney?

2. In which year did cartoonist Carl Giles die?

3. On which ship did murderer Crippen attempt to escape to Canada?

4. Who, at the age of 12, became the youngest father in Britain in January 1998?

5. Who was the second son of Darius II of Persia?

6. Which U.S. interior designer designed the Trellis Room of the Colony Club in New York?

7. What was the nickname of Spanish politician Dolores Ibarurri?

8. What was the middle name of U.S. general Omar N. Bradley?

9. In which year did astronaut Alan Shepard die?

10. Which writer was born Truman Streckfus Persons?

11. What was actress Louise Rose Hovick better known as?

12. Which children's book author and illustrator's works include 1973's *Father Christmas*?

13. Which comedian was born Maxwell Lorimer in 1908?

14. Which actor appeared on the cover of Rolling Stone magazine in 1999 wearing a dress and a rubber glove?

15. Which ex-Spice Girl did disc jockey Chris Evans date in late 1999?

GENERAL KNOWLEDGE

1. Who is the central character in the novel *The History Man* by Malcolm Bradbury?

2. In which county is the port and resort of Felixstowe?

3. In which year was Canadian ice hockey player Bobby Orr born?

4. Which journalist and broadcaster presented the TV show *Question Time* from 1979-89?

5. Which comedy duo starred in the 1932 film *Scram*?

6. Which chart-topping group's hits included the perennial *Merry Xmas Everybody*?

7. In which year did Italian fascist dictator Benito Mussolini die?

8. Who did actor Jack Lord play in the cop series *Hawaii Five-O*?

9. Which French composer's works include the three-act opera *Pénélope*?

10. Which actor played the hero in a 1959 film version of *The 39 Steps*?

11. Which Indian Test cricketer took 5 for 75 against Pakistan at Nagpur in 1983-84?

12. Dundalk is the county town of which county of the Republic of Ireland?

13. Which Biblical herd ran into the sea and drowned after being driven mad?

14. Which 18th Century poet and playwright authored the 1750 tragedy *The Roman Father*?

15. Of which state of North India is Lucknow the capital?

ANSWERS 1. Howard Kirk **2.** Suffolk **3.** 1948 **4.** Sir Robin Day **5.** Laurel and Hardy **6.** Slade **7.** 1945 **8.** Steve McGarrett **9.** Gabriel Fauré **10.** Kenneth More **11.** R. J. Shastri **12.** Louth **13.** The Gadarene swine **14.** William Whitehead **15.** Uttar Pradesh.

ENTERTAINMENT

1. Who directed the 1994 film *Human Traffic*?

2. Who plays Sheriff Chappy in the 1999 film *Happy, Texas*?

3. Who plays the President of the United States in the 1997 film *Absolute Power*?

4. Who composed the 1926 opera *Cardillac*?

5. Which writer scripted the 1957 film *Saint Joan*?

6. In which year was English soprano Joan Carlyle born?

7. Who played *Rob Roy* in the 1995 film?

8. In which opera does bullfighter Escamillo appear?

9. Who plays a sideshow con-man in the 1925 silent film *Sally of the Sawdust*?

10. Which football commentator also provides commentary on the matches in the BBC 2 show *Robot Wars*?

11. In which year was the pilot episode of the comedy show *Are You Being Served?* shown?

12. Who played guest Dr. Ross in the first series of the sitcom *Friends*?

13. Who plays villain Dr. Tolian Soran in the 1994 film *Star Trek: Generations*?

14. Who played Mr. and Mrs. Waltham in series five of the sitcom *Friends*?

15. Who played Josie Packard in the TV series *Twin Peaks*?

SPORT

1. Which boxer was the 1974 Sports Illustrated Sportsman of the Year?

2. Out of a possible 160 points, how many did Montreal Canadiens get in their NHL season in 1976/7?

3. For which side did Adrian Rollins play in the 1999 cricket county championship season?

4. In which city was the 1967 Super Bowl in American Football held?

5. Which duo were 1992 U.S. Open women's doubles tennis champions?

6. What nationality is darts player Raymond Barneveld?

7. In which year did Internazionale first win the Italian league in football?

8. How old was horse Mill House when it won the 1963 Cheltenham Gold Cup?

9. With what sport is Bruno Kernen associated?

10. Which were the first team to be relegated from football's Premier League in 1999/00?

11. In canoeing, what does K2 stand for?

12. What nationality is golfer Mike Weir?

13. Who was 1997 world badminton women's singles champion?

14. What time did Johnny Weissmuller achieve to set a new world record for 100m freestyle swimming on 17th February 1924?

15. What nationality is boxer Vuyani Bungu?

POP

1. Which solo singer had a 1999 No. 1 single with *Livin' La Vida Loca*?

2. Who produced Kool and the Gang's hits *Get Down On It* and *Celebration*?

3. Who is the most famous ex-member of Dublin band Ton Ton Macoute?

4. In which month of 1999 did Cliff Richard's *The Millennium Prayer* enter the singles chart?

5. On which label was E.LP's *Brain Salad Surgery* recorded?

6. Who recorded the 1964 LP *All the News That's Fit To Print*?

7. Which Rolling Stones studio album features the song *Midnight Rambler*?

8. Who recorded the 1983 album *Warriors*?

9. Who had a 1999 No. 1 album with *Rhythm and Stealth*?

10. Which studio album by the Eurythmics features the song *Right By Your Side*?

11. Which group recorded the 1991 album *Spiderland*?

12. Which Status Quo studio album features *Break the Rules*?

13. In which year did Z. Z. Top have a Top 10 single with *Gimme All Your Lovin'*?

14. Who recorded the 1999 dance single *Under the Water*?

15. Which guitarist's albums include *My Feet Are Smiling* and *Chewing Pine*?

ART

1. Who authored the 1855 novel *Harry Coverdale's Courtship*?

2. *A Hall of Mirrors* was the first novel of which New York-born author?

3. In which novel does the character Mr. Flosky appear?

4. Who drew the comic book *Maus*?

5. Who is laird of Monkbarns in Walter Scott's novel *The Antiquary*?

6. Which Russian writer authored *A Theatrical Novel* and *The White Guard*?

7. Who wrote the 1946 novel *Bright Day*?

8. Which playwright and novelist penned 1963's *Radcliffe*?

9. Whose series of woodcuts, *Dance of Death*, was published in 1538?

10. Who painted 1201's *William III on horseback*?

11. What is the butler's name in Graham Greene's short-story *The Fallen Idol*?

12. Where did David Hockney study from 1959-62?

13. Which American author penned the novels *The Car* and *The Gypsy's Curse*?

14. Whose paintings include 1889's *The Yellow Christ*?

15. *The Bluest Eye* was the debut novel of which female author?

GENERAL KNOWLEDGE

1. Who was Conservative defence secretary from 1981-3?

2. What was the name of the Russian secret police set up in 1917 by the Bolshevik government?

3. In which year was German composer Johann Sebastian Bach born?

4. Who wrote the 1960 play *The Dumb-Waiter*?

5. In Christianity, what is the name given to the period of forty weekdays lasting from Ash Wednesday to Holy Saturday?

6. Who were the male and female leads in the 1997 film *Conspiracy*?

7. What was the name adopted by comedian Arthur Marx?

8. In which year was Australian criminal Ned Kelly hanged?

9. In which county is the town of Egham on the River Thames?

10. Who wrote the 1983 book *Ararat*?

11. What is the standard monetary unit of Ecuador?

12. Who wrote the 1943 novel *Double Indemnity*?

13. Who was butler to *The Addams Family* in the TV comedy series?

14. In golf, what is a former name for a No. 3 wood?

15. In which year did U.S. locksmith Linus Yale die?

ANSWERS 1. John Nott **2.** Cheka **3.** 1685 **4.** Harold Pinter **5.** Lent **6.** Mel Gibson and Julia Roberts **7.** Harpo Marx **8.** 1880 **9.** Surrey **10.** D. M. Thomas **11.** Sucre **12.** James M. Cain **13.** Lurch **14.** Spoon **15.** 1868

ENTERTAINMENT

1. Which American Football team has its mascot kidnapped in the 1994 film *Ace Ventura, Pet Detective*?

2. What was Sgt. Wilson's forename in *Dad's Army*?

3. Who play Nicolas Cage's bodyguard in the film *Gone in 60 Seconds*?

4. Who voiced the Ant Hill Mob in cartoon *Wacky Races*?

5. Who directed the 1942 film *Across the Pacific*?

6. In which year was the comedy series *The Darling Buds of May* first shown on TV?

7. Who created the computer games *Quake* and *Doom*?

8. Which comedian played *Lenny* on the London stage in 1999?

9. Who did Bernard Wenton win *Stars in Their Eyes* as in the 1991 final?

10. In which European capital is the 1953 film *Act of Love* set?

11. Who stars in the 1954 film *Yankee Pasha*?

12. Which female impressionist accompanied Bobby Davro in the 1987 series *Bobby Davro's TV Weekly*?

13. Who starred as *A Yank in the R.A.F.* in the 1941 film?

14. Which actor starred in the 1989 film *Vampire's Kiss*?

15. Who directed the 1992 action film *Year of the Comet*?

ANSWERS 1. Miami Dolphins **2.** Arthur **3.** Vinnie Jones **4.** Mel Blanc **5.** John Huston **6.** 1991 **7.** John Romero **8.** Eddie Izzard **9.** Nat King Cole **10.** Paris **11.** Jeff Chandler **12.** Jessica Martin **13.** Tyrone Power **14.** Nicolas Cage **15.** Peter Yates.

SPORT

1. From which Irish county does Hull rugby league player Brian Carney come?

2. How many times did jockey Lester Piggott win the Oaks?

3. Which four teams played in Pool 4 of rugby union's 1999/00 Heineken Cup?

4. Which country were 1997 men's relay world champions at orienteering?

5. What nationality is swimmer Inge de Bruijn?

6. At what sport have Sofiya Kondakova and Inga Artamonova been world champions?

7. Who finished 2nd in the 1999 German Grand Prix in Formula 1?

8. What was the full name of the European football competition known as the Fairs Cup?

9. Which golfer won the $1m N.E.C. Invitational in August 1999?

10. Who was men's triple jump winner at the I.A.A.F. World Cup from 1977-81?

11. How many golds did North Korea win at the 1999 World Athletics Championships?

12. In cricket, who scored 206 for Warwickshire vs. Oxfordshire in their July 1984 NatWest Bank Trophy game?

13. In which sport were Cai Zhenhua and Cao Yanhua world champions in 1985?

14. Who was 1997 British women's Open Amateur champion in golf?

15. By what score did Ireland beat Argentina at rugby union in August 1999?

POP

1. Who produced Joan Armatrading's 1972 album *Whatever's For Us*?

2. Who is lead singer in the group *Coldplay*?

3. In which year did Ian Dury release the single *Sex and Drugs and Rock and Roll*?

4. Which studio album by Shack features *Cornish Town* and *Since I Met You*?

5. Who released the 1988 album *Rehab Doll*?

6. Who had a 1999 No. 1 single with *Mambo No. 5*?

7. Which group recorded the 1994 album *Zingalamaduni*?

8. Which girl group recorded the album *Fan Mail*?

9. Which Bob Dylan studio album features the song *A Hard Rain's A-Gonna Fall*?

10. Which solo artist had a 1984 Top 10 single with *Missing You*?

11. Which group recorded the 1994 singles *Swamp Thing* and *Rollercoaster*?

12. Who had a 1999 Top 10 single with *If I Could Turn Back the Hands on Time*?

13. Which journalist was a member of the group The Art of Noise?

14. Who recorded the 1995 hit single *Push the Feeling On*?

15. What did group The Dollar Bills change their name to in 1963?

ANSWERS 1. Gus Dudgeon **2.** Chris Martin **3.** 1977 **4.** H.M.S. Fable **5.** Green River **6.** Lou Bega **7.** Arrested Development **8.** TLC **9.** The Freewheelin' Bob Dylan **10.** John Waite **11.** The Grid **12.** R.Kelly **13.** Paul Morley **14.** The Nightcrawlers **15.** John Lee's Groundhogs.

GEOGRAPHY

1. On which river is the Welsh village of Betws-y-coed?

2. Wellesley is part of which state of Malaysia?

3. What is the highest peak in the Graian Alps in West Europe?

4. Pegu was capital of which country in the 16th century?

5. Rossan Point is in which county of the Republic of Ireland?

6. Which North American river flows from Lake St. Clair to Lake Erie?

7. Bastia is on which European island?

8. In which African country is the port of Sekondi?

9. Which city became Chemnitz in 1990?

10. Of which French department is Rouen the capital?

11. Mt. del Gennargentu is the highest point of which European island?

12. Deurne is a suburb of which Belgian port?

13. Malaga is on which Spanish coastal resort?

14. The chalk figure called Wilmington Long Man is cut into the side of which hill?

15. Varna in Bulgaria is on which sea coast?

GENERAL KNOWLEDGE

1. Which port in southern England is informally called Pompey?

2. Who wrote the 1946 play *The Iceman Cometh*?

3. Who played criminal Willie Parker in the 1984 film *The Hit* directed by Stephen Frears?

4. Which England Test cricketer took 7 for 40 against Australia at Sydney on the 1970-1 tour?

5. On which firth is the port and resort of Oban in Argyll and Bute?

6. What is the name of the chapel of the pope in the Vatican at Rome?

7. Which woman starred as a rock singer in the 1979 film *The Rose*?

8. In literary terms what is the word used to describe an epigrammatic effect by which contradictory terms are used in conjunction?

9. What was the name of the 1980s TV drama series set in Malayan female prisoner of war camps?

10. Who directed the 1997 film *Lost Highway* starring Bill Pullman?

11. Who directed the 1993 film *Cliffhanger* which starred Sylvester Stallone as a mountain rescuer?

12. Who is the lover of Portia in the play *The Merchant of Venice*?

13. Who penned the 1982 play *Noises Off*?

14. What is the seventh sign of the zodiac?

15. Which genus of cacti includes the prickly pear?

15. Opuntia.
10. David Lynch 11. Renny Harlin 12. Bassanio 13. Michael Frayn 14. Libra
5. Firth of Lorne 6. Sistine Chapel 7. Bette Midler 8. Oxymoron 9. Tenko
ANSWERS 1. Portsmouth 2. Eugene O'Neill 3. Terence Stamp 4. John Snow

ENTERTAINMENT

1. Who directed the 1952 British film *The Yellow Balloon*?

2. Which playwright and director does Jason Robards play in the 1963 film *Act One*?

3. Who played Claudius in the 1990 Franco Zeffirelli film *Hamlet*?

4. Which comedy writing duo penned the 1975 series *Dawson's Weekly* for Les Dawson?

5. Actress Anne Baxter was granddaughter of which architect?

6. Who directed the 1974 film *The Parallax View*?

7. Who directed the 1995 film *The Addiction*?

8. In which year did actor Wallace Beery die?

9. Who played Nick Brim in the sitcom *Just A Gigolo*?

10. In which year did *The Sky At Night* first appear on BBC TV?

11. Which actor plays a would-be boxing promoter in the 1992 film *Night and the City*?

12. Who played Anne of Cleves in the 1970 TV drama *The Six Wives of Henry VIII*?

13. Which actor played political cartoonist Brant on the BBC 2 satire show *The Day Today*?

14. In which year was actor Jean-Paul Belmondo born?

15. Who played Crewman Sparks in the TV series *Voyage to the Bottom of the Sea*?

SPORT

1. In which car did Jochen Rindt win the 1970 British Grand Prix in Formula 1?
2. What is the name of Gloucester rugby union team's home ground?
3. Which rugby league club have won the Yorkshire Cup most times?
4. In which year did British tennis player Dorothea Chambers die?
5. With which winter sport would you associate Susi Erdmann and Gerda Weissensteiner?
6. Who did Cédric Pioline beat in the quarter-finals of the 1999 U.S. Open singles tennis tournament?
7. Which horse won the 1916 Grand National?
8. What nationality is swimmer Therese Alshammar?
9. Which team won the 1964 Olympic women's 4 x 100m relay?
10. Who partnered Kathy Jordan to victory in the 1981 Australian Open women's doubles tennis championship?
11. On which horse did show jumper Marion Coakes win the 1965 individual world championship title?
12. What position does Sean Long play for St. Helens rugby league team?
13. Who was 1924 Olympic men's 400m freestyle swimming champion?
14. Who was the Football Writers' Player of the Year in England in 1993?
15. What nationality is runner Paul Kergat?

ANSWERS 1. Lotus **2.** Kingsholm **3.** Leeds **4.** 1960 **5.** Luge tobogganning **6.** Gustavo Kuerten **7.** Vermouth **8.** Swedish **9.** Poland **10.** Anne Smith **11.** Stroller **12.** Scrum half **13.** Johnny Weissmuller **14.** Chris Waddle **15.** Kenyan.

POP

1. What is the name of Neil Hannon's wife?

2. The Yardbirds had two Top 10 hits in 1966 – what were they?

3. Which female singer recorded the album *Da Real World*?

4. Who was drummer with the rock group The Eagles?

5. In which year was *Life Begins at the Hop* a hit single for X.T.C.?

6. With which Johnny Kidd and the Pirates' song did Chad Allan and the Expressions have a 1965 No. 1 single in Canada?

7. Four of Mark Wynter's top 30 hit singles featured the word *girl*. What were they?

8. Who was frontman with The Wurzels on their 1967 hit *Drink Up Thy Zider*?

9. Which group's albums include *Bee Thousand* and *Alien Lanes*?

10. Which D.J. had a hit in 1984 with *The Gay Cavalieros (The Story So Far)*?

11. In which city did the Foo Fighters record the album *The Colour and the Shape*?

12. Which group had a 1999 No. 1 single with *Flying Without Wings*?

13. Which U.S. group recorded 1990 album *Pastoral Hide and Seek*?

14. Which foodstuff provided a 1994 hit single for Y?N-Vee?

15. Which Suede album features the songs *Down* and *He's Gone*?

HISTORY

1. In which year did Diocletian become Emperor of Rome?

2. In which year was F.W. de Klerk elected to the South African parliament?

3. In which year did Oswald become king of Northumbria?

4. The War of the Spanish Succession opened with the invasion by Austria of which country?

5. In which year did Brian Boru win the Battle of Clontarf?

6. Who was Roman emperor from 306 to 337A.D.?

7. Future president James Buchanan became Secretary of State in 1845 under which president?

8. In which year did El Cid die?

9. In which year was the Battle of Vouillé?

10. In which year in the 13c was the 'children's crusade'?

11. In which year did Oliver Cromwell first represent Huntingdon as Member of Parliament?

12. In which year did Robert Clive commit suicide?

13. In which year did Frederick Barbarossa become Holy Roman Emperor?

14. Who was Horatio Nelson second-in-command to at the Battle of Copenhagen?

15. In which year did Robert Walpole become Chancellor of the Exchequer?

GENERAL KNOWLEDGE

1. What is another name for the European sea eagle?

2. What is the name of the racecourse near Esher in North East Surrey?

3. Who wrote the 1987 novel *Empire*?

4. Who wrote the 1958 novel *A Ripple from the Storm*?

5. Which animal represents the zodiac sign Cancer?

6. Which English conductor authored the autobiography *My Own Trumpet*?

7. Who composed the 1849 narrative poem *Evangeline*?

8. On which river is the North East Bulgarian city of Ruse which is a chief river port of the country?

9. Who was Conservative Home Secretary from 1972-4?

10. Who was a Best Actress Oscar winner for her role as *Kitty Foyle*?

11. Which harbour in North Devon was devastated by flooding in 1952?

12. In which year did Albert Speer, architect and Nazi government official, die?

13. Who was author of the novel *Gormenghast*?

14. Who was author of *The Autobiography of Alice B. Toklas*?

15. To which genus does the mulberry tree belong?

ANSWERS 1. Erne 2. Sandown Park 3. Gore Vidal 4. Doris Lessing 5. Crab 6. Sir Adrian Boult 7. Longfellow 8. Danube 9. Robert Carr 10. Ginger Rogers 11. Lynmouth 12. 1981 13. Mervyn Peake 14. Gertrude Stein 15. Morus.

ENTERTAINMENT

1. Who scripted the 1985 film *Year of the Dragon*?

2. Who directed the 1990 film *Nightbreed* based on his novel *Cabal*?

3. In the 1995 sketch show *Jack and Jeremy's Police 4*, who played Jack and Jeremy?

4. Who directed the 1996 film *The Van*?

5. On which island is the 1957 film *Ill Met By Moonlight* set?

6. Which singer plays a singing nun in the 1974 film *Airport 1975*?

7. Which comedy duo hosted the 1999 quiz show *Casting Couch*?

8. Which comedian created the puppet series *The Bumblies*?

9. The 1998 film *The Alarmist* is based on which play by Keith Reddin?

10. Who scored the 1968 film *Inadmissible Evidence*?

11. *Shining in the Dark* was a 1999 *Omnibus* programme about which author?

12. In which year did comedienne Beryl Reid die?

13. Who does Kevin Kennedy play in *Coronation Street*?

14. Who starred as Tarzan in the 1918 film *Tarzan of the Apes*?

15. Who was first choice to play opposite James Stewart in the Hitchcock film *Vertigo*?

ANSWERS 1. Oliver Stone **2.** Clive Barker **3.** Jack Dee and Jeremy Hardy **4.** Stephen Frears **5.** Crete **6.** Helen Reddy **7.** Mel and Sue **8.** Michael Bentine **9.** Life During Wartime **10.** Dudley Moore **11.** Stephen King **12.** 1996 **13.** Norman 'Curly' Watts **14.** Elmo Lincoln **15.** Vera Miles.

SPORT

1. With which sport are Gustavo Thoeni and Hermann Maier associated?

2. For which rugby league team does Richard Horne play?

3. Franck Adisson and Wilfried Forgues won the men's C2 slalom event at the Canoe Slalom world championships in 1997. Which country did they represent?

4. Which sport do Cardiff Devils and Nottingham Panthers play?

5. Who was 1978 All-England Championships badminton women's singles title winner?

6. Who was 2000 All-England Championships badminton men's singles title winner?

7. Which jockey rode the 1978 St. Leger winner Julio Mariner?

8. Which male squash player won the 2000 Irish Open?

9. Which country were 1964 men's world champions in pétanque?

10. How old was Pete Sampras when he won his first Grand Slam tennis title?

11. With which sport do you associate Anni Friesinger and Gunda Niemann-Stiernemann?

12. Who knocked Siddal out of the 2000 Silk Cut Challenge Cup in rugby league?

13. By what aggregate score did Liverpool win the 1973 U.E.F.A. Cup?

14. In which Australian city was cricketer I.N. Blanchett born?

15. Which women's field event did Ilona Slupianek win at the I.A.A.F. World Cup from 1977-81?

ANSWERS 1. Skiing 2. Hull 3. France 4. Ice hockey 5. Gillian Gilks 6. Xia Xuanze 7. Eddie Hide 8. Peter Nicol 9. Algeria 10. 19 11. Speed skating 12. Leigh 13. 3-2 14. Melbourne 15. Shot.

POP

1. Which female singer had Top 10 single hits with *Fine Time* and *Stand Up For Your Love Rites*?

2. On which label is Belle and Sebastian's album *Tigermilk*?

3. Which group's B-sides include *Astral Conversations with Toulouse-Lautrec*?

4. Who had a 1999 Top 10 single with *(Much Mambo) Sway*?

5. From which country do the group Sigur Ros come?

6. Which group had a 1984 hit single with *Pearly-Dewdrops Drop*?

7. Which group recorded the 1979 single *Life in Tokyo*?

8. Which female singer had a No. 1 hit with *Mi Chico Latino*?

9. What was Bernard Butler's second solo album called?

10. Who composed the soundtrack for the film *Titanic*?

11. In which year did Sonia have a Top 10 single with *You'll Never Stop Me Loving You*?

12. Which female singer did Gregg Allman marry in 1975?

13. Who had a 2000 Top 10 hit with *Sitting Down Here*?

14. Which studio album by Leonard Cohen features the song *Hallelujah*?

15. Who recorded the 1999 album *The Writing's on the Wall*?

WORDS

1. What is the massage technique of acupressure also known as?

2. If you kvetch, what do you do?

3. What would you do with a homburg?

4. What type of farm animal is a hogget?

5. How many legs does a teapoy have?

6. What is hi-fi short for?

7. What is voile, a type of drink or a type of fabric?

8. Which branch of chemistry is concerned with fermentation processes in brewing?

9. What would Ugandan women do with a busuuti?

10. In biology, if something is acauline, what does it lack?

11. If you berate somebody what do you do to them?

12. How old is a sheep known as a teg?

13. What is a bilbo?

14. What in Australia is a bingle?

15. What word for a discriminating eater do we get from the Old French word *gromet* meaning *serving boy*?

ANSWERS 1. Shiatsu **2.** Incessantly complain **3.** Wear it – it's a hat **4.** A sheep **5.** Three **6.** High fidelity **7.** Fabric **8.** Zymurgy **9.** Wear it - it's a long short-sleeved garment **10.** A stem **11.** Scold them **12.** Two **13.** A type of sword **14.** A minor surfboard crash or car crash **15.** Gourmet.

GENERAL KNOWLEDGE

1. Pb is the symbol of which bluish-white element?

2. In Greek mythology, which hero of Corinth captured the horse Pegasus?

3. Which British animator's short films include 1993's *The Wrong Trousers*?

4. Whose poem, *Goblin Market*, was published in 1862?

5. Which country administered the coral island of Okinawa from 1945-72?

6. What is the name of the raven in the novel *Barnaby Rudge* by Charles Dickens?

7. In philately, what is a cachet?

8. Who wrote the 1973 play *Habeas Corpus*?

9. Which dark glassy volcanic rock is also called Iceland agate?

10. Which king in Greek legend was able to turn that which he touched into gold?

11. Who was the first man to swim the English Channel?

12. In which London borough is the TV soap opera *EastEnders* set?

13. Which British unit of weight is equal to 2240 pounds?

14. In which year was U.S. Democrat politician Jesse Jackson born?

15. Who starred as *Wyatt Earp* in the 1994 film *Tombstone*?

ANSWERS 1. Lead **2.** Bellerophon **3.** Nick Park **4.** Christina Rossetti **5.** The United States **6.** Grip **7.** A mark stamped by hand on mail for commemorative purposes **8.** Alan Bennett **9.** Obsidian **10.** King Midas **11.** Matthew Webb **12.** Walford **13.** A ton **14.** 1941 **15.** Kurt Russell.

ENTERTAINMENT

1. Which actor directed the 1997 film *Albino Alligator*?

2. Which private detective did Kathleen Turner play in a 1991 film based on novels by Sara Paretsky?

3. Which comedian played Danny McGlone in the 1987 TV drama *Tutti Frutti*?

4. Who played the lead in the 1956 film *The Eddy Duchin Story*?

5. Which former *EastEnders* actress formerly appeared on the children's show *The Saturday Banana*?

6. Who directed the 1992 film *Damage*?

7. In the 1976 film *Alex and the Gypsy*, who plays the gypsy?

8. Which TV company replaced Westward Television as ITV contractor for the Southwest of England in 1981?

9. Who played the Duke of Norfolk in the TV drama series *The Six Wives of Henry VIII*?

10. Who directed the 1959 film *Edge of Eternity*?

11. In which year did the BBC TV drama series *Mogul* begin?

12. Who directed the 1950 film *In a Lonely Place*?

13. Who created the sitcom *Tripper's Day*?

14. Who played Judy, the Judy in the 1975 TV drama *Trinity Tales*?

15. Who played Dr. Jekyll in the 1989 film *Edge of Sanity*?

SPORT

1. Who did Harlequins play in the 5th round of rugby union's Tetley's Bitter Cup in 2000?

2. Which wicket-keeper made seven dismissals for Derbyshire against Lancashire in their 1975 John Player League game?

3. In which city was footballer Paolo di Canio born?

4. In which year was the Amateur Gymnastics Association formed in Britain?

5. With which sport is Vladimir Samsonov associated?

6. Who won the 1952 and 1953 Dutch Grand Prix in Formula 1?

7. In which city in the southwest was cricketer P. D. Bowler born in 1963?

8. How many tries did George West score for Hull K. R. against Brookland Rovers in the rugby league Challenge Cup in 1905?

9. In which county is the National Federation of Anglers based?

10. Which country were 1979 men's ten-pin bowling doubles world champions?

11. Which athlete was 1978 BBC Sports Personality of the Year?

12. Which horse won the 1989 Cheltenham Gold Cup?

13. Who was the first Australian to be bowled out for 99 twice in Test cricket?

14. Who was 1976 Olympic women's 100m champion?

15. Which country won the 1939 Davis Cup in tennis?

ANSWERS 1. Darlington Mowden Park **2.** Bob Taylor **3.** Rome **4.** 1888 **5.** Table tennis **6.** Alberto Ascari **7.** Plymouth **8.** Eleven **9.** Derbyshire **10.** Australia **11.** Steve Ovett **12.** Dessert Orchid **13.** Greg Blewett **14.** Annegret Richter **15.** Australia.

POP

1. In which city did David Bowie propose to his wife Iman?

2. What is Joe Strummer's backing band called?

3. On which railway station did Paul Simon write the song *Homeward Bound*?

4. Which group recorded *Southern Mark Smith* on the album *Scandal in Bohemia*?

5. Who recorded the 1971 album *Songs for Beginners*?

6. Which artist is 'C' in the group C.P.R.?

7. Who were Marc Almond's backing band on the album *Vermin in Ermine*?

8. What is Public Enemy's singer Flavor Flav's real name?

9. Who recorded the 1985 album *Psychocandy*?

10. Who was guitarist in the group Fat Mattress?

11. Which male singer recorded the 1999 album of covers *My Beauty*?

12. Which ex-Beatle recorded the album *Run Devil Run*?

13. After which singer were band Jefferson Airplane named?

14. Which group had a 1999 Top 10 single with *Summer Son*?

15. Who produced the debut album by the group Alternative T.V., *The Image Has Cracked*?

THE CARLING PUB QUIZ BOOK

SCIENCE

1. Who discovered Thebe, a satellite of Jupiter in 1980?

2. In which year was Tethys, a moon of the planet Saturn, discovered?

3. In which city did Sir Humphry Davy die in 1829?

4. Which Russian chemist became director of the Bureau of Weights and Measures in St. Petersburg in 1893?

5. Which Austrian scientist founded the spiritual movement named anthroposophy?

6. In which city was British scientist Paul Dirac born?

7. What is the name of the daughter of Marie and Pierre Curie who contributed to the discovery of the neutron?

8. The moon Ariel orbits Uranus approximately how often?

9. What was the nickname given to the Lockheed F-117A aircraft by the U.S.A.F.?

10. Which British scientist won the 1921 Nobel prize for chemistry?

11. What is the atomic number of argon?

12. Who was Professor of Physics at McGill University in Montreal from 1898-1907?

13. In which year did the first Spacelab fly?

14. What, on the internet, do the initials www stand for?

15. What, in the field of parapsychology, do the initials P.K. represent?

ANSWERS 1. Stephen Synnott 2. 1684 3. Geneva 4. Mendeleyev 5. Rudolf Steiner 6. Bristol 7. Irène 8. 2.5 days 9. Wobblin' Gobblin' 10. Frederick Soddy 11. 18 12. Ernest Rutherford 13. 1983 14. World Wide Web 15. Psychokinesis.

GENERAL KNOWLEDGE

1. Who was second son of Adam and Eve in the Old Testament?

2. On which river is the Texas city of Laredo?

3. In which year was British fashion designer Mary Quant born?

4. For which 1960 film was Spencer Tracy a Best Actor Oscar nominee?

5. Which city in South Africa is capital of the former Transkei Bantu homeland?

6. In which year did German idealist philosopher Immanuel Kant die?

7. Which comic servant is lover of Columbine in the commedia dell'arte?

8. Who authored the play *Loot*?

9. In which year did playwright and actor Noël Coward die?

10. What is the name of the range of mountains in Antarctica on the coast of Victoria Land northwest of the Ross Sea?

11. Which estuary in France is formed by the confluence of the Rivers Dordogne and Garonne?

12. Who was the Austrian author of the novel *The Man Without Qualities*?

13. Who was a Best Actress Oscar nominee for the film *Leaving Las Vegas*?

14. What was the name of the character played by Antonio Fargas in the TV cop show *Starsky and Hutch*?

15. What is the fourth letter in the Greek alphabet?

THE CARLING PUB QUIZ BOOK

ENTERTAINMENT

1. Which comedian's catchphrases included "You Lucky People"?

2. Who was Milburn Drysdale's P.A. at the Commerce Bank in the sitcom *The Beverly Hillbillies*?

3. Who played Matt Taylor in the 1980s TV drama *Triangle*?

4. Which tennis player replaced Anneka Rice on the Channel 4 show *Treasure Hunt*?

5. Who plays Edith Piaf in the 1983 film *Edith and Marcel*?

6. Which former *EastEnders* actor was Sidney the Milkman in the radio soap *Mrs. Dale's Diary*?

7. Who directed the 1940 film *Santa Fe Trail*?

8. What was the name of Lomax's canal boat in the 1980s TV drama *Travelling Man*?

9. Who created the sitcom *Bewitched*?

10. Who performed the theme song to the BBC TV drama series *Trainer*?

11. Which playwright scripted the 1997 film *Alive and Kicking*?

12. Who directed the 1999 film *Pushing Tin*

13. Which disc jockey starred in the 1971 TV sketch show *Ev*?

14. Who plays Hayley in Radio 4's *The Archers*?

15. Who played patriarch John Walton in TV's *The Waltons*?

SPORT

1. Which team won the 1952 Olympic football tournament?

2. Who scored a hat-trick of tries for Ireland in their 2000 Six Nations victory over France?

3. With which sport are Vladimir Salnikov and Adrian Moorhouse associated?

4. In golf, at which course in Scotland was the 1923 Walker Cup held?

5. Which team were champions of Division 1 in football in 1999/00?

6. Which Briton was 1997 world long-track speedway champion?

7. Who is trainer of the horse Istabraq?

8. What nationality was the cricketer Mike Procter?

9. By what score did England beat France in Paris in the 2000 Six Nations tournament?

10. Which man won the 1986 Biathlon World Cup?

11. At which sport does Winston Gordon represent Britain?

12. Which horse won the 1972 Prix de l'Arc de Triomphe?

13. Who beat Marco Antonio Barrera to retain his W.B.C. super-bantamweight boxing title in February 2000?

14. In rugby league, which club won the 1997 Super League World Club Championship?

15. What nationality was 1973 women's European water-skiing champion Sylvie Maurial?

ANSWERS 1. Hungary **2.** Brian O'Driscoll **3.** Swimming **4.** St. Andrews **5.** Charlton **6.** Steve Schofield **7.** Aidan O'Brien **8.** South African **9.** 15-9 **10.** André Sehmisch **11.** Judo **12.** San San **13.** Erik Morales **14.** Brisbane Broncos **15.** French.

POP

1. On which label is the album *To Venus and Back* by Tori Amos?

2. Which group's singles include *Real, Real, Real* and *Right Here, Right Now*?

3. Who produced Muse's album *Showbiz*?

4. Who recorded the 1999 album *Mobile Home*?

5. Who replaced Keith Dayton in group Sneaker Pimps?

6. Adam Duritz is lead singer with which group?

7. Who won the 1999 Mercury Music Prize with the album *OK*?

8. Which group recorded the 2000 album *WYSIWYG*?

9. Which group recorded the 1985 album *Easy Pieces*?

10. Who had a 1999 Top 10 single with *Unpretty*?

11. Whose debut album is entitled *The Magic Treehouse*?

12. In which year did Elton John have a Top 10 single with *Passengers*?

13. What is the surname of Melanie C of the Spice Girls?

14. Who had a Top 10 single in 1985 with *Things Can Only Get Better*?

15. Which Welsh band headlined a Millennium gig at Cardiff Arms Park on December 31st 1999?

ANSWERS 1. EastWest **2.** Jesus Jones **3.** John Leckie **4.** Longpigs **5.** Chris Corner **6.** Counting Crows **7.** Talvin Singh **8.** Chumbawamba **9.** Lloyd Cole and the Commotions **10.** TLC **11.** Oobermann **12.** 1984 **13.** Chisholm **14.** Howard Jones **15.** Manic Street Preachers.

PEOPLE

1. In which century did Kublai Khan live?

2. In which year was designer Tommy Hilfiger born?

3. Of which country was Babrak Karmal president from 1979-86?

4. What was the nickname of U.S. senator Albert Benjamin Chandler, who died in 1991?

5. Which singer-actor has written the autobiography *True*?

6. In which year was singer George Harrison born?

7. Which Cornishman predicted the existence of the planet Neptune in 1845?

8. In which English county was Arctic explorer Sir John Franklin born?

9. What was boxer Joe Louis's original surname?

10. Who was awarded the Nobel prize for economics in 1976?

11. What was the nickname of businessman and entrepreneur R.W. Rowland who died in 1998?

12. Which member of the royal family suffered a stroke whilst on holiday in Mustique in February 1998?

13. In which year was fashion designer Giorgio Armani born?

14. Which theatrical impressario built the Savoy Theatre in 1881?

15. In which year did Mother Teresa die?

GENERAL KNOWLEDGE

1. From which city of the Philistines did the giant Goliath come?

2. What is the name given to the branch of medicine concerned with childbirth?

3. In which year was New Zealand cricketer Sir Richard Hadlee born?

4. In which year did U.S. saxophone player Stan Getz die?

5. Who wrote the 1910 novel *The History of Mr.Polly*?

6. What unit of length is equal to 0.621 mile?

7. Which Finnish architect invented bent plywood furniture?

8. What is the colour of the ball worth seven points in snooker?

9. Who wrote the 1881 play *Ghosts*?

10. Which Czechoslovakian-born tennis player was U.S. Open men's singles champion from 1985-7?

11. Who was Australian prime minister from 1966-7?

12. Who was world middleweight boxing champion from 1980-7?

13. In which novel by Thomas Hardy is Gabriel Oak a character?

14. Which city in central Portugal was the residence of the Portuguese court in the 15th and 16th centuries?

15. What is the name by which Indian leader Jawaharlal Nehru was known?

ANSWERS 1. Gath **2.** Obstetrics **3.** 1951 **4.** 1991 **5.** H.G. Wells **6.** Kilometre **7.** Alvar Aalto **8.** Seven **9.** Henrik Ibsen **10.** Ivan Lendl **11.** Harold Holt **12.** Marvin Hagler **13.** Far from the Madding Crowd **14.** Evora **15.** Pandit.

ENTERTAINMENT

1. Which comedian played a fruit-selling barrow boy in the 1955 film *The Lady Killers*?

2. Who played the lead in the 1987 film *Allan Quatermain and the Lost City of Gold*?

3. Which singer did Gary Mullen, the winner of the 2000 *Stars in Their Eyes* grand final, impersonate?

4. Which actor played the lead in the 1950s TV show *Cheyenne*?

5. Who play the Gecko Brothers in the 1996 film *From Dusk Till Dawn*?

6. Which French singer starred in the 1991 biopic *Van Gogh*?

7. Who played Warren Beatty's parents in the 1962 film *All Fall Down*?

8. Which comedian starred as *Bob Martin* in the 2000 ITV drama?

9. What was car no. 1 in the cartoon series *Wacky Races*?

10. Who directed 1979 film *Agatha*?

11. What nationality was opera singer Brigitte Fassbaender?

12. Who directed the 1946 spy film *Cloak and Dagger*?

13. Who played Burt Lancaster's father in the 1948 film *All My Sons*?

14. Who directed the 1960 film *Tunes of Glory*?

15. Which comedy actress played Caroline Fairchild in the sitcom *Executive Stress*?

ANSWERS 1. Frankie Howerd **2.** Richard Chamberlain **3.** Freddie Mercury **4.** Clint Walker **5.** Quentin Tarantino and George Clooney **6.** Jacques Dutronc **7.** Karl Malden and Angela Lansbury **8.** Michael Barrymore **9.** The Boulder Mobile **10.** Michael Apted **11.** German **12.** Fritz Lang **13.** Edward G. Robinson **14.** Ronald Neame **15.** Penelope Keith.

THE CARLING PUB QUIZ BOOK

SPORT

1. Who, in 1996, won four TT wins on the Isle of Man?

2. What is the nickname of Whitwell-born cricketer C. J. Adams?

3. Which club won the 1973/4 Scottish First Division?

4. What nationality is rugby league player Yacine Dekkiche?

5. Who won the 1987 Fukuoka men's marathon?

6. What nationality is rugby union referee Stuart Dickinson?

7. The road known as the Koppenberg is a feature of which cycle race?

8. At what age did cricketer John Blain make his debut for Scotland?

9. How many times did jockey John Osborne win the 2000 Guineas from 1857-88?

10. Who did Wasps play in the quarter-finals of the Tetley's Bitter Cup in rugby union in 2000?

11. In which car did Gerald Burgess and Sam Croft-Pearson win the 1959 R.A.C. Rally?

12. In which year did French tennis player Max Decugis die?

13. At what Olympic sport have Henry Bailey and Jean-Pierre Amat been champions?

14. In which year was the British Olympic Association founded?

15. At which weight did Leo Randolph win a 1976 Olympic boxing gold?

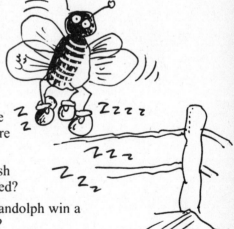

ANSWERS 1. Phillip McCallen **2.** Grizzly **3.** Celtic **4.** French **5.** Takeyuki Nakayama **6.** Australian **7.** Tour of Flanders **8.** 17 years **9.** Six **10.** Manchester **11.** Ford Zephyr **12.** 1978 **13.** Shooting **14.** 1905 **15.** Flyweight.

POP

1. Who was drummer in the group The Only Ones?

2. Who co-wrote the punk song *Chinese Rocks*?

3. In which year was songwriter Fred Neil born?

4. What is D.J. Eric B.'s surname?

5. Who recorded the 2000 solo album *The Secret Language of Birds*?

6. Which former members of the Human League produced Tina Turner's hit *Let's Stay Together*?

7. What is the title of the 2000 album by the Blue Aeroplanes?

8. The group Cosmic Rough Riders are from which Scottish city?

9. Who recorded the 1999 album *Us and Us Only*?

10. Which solo artist had a 1989 Top 10 single with *Leave A Light On*?

11. Which punk singer was born Richard Meyers in 1949?

12. Which Irish group recorded the 2000 album *Water from the Well*?

13. Which Scottish group's only album was *Morning Dove White*?

14. Which singer-songwriter recorded the albums *Blue Afternoon* and *Starsailor*?

15. In which year was Jimi Hendrix's album *Are You Experienced?* released?

ANSWERS 1. Mike Kellie **2.** Dee Dee Ramone and Johnny Thunders **3.** 1937 **4.** Barrier **5.** Ian Anderson **6.** Ian Craig Marsh and Martyn Ware **7.** Cavaliers **8.** Glasgow **9.** The Charlatans **10.** Belinda Carlisle **11.** Richard Hell **12.** The Chieftains **13.** One Dove **14.** Tim Buckley **15.** 1967.

ART

1. Which sculptor's busts include 1934's *George Bernard Shaw* and 1945's *Yehudi Menuhin*?

2. In which city is El Greco buried?

3. Dorothea Brooke features in which novel by George Eliot?

4. In which year did Leonardo da Vinci enter the service of Cesare Borgia?

5. What is the sequel to Mikhail Sholokhov's *And Quiet Flows the Don*?

6. In which year was George Eliot's novel *Felix Holt* first published?

7. In which city was painter Sir John Everett Millais born?

8. What was Anne Brontë's first novel?

9. In which century did painter Bartolomé Murillo live?

10. What was the first novel of U.S. author Ralph Ellison?

11. Which painter's works include 1949's *Rectangular Motif in Black and White*?

12. Which U.S. author's short stories include *Go Down, Moses*?

13. In which city was Picasso born in 1881?

14. Which film director authored the stories *Night in Tunisia* and *The Dream of a Beast*?

15. Which French artist's works include 1634's *Adoration of the Golden Calf*?

GENERAL KNOWLEDGE

1. What is the standard monetary unit of Iceland?

2. Who was a Best Actor Oscar nominee for the 1954 film *A Star is Born*?

3. Which Greek hero of the Trojan War killed himself when the armour of Achilles was given to Odysseus?

4. Who was the 1960 Olympic men's 1500m champion?

5. What is the name of the Royal house that ruled in England from 1603-1714?

6. In which year did J. Paul Getty, U.S. millionaire oil executive and art collector, die?

7. What is the name of the Liverpool railway station built in 1867?

8. What type of bird is a nene?

9. Who was a Best Supporting Actress Oscar winner for the film *West Side Story*?

10. Who were the male and female leads in the 1939 film western *Dodge City*?

11. Oxon is an abbreviation for which English county?

12. Which playwright directed and scripted the 1991 film *Homicide*?

13. In which novel by Thackeray does the character Blanche Amory appear?

14. What is the largest lake in Italy?

15. For which 1993 film was Holly Hunter a Best Actress Oscar nominee?

ANSWERS 1. Krona **2.** James Mason **3.** Ajax **4.** Herb Elliott **5.** Stuart **6.** 1976 **7.** Lime Street **8.** A black-and-grey Hawaiian goose **9.** Rita Moreno **10.** Errol Flynn and Olivia de Havilland **11.** Oxfordshire **12.** David Mamet **13.** The History of Pendennis **14.** Lake Garda **15.** The Piano.

THE CARLING PUB QUIZ BOOK

ENTERTAINMENT

1. In which opera does the giant Fasolt appear?

2. Who directed the 1999 film *The Winslow Boy*?

3. Who composed the 1859 opera *Faust*?

4. Which female U.S. musician starred in the 1987 film *The Allnighter*?

5. Who wrote the 1990 comedy serial *The Gravy Train*?

6. Which comedy actress played Jane Edwards in the sitcom *Waiting For God*?

7. Who played a martian in the 1989 Channel 4 show *The Groovy Fellers*?

8. Who played Flint McCullough in the U.S. TV show *Wagon Train*?

9. Who composed the 1888 opera *The Fairies*?

10. Who starred as the abductor of Kiefer Sutherland's girlfriend in the 1993 film *The Vanishing*?

11. Who played poet Roland Milk in the 1970s comedy show *Grub Street*?

12. In which year did comedian Harry H. Corbett die?

13. Who played Brother Benjamin in the 1980s sitcom *Hallelujah!*?

14. Who composed the 1840 opera *The Favourite?*

15. Who directed the 1950 film *Panic in the Streets*?

ANSWERS 1. Das Rheingold **2.** David Mamet **3.** Gounod **4.** Susanna Hoffs **5.** Malcolm Bradbury **6.** Janine Duvitski **7.** Roland Rivron **8.** Robert Horton **9.** Wagner **10.** Jeff Bridges **11.** Julian Orchard **12.** 1982 **13.** David Daker **14.** Donizetti **15.** Elia Kazan

SPORT

1. Where were the 1985 World Student Games held?

2. In which city were the first figure skating world championships held in 1896?

3. Which boxer was 1985 BBC Sports Personality of the Year?

4. Who were Eastern Division winners of the A.F.C. Conference in American Football in 1970?

5. Sherwood Stewart and Ferdi Taygan won the 1982 French Open men's doubles tennis championship. Which country are they from?

6. Albert Iten was 1991 men's downhill mountain biking champion. Which country did he represent?

7. What sport do Michelle Rogers and Chloe Cowen take part in?

8. Which man was British Open squash champion in 1938?

9. Who lost the 1979 Scottish F.A. Cup Final on a second replay?

10. What nationality is Formula 1 driver Marc Gené?

11. How many Olympic gold medals did shooter Otto Olsen win from 1920-4?

12. What nationality is tennis player Marat Safin?

13. With what Olympic sport do you associate Olaf Heukrodt and Larry Cain?

14. Who was captain of the Zimbabwe touring cricket side in the West Indies in 2000?

15. Who was 1925 men's world cross-country champion?

POP

1. On which label is Asian Dub Foundation's *Community Music* album?

2. Which U.S. punk group recorded the LP *Young Loud and Snotty*?

3. Who recorded the 1999 album *This Constant Chase for Thrills*?

4. Which Welsh group recorded the 1974 LP *Wish You Were Here*?

5. With which group did Tom Jones record the Talking Heads song *Burning Down the House*?

6. Of which band is Hanin Elias lead singer?

7. Who recorded the 2000 album *The Noise Made By People*?

8. Who is writer and lead singer with the group The Mighty Wah!?

9. Which singer recorded the 2000 album *Voodoo*?

10. Which singer recorded the 1999 album *hours ...*?

11. Which group recorded the 1968 LP *The Third Testament*?

12. In which year did guitarist Danny Gratton kill himself?

13. On which label did Gorky's Zygotic Mynci record the 1999 album *Spanish Dance Troupe*?

14. In which year did Depeche Mode have a Top 10 single with *Master and Servant*?

15. What was the second album by the Eurythmics?

GEOGRAPHY

1. Which country is to the immediate north of Bulgaria?

2. Dalmatia is a region of which European country?

3. Rousay and Stronsay are part of which island group?

4. What is the name of the inlet of the Bosporus in Turkey which forms the harbour of Istanbul?

5. Girdle Ness is south-east of which Scottish city?

6. Which Irish county is south-east of County Carlow?

7. In which ocean is the volcanic island of Ascension?

8. Which inland port in Yorkshire lies at the confluence of the Rivers Don and Ouse?

9. What is the name of the strait in Denmark linking the Baltic Sea with the Kattegat?

10. Bantry is in which county of the Republic of Ireland?

11. To the nearest mile, how long is Coniston Water?

12. Which town houses Israel's chief airport?

13. The coral islands called the Dry Tortugas are part of which U.S. state?

14. The town of Llandaff is a suburb of which Welsh city?

15. In which year did Bahrain become an independent state?

ANSWERS 1. Romania **2.** Croatia **3.** Orkneys **4.** Golden Horn **5.** Aberdeen **6.** Wexford **7.** Atlantic **8.** Goole **9.** Great Belt **10.** Cork **11.** Five miles **12.** Lod **13.** Florida **14.** Cardiff **15.** 1971.

GENERAL KNOWLEDGE

1. In which county is the town of High Wycombe?

2. Which sailing competition culminates in the Fastnet Race?

3. Who was Best Actor Oscar-winner for the film *Patton*?

4. Who is the central character in the novel *The Honourable Schoolboy* by John Le Carré?

5. In which year did U.S. jazz musician Count Basie die?

6. Which port lies on the Atlantic at the easternmost point of Brazil?

GEORGE

7. Who was the father of Icarus in Greek mythology?

8. Which leguminous West Indian shrub is a source of indigo?

9. Who authored the 1973 novel *The Irish Witch*?

10. Who was 1976 Olympic men's downhill skiing champion?

11. Who authored the 1936 novel *Maiden Castle*?

12. Who was a Best Actress Oscar nominee for the film *The Collector*?

13. Which actor played a child murderer in the 1931 film *M*?

14. Who was prime minister of Rhodesia from 1964-79?

15. Which river forms most of the border between Cornwall and Devon?

ANSWERS 1. Buckinghamshire **2.** The Admiral's Cup **3.** George C. Scott **4.** George Smiley **5.** 1984 **6.** Recife **7.** Daedalus **8.** Anil **9.** Dennis Wheatley **10.** Franz Klammer **11.** John Cowper Powys **12.** Samantha Eggar **13.** Peter Lorre **14.** Ian Smith **15.** Tamar.

ENTERTAINMENT

1. Which actor/singer narrates the *The Legend of Sleepy Hollow* segment of the 1949 Disney film *The Adventures of Ichabod and Mr. Toad*?

2. In which year did the opera *Eugene Onegin* premier?

3. Who played Alan Brady in the 1960s sitcom *The Dick Van Dyke Show*?

4. Who played Lt. Colonel Ian Jennings in the TV drama *Soldier, Soldier*?

5. Who did Jacqui Cann impersonate to win *Stars in Their Eyes* in 1993?

6. Who directed the 1952 film *Adventures of Robinson Crusoe* starring Dan O'Herlihy?

7. In which year was newsreader Jon Snow born?

8. Which comedian starred in the film *Me, Myself and Irene*?

9. What was the number of Dick Dastardly's car 'The Mean Machine' in the cartoon show *Wacky Races*?

10. Who won Best Original Song Oscar in 2000 for *You'll Be In My Heart*?

11. Which veteran actress died shortly after the film *Valmont*, in which she appeared, was released in 1989?

12. What is the title of Harry Enfield's 2000 cinema release?

13. Which *Blue Peter* presenter announced she was to leave the show in 2000?

14. Who played the lead in the 1944 film *The Adventures of Mark Twain*?

15. Who played Kimberly Drummond in the sitcom *Different Strokes*?

SPORT

1. Who knocked Batley out of the 2000 Silk Cut Challenge Trophy in rugby league?

2. Which jockey rode the Epsom Derby winner from 1921-3?

3. Who beat Yevgeny Kafelnikov in the final of the A.T.P. Legg Mason Classic in August 1999?

4. Where were the 1952 Winter Olympic Games held?

5. At what weight did Audley Harrison box?

6. Who was 1992 Olympic women's 5000m speed skating champion?

7. Which sport do you associate with Carlos Sainz and Marcus Gronholm?

8. Who scored Liverpool's winner in the 1978 European Champion Clubs' Cup Final?

9. Who won the 1999 Rally of Finland to take his twenty-third world championship rally?

10. In which year were the World Indoor Championships for athletics first held, in Bercy, France?

11. Which football team won the Scottish Premier League in 1999/00?

12. How many dismissals did Australian wicket-keeper Tim Zoehrer make in his career from 1980-94?

13. Which motorcyclist won the Czech 500cc Grand Prix in August 1999?

14. Which woman golfer won the 1990 Nabisco Dinah Shore tournament?

15. With which sport are Brigitte Bécue and Agnes Kovacs associated?

ANSWERS 1. Oldham St. Annes **2.** Steve Donoghue **3.** Andre Agassi **4.** Oslo **5.** Super-heavyweight **6.** Gunda Niemann **7.** Rallying **8.** Kenny Dalglish **9.** Juha Kankkunen **10.** 1985 **11.** Rangers **12.** 461 **13.** Tadayuki Okada **14.** Betsy King **15.** Swimming.

POP

1. *Pod* was the 1990 debut album from which group?

2. Which former member of the Beatles recorded the 1993 album *Off the Ground*?

3. Who had a 2000 Top 10 single with *Cartoon Heroes*?

4. At which Liverpool club did Echo and the Bunnymen play their first gig?

5. Neu! members Klaus Dinger and Michael Rother were formerly in which German group?

6. Which solo artist had a 1989 Top 10 single with *Right Here Waiting*?

7. On which label did Simply Red record the album *Love and the Russian Winter*?

8. Who had a Top 10 single in March 2000 with *Killer*?

9. In which year did Brinsley Schwarz play their last gig?

10. In which year was Fern Kinney's *Together We Are Beautiful* a Top 10 hit?

11. Who is leader of the group Half Man Half Biscuit?

12. In which year did Johnny Ace die whilst playing Russian Roulette?

13. Which former singer with Duke Ellington's band died in prison in 1968?

14. Who was organ player in the group Inspiral Carpets?

15. Amoo, Amoo, Lake, Smith. Which 1970s chart-topping group?

ANSWERS 1. The Breeders **2.** Paul McCartney **3.** Aqua **4.** Eric's **5.** Kraftwerk **6.** Richard Marx **7.** EastWest **8.** ATB **9.** 1975 **10.** 1980 **11.** Nigel Blackwell **12.** 1954 **13.** Little Willie John **14.** Clint Boon **15.** Real Thing.

HISTORY

1. In which U.S. state was the Battle of Cedar Mountain fought in 1862?

2. In which year was Johann Friedrich Struensee, German-born Danish statesman, executed?

3. In which year was the Vinegar Hill rebellion in Ireland?

4. Who commanded the German 6th Army which advanced into Stalingrad in August 1942?

5. In which year was Eleanor Roosevelt born?

6. In which year did Henry VIII's adviser Thomas Cromwell die?

7. Who succeeded Antonius Pius as Roman emperor in 161?

8. Who commanded U.S. forces in South Vietnam from 1964-68?

9. In which year did Napoleon I die?

10. What was the sister company of the Dutch East India Company?

11. In which year was Giuseppe Garibaldi born?

12. Which Kent-born statesman discovered the Babington Plot?

13. Who became mayor of Plymouth in 1581?

14. In which year did Prince Rudolf of Austria die at Mayerling?

15. Which German army officer tried to assassinate Hitler in 1944?

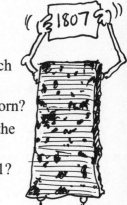

GENERAL KNOWLEDGE

1. Who was the 1964 Olympic men's 1500m champion?

2. Who was the first president of the Republic of Indonesia?

3. Who authored the 1929 novel *The Near and the Far*?

4. Who was the 1993 U.S. Open women's singles tennis champion?

5. What is the name given to the third epoch of the Tertiary period of geological time?

6. What is the name of the tiger in Kipling's *The Jungle Book*?

7. For which 1947 film were Robert Ryan and Gloria Grahame Best Supporting Actor and Actress nominees?

8. Who wrote the 1951 story collection *The Ballad of the Sad Café*?

9. What, in Japan, is a kakemono?

10. In which county is the market town of Pontefract, which houses a racecourse?

11. Who was the Welsh author of the play *Night Must Fall*?

12. Which German poet authored the novel *The Sorrows of Young Werther*?

13. Who was a Best Actor Oscar nominee for the film *The Prince of Tides*?

14. Which river of North Yorkshire flows to the Swale to form the Ouse?

15. What is the longest river in France?

ANSWERS 1. Peter Snell **2.** Achmed Sukarno **3.** L. H. Myers **4.** Steffi Graf **5.** Oligocene **6.** Shere Khan **7.** Crossfire **8.** Carson McCullers **9.** A paper or silk wall hanging with a roller at the bottom of it **10.** West Yorkshire **11.** Emlyn Williams **12.** Johann Wolfgang von Goethe **13.** Nick Nolte **14.** Ure **15.** Loire.

ENTERTAINMENT

1. Which actress played a palaeontologist in the film *Lake Placid*?

2. Who directed the 1995 film *Vampire in Brooklyn*?

3. Who were Harry Hill's backing group on his 2000 Channel 4 TV show?

4. In which year did opera singer Sir Geraint Evans make his London debut?

5. Who did Peter O'Brien play in the soap opera *Neighbours*?

6. In which Verdi opera does Roman general Ezio appear?

7. Who played Karen Betts in the TV show *Bad Girls*?

8. Who directed the film *Any Given Sunday*?

9. Which actress played the wife of Clint Eastwood and Lee Marvin in the film *Paint Your Wagon*?

10. Who directed the 1975 film *The Yazuka*?

11. Who played Greta Garbo's husband in the 1934 film *The Painted Veil*?

12. Which comedian played historian David Oxley in the spoof TV show *We Are History*?

13. Which comedy duo star in the 1932 film *Pack Up Your Troubles*?

14. Who played Fanny Price in the 2000 film *Mansfield Park*?

15. Who directed the 1990 film *Pacific Heights*?

SPORT

1. Which New Zealander won the 1960 Argentine Grand Prix in Formula 1?

2. How many golds did Spain win in the 1999 World Athletics Championships?

3. Which club have won the rugby league Challenge Cup the most times?

4. Who beat England men's hockey team in the semi-finals of the 1999 European Cup?

5. Nobuaki Kobayashi was 1984 world champion at what ball game?

6. Which athlete was 1987 BBC Sports Personality of the Year?

7. Which horse was leading moneywinner in Britain in 1966?

8. By what score did Argentina beat Scotland at rugby union in August 1999?

9. Who was women's marathon champion at the 1983 world athletics championships?

10. Who partnered Anne Smith in their 1980 French Open mixed doubles tennis championship victory?

11. In which city was the international governing body of fencing, the F.I.E., founded in 1913?

12. Cypheus Bunton is captain of which UK basketball team?

13. Who was 1988 Olympic women's 400m individual medley swimming champion?

14. Which Spanish golfer won the 1994 U.S. Masters tournament?

15. Who was manager of Birmingham City in football in 1999/00?

ANSWERS 1. Bruce McLaren **2.** Two **3.** Wigan **4.** Germany **5.** Three-Cushion Billiards **6.** Fatima Whitbread **7.** Charlottetown **8.** 31-22 **9.** Grete Waitz **10.** Bill Martin **11.** Paris **12.** Derby Storm **13.** Janet Evans **14.** José-Maria Olazabal **15.** Trevor Francis.

POP

1. For which label did Bronski Beat record the 1984 Top 10 single *Why??*

2. In which year was Chris Rea born?

3. Who had a 1992 hit single with *Searchin' For My Rizla*?

4. 1993's *Bellyache* was the debut of which group?

5. Who featured on Eddie Murphy's 1993 single *I Was A King*?

6. Which group recorded the 1990 album *Nomads Indians Saints*?

7. Who features on Dr. Dre's 2000 Top 10 single *Still Dre*?

8. In which year did Alex Harvey die?

9. In which year did Maria McKee form Lone Justice?

10. *It's Her Factory* is the B-side of which single by the Gang of Four?

11. In which year was Chic's album *C'est Chic* released?

12. Which group were the first signings to The Beastie Boys' *Grand Royal* record label?

13. Who is the mother of singer Kirsty MacColl?

14. *All Night Party* was the debut single of which Manchester group?

15. What is the surname of Katrina of the group Katrina and the Waves?

ANSWERS 1. Forbidden Fruit **2.** 1951 **3.** Ratpack **4.** Echobelly **5.** Shabba Ranks **6.** Indigo Girls **7.** Snoop Dogg **8.** 1982 **9.** 1982 **10.** At Home He's A Tourist **11.** 1978 **12.** Luscious Jackson **13.** Peggy Seeger **14.** A Certain Ratio **15.** Leskanich.

WORDS

1. What is a kris in Indonesia?

2. What is the U.S. equivalent of the game hide-and-seek?

3. What is a lanneret - a bird or an insect?

4. What is a lickspittle?

5. Who would work with a matched sample?

6. What is a temblor in the U.S.?

7. What is the name given to petroleum before it has been refined?

8. What type of creature is an ai?

9. What two-letter word describes a loose-fitting suit worn in martial arts?

10. The illness croup affects which part of a child's body?

11. What would a priest do with an alb?

12. What would you do with a ländler in Austria - dance it or ride in it?

13. What, specifically, in U.S. slang is a top banana?

14. What would a woman have done with a peplos in ancient Greece?

15. Numbles is food taken from which animal?

GENERAL KNOWLEDGE

1. Which two actors played the Riddler in the 1960s TV show *Batman*?

2. Who wrote the 1984 novel *Money*?

3. What is the 16th letter in the Greek alphabet?

4. Who wrote the 1980 novel *Snow Falcon*?

5. Which pop group had a 1974 No. 1 single with *Tiger Feet*?

6. Who was 1998 Commonwealth Games men's 400m champion?

7. In which ship did Francis Drake circumnavigate the world?

8. Who was a Best Actress Oscar nominee for the film *Little Women*?

9. What is the name given to the system of training to music originally taught by Émile Jacques-Dalcroze?

10. Who was 1981 U.S. P.G.A. golf champion?

11. In which European country is the port of Setubal?

12. Of which county of the Republic of Ireland is Tralee the county town?

13. Who wrote the 1953 play *The Lark*?

14. Which Florentine painter's works include *The Battle of San Romano, 1432*?

15. Which daughter of *King Lear* poisons her sister Regan in a play by Shakespeare?

ANSWERS 1. Frank Gorshin and John Astin **2.** Martin Amis **3.** Pi **4.** Craig Thomas **5.** Mud **6.** Iwan Thomas **7.** The Golden Hind **8.** Winona Ryder **9.** Eurythmics **10.** Larry Nelson **11.** Portugal **12.** Kerry **13.** Jean Anouilh **14.** Paolo Uccello **15.** Goneril.

ENTERTAINMENT

1. Who was the announcer on the sitcom *Soap*?

2. The 1988 science-fiction film *Nightfall* is based on whose classic short story?

3. In which year did Richard Digance become a professional entertainer?

4. Who directed the 1970 Hammer horror film *The Vampire Lovers*?

5. Who directed the 1972 film *The Nightcomers* starring Marlon Brando?

6. Which city is the setting for Pier Paolo Pasolini's 1961 film *Accatone*?

7. Which pop star narrated the 1999 animated film *Hooves of Fire*?

8. Which actor played Mr. Goldberg in the sitcom *Are You Being Served?*?

9. In the 1974 film *Earthquake*, what relationship is Ava Gardner's character to that of Lorne Greene?

10. Who wrote the score for the 1976 film *Taxi Driver*?

11. What is Kevin Kline's profession in the 1990 film *I Love You To Death*?

12. What is James Stewart's character name in the film *Harvey*?

13. What is Elvis Presley's profession in the 1967 film *Easy Come, Easy Go*?

14. Who directedthe 1956 film *Tea and Sympathy*?

15. Which silent comedy star played a bus driver in the 1944 film *San Diego, I Love You*?

ANSWERS 1. Rod Roddy **2.** Isaac Asimov **3.** 1973 **4.** Roy Ward Baker **5.** Michael Winner **6.** Rome **7.** Robbie Williams **8.** Alfie Bass **9.** Daughter **10.** Bernard Herrmann **11.** Owner of a pizzeria **12.** Elwood P. Dowd **13.** Frogman **14.** Vincente Minnelli **15.** Buster Keaton.

SPORT

1. With which winter sport is the Worldloppet Cup associated?

2. Who was 1999 winner of the Australian Grand Prix in Formula 1?

3. In which country was cricketer Mike Procter born?

4. What nationality is runner Kutre Dulecha?

5. Between 15th May - 16th July 1941, how many consecutive games did baseball player Joe DiMaggio bat safely?

6. Which country did athlete Juliet Cuthbert represent?

7. Which horse won the 1994 Haydock Park Sprint Cup?

8. Which country did athlete Silvio Leonard represent?

9. At what sport was James Dear world champion from 1955-7?

10. In which year did cricketer Rupesh Amin make his county debut for Surrey?

11. How many nations were there in the Fédération Internationale de Korfball in 1970?

12. Which country is host to the international governing body of trampolining, the F.I.T.?

13. In which year did England's football team last win the British Home International Championship?

14. What nationality is weightlifter Li Feng-Ying?

15. Which man set a world record of 26:43.53 for the 10,000m on 5th June 1995?

POP

1. What is the debut album of Manchester group Doves?

2. Which studio album by Genesis includes the tracks *Cuckoo Cocoon* and *In the Rapids*?

3. Which group recorded the track *Disneyland Forever* on the album *Songs of Strength & Heartbreak*?

4. Which drummer with Chilli Willi and the Red Hot Peppers later became a member of The Attractions?

5. Who played tenor banjo on the 1994 debut album by The Popes?

6. Which group went to No. 1 in 1999 with the song *If I Let You Go*?

7. Who recorded song *Nazi Girlfriend* on album *Avenue B*?

8. Which band recorded the live album *Viva Wisconsin*?

9. Which group recorded the 1969 album *One Step Beyond*?

10. Who had a 2000 Top 10 hit with *In Your Arms (Rescue Me)*?

11. Which former member of Orange Juice appeared on the song *Endless Art* by A House?

12. Which Scottish group recorded the 2000 album *Weather Underground*?

13. Who had a 1990 Top 10 hit single with *Infinity*?

14. What is the title of Supergrass's third album?

15. Which songwriter records under the name of East River Pipe?

SCIENCE

1. On which moon of Jupiter is the volcano Prometheus?

2. In which European city was Erwin Schrödinger born in 1887?

3. What, in computer science, is time-sharing?

4. In what year did TAT9, a fibre-optic cable used in telecommunications, come into operation?

5. In which century did French physiologist Claude Bernard live?

6. 71% of the sun is composed of which element?

7. Which inventor died in West Orange, New Jersey in 1931?

8. Of what is epigraphy the science?

9. Which biologist authored the 1986 book *The Blind Watchmaker*?

10. In which year was U.S. psychologist William James born?

11. In which European capital was physical chemist Wilhelm Ostwald born in 1853?

12. In which town was Charles Darwin born in 1809?

13. In which country was the element Dubnium first created in 1967?

14. In which year did British physicist Sir John Douglas Cockcroft die?

15. In computing, what does the acronym BASIC stand for?

GENERAL KNOWLEDGE

1. Who was a Best Actor Oscar winner for the film *It Happened One Night*?

2. Which play by Shakespeare features the character Ariel?

3. What is the eleventh sign of the zodiac?

4. Who wrote the poem *The Jumblies*?

5. Which river flows to the North Sea at Sunderland?

6. Des Moines is the capital of which U.S. state?

7. On which river is the Italian town of Schio, which lies at the foot of the Alps?

8. Who was 1983 French Open men's singles tennis champion?

9. Which pop singer had a No. 1 single with the song *When the Going Gets Tough, the Tough Get Going*?

10. Who was 1988 Olympic men's 200m butterfly swimming champion?

11. Who wrote the 1820 novel *The Abbot*?

12. Who wrote the 1880 novel *The Duke's Children*?

13. On which river is the town of Mold in North Wales?

14. Who was 1996 Australian Open men's singles tennis champion?

15. Abuja is the capital of which West African republic?

ENTERTAINMENT

1. What was Kerry Gardner's character name in the sitcom *Up Pompeii*?

2. The 1967 film *Accident* is based on a novel by which author?

3. The 1950 film *Tea for Two* was loosely based on which stage play?

4. Which oft-paired duo starred in the 1942 film *I Married an Angel*?

5. In which year was *University Challenge* first shown on TV?

6. Who played Cupcake in the sitcom *The Army Game*?

7. Who wrote the 1937 comedy film *Easy Living*?

8. The 1965 BBC TV soap opera *United!* was about which fictional football team?

9. Who played Oscar Wilde in the 1988 film *Salome's Last Dance*?

10. Who played Lt. Gay Ellis in the 1970s TV show *UFO*?

11. Who directed the 1951 film *An American in Paris*?

12. Who directed the 1976 film *Aces High*?

13. Who played Frederick in the drama series *Upstairs Downstairs*?

14. Which TV comedian's characters include Oscar Pennyfeather?

15. In which year did Tyne Tees Television first appear on our screens?

SPORT

1. In which year did German tennis player Hilde Krahwinkel die?

2. In which year was the Croquet Association founded in England?

3. In which year was athlete Daniel Effiong born?

4. Who was women's overall champion at the 1975 gymnastics World Cup?

5. By what score did Wales beat Scotland in the 2000 Six Nations tournament in rugby union?

6. Who won the the 1998 Spanish Grand Prix in Formula 1 driving a McLaren?

7. Which country did runner Chidi Imo represent?

8. By what score did rugby union team the British Lions beat Australia at Brisbane in June 1966?

9. What nationality is runner Zahra Ouaziz?

10. Who took over from Joe Walcott in 1906 as undisputed world welterweight boxing champion?

11. In which year was athlete Koji Ito born?

12. In which month is the Kentucky Derby run in the U.S.A.?

13. In which year was athlete Jeff Laynes born?

14. Who was 1969 women's individual world archery champion?

15. In which year did L. R. Erskine and Herbert Lawford win the men's doubles tennis title at Wimbledon?

ANSWERS 1. 1981 2. 1897 3. 1972 4. Lyudmila Tourischeva 5. 26-18 6. Mika Hakkinen 7. Nigeria 8. 31-0 9. Moroccan 10. Honey Mellody 11. 1970 12. May 13. 1970 14. Dorothy Lidstone 15. 1879.

POP

1. Which Leeds group recorded the 1994 album *Anarchy*?

2. Which female singer's albums include *Truth From Lies* and *A Crash Course in Roses*?

3. Which member of the group Lush is half-Hungarian and half-Japanese?

4. Tetsu Yamauchi replaced Ronnie Lane in which group in the 1970s?

5. Tabitha Tinsdale and Vinny Cafiso record under what name?

6. Who played saxophone on Gerry Rafferty's track *Baker Street*?

7. Which New York group recorded the 1994 album *Panic On*?

8. Which group had a Top 10 single in 1999 with *Drinking in L.A.?*

9. Which duo had a 2000 Top 10 hit with *A Lttle Bit of Luck*?

10. Which band's second album is called *Liquid Skin*?

11. Who featured on the 1989 single *Pump up the Jam* by Technotronics?

12. Which studio album by Sting includes the song *Russians*?

13. Which guitarist recorded the 1978 album *Casino*?

14. Which song opens the 1974 album *Second Helping* by Lynyrd Skynyrd?

15. What is rapper Jonathan David better known as?

PEOPLE

1. In which country was actress Vivien Leigh born?

2. Which opponent of apartheid married Joe Slovo in 1949?

3. What was the nickname of U.S. pacifist Elihu Burritt?

4. Lisa Scott Lee is a member of which pop group?

5. Jennifer Flavin is the wife of which Hollywood actor?

6. In which Louisiana town was Britney Spears born?

7. What is the middle name of South African religious leader Desmond Tutu?

8. In which city was Holy Roman Emperor Leopold I born?

9. Kate Winslet's sister acted in the BBC TV drama *The Scold's Bridle*. What is her name?

10. Who did Katharine Worsley marry in 1961?

11. Who is female presenter of the Channel 4 comedy show *dotcomedy*?

12. Who played Screech in the TV comedy *Saved by the Bell*?

13. Which pop star wrote the 1999 autobiography *A Cure for Gravity*?

14. In which northern city was aircraft designer Robert Blackburn born in 1885?

15. Who became president of the National American Woman Suffrage Association in 1892?

GENERAL KNOWLEDGE

1. Which unit of distance in navigation is equal to one tenth of a sea mile?

2. The 1998 film *Apt Pupil* by Bryan Singer is based on a novella by which author?

3. On whose play is the 1948 film *Rope* by Alfred Hitchcock based?

4. Ipswich is the administrative centre of which English county?

5. Who was 1998 Commonwealth Games men's high jump champion?

6. What was the name of the Kampuchean communist party which seized power in 1975?

7. Who directed the 1982 science fiction film *Blade Runner*?

8. Who authored the 1961 novel *Fear is the Key*?

9. Which British admiral defeated the Spanish fleet off Messina in 1717?

10. Which French painter's works include *Dimanche à la Grande-Jatte*?

11. Who was 1936 Olympic men's 100m & 200m champion?

12. What was the name of the former secret police in East Germany?

13. In which group of islands in the central Philippines is the island of Cebu?

14. Who was the Roman goddess of abundance and fertility?

15. Which actor played Sherlock Holmes on film in 1939's *The Hound of the Baskervilles*?

ENTERTAINMENT

1. Who plays the witch in the 1942 film *I Married a Witch*?

2. Who played butler Robert Hiller in the 1970's sitcom *Two's Company*?

3. Who directed the 1954 film *White Christmas*?

4. Who played Bill's mum Bette in the sitcom *2 Point 4 Children*?

5. Who directed the 1999 film *Tea with Mussolini*?

6. Who directed the 1991 film *The Adjuster*?

7. Which comedy team co-wrote the 1969 sitcom *Two in Clover*?

8. Which comedian's catchphrases included "Doesn't it make you want to spit?"?

9. What was Kenneth Welsh's character name in the television drama series *Twin Peaks*?

10. Which animal is the star of the 1973 film *Salty*?

11. Who is the female lead in the 1967 film *Caprice*?

12. Which former *Coronation Street* actress played Kathy Starkie in the 1999 drama series *Four Fathers*?

13. Who plays the title role in the 1984 film *Iceman*?

14. Which 'James Bond' actor starred in the 1988 film *Taffin*?

15. Who did John Ratzenberger play in the sitcom *Cheers*?

ANSWERS 1. Veronica Lake **2.** Donald Sinden **3.** Michael Curtiz **4.** Liz Smith **5.** Franco Zeffirelli **6.** Atom Egoyan **7.** Vince Powell and Harry Driver **8.** Arthur Askey **9.** Windom Earle **10.** Sea-lion **11.** Doris Day **12.** Eva Pope **13.** John Lone **14.** Pierce Brosnan **15.** Cliff Clavin

SPORT

1. Who was men's show jumping champion at the 1957 European championships?

2. What nationality is runner Charles Kamathi?

3. Who was 1920 Olympic men's 400m freestyle swimming champion?

4. Which Aberdeen footballer was 1971 Scottish P.F.A. Player of the Year?

5. Which women's tennis players met in the final of the Champions Cup at Indian Wells in March, 2000?

6. Which county were women's world champions in pétanque in 1996?

7. Flintshire Fleece and Whitley Warriors compete at which sport?

8. Which country won the women's K1 team event from 1989-95 at the Canoe Slalom World Championships?

9. What nationality is skier Bente Martinsen?

10. Finn Kobbero and Per Neilsen were 1960 All-England Championships men's doubles badminton champions. Which country did they represent?

11. Who succeeded Ellery Hanley as coach of St. Helens rugby league team in 2000?

12. How many times did trainer John Scott win the St. Leger?

13. What nationality is tennis player Lleyton Hewitt?

14. Between 1948 and 1973, how many classic races did Noel Murless win?

15. For which rugby league side does Brett Goldsprink play?

ANSWERS 1. Hans Günter Winkler **2.** Kenyan **3.** Norman Ross **4.** Martin Buchan **5.** Martina Hingis and Lindsay Davenport **6.** Spain **7.** Ice hockey **8.** France **9.** Norwegian **10.** Denmark **11.** Ian Millward **12.** Sixteen **13.** Australian **14.** Nineteen **15.** Halifax Blue Sox.

POP

1. What is Nine Inch Nails' singer Trent Reznor's first name?

2. Who featured on Puff Daddy's 2000 hit single *Satisfy You*?

3. Which Liverpool band released the 1983 album *The White Album*?

4. The group Main formed in 1991 after the demise of which group?

5. In which year did the Climax Chicago Blues Band drop the word 'Chicago' from their name?

6. Which group had a 1989 Top 10 single with *You Keep It All In*?

7. What were vocal group Ripple and Waves Plus Michael renamed?

8. Which artist's albums include *Wild Dogs* and *Tulsa*?

9. Who duetted with Paul Weller on the Jam's single *The Bitterest Pill*?

10. Who recorded the 1987 album *Never Let Me Down*?

11. In which year did Liza Minnelli have a Top 10 single with *Losing My Mind*?

12. In which year was Kevin Rowland born?

13. Who had a 2000 Top 10 single with *Glorious*?

14. Who penned the autobiography *The Long Hard Road out of Hell*?

15. Who recorded the 1999 solo album *Flatlands*?

ANSWERS 1. Michael **2.** R. Kelly **3.** Afraid of Mice **4.** Loop **5.** 1972 **6.** The Beautiful South **7.** The Jackson Five **8.** Dwight Twilley **9.** Jenny McKeown **10.** David Bowie **11.** 1989 **12.** 1953 **13.** Andreas Johnson **14.** Marilyn Manson **15.** Dr. Robert.

THE CARLING PUB QUIZ BOOK

ART

1. Which Nobel prize winner authored *Group Portrait with Lady*?

2. In which year did Henry Raeburn become a member of the Royal Academy?

3. Whose fables include *The Cat That Walked By Himself* and *The Crab That Played With The Sea*?

4. In which city did Raphael die in 1520?

5. Which journalist compiled the *Devil's Dictionary* before setting off for Mexico in 1913 and disappearing?

6. Where did Stanley Spencer study from 1908-12?

7. What was the debut novel of Rosamond Lehmann?

8. In which city was French artist Georges Henri Rouault born?

9. In which year was D.H. Lawrence's novel *Women in Love* first published?

10. Which cartoonist created *The Bash Street Kids*?

11. Who authored the 1985 novel *A Maggot*?

12. Who wrote the 1837 novel *Ethel Churchill*?

13. Who wrote the 1988 novel *The Truth About Lorin Jones*?

14. Which book won the 1996 Booker prize?

15. Who wrote the 1973 novel *Forgetting Elena*?

GENERAL KNOWLEDGE

1. Which former Manchester United footballer appeared in the 1998 historical film *Elizabeth*?

2. Who wrote the 1977 novel *Shall We Tell the President?*?

3. Who wrote the 1872 novel *Erewhon*?

4. Who directed and acted in the 1996 film *Trees Lounge*?

5. Which ornamental shrub is also called a butterfly bush?

6. Who wrote the 1970 novel *Love Story*?

7. In which year did German composer Max Reger die?

8. Which contagious skin infection is caused by the mite *Sarcoptes scabiei*?

9. On which river is the Austrian town of Melk?

10. Who was Best Actress Oscar winner for the film *It Happened One Night*?

11. Who wrote the 1981 novel *Cujo*?

12. Which playwright scripted the 1997 film *The Edge*, starring Anthony Hopkins?

13. What, in Russia, is kvass?

14. What is the name of the rudimentary bone in horses which occurs on each side of the cannon bone?

15. Which plant is the national symbol of Ireland?

ANSWERS 1. Eric Cantona **2.** Jeffrey Archer **3.** Samuel Butler **4.** Steve Buscemi **5.** Buddleia **6.** Erich Segal **7.** 1916 **8.** Scabies **9.** Danube **10.** Claudette Colbert **11.** Stephen King **12.** David Mamet **13.** An alcoholic drink made from cereals and stale bread **14.** Splint bone **15.** Shamrock.

ENTERTAINMENT

1. Which political figure did Robert Donat play in the 1947 film *Captain Boycott*?

2. The 1986 film *Tai-Pan* is based on whose novel?

3. Which mother and daughter team were in the 1991 film *Rambling Rose*?

4. Which Scottish actor is associated with the company Fountainbridge Films?

5. Which duo wrote the sitcom *Chelmsford 123*?

6. Who directed the 1970 film *Take a Girl Like You*?

7. Which actress starred in the 1981 sitcom *Chintz*?

8. How much did the film *The Blair Witch Project* take at the U.K. box office in the first weekend of its release?

9. Which duo dance and sing the number *At the Codfish Ball* in the 1936 film *Captain January*?

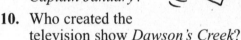

10. Who created the television show *Dawson's Creek*?

11. Who directed the 1996 film *Carla's Song*?

12. Which two actors fight for the love of Elsa Martinelli in the 1963 film *Rampage*?

13. Who directed 1999 film *Flawless* starring Robert De Niro?

14. Which comedian voiced the role of Jasper the Owl in the children's television drama *The Magician's House*?

15. Which Oscar-nominated actress played Alison Little in the sitcom *Chance in a Million*?

ANSWERS 1. Charles Parnell 2. James Clavell 3. Diane Ladd and Laura Dern 4. Sean Connery 5. Rory McGrath and Jimmy Mulville 6. Jonathan Miller 7. Michele Dotrice 8. £5.87m 9. Buddy Ebsen and Shirley Temple 10. Kevin Williamson 11. Ken Loach 12. Robert Mitchum and Jack Hawkins 13. Joel Schumacher 14. Stephen Fry 15. Brenda Blethyn

SPORT

1. At what sport have Michel Daignault and Maryse Perreault been world champions?

2. What nationality is tennis player Hicham Arazi?

3. Which teams met in the 1984 U.E.F.A. Cup Final in football?

4. Who was women's singles champion at badminton at the All-England Championships in 2000?

5. Which country's team won the men's I.A.A.F. world half-marathon championship in 1992 and 1993?

6. Which German cyclist won the 2000 Paris-Nice 'race to the sun'?

7. Who scored 917 runs in the Refuge Assurance League for Warwickshire in 1991?

8. How old was Andre Agassi when he first won a Wimbledon singles title?

9. Who was men's combined exercises champion in gymnastics at the 1956 Olympic Games?

10. How many nations contested the men's events at the 1993 Taekwondo World Championships?

11. Who won the 1952 French Grand Prix in Formula 1?

12. By what score did Italy beat Scotland in the 2000 Six Nations tournament in rugby union?

13. How many goals did Jim Sullivan score for Wigan against Flimby and Fothergill in a 1925 rugby league Challenge Cup?

14. Who knocked Sheffield out of the 2000 Silk Cut Challenge Cup in rugby league?

15. Who won the professional Bowlers' Association's Tournament of Champions in 1987?

POP

1. Which Welsh group recorded the 1972 album *Be Good To Yourself At Least Once A Day*?

2. What is the title of Melanie C's debut solo album?

3. Bap Kennedy was lead singer in which Belfast group?

4. Which Welsh group's debut L.P. in 1984 was *Declaration*?

5. Paul Kelly and Debsey Wykes comprise which duo?

6. Which song by the Four Seasons does Kevin Rowland cover on a 1999 album?

7. Which group's debut release was the 1992 *Drill* E.P.?

8. Which duo recorded the album *Western Wall: The Tucson Sessions*?

9. Which songwriter's albums include *Spirits Colliding* and *Hard Station*?

10. In which city did Alberto Y Lost Trios Paranoias form?

11. Which U.S. group recorded the album *Bali*?

12. Vocal group The Coasters evolved from which Los Angeles-based band?

13. Who recorded the 1999 album *The Singing Hatchet*?

14. Who produced the 1993 album *Laid* by James?

15. Who recorded the 1999 album *Jewels for Sophia*?

ANSWERS 1. Man **2.** Northern Star **3.** Energy Orchard **4.** The Alarm **5.** Birdie **6.** Rag Doll **7.** Radiohead **8.** Emmylou Harris & Linda Ronstadt **9.** Paul Brady **10.** Manchester **11.** The Wondermints **12.** The Robins **13.** Radar Brothers **14.** Brian Eno **15.** Robyn Hitchcock.

GEOGRAPHY

1. In which European country is the village of Quatre Bras?

2. If you travelled due south from Malta, which African country would you reach first?

3. Which Tropic runs through Paraguay?

4. Which Canadian port was capital of Cape Breton Island until 1820?

5. On which river is the city of Canterbury?

6. In which year was Dakota divided into North and South?

7. On which river is the Netherlands town of Arnhem?

8. The Isle of Thanet is in the north-east tip of which county?

9. The Irish port of Drogheda lies near the mouth of which river?

10. On which Pacific island is Mount Suribachi?

11. On which river does Gloucester stand?

12. The city of Gondar was a former capital of which country?

13. Which port is more populated - San Francisco or Shanghai?

14. In which county is Burghley House, setting of one of three-day eventing's famous horse trials?

15. Dungeness is part of which marshy area of Kent?

GENERAL KNOWLEDGE

1. Which horse won the 1979 Epsom Derby?

2. Who was British prime minister from 1804-6?

3. Which food fish is also called an eulachon?

4. Which town in N.E. Iran was the birthplace of Omar Khayyam?

5. Who was a Best Actress Oscar nominee for the film *The L-Shaped Room*?

6. Who authored the 1960 play *Ross*?

7. In mathematics, what is the name given to an angle of less than 90°?

8. Who was author of the novel *The Girls of Slender Means*?

9. What is the 22nd letter of the Greek alphabet?

10. Flush was the dog of which 19th Century writer?

11. Who was a Best Actor Oscar winner for the film *Scent of a Woman*?

12. Who was the composer of the oratorio *The Dream of Gerontius*?

13. Who was 1990 & 1991 World Fresh Water angling individual champion?

14. In classical mythology, which princess of Tyre founded Carthage?

15. In which year did British landscape painter J.M.W. Turner die?

Nudd **14.** Dido **15.** 1851.
10. Elizabeth Barrett Browning **11.** Al Pacino **12.** Sir Edward Elgar **13.** Bob
5. Leslie Caron **6.** Terence Rattigan **7.** An acute angle **8.** Muriel Spark **9.** Chi
ANSWERS 1. Troy **2.** William Pitt (the Younger) **3.** Candlefish **4.** Nishapur

ENTERTAINMENT

1. Which duo presented the Channel Four show *The Priory* in 1999?

2. What are the comedy team Paul and Barry Elliott better known as?

3. Which actress and actor were dating when they made the film *Kalifornia*?

4. Which comedy team wrote the first series of the 1960 sitcom *Citizen James* starring Sid James?

5. Who played lawyer Atticus Finch in the 1962 film *To Kill a Mockingbird*?

6. Which stand-up comedian performed the show *Urban Trauma* in Edinburgh in 1998?

7. Who played Captain Nemo in the 1961 film *Mysterious Island*?

8. Who played actress Donna Sinclair in the spoof sitcom *Dr. Willoughby* in 1999?

9. What is Alexander Siddig's character name in *Star Trek: Deep Space Nine*?

10. Herbert's of Liverpool was the hairdressing salon featured in which fly-on-the-wall documentary in 1999?

11. Which duo host the television show *Friends Like These*?

12. On which channel does the soap *Hollyoaks* appear?

13. Who directed the 1968 film *Ice Station Zebra*?

14. The 1978 film *Take Down* is about which sport?

15. An episode of which sitcom, in 1979, was entitled *Only Fools and Horses*?

SPORT

1. At what weight does boxer Joe Calzaghe fight?

2. Which horse won the 1990 Cheltenham Gold Cup?

3. What nationality is cyclist Tom Steels?

4. Balazs Kiss was 1996 Olympic hammer champion. Which country did he represent?

5. Which country won the 1975 Davis Cup in tennis?

6. Cindy Devine was 1990 women's downhill mountain biking champion. Which country did she represent?

7. Which sport do Will Green, Spencer Brown and Roy Winters partake in?

8. Mahmoud Karim was 1946-9 British Open squash champion. Which country did he represent?

9. Which team won the 1980 Scottish F.A. Cup Final?

10. Which Australian motor cyclist is manager of the Nastro Azzurro Honda team?

11. What nationality was Olympic shooting champion Gudbrand Skatteboe?

12. How many laps did Jenson Button complete in his Formula 1 Grand Prix debut at Melbourne in 2000?

13. What nationality are Olympic canoeists Ulrich Papke and Ingo Spelly?

14. For which international Test cricket side does Trevor Gripper play?

15. Who was 1980 men's world cross-country champion?

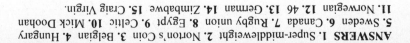

ANSWERS 1. Super-middleweight **2.** Norton's Coin **3.** Belgian **4.** Hungary **5.** Sweden **6.** Canada **7.** Rugby union **8.** Egypt **9.** Celtic **10.** Mick Doohan **11.** Norwegian **12.** 46 **13.** German **14.** Zimbabwe **15.** Craig Virgin.

POP

1. Who had a 2000 Top 10 single with *Girl on TV*?

2. Who recorded the 1968 solo album *Oar*?

3. Who recorded the 1999 album *Approaching Silence*?

4. Why did Nick Lowe entitle an E.P. of his *Bowi*?

5. Who had a 1989 Top 10 single with *Girl I'm Gonna Miss You*?

6. Which 1986 hit single featured the lyrics "We don't have the time for psychological romance"?

7. Who had a No.1 single in 1989 with *All Around the World*?

8. In which Australian city were the group The Hoodoo Gurus formed?

9. Which progressive rock group recorded the 1978 album *Love Beach*?

10. Who had a No. 1 single in 2000 with *Pure Shores*?

11. To which label did John Lee Hooker sign in 1955?

12. Which reggae artist released the 1979 compilation album *Harder Than the Best*?

13. What was the title of the second album by EMF?

14. Who had a 1999 No. 1 single with *Blue (Da Ba Dee)*?

15. What was The Royal Guardsmen's April 1967 follow-up to the single *Snoopy vs. the Red Baron*?

HISTORY

1. Who led the Russian army in the Battle of Borodino?

2. In which month of 1909 did Louis Blériot cross the English Channel in an aeroplane?

3. In which year was the Battle of Friedland?

4. Who did Louis VII of France marry in 1137?

5. In which year did the Free-Soil Party originate in the U.S.?

6. In which year did President Nixon resign?

7. Who was vice-president of the U.S. from 1825-32?

8. What was the Barebones Parliament of 1653 previously known as?

9. In which year did Thomas Paine emigrate to Philadelphia?

10. In which year of World War One was the Battle of Caporetto?

11. What was the Prisoners (Temporary Discharge for Ill-Health) Act of 1913 better known as?

12. In which county was Sir Walter Raleigh born?

13. In which year did British naval officer George Vancouver die?

14. At what age did Edward I marry Eleanor of Castile?

15. Who was U.S. secretary of state from 1977-80?

GENERAL KNOWLEDGE

1. What was the name of the U.S. secretary of state who purchased Alaska?

2. What was the name of the chief of the Ottawa Indians who led a rebellion against the British from 1763-6?

3. Who was the author of the novel *The Cloister and the Hearth*?

4. Which 18th Century composer and organist composed the oratorio *Jephtha*?

5. Which Norwegian painter's works include 1893's *The Scream*?

6. Which city in central India was the site of a poisonous gas leak in 1984?

7. Which English soldier became military governor of Montreal in 1760?

8. Which actor's television roles included McLaren in the sitcom *Porridge*?

9. Who was a Best Supporting Actor Oscar nominee for the film *Driving Miss Daisy*?

10. Who wrote the 1965 novel *The Looking-Glass War*?

11. Who was 1984 & 1988 Olympic men's springboard diving champion?

12. Who was the Mogul emperor of India from 1556-1605?

13. How many wickets did Alec Bedser take in his England Test career?

14. Who was the goddess of youth and spring in Greek mythology?

15. In which year did Roman historian Livy die?

ANSWERS 1. William Henry Seward 2. Pontiac 3. Charles Reade 4. John Stanley 5. Edvard Munch 6. Bhopal 7. Thomas Gage 8. Tony Osoba 9. Dan Aykroyd 10. John Le Carré 11. Greg Louganis 12. Akbar 13. 236 14. Hebe 15. 17 A.D.

ENTERTAINMENT

1. Which actor directed and starred in the 1966 film *The Naked Prey*?
2. In which year was comedian Lou Costello born?
3. Which film won Best Picture (Comedy/Musical) at the 2000 Golden Globes?
4. Who plays Linda Sykes in *Coronation Street*?
5. Which musician directed and starred in the 1986 film *Under the Cherry Moon*?
6. In which television puppet series did the character Atlanta Shore appear?
7. Who directed the 1961 film *Underworld USA*?
8. Which *Emergency - Ward 10* actress replaced Ray Martine as presenter of the 1960's variety show *All Stars and Garters*?
9. Who won a Best Supporting Actor Oscar for the film *Unforgiven*?
10. Who did Grace Lee Whitney play in the 1960's television series *Star Trek*?
11. Which Scot stars in the 1986 film *The Name of the Rose*?
12. Which comedienne was one of the six main cast members in the Channel Four sketch show *Absolutely*?
13. Which Hollywood director's animated creations include *The Stain Boy*?
14. What nationality is the tenor Giuseppe Di Stefano?
15. Which two comic actors star in show *The Strangerers* on satellite television?

SPORT

1. What nationality is tennis player Juan Carlos Ferrero?

2. Who rode the 1978 Epsom Derby winner Shirley Heights?

3. Who knocked Castleford Lock Lane out of the 2000 Silk Cut Challenge Cup in rugby league?

4. How many medals did gymnast Larisa Latynina win at the Olympics from 1956-64?

5. Which golfer was 1957 B.B.C. Sports Personality of the Year?

6. What time did Claudia Pechstein take to win the 1994 Olympic 5000m speed skating gold?

7. What nationality is motorcyclist Alex Criville?

8. What nationality was sprinter Ray Stewart?

9. How many golds did Kenya win at the 1999 World Athletics Championships?

10. Who was men's long jump champion at the 1991 world indoor championships?

11. Who beat Lindsay Davenport in the 1999 U.S. Open tennis singles semi-final?

12. How many dismissals did South African wicket-keeper Richard Ryall make in his career from 1980-95?

13. Which city is headquarters of the World Professional Billiards and Snooker Association?

14. Which women's golfer won the 1955 Du Maurier Classic?

15. In which sport do Britons Carolyn Wilson and Amanda Dodd partake?

POP

1. In which year did blues singer Lightnin' Hopkins die?

2. Which reggae artist released the 1984 album *Statement*?

3. Marie Fredriksson and Per Gessle comprise which duo?

4. Damo Suzuki left German group Can in 1973 to join which religious organisation?

5. What was the debut album by Hothouse Flowers?

6. What was the lead track on 1976's No. 1 *The Roussos Phenomenon E.P.*?

7. Who was the original drummer with the group The House of Love?

8. Who recorded the 1989 Top 10 single *I Feel the Earth Move*?

9. Which female singer had a 1995 hit single with *Sexual*?

10. Who played bass in The Housemartins?

11. Which member of Canned Heat died of a drug overdose in 1970?

12. What has been David Lee Roth's only Top 30 U.K. single?

13. In which year did blues singer Howlin' Wolf die?

14. What is the real name of Diana Ross?

15. In which year did Ron Wood join the Rolling Stones?

ANSWERS 1. 1982 **2.** Ini Kamoze **3.** Roxette **4.** Jehovah's Witnesses **5.** People **6.** Forever and Ever **7.** Pete Evans **8.** Martika **9.** Maria Rowe **10.** Norman Cook **11.** Al Wilson **12.** Just Like Paradise **13.** 1976 **14.** Diana Earle **15.** 1975.

WORDS

1. The adjective crural refers to which part of the body?

2. What is the plural of radius?

3. What type of creature is a kelt?

4. How many points does a pentagram have?

5. What does the Italian food *crostini* translate as?

6. What does the phrase *per contra* mean?

7. What in Scotland is a plouk?

8. What in Australia does a jinker transport?

9. What in the U.S. is a musette bag?

10. What in India is numdah?

11. What type of creature is a ringlet?

12. In which part of the body would a labret be inserted as an ornament?

13. If something is saline, what does it contain?

14. What type of creature is a launce?

15. What is a female tiger called?

ANSWERS 1. Leg or thigh **2.** Radii **3.** Salmon **4.** Five **5.** Little crusts **6.** On the contrary **7.** Pimple **8.** Timber **9.** An army officer's haversack **10.** A type of coarse felt **11.** Butterfly **12.** Lip **13.** Common salt **14.** An eel **15.** Tigress.

GENERAL KNOWLEDGE

1. What was Honor Blackman's character called in the television show *The Avengers*?

2. Which unit of area is equivalent to 2.471 acres?

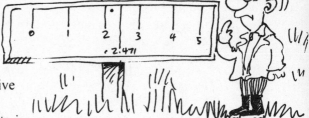

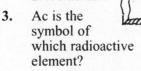

3. Ac is the symbol of which radioactive element?

4. The port of Salto is the second largest city in which South American country?

5. Who was the English soldier who commanded the British capture of Quebec in the 18th Century?

6. In which year was German painter Max Ernst born?

7. Which Russian revolutionary leader became premier in July 1917?

8. The 1978 film *The Shout*, starring Alan Bates, was based on a short story by which writer?

9. In which year was American avant-garde pianist and jazz composer Cecil Taylor born?

10. At which racecourse is the English Grand National run?

11. Which word used in signalling indicates that a message received will be complied with?

12. Who was 1974-7 champion flat race jockey?

13. The 1964 film *Woman of Straw*, starring Sean Connery, was based on a novel by which writer?

14. In which year did British sculptor, typographer and engraver Eric Gill die?

15. Which tennis player won the 1980 Wimbledon men's doubles title with Paul McNamee?

ANSWERS 1. Cathy Gale 2. Hectare 3. Actinium 4. Uruguay 5. James Wolfe 6. 1891 7. Alexander Kerensky 8. Robert Graves 9. 1933 10. Aintree 11. Wilco 12. Pat Eddery 13. Catherine Arley 14. 1940 15. Peter McNamara.

ENTERTAINMENT

1. Who plays Rita Sullivan in *Coronation Street*?

2. Who is the female star of the film *You've Got Mail*?

3. Who appeared as Jill, Rachel's younger sister in the sitcom *Friends* in 2000?

4. Who composed the 1872 opera *Djamileh*?

5. Who are the two female leads in the film *Practical Magic*?

6. What is comedienne Dora Bryan's real name?

7. Who directed the 1922 film *Nanook of the North*?

8. Who stars in the 2000 film *Erin Brockovich*?

9. Which Hollywood actress was born Ruby Stevens?

10. Who directed the film *Pi*?

11. Who plays Geoff, Vinnie, and Olive in television's *The League of Gentlemen*?

12. In which opera by Rimsky-Korsakov does King Dodon appear?

13. Who directed the 2000 film *The Beach*?

14. Which actress played Vera Hopkins in *Coronation Street*?

15. Who directed the 2000 film *The End of the Affair*?

THE CARLING PUB QUIZ BOOK

SPORT

1. Which Finn was 1998 Australian Grand Prix winner in Formula 1?

2. In cricket, who scored 160 for Lancashire vs. Yorkshire in the 1st innings of their 1999 county championship match?

3. Which club have played in the most rugby league Challenge Cup finals?

4. In which year did tennis player Wilfred Baddeley die?

5. What nationality were the 1968 Olympic two-man bobsleigh champions?

6. How many runs did Graham Thorpe score in his three Tests against South Africa in 1998?

7. Which horse was leading moneywinner in Britain in 1967?

8. Who did Todd Martin beat in the quarter-finals of the 1999 U.S. Open tennis singles championship?

9. Zhanna Pintusevich was women's 200m champion at the 1997 world championships. Which country did she represent?

10. Who partnered Arantxa Sanchez to victory in the 1992 French Open mixed doubles championships?

11. By what score did Germany beat Mexico in the 1998 football World Cup finals 2nd round?

12. Who coached Scotland to their 1990 rugby union Grand Slam?

13. At which sport were Teresa Andersen and Gail Johnson 1973 world champions?

14. What nationality is golfer John Cook, who has earned more than $6m dollars on the U.S. tour?

15. Who was named as coach of France's rugby union team in November 1999?

POP

1. Which band did Caravan's Dave Sinclair join after leaving the group in 1971?

2. Which member of Depeche Mode recorded the album *Liquid* under the name Recoil?

3. Which reggae artist had a posthumous 1999 Top 10 single with *Sun is Shining*?

4. In which city was country star Kenny Rogers born?

5. For how many years did Lionel Ritchie front The Commodores before going solo in 1982?

6. On which label did Rich Kids have a 1978 Top 30 hit with *Rich Kids*?

7. In which year did Roxy Music have a Top 10 single with *Both Ends Burning*?

8. Which female singer recorded the 1956 Top 20 single *Jimmy Unknown*?

9. Who produced Talk Talk's 1991 album *Laughing Stock*?

10. Who recorded the 1977 album *Before and After Science*?

11. Which reggae legend recorded the 1999 album *Living in the Flood*?

12. From which group did drummer John Hinch join Judas Priest?

13. Which solo artist had a 2000 Top 10 hit with *Dolphins Were Monkeys*?

14. In which year did Black Lace first hit the Top 10 with the single *Agadoo*?

15. Greg Ginn was leader of which 1980s band?

SCIENCE

1. In which year did scientist André Marie Ampère die?

2. Which branch of physical science deals with the behaviour of light?

3. In which year was computer company Sun Microsystems Inc. founded?

4. What was the middle name of scientist James Joule?

5. In which year was the first smart card introduced, in France?

6. What is the only known satellite of the planet Pluto?

7. In which year did German scientist Franz Joseph Müller discover Tellurium?

8. In which European capital was surgeon Sir Charles Bell born in 1774?

9. In which year was engineer Sir Clive Sinclair knighted?

10. Which British optician invented the achromatic object glass in 1757?

11. In which century did French neurologist Jean Martin Charcot live?

12. What is SETI an acronym for?

13. What in computer science is OCR?

14. In which Australian city is the Powerhouse Museum?

15. Which company originally developed the computer mouse?

GENERAL KNOWLEDGE

1. How many first-class wickets did cricketer Fred Trueman take in his career?

2. Stoop Memorial Ground is the home ground of which rugby union club?

3. What is the name of the newspaper which features in Evelyn Waugh's novel *Scoop*?

4. 'Old Rowley' was the nickname of which king of England?

5. Who was president of Zambia from 1964-91?

6. Who was director of the 1983 film *Gorky Park*?

7. The French port of St. Nazaire is at the mouth of which river?

8. Which saint and Roman monk was the first archbishop of Canterbury?

9. What is the name of the central character in the play *Death of a Salesman*?

10. What is the capital of Nicaragua?

11. Who wrote the 1970 one-act play *After Magritte*?

12. In which year did British iron manufacturer Abraham Darby die?

13. Which tennis player won the 1998 Australian Open women's doubles title with Martina Hingis?

14. Which city in California is the 'city of angels'?

15. Who was 1972 Wimbledon men's singles tennis champion?

ANSWERS 1. 2,304 2. Harlequins 3. The Beast 4. Charles II 5. Kenneth Kaunda 6. Michael Apted 7. Loire 8. St. Augustine 9. Willy Loman 10. Managua 11. Tom Stoppard 12. 1717 13. Mirjana Lucic 14. Los Angeles 15. Stan Smith.

ENTERTAINMENT

1. Who plays Stuart in the television drama *Queer as Folk*?

2. Who directed the 1996 film *Unforgettable* which starred Ray Liotta?

3. Who plays Terry Duckworth in *Coronation Street*?

4. Which actress played John Gordon-Sinclair's girlfriend in the 1991 sitcom *An Actor's Life For Me*?

5. What is James Stewart's profession in the 1953 film *The Naked Spur*?

6. Who plays King Louis XI of France in the 1938 film *If I Were King*?

7. Who plays school librarian Giles in television's *Buffy the Vampire Slayer*?

8. At which London Underground station was the picture *Deathline* filmed?

9. Which cast member of *The Fast Show* presented the television fashion show *She's Gotta Have It*?

10. Which comedienne played Mrs. Leo Hunter in the 1952 film *The Pickwick Papers*?

11. Who impersonated Elvis Costello in a *Stars in Their Eyes* celebrity special?

12. On which island is the 1949 British film *If This Be Sin* set?

13. Who plays PC Natalie Metcalf in the television series *The Cops*?

14. Who played Joe Purvis in the television series *Grafters*?

15. Who directed 1983 film *Daniel* based on the novel *The Book of Daniel*?

SPORT

1. Which country were 1996 world champions at speedway?

2. Which country won the golf World Cup in November, 1999?

3. In his 36,012 First-class runs scored from 1894-1928, how many double centuries did Billy Quaife make?

4. For which rugby league team do Gavin Wood and Dan Potter play?

5. At which sport have Eirik Kvalfoss and Frank Ullrich been world champions?

6. Who was named top male athlete of the 20th Century by the I.A.A.F. in November, 1999?

7. Which horse won the 1971 Prix de l'Arc de Triomphe?

8. What nationality is high jumper Javier Sotomayor?

9. Which rowing club won the 1989 & 1990 Grand Challenge Cup at Henley?

10. Which football club won the 1999/00 League Cup?

11. Who won the Isle of Man Senior TT in 1991 and 1992?

12. Which team won the 1999 cricket county championship?

13. How many times have Bolton been placed third in the Football League Division 1?

14. Who took over captaincy of Northamptonshire C.C.C. in 1996?

15. Who won the 1975 Boston men's marathon?

ANSWERS 1. Poland 2. U.S.A. 3. Four 4. Dewsbury Rams 5. Biathlon 6. Carl Lewis 7. Mill Reef 8. Cuban 9. Hansa Dortmund RC 10. Leicester City 11. Steve Hislop 12. Surrey 13. Three 14. R.J. Bailey 15. Bill Rodgers.

POP

1. Which female singer recorded the song *I Belong to a World That's Destroying Itself* in 1968?

2. Who recorded the 1999 album *The Science of Things*?

3. Which Irish solo artist once fronted the group *Ten Past Seven*?

4. Which two musicians recorded the 1966 album *Bert and John*?

5. In which year did Paul McCartney have a Top 10 single with *No More Lonely Nights*?

6. Ed Kuepper and Chris Bailey were members of which Australian punk band?

7. In which U.S. city did Pere Ubu form in 1975?

8. Who replaced Dave Krusen as drummer in the group Pearl Jam?

9. Who comprised the 'Million Dollar Quartet' at Sun Records?

10. Which of the Pet Shop Boys is older - Chris Lowe or Neil Tennant?

11. What is the title of the debut album by the group *Cousteau*?

12. Who produced the 1987 album *Little Baby Buntin'* by Killdozer?

13. In which year did Tom Petty & the Heartbreakers release their debut album?

14. Which group recorded the album *The Evil Powers of Rock 'N' Roll*?

15. What was the title of The Penguin Café Orchestra's second album?

ANSWERS 1. Annette Peacock **2.** Bush **3.** Brian Kennedy **4.** Bert Jansch & John Renbourne **5.** 1984 **6.** The Saints **7.** Cleveland **8.** Dave Abbruzzese **9.** Elvis Presley, Johnny Cash, Jerry Lee Lewis and Carl Perkins **10.** Neil Tennant **11.** Cousteau **12.** Butch Vig **13.** 1976 **14.** Supersuckers **15.** Penguin Café Orchestra.

PEOPLE

1. In which year did actor Burgess Meredith die?

2. What was the middle name of U.S. union leader Jimmy Hoffa?

3. In which year did alleged murderess Lizzie Borden die?

4. In which year did Johnny Depp and Kate Moss start dating?

5. In which year was the Duke of Edinburgh born?

6. Who was Foreign Secretary from 1989-95?

7. Who was married from 1973-8 to actress Ali McGraw?

8. Irish nationalist Charles Gavan Duffy became prime minister of which Australian state in 1871?

9. In which year did actor John Wells die?

10. Which football club does actor Joseph Fiennes support?

11. Which Radio 1 disc jockey was shot in July, 1999?

12. Which illness did actor Michael J. Fox announce himself as having in 1999?

13. In which country was writer Jonas Lie born?

14. Which actress wrote the book *How Was It For You*?

15. Which architect did Harry Kendall Thaw murder in 1906?

GENERAL KNOWLEDGE

1. Who is sister of Meg, Jo and Beth March in the novel *Little Women*?

2. In which year did British art historian and Soviet spy Anthony Blunt die?

3. What is the third brightest star in the constellation Orion?

4. Which Scottish jockey was 1983 flat racing champion?

5. Which golfer was winner of the 1998 Philips PFA Golf Classic on the PGA European Seniors Tour?

6. Which town in the Ukraine was the site of a nuclear power accident in 1986?

7. Who was Best Actor Oscar winner for the film *The Color of Money*?

8. Who were the male and female stars of the 1935 film *Top Hat*?

9. In which year did French impressionist painter and sculptor Edgar Degas die?

10. Who was 1952 Olympic men's 5,000m champion?

11. Who was prime minister of New Zealand from 1928-30?

12. On which gulf in Italy is the small port of Imperia?

13. Who was president of the African National Congress from 1977-91?

14. Which Bohemian composer and violinist was Dvorak's son-in-law?

15. Who was 1996 British Open golf champion?

ANSWERS 1. Amy **2.** 1983 **3.** Bellatrix **4.** Willie Carson **5.** Neil Coles **6.** Chernobyl **7.** Paul Newman **8.** Fred Astaire and Ginger Rogers **9.** 1917 **10.** Emil Zatopek **11.** Joseph Ward **12.** Gulf of Genoa **13.** Oliver Tambo **14.** Josef Suk **15.** Tom Lehman.

ENTERTAINMENT

1. Who play the Three Musketeers in the 1997 film *The Man in the Iron Mask*?

2. Which comedian sang the title song of the 1960 film *Raymie*?

3. Who voiced Stinky Pete in the film *Toy Story 2*?

4. In which city was comedian Brian Conley born?

5. Who plays movie producer *Bowfinger* in a 1999 film?

6. Which comedian played Gudrun in the 1999 comedy show *Dark Ages*?

7. Which French actor played the lead in the 1982 film *Danton*?

8. Which Hollywood star played Flynn in the 1997 film *Welcome to Sarajevo*?

9. Who directed the 1999 film *Man on the Moon*?

10. The 1987 film *Dark Eyes* which stars Marcello Mastroianni, is based on stories by which author?

11. Who played Quaker Jess Birdwell in the 1956 film *Friendly Persuasion*?

12. Who played Matthew in the soap *EastEnders*?

13. Who directed the 1997 film *I Know What You Did Last Summer*?

14. What was the title of Bill Forsyth's 1999 follow-up to the film *Gregory's Girl*?

15. The 1956 film *Reach for the Sky* is based on whose life story?

ANSWERS 1. Jeremy Irons, Gérard Depardieu and John Malkovich **2.** Jerry Lewis **3.** Kelsey Grammer **4.** London **5.** Steve Martin **6.** Phill Jupitus **7.** Gérard Depardieu **8.** Woody Harrelson **9.** Milos Forman **10.** Anton Chekhov **11.** Gary Cooper **12.** Joe Absolom **13.** Jim Gillespie **14.** Gregory's Two Girls **15.** Douglas Bader.

SPORT

1. Who was coach at the L'Aquila rugby club in Italy from 1989-91?

2. Which Italian cyclist won the 1983 Giro d'Italia?

3. At what sport have Jeanette Brown and Guyonne Dalle been world champions?

4. Quick as Lightning won the 1980 1000 Guineas. Who was the rider?

5. For which club side do French rugby union players Jean Daud and Sébastien Chabal play?

6. In which vehicle did Gatsonides and Worledge win the 1953 Monte Carlo Rally?

7. For which First Division football club does defender Darren Moore play?

8. U.I.T. is the international governing body of which sport?

9. Which Ryder Cup saw Lee Westwood's first appearance?

10. At what weight did Sugar Ray Leonard win a 1976 Olympic boxing title?

11. Which tennis player was 1992 Sports Illustrated Sportsman of the Year?

12. Who was women's figure skating champion at the 1998 Olympics?

13. How many golds did Morocco win at the 1999 World Athletics Championships?

14. Who were Eastern Division winners of the NFC Conference in American Football in 1980?

15. In which year did Gottfried Van Cramm win the French Open singles tennis title for the second time?

ANSWERS 1. Brad Johnstone **2.** Giuseppe Saronni **3.** Water-skiing **4.** Brian Rouse **5.** Bourgoin **6.** Ford Zephyr **7.** Portsmouth **8.** Shooting **9.** 1997 **10.** Light-welterweight **11.** Arthur Ashe **12.** Tara Lipinski **13.** Two **14.** Philadelphia Eagles **15.** 1936.

POP

1. Which duo recorded the album *Dark Edison Tiger*?

2. With which song, originally a 1959 hit for Phil Phillips, did Robert Plant have a U.S. Top 10 single?

3. Which singer recorded the album *Anytime Tomorrow*?

4. What band recorded the 1999 album *Tilt*?

5. Which punk group's debut album included the tracks *Requiem* and *War Dance*?

6. Which group recorded the album *Home* featuring *Take Your Place*?

7. The group Knife in the Water take their name from a film by which director?

8. Who had a 1984 hit single with *Like To Get To Know You Well*?

9. How old was Curtis Mayfield when he died in 1999?

10. Who recorded the 1995 album *Whip-Smart*?

11. Which studio album by The Clash includes song *The Last Gang in Town*?

12. Murray, Blamire, Chaplin, Smallman. Which punk group?

13. Which guitarist recorded the 1986 album *When a Guitar Sings the Blues*?

14. Which jazz artist's real name is Herman Poule Blount?

15. Which blues artist is nicknamed *The Beale Street Blues Boy*?

ART & LITERATURE

1. In which novel by Charles Dickens does Fagin appear?

2. In which year was Virginia Woolf's novel *Orlando* first published?

3. Who wrote the children's tale *Martin Pippin in the Apple-Orchard*?

4. Which Edinburgh-born author's stories include *The Beach of Falesa*?

5. In which city did artist Tiepolo die in 1770?

6. In which year was Charlotte Brontë's novel *Shirley* published?

7. In which year did author Malcolm Lowry die?

8. Which U.S. author's short stories include *The Mystery of Marie Rogêt* and *The Sphinx*?

9. In which U.S. state was painter Jackson Pollock born?

10. *Temples of Delight* is the third novel of which South Africa-born writer?

11. In which year was painter and poet William Blake born?

12. Which cartoonist drew *The Larks*?

13. Which Dutch artist, who died in 1516, painted *The Seven Deadly Sins* and *The Adoration of the Magi*?

14. Who painted *Kitchen Scene with Christ in the House of Martha and Mary*?

15. Which comedian authored the short story collection *Barcelona Plates*?

ANSWERS 1. Oliver Twist **2.** 1928 **3.** Eleanor Farjeon **4.** Robert Louis Stevenson **5.** Madrid **6.** 1849 **7.** 1957 **8.** Edgar Allan Poe **9.** Wyoming **10.** Barbara Trapido **11.** 1757 **12.** Jack Dunkley **13.** Hieronymous Bosch **14.** Diego Velasquez **15.** Alexei Sayle.

GENERAL KNOWLEDGE

1. Who was the first wife of Jacob in the Old Testament?

2. Which Brighton-born animator was known as 'Britain's answer to Walt Disney'?

3. Who was the Roman goddess of love?

4. Which tennis player was 1994 French Open men's doubles champion with Jonathan Stark?

5. Who was second son of Noah in the Old Testament?

6. Who directed the 1992 film satire *The Player*?

7. Which overture by Mendelssohn was first performed in 1832?

8. Who directed the 1963 film *Irma La Douce*?

9. Who was the Czech composer of the opera *The Bartered Bride*?

10. Which U.S. golfer won the 1998 Shell Houston Open?

11. Who was director of the 1946 film *Duel in the Sun* starring Gregory Peck and Jennifer Jones?

12. What is the name of the nest in which a hare lives?

13. Which novel by John Cleland was subtitled *Memoirs of a Woman of Pleasure*?

14. In which year did Scottish architect and artist Charles Rennie Mackintosh die?

15. Who wrote the 1941 novel *N or M?*?

ANSWERS 1. Leah **2.** Anson Dyer **3.** Venus **4.** Byron Black **5.** Japheth **6.** Robert Altman **7.** Fingal's Cave overture **8.** Billy Wilder **9.** Bedrich Smetana **10.** David Duval **11.** King Vidor **12.** Form **13.** Fanny Hill **14.** 1928 **15.** Agatha Christie.

ENTERTAINMENT

1. Who directed the 1999 film *Deep Blue Sea*?

2. Who plays Peggy Butcher in *EastEnders*?

3. In which year was comedian Billy Connolly born?

4. Who directed the 1999 film *The Green Mile*?

5. Which Irish comedian succeeded Ardal O'Hanlon as the host of BBCTV's *The Stand-up Show*?

6. What was John Thomson's character name in Steve Coogan's television film *Three Fights, Two Weddings and a Funeral*?

7. Who played Susie in the 1999 drama series *Real Women*?

8. Who directed the 1999 film *The Talented Mr. Ripley*?

9. Which cast member played Mr. Creosote in the film *Monty Python's Meaning of Life*?

10. Who won a Best Director Oscar in 2000 for the film *American Beauty*?

11. Who plays villainess Fatima Blush in the 1983 Bond film *Never Say Never Again*?

12. What is the name of the family central to the U.S. sitcom *ALF*?

13. Who played Sheila Haddon in the 1980s sitcom *All At No. 20*?

14. Who starred as an American ambassador in the 1963 film *The Ugly American*?

15. Who is quizmaster on Channel Four's *Fifteen to One*?

ANSWERS 1. Renny Harlin **2.** Barbara Windsor **3.** 1942 **4.** Frank Darabont **5.** Tommy Tiernan **6.** Fat Bob **7.** Michelle Collins **8.** Anthony Minghella **9.** Terry Jones **10.** Sam Mendes **11.** Barbara Carrera **12.** Tanner **13.** Maureen Lipman **14.** Marlon Brando **15.** William G. Stewart.

SPORT

1. Who holds the record of 14 goals scored in World Cup finals tournaments?

2. What nationality is golfer Wayne Riley?

3. Who was 1998 women's 200m freestyle swimming world champion?

4. Which U.S. golfer was leading money winner on the European Tour in 1967?

5. For which international side does winger Liam Botham play?

6. In which year did the world championships in snowboarding start?

7. For which side did cricketer Ian Blackwell make his county debut in 1997?

8. In cricket, how many runs did Papua New Guinea score against Gibraltar in their 60 overs match on 18th June 1986?

9. Which rider led Britain to team bronze at the 1998 World Equestrian Games?

10. Michael Jordan was NBA leading scorer in 1993. What was his average per game?

11. In cricket, who scored 125 for Kent against Somerset in the 2nd innings of their 1999 county championship game?

12. In which year was the French Derby first run?

13. What nationality is boxer Marco Antonio Barrera?

14. In which year were the first world rowing championships held?

15. Which country won the men's water polo title at the 1995 FINA World Cup?

ANSWERS 1. Gerd Müller 2. Australian 3. Claudia Poll 4. Gay Brewer 5. England 6. 1993 7. Derbyshire 8. 455 runs 9. Polly Phillips 10. 32.6 points 11. Robert Key 12. 1836 13. Mexican 14. 1962 15. Hungary.

POP

1. What creature features on the cover of the album *The Fat of the Land* by the Prodigy?

2. On which label did the group S Club 7 record single *S Club Party*?

3. Which female singer recorded the 1999 album *On the 6*?

4. Simon Fowler is lead vocalist with which group?

5. Who had a 2000 No. 1 hit with the song *American Pie*?

6. Which studio album by Julian Cope featured the hit single *Beautiful Love*?

7. Which David Bowie studio album features the single *Fashion*?

8. Who recorded the 1991 album *Mighty Like A Rose*?

9. In which year was Beck born?

10. Which song by the Rolling Stones did Tori Amos cover on the 1992 E.P. *Crucify*?

11. What is Kiss frontman Gene Simmons's real name?

12. Who recorded the 1988 album *Bummed*?

13. Which group recorded the album *Wh'Appen*?

14. Which song does Ron Sexsmith sing on the 1999 compilation album *Bleeker Street*?

15. Who duetted with Tom Jones on the song *Baby, It's Cold Outside* in 1999?

ANSWERS 1. A crab **2.** Polydor **3.** Jennifer Lopez **4.** Ocean Colour Scene **5.** Madonna **6.** Peggy Suicide **7.** Scary Monsters (And Super Creeps) **8.** Elvis Costello **9.** 1970 **10.** Angie **11.** Chaim Witz **12.** Happy Mondays **13.** The Beat **14.** Tim Hardin's *Reason to Believe* **15.** Cerys Matthews.

GEOGRAPHY

1. Between which two countries was the former Russian province of Livonia divided in 1918?

2. Paramaribo is the capital of which South American republic?

3. On which French river is the porcelain centre of Limoges?

4. Where are the administrative headquarters of Gwynedd?

5. The city of Laval is a suburb of which Canadian city?

6. The German city of Duisburg lies at the confluence of which two rivers?

7. On which bay is the Spanish town of La Linea?

8. Shaba is a region of which African country?

9. Which river enters the North Sea at Middlesbrough?

10. Which island joined with Tanganyika to form Tanzania?

11. What is the German village of Blindheim better known as?

12. The former penal colony of Devil's Island belongs to which island group?

13. In which Australian state are the Grampian Mountains?

14. Monte Perdido in Spain is in which mountain range?

15. Georgian Bay is in the N.E. part of which North American Great Lake?

GENERAL KNOWLEDGE

1. Who was wife of Cronus and mother of Zeus in Greek mythology?

2. What was the nickname of Richard I of England?

3. Who wrote the 1863 novel *Hard Cash*?

4. Which is the inner and longer of the two bones of the human forearm?

5. Which Argentinian was 1998 W.B.A. flyweight boxing champion?

6. The St. John River, which forms part of the international boundary between the U.S. and Canada, rises in which state?

7. Who wrote 1880 novel *The Tragic Comedians*?

8. Who was prime minister of Israel from 1977-83?

9. Which British field marshal was commander-in-chief of the British forces in France and Flanders from 1915-18?

10. Which Canada-born revue singer's films included 1967's *Thoroughly Modern Millie*?

11. Which playwright's works for television include 1991's *GBH*?

12. Which unit of distance used in astronomy is equal to 0.3066 of a parsec?

13. Which pop group's Top 10 singles included 1971's *My Brother Jake*?

14. Who is narrator of the novel *Brideshead Revisited*?

15. Which 1979 record album by Michael Jackson spent over 170 weeks in the U.K. album chart?

ANSWERS 1. Rhea **2.** The Lion-Heart (or Couer de Lion) **3.** Charles Reade **4.** Ulna **5.** Hugo Soto **6.** Maine **7.** George Meredith **8.** Menachim Begin **9.** Douglas Haig **10.** Beatrice Lillie **11.** Alan Bleasdale **12.** A light year **13.** Free **14.** Charles Ryder **15.** Off the Wall.

ENTERTAINMENT

1. Who composed the 1938 one-act opera *Daphne*?

2. Who plays Pauline Fowler in *EastEnders*?

3. Which actor terrorises Audrey Hepburn in the 1967 film *Wait Until Dark*?

4. Who replaced Peter Jay as presenter of ITV's *Weekend World*?

5. Which comedian starred in the 1989 film *UHF*?

6. Who directed film *Bicentennial Man*?

7. Who scored the 1971 film *Walkabout*?

8. In which European capital is the 1937 film *Dark Journey* set?

9. Which two actors played the Dean in the BBCTV sitcom *All Gas and Gaiters*?

10. Which comedian co-presented the satellite television show *Prickly Heat* with Denise Van Outen?

11. Who played Pamela Lynch in the sitcom *Watching*?

12. Who plays a beekeeper in the 1997 film *Ulee's Gold*?

13. Who plays Nicki in the television drama *Sunburn*?

14. Who plays the title role in the 1954 film *Ulysses*?

15. Who composed the 1954 five-act opera *David*?

ANSWERS 1. Richard Strauss **2.** Wendy Richard **3.** Alan Arkin **4.** Brian Walden **5.** 'Weird Al' Yankovic **6.** Chris Columbus **7.** John Barry **8.** Stockholm **9.** John Barron and Ernest Clark **10.** Julian Clary **11.** Liza Tarbuck **12.** Peter Fonda **13.** Michelle Collins **14.** Kirk Douglas **15.** Milhaud.

THE CARLING PUB QUIZ BOOK

SPORT

1. Who was 1954 and 1956 World Sidecar champion in motorcycling?

2. Where were the 1981 World Student Games held?

3. Which Second Division team appeared in the 1920 F.A. Cup Final?

4. Where were the 1958 Asian Games held?

5. How long did Lorraine Miller take to run 10 miles on 9th January 1993?

6. What nationality is golfer Olivier Edmond?

7. What nationality is champion amateur cyclist Bruno Risi?

8. In which year did British tennis player Lottie Dod die?

9. Which club won the men's English National Inter-League in hockey in 1990?

10. Who did Bristol play in the quarter-finals of the Tetley's Bitter Cup in rugby union in 1990?

11. Which Briton was part of the team that won the 1998 Le Mans 24-Hour Race?

12. Where were the 1983 Pan-American Games held?

13. What was the name of the winning boat in the 1886 America's Cup?

14. Which golfer was 1964 Sports Illustrated Sportsman of the Year?

15. Samuth Sithnaruepol was 1988 IBF boxing champion. At what weight?

ANSWERS 1. Wilhelm Noll **2.** Bucharest **3.** Huddersfield Town **4.** Tokyo **5.** 54:21.8 **6.** French **7.** Swiss **8.** 1960 **9.** Havant **10.** Harlequins **11.** Allan McNish **12.** Caracas **13.** Mayflower **14.** Ken Venturi **15.** Strawweight.

POP

1. Nick Kane is guitarist with which best-selling group?

2. On which label was Tim Hardin's debut L.P. recorded?

3. Matthew Bellamy is singer with which group?

4. Which group recorded the 1999 Top 10 album *Invincible*?

5. Who is the female singer with the group Venini?

6. Who is lead singer with Heaven 17?

7. Which studio album by Laurie Anderson features the song *O Superman*?

8. Dr. John's album *Duke Elegant* is an album of whose songs?

9. On which album cover did baby Spencer Elden feature in 1991?

10. Which group recorded the 1993 album *Gentlemen*?

11. Which solo artist had a 1999 Top 10 single with *Man! I Feel Like A Woman*?

12. With which female singer did Zucchero duet on the 1992 hit *Diamante*?

13. Which duo recorded the 1991 single *Zeroxed*?

14. What is the title of the Divine Comedy's 1999 'Greatest Hits' album?

15. Which group's only hit single was 1965's *She's Lost You*?

ANSWERS 1. The Mavericks **2.** Verve **3.** Muse **4.** Five **5.** Debbie Lime **6.** Glenn Gregory **7.** Big Science **8.** Duke Ellington **9.** *Nevermind* by Nirvana **10.** The Afghan Whigs **11.** Shania Twain **12.** Randy Crawford **13.** Zero Zero **14.** A Secret History **15.** The Zephyrs.

HISTORY

1. The Tripolitan War of 1801-5 was between the North African state of Tripoli and which country?

2. To which islands was Archbishop Makarios of Cyprus exiled in 1956?

3. What was Benito Mussolini's father's occupation?

4. In which month of 1215 did King John sign the Magna Carta?

5. Who was governor of the U.S. state of Georgia from 1971-5?

6. Who was U.S. ambassador to the United Nations from 1971-2?

7. In which year did Henry VIII of England die?

8. In which year was Marie Antoinette guillotined?

9. Which womens' rights leader was born Emmeline Goulden in 1858?

10. Who served as Lord Chancellor from 1660-7?

11. Who was made King of Spain in 1808 by Napoleon?

12. Who did John of Gaunt marry in 1396 after the death of his second wife?

13. In which year was the Beer Hall Putsch initiated by Adolf Hitler?

14. In which year did Iraq invade Kuwait, leading to the Gulf War?

15. In which month of 1982 did Argentina first invade the Falkland Islands?

ANSWERS 1. United States **2.** Seychelles **3.** Blacksmith **4.** June **5.** Jimmy Carter **6.** George Bush **7.** 1547 **8.** 1793 **9.** Emmeline Pankhurst **10.** Edward Hyde, Earl of Clarendon **11.** Joseph Bonaparte **12.** Catherine Swynford **13.** 1923 **14.** 1990 **15.** April.

GENERAL KNOWLEDGE

1. What is the name of the annual ceremony held on the Queen's Birthday on Horse Guards Parade?

2. Who directed the 1984 film *Swann in Love* starring Jeremy Irons?

3. For which 1953 film was Richard Burton a Best Actor Oscar nominee?

4. What character did George Raft play in the 1932 film *Scarface*?

5. Who was German commander-in-chief at the Battle of Jutland in 1916?

6. Which port in the Côte d'Ivoire is the legislative capital of the country?

7. In which year did cricket commentator John Arlott die?

8. What is an oenophile?

9. An aberdevine was the former name for which cagebird?

10. Which genus of plants includes dyer's rocket?

11. Who directed the 1977 World War II film *A Bridge Too Far*?

12. What did Melvil Dewey most famously invent?

13. Which arm of the Atlantic Ocean was formerly known as the German Ocean?

14. What is the name of the white two-piece cotton costume worn to play judo?

15. Who was the Dutch painter of *The Garden of Earthly Delights*?

ANSWERS 1. Trooping the Colour **2.** Volker Schlöndorff **3.** The Robe **4.** Rinaldo **5.** Reinhard Scheer **6.** Abidjan **7.** 1991 **8.** A lover of wines **9.** Siskin **10.** Reseda **11.** Richard Attenborough **12.** A system for the classification of library books **13.** North Sea **14.** Judogi **15.** Hieronymus Bosch

ENTERTAINMENT

1. In which comedy show did German exchange teacher Herr Lipp appear?

2. Who directed the 1988 film *Walker*?

3. Which actress played a wheelchair-bound crime writer in the 1994 sitcom *All Night Long*?

4. Who played Steerpike in the 2000 BBCTV adaptation of *Gormenghast*?

5. Who played Trudy in the 2000 BBCTV drama *Clocking Off*?

6. Which actor played Tom Wedloe in the children's TV show *Gentle Ben*?

7. In which year did conductor Andrew Davis make his debut at Glyndebourne?

8. In which city was the ITV drama *At Home with the Braithwaites* set?

9. Who plays Dot Cotton in *EastEnders*?

10. Who directed the 1993 film *The Dark Half*, which was based on a Stephen King book?

11. Who was originally chosen to play Archie Bunker in the U.S. sitcom *All in the Family*?

12. Who directed the 1975 film *French Connection 2*?

13. Who played the wife of Robert Donat in the 1939 film *Goodbye Mr. Chips*?

14. Who directed the 1992 film *Lorenzo's Oil*?

15. *The New Centurions* is a 1972 film about which U.S. city's police force?

ANSWERS 1. The League of Gentlemen **2.** Alex Cox **3.** Dinah Sheridan **4.** Jonathan Rhys Meyers **5.** Lesley Sharp **6.** Dennis Weaver **7.** 1973 **8.** Leeds **9.** June Brown **10.** George A. Romero **11.** Mickey Rooney **12.** John Frankenheimer **13.** Greer Garson **14.** George Miller **15.** Los Angeles.

SPORT

1. In cricket, who scored 108 for Middlesex vs. Leicestershire in the 2nd innings of their 1999 county championship game?

2. In which sport is the Conn Smythe Trophy awarded?

3. Where were the 1983 World Student games held?

4. Who scored a total of five field goals for the San Francisco 49ers in their two Super Bowl games in 1982 and 1985?

5. Which pair were 1997 U.S. Open men's doubles tennis champions?

6. In football, who did Holland beat in the 1998 World Cup 2nd Round?

7. For which rugby league club do Richie Blackmore and David Barnhill play?

8. In which year was the World Cup in diving first held?

9. How many times did Bobby Jones win the U.S. Amateur Championship in golf?

10. For which French side does Scotland rugby union player Stuart Reid play?

11. Which country were world team champions at speedway in 1995?

12. What is the profession of Mary Reveley?

13. Who scored the two double centuries for Kent against Essex in their cricket match in July 1938?

14. What nationality is golfer Jose Coceres?

15. Which man won the 1984 and 1985 Biathlon World Cup?

POP

1. Which group recorded the 1991 single *My Head's in Mississippi*?

2. Two-thirds of which trio used to be in a band called The Jennifers?

3. In which city did Michael Hutchence die?

4. Who recorded the 1969 album *Folkjokeopus*?

5. In which city was singer Kevin Coyne born?

6. Which group covered David Bowie's song *Ziggy Stardust* in 1982?

7. Which studio album by Lambchop features the track *Your Life As A Sequel*?

8. Which German group released the album *Underwater Sunlight*?

9. Which solo singer had a 1999 Top 10 single with *Wild Wild West*?

10. Who produced Meat Loaf's album *Bat Out of Hell*?

11. Who had a 2000 Top 10 single with *Show Me the Meaning of Being Lonely*?

12. Which studio album by Be-Bop Deluxe contains the song *Maid in Heaven*?

13. Which two women's names provided Marty Wilde with hit singles?

14. What was Dr. Feelgood drummer John Martin better known as?

15. Which unusual pairing had a 1987 hit with *Rockin' Around the Christmas Tree*?

WORDS

1. What is the holding of two nonconsecutive high cards in a suit at bridge called?

2. What type of creature is a goa?

3. What in Canada is muskeg?

4. What would you have done with a johannes in Portugal in the 18c?

5. A howlet is a poetic name for which bird?

6. What type of bird is a koel?

7. If something is caprine, what creature does it resemble?

8. Why might you eat a cheerio in New Zealand?

9. What is a tenterhook used to hold?

10. What is another name for a fever blister?

11. Gnathic refers to which part of the body?

12. What does a thurifer carry?

13. What in Scotland is a hoast?

14. What shape is a tomb called a tholos?

15. What word in ballet is used to describe the tip of the toe?

ANSWERS 1. Tenace **2.** A gazelle or antelope **3.** Undrained boggy land **4.** Spent it **5.** An owl **6.** A cuckoo **7.** A goat **8.** It's a small sausage **9.** Cloth **10.** Cold sore **11.** The jaw **12.** The censer at a religious ceremony **13.** A cough **14.** Beehive-shaped **15.** Pointe.

GENERAL KNOWLEDGE

1. Who were the male and female leads in the 1978 film musical *Grease*?

2. Who wrote the 1958 novel *The Dharma Bums*?

3. Which duo starred in the 1983 comedy film thriller *Two of a Kind*?

4. In philately, what is the name given to a horizontal or vertical row of three or more joined postage stamps?

5. In which year did trombonist and composer Kid Ory die?

6. What is the name given to the great circle of the earth at 0° latitude?

7. Which character actor born in 1894 played Moriarty in the 1945 film *The Woman in Green*?

8. Who wrote the 1953 novel *In the Wet*?

9. Which woman wrote the 1937 book *The Years*?

10. In which year of the 1970s was the Italian city of Udine partially damaged by an earthquake?

11. Which 18th century British admiral captured Martinique in 1762?

12. The 1999 Channel Four drama series *Psychos* was set in a hospital in which city?

13. Which 1985 film by Richard Attenborough starred Michael Douglas as a choreographer?

14. What type of creature is the bharal, which inhabits the Himalayas?

15. On which body of water is the West Somerset port of Watchet?

ANSWERS 1. John Travolta and Olivia Newton-John **2.** Jack Kerouac **3.** John Travolta and Olivia Newton-John **4.** Strip **5.** 1973 **6.** Equator **7.** Henry Daniell **8.** Nevil Shute **9.** Virginia Woolf **10.** 1976 **11.** George Rodney **12.** Glasgow **13.** A Chorus Line **14.** Sheep **15.** Bristol Channel.

ENTERTAINMENT

1. Who directed the 1956 film *Around the World in Eighty Days*?

2. What is Walter Matthau's profession in the 1969 film *Cactus Flower*?

3. Who composed the opera *La Bohème*?

4. Who directed and starred in the 1972 film *Rage*?

5. Who played Clarice Starling in the film *The Silence of the Lambs*?

6. Who plays the lead as a pirate in the 1962 film *The Rage of the Buccaneers*?

7. Which actor starred in the films *The Mummy* and *George of the Jungle*?

8. Who played the lead in the 1952 film *Hans Christian Andersen*?

9. Who composed the 1825 one-act opera *Don Sanche*?

10. What nationality is soprano Barbara Bonney?

11. Who directed the 1970 film *The Arousers*?

12. How many million dollars did Mark Wahlberg earn for the film *Three Kings*?

13. Which *Upstairs Downstairs* actress played *Olivia* in the soap *Sunset Beach*?

14. In which European capital is the 1932 film *Arsène Lupin* set?

15. Which James Bond actor appears in the film *The Long Good Friday* as an Irish terrorist?

SPORT

1. Who scored a 140 break in the 2000 Benson and Hedges Masters snooker tournament to win £19,000?

2. Which jockey won the 1997 Prix Royal Oak on Ebadiyla?

3. Which BNL hockey side signed Canadian Chad MacLeod in September 1999?

4. Which country won the 1975 rugby league World Cup?

5. In which year did Tobin Bailey make his county debut for Northants at cricket?

6. Who won the Isle of Man senior TT in 1993?

7. How many Tests did cricketer Craig White play for England from 1994-7?

8. How many times have Sheffield United won the 1st Division in football?

9. Who was men's European water-skiing champion in 1974 & 1975?

10. Who won the 1985 Chicago men's marathon?

11. What nationality is golfer Riikka Hakkarainen?

12. Which Spaniard won the 1982 Vuelta a España cycle race?

13. With what sport are Pippa Funnell and Karen Dixon associated?

14. My Babu won the 1948 2000 Guineas. Who was the rider?

15. Which cyclist is known as El Yaya?

ANSWERS 1. Ken Doherty 2. Gérald Mosse 3. Milton Keynes Kings 4. Australia 5. 1996 6. Phillip McCallen 7. Eight 8. Once 9. Paul Seaton 10. Steve Jones 11. Finnish 12. Marino Lejarreta 13. Equestrianism 14. Charlie Smirke 15. Laurent Jalabert.

POP

1. What is unusual about the record player on the back cover of Jethro Tull's album *Songs From the Wood?*

2. Which mod-revival group recorded the 1981 album *Ambience?*

3. Which group had a 1975 hit single with *Skiing in the Snow?*

4. Which U2 studio album includes the song *With or Without You?*

5. What was Barry White's first Top 30 hit single?

6. What relationship was Mike Love to Brian, Carl, and Dennis Wilson of the Beach Boys?

7. Which Irish group had a 1996 hit single with *Twinkle?*

8. Who recorded the 1971 album *Sun, Moon and Herbs?*

9. Which solo singer had a 1999 Top 10 single with *My Love is Your Love?*

10. Which female singer had her first solo hit in 1990 with *Livin' in the Light?*

11. What was the second album by The Beastie Boys?

12. Abiodun Oyewole was sentenced to 14 years imprisonment for robbery in 1970. With which group had he been performing prior to his arrest?

13. Which Swedish group had a hit in 1998 with *Four Big Speakers?*

14. On which label is the album *Unplugged* by the Corrs?

15. Which girl group had a hit single in 1986 with *Love is the Slug?*

ANSWERS 1. It's made from a tree stump **2.** The Lambrettas **3.** Wigan's Ovation **4.** The Joshua Tree **5.** I'm Gonna Love You Just A Little Bit More Baby **6.** Cousin **7.** Whipping Boy **8.** Dr. John **9.** Whitney Houston **10.** Caron Wheeler **11.** Paul's Boutique **12.** The Last Poets **13.** Whale **14.** Atlantic **15.** We've Got A Fuzzbox and We're Gonna Use It.

SCIENCE

1. In which European capital was physicist Edward Teller born?

2. Which English scientist discovered benzene in 1825?

3. What, in computing, does ISDN stand for?

4. In which year was J. Robert Oppenheimer awarded the Enrico Fermi Award by the Atomic Energy Commission?

5. What, in computing, does PCMCIA stand for?

6. In which year was Dolly the cloned sheep created?

7. Which was the first element to be created artificially?

8. What nationality was botanist Hugo Marie De Vries?

9. In which capital city is the Institut Pasteur based?

10. With reference to the illness, what does the acronym AIDS stand for?

11. Which naturalist's written works include 1869's *Malay Archipelago*?

12. In which century did British biologist Thomas Henry Huxley live?

13. V is the symbol for which unit of electromotive force?

14. Which British scientist is considered the founder of the science of eugenics?

15. In which century did German physicist Otto von Guericke live?

GENERAL KNOWLEDGE

1. Who wrote the 1858 novel *Doctor Thorne*?

2. Who was author of the book *I, Claudius*?

3. Which plant of the genus Lactuca is cultivated for its large edible leaves?

4. Who played the lead in the 1960s cult science fiction television series *Adam Adamant Lives!*?

5. What name did pop singer Alvin Stardust use when he led the group The Fentones?

6. Kishinev is capital of which republic in S.E. Europe?

7. Who was 1990 Wimbledon women's singles tennis championship runner-up?

8. Who was author of the short story collection *The Day We Got Drunk on Cake*?

9. Which symbol of Joan of Arc was adopted by the free French forces' leader Charles de Gaulle in 1940?

10. The Chianti mountain range in Tuscany is part of which mountain group?

11. Which club were winners of the 1997 Courage Clubs championship in rugby union?

12. Which American theatre director and producer collaborated with Orson Welles in running the Mercury Theatre company?

13. Who wrote the 1909 play *Strife*?

14. Which 18th Century Italian etcher's works include *Imaginary Prisons*?

15. Who authored the 1881 novel *A Laodicean*?

ENTERTAINMENT

1. What was Tommy Lee Jones's character name in the film *Batman Forever*?

2. Who plays Bev McLoughlin in *Brookside*?

3. Who played Neil Hamilton in the television drama-documentary *Justice in Wonderland*?

4. Who directed the 1987 film *Good Morning, Vietnam*?

5. Who directed the 1997 film *As Good As It Gets*?

6. Which actor directed and starred in the 1991 film *Cadence*?

7. Who played *Shaft* in a 1971 film ?

8. Who plays the Angel Gabriel in the 1994 film *The Prophecy*?

9. Who played the lead in the 1965 film *Dr. Zhivago*?

10. Which band won Best Album award at the 2000 Brits?

11. Who played Cleopatra in the 1946 film *Caesar and Cleopatra*?

12. Who won Best Female Artist at the 2000 Brits?

13. What nationality was soprano Xenia Dorliak?

14. Which actress was born Theodosia Goodman in 1890?

15. Who played the lead role in the 1973 film *Cahill - United States Marshal*?

SPORT

1. In which vehicle did Chiron and Basadonna win the 1954 Monte Carlo rally?

2. What nationality is golfer Nina Karlsson?

3. In which year did shooting become part of the Olympic programme?

4. In cricket, who scored 110 for Northants vs. Hants in the 1st innings of their 1999 county championship game?

5. Aleksandr Lebziak was 1997 world amateur boxing champion. At what weight?

6. What nationality is golfer Thomas Bjorn?

7. Anna Hübler and Heinrich Burger were pairs figure skating champions at which Olympics?

8. Which golfer was 1978 Sports Illustrated Sportsman of the Year?

9. Who were Eastern Division winners of the NFC Conference in American Football in 1979?

10. Who was 1988 French Open men's singles tennis title winner?

11. In which city was the 1988 football World Cup Group E game between Belgium and South Korea played?

12. For which country was Linetta Wilson a 1996 Olympic swimming champion?

13. At what sport was Olga Sedakova a 1998 world champion?

14. Who won the Harry Vardon Trophy in golf from 1971-4?

15. In which country was Italy's rugby union player Wilhelmus Visser born?

ANSWERS 1. Lancia-Aurelia **2.** Swedish **3.** 1896 **4.** Russell Warren **5.** Light-heavyweight **6.** Danish **7.** 1908 **8.** Jack Nicklaus **9.** Dallas Cowboys **10.** Mats Wilander **11.** Paris **12.** U.S.A. **13.** Synchronised swimming **14.** Peter Oosterhuis **15.** South Africa.

POP

1. Parker, Schenker, Raymond, Mogg, Way. Which heavy rock group?

2. Which U.S. singer had a 1956 hit single with *Tumbling Tumbleweeds*?

3. Which female singer recorded the 1988 album *Shadowland*?

4. What was the debut single of Birmingham group The Beat?

5. What was Roger Whittaker's first Top 10 single?

6. Which folk artist recorded the 1972 solo album *Myrrh*?

7. On what label was The Who's 1965 hit *I Can't Explain*?

8. In which year was B.A. Robertson's *Knocked It Off* a Top 10 single?

9. In which year did Dollar have a Top 10 single with *Love's Gotta Hold On Me*?

10. What was the debut L.P. by The Beatles?

11. Who is the organiser of the annual Glastonbury Festival?

12. Which German group recorded the 2000 single *Expo 2000*?

13. From which city do the group Subaqwa hail?

14. In which year did Roxy Music have a Top 10 hit single with *Angel Eyes*?

15. Which California group recorded the 1967 album *Headquarters*?

ANSWERS 1. U.F.O. **2.** Slim Whitman **3.** KD Lang **4.** Tears of a Clown **5.** I Don't Believe In If Anymore **6.** Robin Williamson **7.** Brunswick **8.** 1979 **9.** 1979 **10.** Please Please Me **11.** Michael Eavis **12.** Kraftwerk **13.** Birmingham **14.** 1979 **15.** The Monkees.

THE CARLING PUB QUIZ BOOK

PEOPLE

1. Which journalist has written the volume of autobiography *Strange Places, Questionable People*?

2. Which automobile manufacturer introduced the 'Plymouth' motor car?

3. In which year did cookery writer Mrs. Beeton die?

4. Which pop star has written the autobiography *Say Yes!*?

5. In which country was economist J.K. Galbraith born?

6. How old was athlete Florence Griffith-Joyner when she died in 1998?

7. In which year did naturalist Charles Darwin die?

8. In which year was President Lincoln assassinated?

9. Scientist Peter Artedi was known as the 'father of ichthyology'. What nationality was he?

10. Which actress was born Lucille Le Sueur in 1906?

11. In which year was sports administrator Ali Bacher born?

12. In which year did broadcaster Hughie Green die?

13. What was the name of the first person to win £500,000 on the television quiz *Who Wants To Be A Millionaire?*

14. What is the name of singer-actress Courtney Love's daughter?

15. Jane Goldman is the wife of which television presenter?

ANSWERS 1. John Simpson **2.** Walter Chrysler **3.** 1865 **4.** Rick Wakeman **5.** Canada **6.** 38 **7.** 1882 **8.** 1865 **9.** Swedish **10.** Joan Crawford **11.** 1942 **12.** 1997 **13.** Peter Lee **14.** Frances Bean **15.** Jonathan Ross.

GENERAL KNOWLEDGE

1. What is the name given to the set of chalk stacks off the west coast of the Isle of Wight?

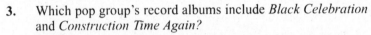

2. What is the chief port of Tanzania?

3. Which pop group's record albums include *Black Celebration* and *Construction Time Again?*

4. Who was the male star of the 1989 film *How to Get Ahead in Advertising,* directed by Bruce Robinson?

5. Who was the 1950-9 British Open women's squash champion?

6. Which jockey won the St. Leger in 1995 and 1996 on horses Classic Cliche and Shantou respectively?

7. Who wrote the 1963 novel *The Unicorn?*

8. What is the name given to the artistic distribution of light and dark masses in a painting?

9. Who wrote the 1988 novel *The Satanic Verses?*

10. What is the name given to the South African coin containing 1 troy ouce of gold?

11. What was the former name, until 1973, of the island Bioko?

12. Who was the author of the poem *The Lady of Shalott?*

13. In which year was British cartoonist Gerald Scarfe born?

14. What is the name of the fielding position in cricket between cover and mid-off ?

15. What Israeli monetary unit is worth one hundredth of a shekel?

ENTERTAINMENT

1. Who was the first husband of actress Brigitte Bardot?

2. Who played *Little Lord Fauntleroy* in the 1936 film?

3. Who starred opposite Pierce Brosnan in the remake of *The Thomas Crown Affair*?

4. In which city was actor John Barrymore born?

5. Which actor stars opposite Jennifer Aniston in the film *Metal God*?

6. Which actor directed and starred in the 1973 film *Antony and Cleopatra*?

7. Who plays Ron in the soap *Brookside*?

8. Who played gangster John Dillinger in 1979 film *The Lady in Red*?

9. Who directed the 1988 film *Talk Radio*?

10. Who directed the 1936 film musical *Anything Goes*?

11. Which duo wrote the 1974 sitcom *Thick As Thieves*?

12. In which year in the future is the 1982 film *Blade Runner* set?

13. Which actress played Ophelia in the 1996 film *Hamlet*?

14. Which actor voiced Sgt. Major Zero in the 1980s children's puppet show *Terrahawks*?

15. Which 1972 film by Ken Russell is about sculptor Henri Gaudier-Brzeska?

SPORT

1. Who was the 1980 individual world speedway champion?

2. Who was Scotland rugby union coach for their 2000 Six Nations game against France?

3. In his 36,049 first-class runs total from 1957-83, how many tons did Alan Jones make?

4. In which year was athlete Dawn Sowell born?

5. Who was the 1968 Olympic men's 20km biathlon champion?

6. In which year was athlete Gail Devers born?

7. In which month is the Prix de l'Arc de Triomph run?

8. In which year was athlete Sheila Echols born?

9. In which year was the Henley Royal Regatta inaugurated?

10. Who was named top female athlete of the 20th Century by the I.A.A.F. in November 1999?

11. Who was Wimbledon men's singles tennis champion in 1946?

12. In which year was wicket-keeper A.N. Aymes born?

13. Who won the 1995 League Cup in football?

14. Which players met in the 2000 Thailand Masters snooker final?

15. How long did Ann Jansson take to walk 15,000 metres on 25th October 1987?

ANSWERS 1. Michael Lee 2. Ian McGeechan 3. 56 4. 1966 5. Magnar Solberg 6. 1966 7. October 8. 1964 9. 1839 10. Fanny Blankers-Koen 11. Yvon Petra 12. 1964 13. Liverpool 14. Mark Williams & Stephen Hendry 15. 1hr 15:37.9.

POP

1. On which label did the Eurythmics record their album *Peace*?

2. Which unlikely duo sang song *Where the Wild Roses Grow* at Nick Cave's Meltdown Festival in 1999?

3. Who featured on the 1990 Top 10 single *Got to Have Your Love* by Mantronix?

4. Bid was the singer in which London-based group formed in 1978?

5. What were the forenames of the Louvin Brothers?

6. Nick Hallam and Rob Birch comprise which group?

7. Who was the singer in the group *The Left Banke*?

8. Which comedian was responsible for the reformation of the group The Cult in 2000?

9. Who is the eldest member of the group Travis?

10. Which Rolling Stones song did Eddie and the Hot Rods cover on their *Live At The Marquee* E.P.?

11. On which label did Alanis Morissette record the 1995 L.P. *Jagged Little Pill*?

12. Which of his own compositions is on the B-side of Bryan Ferry's single *Let's Stick Together*?

13. Which songwriter recorded the album *Pink Moon*?

14. Which pair wrote the Echo and the Bunnymen song *Read it in Books*?

15. Simon Mills and Nail comprise which duo?

ANSWERS 1. RCA **2.** Kylie Minogue and Sir Les Patterson **3.** Wondress **4.** The Monochrome Set **5.** Ira and Charlie **6.** Stereo MC's **7.** Steve Martin **8.** Vic Reeves **9.** Neil Primrose **10.** Satisfaction **11.** Maverick **12.** Sea Breezes **13.** Nick Drake **14.** Ian McCulloch and Julian Cope **15.** Bent.

ART

1. In which year did artist Henri Fantin-Latour die?

2. In which year did Peter Paul Rubens, born in 1577, marry 16 year-old Hélène Fourment?

3. Who penned the story *The Minister's Wooing*?

4. Who wrote the 1999 book *Adrian Mole: The Cappuccino Years*?

5. Who wrote *Day of the Triffids*?

6. Who is the author of the 2000 novel *Dark Hollow*?

7. Who wrote *Invasion of the Body Snatchers*?

8. Who painted 1660's *Maidservant Pouring Milk*?

9. Who wrote the 2000 crime novel *Dreamworld*?

10. In which century did painter Georges Seurat live?

11. Who wrote the thriller novel *The Houdini Girl*?

12. In which year did the artist Jean Antoine Watteau die?

13. Who wrote the novel *The Skull Mantra*?

14. Which German Expressionist painter's works include the triptych *Departure*?

15. Which character narrates the 1899 novel *The Amateur Cracksman* by E.W. Hornung?

ANSWERS 1. 1904 **2.** 1630 **3.** Harriet Beecher Stowe **4.** Sue Townsend **5.** John Wyndham **6.** John Connolly **7.** Jack Finney **8.** Jan Vermeer **9.** Jane Goldman **10.** 19th **11.** Martyn Bedford **12.** 1721 **13.** Eliot Pattison **14.** Max Beckmann **15.** Bunny.

THE CARLING PUB QUIZ BOOK

GENERAL KNOWLEDGE

1. Which island in Indonesia is the largest of the Lesser Sunda Islands?

2. What is the name given to the study of the composition and formation of rocks?

3. Which 1990 film was a belated follow-up to *Chinatown* starring Jack Nicholson?

4. For which 1995 film was Sharon Stone a Best Actress Oscar nominee?

5. In Hindu mythology, what is the food of the gods that bestows immortality?

6. What was the name of the character played by Rodney Bewes in the sitcom *The Likely Lads*?

7. What was the first Top 10 single, in 1967, by the group the Jimi Hendrix Experience?

8. Who was the author of the 1934 novel *Gaudy Night*?

9. Which actor played Officer Francis Poncherello in the television police drama *CHiPS*?

10. Who was a Best Supporting Actress Oscar winner for her role as Mrs. Van Daan in *The Diary of Anne Frank*?

11. Which flower of Greek legend was said to cover the Elysian fields?

12. For which 1994 film did Jessica Lange win a Best Actress Oscar?

13. Which former Pakistan Test cricket captain scored 211 against Australia at Karachi in 1988-9?

14. Who directed the 1991 film *Thelma & Louise*?

15. Who was president of South Africa from 1984-9?

ANSWERS 1. Timor **2.** Petrology **3.** The Two Jakes **4.** Casino **5.** Amrita **6.** Bob Ferris **7.** Hey, Joe **8.** Dorothy L. Sayers **9.** Erik Estrada **10.** Shelley Winters **11.** Asphodel **12.** Blue Sky **13.** Javed Miandad **14.** Ridley Scott **15.** P.W. Botha.

ENTERTAINMENT

1. Which actress played Blanche Simmons in the television drama *Tenko*?

2. Who directed the 1972 film *Hammersmith is Out*?

3. In which year did *Telly Addicts* begin on BBCTV?

4. Who directed the 1955 film *Apache Woman*?

5. Who created the sitcom *Tell it to the Marines* which began in 1959?

6. Who directed the 1985 historical film *Lady Jane*?

7. Who played Latka Gravas in the sitcom *Taxi*?

8. Which actress provides the love interest in the 1955 film *The Tall Men*?

9. Who played author Knut Hamsun in the 1996 film *Hamsun*?

10. What is *Coronation Street* actor Bill Tarmey's real name?

11. In which South American capital is the 1988 film *Apartment Zero* set?

12. What was the name of the guinea pig in the 1960s children's show *Tales of the Riverbank*?

13. In which year did Victor Borge make his British television debut?

14. Who played Jenny in the BBC TV drama *Take Three Girls*?

15. Who presented the 1960s game show *Take A Letter*?

SPORT

1. In which year did cricketer Douglas Brown make his county debut for Warwickshire?

2. Which Italian won the 1925 Tour de France?

3. At what sport have Janelle Kirkley, Sylvie Hulsemann and Renate Hansluvka been world champions?

4. Tudor Minstrel won the 1947 2000 Guineas. Who was the rider?

5. What nationality is tennis player Francisco Clavet?

6. Over what distance, in yards, is a drag race?

7. In which year did U.S. tennis player Hazel Hotchkiss die?

8. Which American won the 1980 single-handed transatlantic yacht race?

9. In which year did cricketer Jason Brown make his county debut for Northamptonshire?

10. Ulderico Sergo was 1936 Olympic bantamweight champion. Which country did he represent?

11. In which sport do Simon Archer and Joanne Goode play as a doubles team?

12. Who was men's figure skating champion at the 1998 Olympics?

13. In which year did wicket-keeper Keith Brown make his county debut for Middlesex?

14. Who scored seven field goals for Minnesota against Los Angeles in their American Football game in November 1989?

15. Who partnered Bob Hewitt to victory in the 1979 U.S. Open mixed doubles tennis championship?

ANSWERS 1. 1992 **2.** Ottavio Bottecchia **3.** Water skiing **4.** Gordon Richards **5.** Spanish **6.** 440 yards **7.** 1974 **8.** Phil Weld **9.** 1996 **10.** Italy **11.** Badminton **12.** Ilya Kulik **13.** 1984 **14.** Rich Karlis **15.** Greer Stevens.

POP

1. Which label did Leiber and Stoller launch in 1964?

2. Which Bob Dylan studio album features the song *Gates of Eden*?

3. Which 1990 Kylie Minogue hit does Nick Cave recite on the 2000 spoken-word C.D. release *The Secret Life of the Love Song*?

4. Which duo wrote the song *Hit Me With Your Rhythm Stick*?

5. What was the nickname of producer George Morton?

6. Lee Gorton and Ian Smith are members of which Salford group?

7. On which label did Steve Earle record his album *Guitar Town*?

8. Who had a 1966 hit with the song *Sweet Talking Guy*?

9. Blade, Chevette, Woodcock, Generate. Which punk group?

10. Who is the keyboard player with the group Embrace?

11. Who was the female singer in the Leeds group Girls at Our Best*?*

12. Kenny Pickett was lead singer in which 1960s group?

13. Who is the lead singer in the group Hefner?

14. On which label did Melanie C record her debut solo album?

15. Who recorded the 1999 album *In Reverse*?

GEOGRAPHY

1. Santa Fé is the capital of which U.S. state?

2. The Shiré Highlands is an upland area of which African country?

3. In which European country is the town of Schwyz?

4. What did the Netherlands East Indies become in 1945?

5. In which English county is the textile town of Nelson?

6. What is the name of the 19c castle five miles N.W. of Cardiff?

7. The Rio Negro forms part of the border between which two countries?

8. Over which canal in Venice does the Rialto Bridge cross?

9. Into which sea does the River Scheldt flow?

10. Into which river does the River Neckar flow at Mannheim?

11. What is the highest point on Bodmin Moor?

12. How many islands comprise the Cayman Islands in the West Indies?

13. In which Asian country is the village of My Lai?

14. In which year did Burma become Myanmar?

15. Gerlachovka is the highest peak of which mountain system?

ANSWERS 1. New Mexico **2.** Malawi **3.** Switzerland **4.** Indonesia **5.** Lancashire **6.** Castle Coch **7.** Colombia and Venezuela **8.** Grand Canal **9.** North Sea **10.** Rhine **11.** Brown Willy **12.** Three **13.** Vietnam **14.** 1989 **15.** Carpathian Mountains.

GENERAL KNOWLEDGE

1. Who was 1988 U.S. Open men's singles tennis champion?

2. Which poet's volumes included 1889's *Days and Nights*?

3. Who was the 26th president of the U.S.?

4. Who wrote the 1894 play *Little Eyolf*?

5. Which England Test bowler took a hat-trick against West Indies at Leeds in 1957?

6. Who was the author of the 1904 volume *Ghost Stories of an Antiquary*?

7. Which politician was elected M.P. for Edinburgh East and Musselburgh in 1997?

8. Which poisonous marsh plant is also called water hemlock?

9. What is the name of the Polish river upon which Poznan stands?

10. Which English ballerina was born Lilian Alicia Marks?

11. Which actor's television roles included Chris Hawthorne in the comedy *The Cuckoo Waltz*?

12. Who won a Best Supporting Actor Oscar for the film *The Fugitive*?

13. Who wrote the 1981 novel *A Good Man in Africa*?

14. Which British aircraft designer was chairman of the Hawker Siddeley Group from 1935-63?

15. Who wrote the 1936 novel *A Gun for Sale*?

ENTERTAINMENT

1. Who directed the 1988 film *A Handful of Dust*?

2. Who produced the 1993 fly-on-the-wall programme *Sylvania Waters*?

3. Who starred in, and directed, the 1974 film *The Savage is Loose*?

4. Which actress played Angelica in the ITV adventure series *Sword of Freedom*?

5. Who directed the 1995 film *Apollo 13*?

6. Who created the 1970s science fiction show *Survivors*?

7. Which Oscar-winning actor starred in the 1980s U.S. sitcom *Bosom Buddies*?

8. In which year did *Survival* begin on British television?

9. Who played Cory Matthews in the U.S. sitcom *Boy Meets World*?

10. Who directed the 1989 comedy film *The Tall Guy*?

11. Who directed the 1998 film *American History X*?

12. Who starred as *Father Charlie* in the 1982 sitcom?

13. Which pop star hosted the TV show *Victoria's Secrets* in 2000?

14. In which European capital city is the 1988 film *American Roulette* set?

15. Who plays Shula in Radio Four's *The Archers*?

THE CARLING PUB QUIZ BOOK

SPORT

1. Which country won the 1956 Olympic football tournament?

2. How many horses have won Cheltenham's Champion Hurdle three years in a row?

3. Who did Leeds Rhinos beat in the 2000 rugby league Challenge Cup quarter-finals?

4. By what score did the U.S.A. win the 1924 Walker Cup?

5. Which golfer won the Catalonia Open in 1994?

6. With what sport are Hans Nielsen and Erik Gundersen associated?

7. Who knocked Leigh Centurions out of the rugby league Challenge Cup in February 2000?

8. Colin Blythe took 17 wickets for Kent against Northants in June 1907. For how many runs?

9. What nationality is athlete Leonard Myles-Mills?

10. Willie Smith was a 1923 world professional champion. At what ball game?

11. Which snooker player won the 2000 Benson & Hedges Masters?

12. Who was flat racing champion jockey from 1909-1912?

13. At what sport do Mark Covell and Ian Walker compete?

14. Which club won the first rugby league Challenge Cup Final?

15. In cricket, who took 14-169 against Somerset for Gloucestershire in 1993?

POP

1. From which city do U.S. girl group The Donnas hail?

2. Which 22 minute song features on the 1971 Focus album *Moving Waves*?

3. Who had a 2000 Top 10 single with *Aisha*?

4. What was the debut single of the group The Mekons?

5. In which year did Corona have a Top 10 single with the song *The Rhythm of the Night*?

6. Which country artist recorded the album *New Day Dawning*?

7. From which country do dance duo Impulsion hail?

8. Which group had a U.S. Top 40 single in 1970 with *Mississippi Queen*?

9. In which year did Foghat form?

10. The band Mudhoney are named after a film by which cult director?

11. In which city were the group New Fast Automatic Daffodils formed?

12. Which two members of the Foo Fighters were formerly in the group Sunny Day Real Estate?

13. Who wrote the 1971 song *Can Someone Please Direct Me Back to Earth*?

14. Who recorded the 1999 No. 1 album *Steptacular*?

15. Who recorded the 1978 single *Private Plane*?

ANSWERS 1. San Francisco **2.** Eruption **3.** Death in Vegas **4.** Never Been in a Riot **5.** 1994 **6.** Wynonna Judd **7.** France **8.** Mountain **9.** 1970 **10.** Russ Meyer **11.** Manchester **12.** William Goldsmith and Nate Mendel **13.** John Kongos **14.** Steps **15.** Thomas Leer.

HISTORY

1. In which year did Ethelbert, Anglo-Saxon king of Kent die?

2. Which pope crowned Charlemagne Emperor of the Romans in 800?

3. The Onin War in 15c Japan was fought in and around which city?

4. How did French minister Léon Gambetta escape Paris in 1870 during the Franco-Prussian War?

5. In which year did Elizabeth I succeed Mary as queen?

6. In which battle was Richard Neville, Earl of Warwick, slain?

7. In which year did Edward III of England die?

8. Who was vice-president of the U.S. from 1905-9?

9. Who was president of South Korea during the Korean War?

10. In which year did Burma gain independence?

11. In which year did Khrushchev replace Bulganin as premier of the Soviet Union?

12. Which smuggler, captain of the brig *Rebecca,* reputedly had an ear cut off by Spanish coastguards in 1731?

13. In which month of 1949 was the Berlin Blockade lifted?

14. In November, 1853 the Russians destroyed the Turkish fleet at which Black Sea port?

15. Which two South American countries fought the Chaco War from 1932-5?

ANSWERS 1. 616 **2.** Pope Leo III **3.** Kyoto **4.** By balloon **5.** 1558 **6.** Battle of Barnet **7.** 1377 **8.** Charles Warren Fairbanks **9.** Syngman Rhee **10.** 1948 **11.** 1958 **12.** Robert Jenkins **13.** May **14.** Sinope **15.** Bolivia and Paraguay.

GENERAL KNOWLEDGE

1. In which year did the saint known as 'the Venerable Bede' die?

2. Of which French overseas region in N.E. South America is Cayenne the capital?

3. Which trio of actors were cell-mates in the 1960 film comedy *Two Way Stretch*?

4. Which town in N.W. England is administrative centre of Lancashire?

5. Which television talent show was hosted from 1956-78 by Hughie Green?

6. Who directed the 1995 film *Heat* which starred Al Pacino?

7. Who was the author of the 1945 poetry collection *The North Ship*?

8. Which comedy actor's television roles included Dennis Dunstable in *Please Sir!*?

9. Who were the four members of the pop group the Monkees?

10. Which woman is Labour M.P. for Birmingham Ladywood?

11. In which year did Welsh actor, songwriter and dramatist Ivor Novello die?

12. Who wrote the 1934 novel *A Man Lay Dead*?

13. In which year did David Koresh and the Branch Davidians Christian cult hold a siege in Waco, Texas?

14. Which New York-born actor-comedian played Nicely-Nicely Johnson in the film *Guys and Dolls*?

15. Which 1971 book by Hunter S. Thompson is subtitled *A savage journey to the heart of the American Dream*?

ANSWERS 1. 735 A.D. **2.** French Guiana **3.** Peter Sellers, David Lodge and Bernard Cribbins **4.** Preston **5.** Opportunity Knocks! **6.** Michael Mann **7.** Philip Larkin **8.** Peter Denyer **9.** Davy Jones, Micky Dolenz **10.** Clare Short **11.** 1951 **12.** Ngaio Marsh **13.** 1993 **14.** Stubby Kaye **15.** Fear and Loathing in Las Vegas.

ENTERTAINMENT

1. Which actor stars in the 1989 film *The Rachel Papers*?

2. What was the nickname of Welsh theatre manager Hugh Beaumont?

3. Which former *M*A*S*H* actor appeared in *E.R.* in 1999 as a doctor?

4. Who did the Oscar-winning make-up effects in the 1981 film *An American Werewolf in London*?

5. Which former *Monty Python* member appears as a magazine editor in the sitcom *Suddenly Susan*?

6. In which year did English tenor Geoffrey Dunn die?

7. Which actress played Lauren Miller in the 1980s sitcom *Family Ties*?

8. Who plays Julia in Radio Four's soap *The Archers*?

9. Who plays former president John Quincy Adams in the 1997 film *Amistad*?

10. Who composed the 1955 opera *The Fiery Angel*?

11. Who is the director of the film *Mission: Impossible 2*?

12. In which New York theatre was Edward Albee's play *The Death of Bessie Smith* first performed?

13. Who directed the 1999 film *Analyze This*?

14. Who played Father O'Malley in the 1960s U.S. sitcom *Going My Way*?

15. Who plays Bob Fleming in the TV sketch series *The Fast Show*?

SPORT

1. At what sport was Dave Thorpe a world champion in 1989?

2. What sport do Newcastle Riverkings play?

3. Which club has won the Scottish First Division/Premier Division the most times?

4. What nationality was 1972 women's European water-skiing champion Willi Stahle?

5. Who won the 1996 London women's marathon?

6. Who did Peter Nicol beat in the quarter-finals of the Flanders Open squash tournament in 2000?

7. How many times did Eddy Merckx win the Liége-Bastogne-Liége cycle race?

8. How many cricket Tests did Dermot Reeve play for England?

9. Which horse was Jem Robinson's last winning mount in the 2000 Guineas?

10. How many times did Will Carling lead England in Tests at rugby union?

11. Which driver was a member of the R.A.C. Rally-winning team from 1960-2?

12. Which jockey was 1977 Sports Illustrated Sportsman of the Year?

13. At what Olympic sport have Louis Debray and Yevgeny Petrov been champions?

14. Who did rugby league side Wigan play on 5th September 1999 in the last game at Central Park?

15. Which Cuban was 1974 world amateur flyweight boxing champion?

ANSWERS 1. Moto-cross **2.** Ice hockey **3.** Rangers **4.** Holland **5.** Liz McColgan **6.** David Evans **7.** Five **8.** Three **9.** Flatcatcher **10.** 59 **11.** Erik Carlsson **12.** Steve Cauthen **13.** Shooting **14.** St. Helens **15.** Douglas Rodriguez.

POP

1. Which rap group recorded the 1999 album *There's a Poison Goin' On...*?

2. What is the B-side of the 1974 John Lennon single *Whatever Gets You Through the Night*?

3. Which singer's early groups included Crepe Soul and Snakepit Banana Barn?

4. What is the B-side of Jona Lewie's single *The Baby, She's on the Street*?

5. Which group recorded the 1999 country album *Fly*?

6. Who produced B. Bumble and the Stingers' single *Nut Rocker*?

7. On which label did Lew Lewis record his 1978 single *Lucky Seven*?

8. Which group recorded the 1991 live album *Raw Melody Men*?

9. Who is eldest of the four Neville Brothers?

10. Which guitarist recorded the album *After the Satellite Sings*?

11. Which U.S. group recorded the 1999 album *Villa Elaine*?

12. Who recorded the 1999 album *Awake and Breathe*?

13. What did the Four Tops change their name from?

14. Jackie Mittoo was a founder member of which reggae group?

15. In which year did the German group *Nektar* form?

WORDS

1. Where does an Orcadian live?

2. What would you keep in a frail?

3. What is the resin olibanum better known as?

4. Who might use a roband?

5. The branch of science called odontology refers to which part of the body?

6. What is the plural of monsieur?

7. What in film-making is a foley?

8. What in Ireland is a loy?

9. If you perform hongi in New Zealand, how do you greet someone?

10. For what sporting activity would you wear salopettes?

11. The word honcho meaning boss derives from which language?

12. What is an opsimath?

13. What would you do in Papua New Guinea with a toea?

14. In which game would you employ a zwischenzug?

15. What does the phrase *foie gras* mean as in the food pâté de fois gras?

ANSWERS 1. The Orkney Islands **2.** Figs or raisins **3.** Frankincense **4.** A sailor - it is used for fastening a sail to a spar **5.** Teeth **6.** Messieurs **7.** A technician who adds sound effects **8.** A spade **9.** By touching noses **10.** Skiing **11.** Japanese **12.** A person who learns late in life **13.** Spend it **14.** Chess **15.** Fat liver.

GENERAL KNOWLEDGE

1. Who wrote the 1975 novel *The Shepherd*?

2. Which rider was the 1994 & 1996 winner of the Badminton Horse Trials?

3. Which American singer released the 1975 record album *Desire*?

4. Who wrote the 1989 novel *A Prayer for Owen Meany*?

5. Which unit of weight is equal to 24 grains in the Troy system?

6. Who wrote the 1983 novel *Ancient Evenings*?

7. Which 1876 novel by Mark Twain features the character Becky Thatcher?

8. Which actor's television roles included the lead in the 1979 series *Charles Endell Esquire*?

9. Which Indian Test cricketer scored 121 against England in Bombay in the 1972-73 season?

10. What is the third sign of the zodiac?

11. In which year was English guitarist and lutenist Julian Bream born?

12. What is the U.S. name for the card game patience?

13. Who was the 37th president of the U.S.?

14. Who is the American composer of the opera *Akhnaten*?

15. With which Olympic field event is Sergey Bubka associated?

ENTERTAINMENT

1. Who played Chuy Castillos in the 1990s sitcom *The Golden Palace*?

2. In which year did American actor-manager David Belasco die?

3. Who plays Jack in Radio Four's *The Archers*?

4. Which playwright's works include the 1986 play *Kafka's Dick*?

5. Which comic actress played Susie Deruzza in the 1990s sitcom *Good Advice*?

6. Which playwright was replaced by Stephen Zaillian as the writer of the film *Hannibal*, the follow-up to *The Silence of the Lambs*?

7. In which town was Larry Grayson born in 1923?

8. In which year was Scottish mezzo-soprano Linda Finnie born?

9. What was the real name of comedienne Joyce Grenfell?

10. Who played Mrs. Chapman in the 1978 sitcom *Going Straight*?

11. Which actor directed wife Joanne Woodward in the 1968 film *Rachel Rachel*?

12. Who composed the 1775 opera *The Feigned Gardener*?

13. Who plays Lilith in the TV sitcom *Frasier*?

14. Which actor directed the 1981 film *Race to the Yankee Zephyr*?

15. In which year did Bill Maynard make his stage debut, with comedian Terry Scott?

ANSWERS 1. Cheech Marin **2.** 1931 **3.** Arnold Peters **4.** Alan Bennett **5.** Shelley Long **6.** David Mamet **7.** Bolton **8.** 1952 **9.** Joyce Phipps **10.** Rowena Cooper **11.** Paul Newman **12.** Mozart **13.** Bebe Neuwirth **14.** David Hemmings **15.** 1951.

SPORT

1. At what sport does Troy Corser compete?

2. Which Briton was 1906-7 world figure skating champion?

3. In cricket, who scored 167 for Somerset vs. Glamorgan in the 2nd innings of their 1999 county championship game?

4. Which two teams met in the 1947 play-off for the NFL championship in American Football?

5. Who was 1961 French Open women's singles tennis champion?

6. By what score did Brazil beat Morocco in their 1998 football World Cup Group A game?

7. For which Test cricket team does wicket-keeper Chris Nevin play?

8. Who was 1978 women's 100m breaststroke swimming world champion?

9. Which U.S. golfer was leading money winner on the 1952 U.S. tour?

10. Who captained England's rugby union side in their 2000 Six Nations game against Wales?

11. How many players are there in a softball side?

12. In which year was runner Ato Boldon born?

13. How many minutes did Ravi Shastri take to hit 200 runs in Bombay's cricket game against Boroda in January 1985?

14. In which year was runner Linford Christie born?

15. Who was voted basketball's most valuable player in the NBA in 1992?

POP

1. *5.22* was an album of which group's B-sides and rarities?

2. Which group did Lee Dorrian form after quitting Napalm Death?

3. What was the debut single of The Members?

4. Colm O'Ciosoig was drummer with which Creation Records artists?

5. Which Hull-based group released the 1999 album *Musicality*?

6. Who was the original drummer in the heavy metal group Black Sabbath?

7. Which group recorded the single *The Diary of Horace Wimp*?

8. Which jazz player contributed a trumpet solo to Scritti Politti's song *Oh Patti (Don't Feel Sorry For Loverboy)*?

9. Which group released the 1973 album *Dixie Chicken*?

10. Which U.S. group recorded the 1998 album *Pennsylvania*?

11. Which blues singer recorded the 1956 single *Little Boy Blue*?

12. Which female singer had a 1999 Top 10 single with *Goin' Down*?

13. In which year did The Spencer Davis Group first release the single *Keep On Running*?

14. Which group's singles include 1997's *Happy* and *Tied to the 90s*?

15. During a tour of which country in 1957 did Little Richard convert to Christianity?

ANSWERS 1. Ned's Atomic Dustbin **2.** Cathedral **3.** Solitary Confinement **4.** My Bloody Valentine **5.** Salako **6.** Bill Ward **7.** E.L.O. **8.** Miles Davis **9.** Little Feat **10.** Pere Ubu **11.** Bobby Bland **12.** Melanie C **13.** 1965 **14.** Travis **15.** Australia.

SCIENCE

1. What percentage of the atmosphere of the planet Venus is carbon dioxide?

2. In which year did Austrian psychoanalyst Sigmund Freud die?

3. Which physicist was Governor of South Australia from 1971-6?

4. Approximately how many days does the moon Deimos take to orbit Mars?

5. James Hutton is often called the 'father of geology'. In which European capital was he born?

6. In which U.S. state was archaeologist Lewis Binford born?

7. Which moon of Uranus has areas which have been named the Chevron, Circus Maximus, and the Racetrack?

8. In which year was the Lotus Development Corporation founded?

9. Which British mathematician proved Fermat's Last Theorem in 1995?

10. What is the name given to the chemical elements of atomic number greater than 92?

11. In which year did Trevor Bayliss invent the clockwork radio?

12. In which year was the compact disc invented?

13. In which year was the Hubble Space Telescope launched?

14. What is the largest of Saturn's moons?

15. In the term CAT scanner, what does the acronym CAT stand for?

ANSWERS 1. 97% **2.** 1939 **3.** Mark Laurence Oliphant **4.** 1.26 days **5.** Edinburgh **6.** Virginia **7.** Miranda **8.** 1982 **9.** Andrew Wiles **10.** Transuranic elements **11.** 1993 **12.** 1979 **13.** 1990 **14.** Titan **15.** Computerized axial tomography.

GENERAL KNOWLEDGE

1. Actor Nicholas Hannen was the second husband of which English comedy actress?

2. In which year did U.S. painter Edward Hopper die?

3. Who was the author of the novel *Lorna Doone*?

4. Who was the archbishop of Canterbury from 1980-91?

5. In which year did Austrian psychiatrist Alfred Adler die?

6. Who wrote the 1982 novel *Light Thickens*?

7. Which motor racing driver won the 1975 Spanish Grand Prix in Formula 1?

8. Who did Guillermo Vilas beat in the 1977 French Open men's singles tennis championship final?

9. Who was 1946/7 National Hunt champion jockey?

10. Who was Labour Secretary of State for Trade from 1974-6?

11. Which Old Testament brother of Moses was first high priest of the Israelites?

12. Which plant with pinkish-white flowers is a hybrid of *Saxifraga umbrosa* and *Saxifraga spathularis*?

13. Who is the cartoon adversary of Road Runner?

14. Leopold Bloom is the central character in which novel?

15. In which year was *True Blue* a No. 1 single by Madonna?

ANSWERS 1. Athene Seyler **2.** 1967 **3.** R.D. Blackmore **4.** Robert Runcie **5.** 1937 **6.** Ngaio Marsh **7.** Jochen Mass **8.** Brian Gottfried **9.** Jack Dowdeswell **10.** Peter Shore **11.** Aaron **12.** London Pride **13.** Wile E. Coyote **14.** Ulysses **15.** 1986.

ENTERTAINMENT

1. Which comedy duo starred in the 1937 film *All Over Town*?

2. What is Dawn French's character name in *The Vicar of Dibley*?

3. What is Fred McMurray's profession in the 1947 film *The Egg and I*?

4. Which actor plays a Spanish police chief in the 1984 film *Target Eagle*?

5. What is Rock Hudson's job in the 1955 film *All That Heaven Allows*?

6. Who starred as television show host Ben Black in the 1999 television drama *Sex 'N' Death*?

7. Who directed the 1981 film *Excalibur*?

8. Who appears as sports writer Ring Lardner in the 1988 film *Eight Men Out*?

9. Who directed the 1983 film *Local Hero*?

10. Who plays Roz Doyle in the sitcom *Frasier*?

11. The 1960 film *All the Fine Young Cannibals* was inspired by the life of which jazz musician?

12. Which Hollywood actress played Max in the 1990 sitcom *Freddie and Max*?

13. Which actor plays a sleazy tabloid publisher in the 1997 film *L.A. Confidential*?

14. Rowland Rivron and Simon Brint comprise which musical comedy act?

15. Who plays the vet James Herriot in the 1979 film *All Things Bright and Beautiful*?

SPORT

1. Which country does Obadele Thompson run for?

2. Which American rode Northern Trick to victory in the 1983 Prix de Diane Hermès?

3. In which year was athlete Bruny Surin born?

4. For which university did Boris Rankov row in the University Boat Race from 1978-83?

5. In cricket, who was Man of the Match in the 1998 NatWest Final for Lancashire?

6. How many Grand Prix wins did motorcyclist Mike Hailwood achieve in total?

7. Who was named female athlete of 1999 by the I.A.A.F.?

8. Who scored West Bromwich Albion's goal in their 1970 League Cup Final defeat?

9. In which year was athlete Dennis Mitchell born?

10. What nationality is athlete Masako Chiba?

11. Who was men's overall water-skiing world champion in 1957?

12. What nationality is women's cyclist Barbara Heeb?

13. In which year was 100m runner Andre Cason born?

14. In which year was the jockey club formed in England?

15. For which Test cricket side do Damien Martyn and Matthew Hayden play?

POP

1. Who had a Christmas 1999 hit with *Say You'll Be Mine/Better the Devil...*?

2. What was Transvision Vamp's last Top 20 hit, in August 1989?

3. What were Traffic's three Top 10 hit singles in 1967?

4. Which song made famous by Johnny Cash did Blondie perform in the film *Roadie*?

5. Which studio album by Warren Zeavon features *Dirty Little Religion* and *Porcelain Monkey*?

6. Which singer joined the group Living Colour in 1985?

7. How old was singer Doug Sahm when he died in 1999?

8. Which duo had a 2000 Top 10 single with *You Only Tell Me You Love Me When...*?

9. Who played electric organ on Bob Dylan's single *Like A Rolling Stone*?

10. Who had a Top 10 single in 1979 with *Born to Be Alive*?

11. Douglas Vipond was drummer with which late 1980s Scottish band?

12. Which member of Morphine died in July 1999?

13. What Tom Waits song features at the start of the film *Down By Law*?

14. Which rapper recorded the 1995 album *Mr. Smith*?

15. Which song by The Young Rascals did Birth cover on his debut E.P. *Sweet Idol*?

PEOPLE

1. In which year did Christopher Reeve become paralysed from the neck down following an accident?

2. Which singer has been given exclusive use of island Ellidaey by the Iceland government?

3. In which U.S. prison is Robert Downey Jr. serving a 14 month sentence on drug-related charges?

4. In which country was landscape painter John La Farge born in 1835?

5. How was actress Grace Kelly killed?

6. Who was U.S. secretary of state from 1949-53?

7. Which writer was born Leslie Charles Bowyer Yin?

8. In which year was composer Richard Rodney Bennett born?

9. *Little Girl Lost* is a biography of which current Hollywood actress?

10. Which blues guitarist was born in Itta Bena, Mississippi in 1925?

11. Which actress wrote the memoir *White Cargo*?

12. Which politician has written the autobiography *Pride and Perjury*?

SURBITON

13. What is the middle name of actress Joan Collins?

14. On what day of 1997 did the funeral of Diana, Princess of Wales, take place?

15. With which card game is Ely Culbertson associated?

GENERAL KNOWLEDGE

1. Who wrote the 1963 novel *Inside Mr. Enderby*?

2. Who wrote the 1970 novel *The Naked Face*?

3. Who directed the 1985 comedy film *After Hours*?

4. In which year was *Radio Gaga* a Top 10 single for pop group Queen?

5. Which Polish-born British property developer was involved in the Profumo scandal?

6. In ancient Greek drama what was the name given to the first of two movements made by a chorus during the performance of a choral ode?

7. What was the name of the character played by Ronald Allen in the TV soap *Crossroads*?

8. Who was the 1997 Wimbledon women's singles tennis champion?

9. Who wrote the 1978 play *Plenty*?

10. Which TV conjuror is married to his former assistant Debbie McGee?

11. In which year did U.S. singer and jazz pianist Nat 'King' Cole die?

12. Which U.S. food manufacturer invented the advertising slogan '57 Varieties'?

13. Which city in New South Wales, Australia, was scene of a gold rush in 1851?

14. Who wrote the 1978 novel *The Sea, the Sea*?

15. Which imaginary creature is depicted as a white horse with one long spiralled horn growing from its forehead?

ENTERTAINMENT

1. Who played Billy Joe Bobb in the 1980s spoof serial *Fresno*?

2. Who directed and starred in the 1961 comedy film *The Ladies' Man*?

3. In which year did comedy show *The Frost Report* first appear on BBCTV?

4. Which duo created the 1980s sitcom *Full House*?

5. Who played God in the 1990 film *Almost an Angel*?

6. Which actress played WPc Pamela Purvis in the 1970s sitcom *The Fuzz*?

7. Who directed the 1960 film *La Dolce Vita*?

8. Which actor took over from Alec Guinness in the 1961 stage production of *Ross*?

9. The 1993 film *Eight Hundred Leagues Down the Amazon* is based on a novel by which author?

10. In which year did Jack Buchanan make his stage debut in New York?

11. *The Lady and the Bandit* is a 1951 film about which criminal?

12. In which year did Richard Burton make his stage debut?

13. The 1984 film *The Ambassador* is based on which Elmore Leonard novel?

14. In which city was theatre and coffee-house Caffé Cino opened in 1958?

15. Who directed the 1965 film *The Satan Bug*, based on an Alistair MacLean novel?

SPORT

1. Which American won the 1953 & 1954 Indianapolis 500 race?

2. In which year did French tennis player Rene Lacoste die?

3. Which country were 1996 Olympic yachting champions at soling class?

4. In which year was athlete Jon Drummond born?

5. Who was 1984 Olympic super-heavyweight boxing champion?

6. In which year was athlete Tim Montgomery born?

7. In which sport is the James Norris Memorial Trophy awarded?

8. In which city are American football team Carolina Panthers based?

9. Which country does athlete Mel Lattany represent?

10. Which duo were U.S. Open women's doubles tennis champions in 1993?

11. On which horse did Alwin Schockemöhle win the 1976 Olympic individual show jumping gold?

12. In golf, which U.S. city hosted the Bay Hill Invitational Tournament in March 2000?

13. At what sport is Australian Kieren Perkins a former world record holder?

14. Which Italian was 1993 World Footballer of the Year?

15. In which year was boxer Naseem Hamed born?

ANSWERS 1. Bill Vukovich 2. 1996 3. Germany 4. 1968 5. Tyrell Biggs 6. 1975 7. Ice hockey 8. Charlotte 9. U.S.A. 10. Arantxa Sanchez and Helena Sukova 11. Warwick Rex 12. Orlando 13. Swimming 14. Roberto Baggio 15. 1974.

POP

1. Which jazz artist recorded the album *Classics in the Key of G*?

2. Which Van Morrison studio album features the songs *Precious Time* and *Philosopher's Stone*?

3. Who had a 1989 hit single with *Dear Jessie*?

4. Davey Ray Moor is songwriter with which group?

5. Which member of band Blood, Sweat & Tears wrote the much-covered song *Spinning Wheel*?

6. Which female vocal group had a 1966 hit single with *Attack*?

7. Which group had a 1980 Top 10 single with *Someone's Looking At You*?

8. Which female singer had a 1999 Top 10 single with *Sunshine*?

9. In which city was guitarist Nils Lofgren born?

10. New York band Blue Oyster Cult were the brainchild of which journalist?

11. In which year was Tracy Chapman's album *Tracy Chapman* released?

12. Who produced the first album by Family, *Music in a Doll's House*?

13. Which Rolling Stones studio album includes the track *Start Me Up*?

14. Who recorded the 1984 album *Fans*?

15. On which label did Supergrass record their Top 10 single *Moving*?

ART

1. In which city did sculptor Constantin Brancusi die in 1957?

2. Who authored *The Great Gatsby*?

3. Which cartoonist created the *Doonesbury* comic strip?

4. In which novel by Charles Dickens does the character Estella appear?

5. Which 19th century artist's works include *Pilot Boats*?

6. Who wrote *For Whom the Bell Tolls*?

7. Whose paintings include *Cheyne Walk: The Corner of Beaufort Street*?

8. Who authored the 2000 crime novel *God is a Bullet*?

9. Who painted 1901's *Peaches and Almonds*?

10. Who authored the novel *Adeline Mowbray*?

11. Emma Hamilton was the most famous sitter of which Lancashire-born painter?

12. Who painted the work *The Execution of Maximilian* in about 1867?

13. For how many francs did Pierre Auguste Renoir sell his painting *La Loge* in 1875?

14. Which artist created the *Jane* strip cartoon?

15. Which 20th-century English painter's works include 1942's *Soldiers*?

GENERAL KNOWLEDGE

1. Who was the French author of the novel *Eugénie Grandet*?

2. Who was the 1986 Commonwealth women's 100m hurdles champion?

3. In which year was veteran Northern Ireland politician Ian Paisley born?

4. Which industrial city and port in Belgium is at the confluence of the Rivers Lys and Scheldt?

5. Of which U.S. state is Boise the capital?

6. Port Blair is the capital of which territory of India?

7. Which former standard monetary unit of Thailand was replaced in 1928 by the baht?

8. Which port in central Vietnam was former capital of the kingdom of Annam?

9. Who wrote the 1932 novel *Tobacco Road*?

10. Munich is the capital of which state of Germany?

11. Which chesspiece moves in an L-shaped direction?

12. On which river is the market town of Settle in North Yorkshire?

13. Who was a Best Actor Oscar nominee for his role in the 1984 film *Under the Volcano*?

14. In which year was U.S. poet Ezra Pound indicted for treason by the U.S. government?

15. Who was 1932-3 world heavyweight boxing champion?

ANSWERS 1. Honoré de Balzac **2.** Sally Gunnell **3.** 1926 **4.** Ghent **5.** Idaho **6.** The Andaman and Nicobar Islands **7.** Tical **8.** Hué **9.** Erskine Caldwell **10.** Bavaria **11.** Knight **12.** River Ribble **13.** Albert Finney **14.** 1945 **15.** Jack Sharkey.

ENTERTAINMENT

1. What nationality is stage actress Zoë Caldwell?

2. Which star of the 1992 sitcom *The Big One* co-wrote the series?

3. What was the maiden name of actress Mrs. Patrick Campbell?

4. Who played Simon Sparrow in the 1954 film *Doctor in the House*?

5. Who played Jane in the 1934 film *Tarzan and his Mate*?

6. Who played Moriarty in the 1939 film *The Adventures of Sherlock Holmes*?

7. Who played Duggie Ferguson in *Coronation Street*?

8. Which actor played the lead in the 1958 film *I, Mobster*?

9. Who directed the 1961 film *A Taste of Honey*?

10. Who wrote and directed the 1997 film *Afterglow*?

11. Who directed the 2000 film *American Psycho*?

12. Who directed the 1952 film *The Importance of Being Earnest?*

13. Which comedy team wrote the 1960s sitcom *Barney is my Darling*?

14. Who made his debut as Tarzan in the 1955 film *Tarzan's Hidden Jungle*?

15. The 1999 movie *The Insider* is based on whose life story?

SPORT

1. At what sport did Otto Furrer win a world title in 1932?

2. In which sport were Hui Jun & Geng Lijuan world champions in 1987?

3. In canoeing, what does C4 stand for?

4. Which Welsh rugby union side play at the Gnoll?

5. Steen Stovgaard & Lene Køppen were 1977 world badminton mixed doubles champions. Which country were they from?

6. Which sport do Canterbury Crusaders and Auckland Blues play in New Zealand?

7. Which 19th-century horserace trainer won the Oaks 12 times?

8. In which city was Australian cricketer Michael Bevan born?

9. Which country were women's relay orienteering world champions in 1997?

10. In which sport might the Sheffield Sharks play the Chester Jets?

11. Which British side lost the 1961 Fairs Cup in football?

12. What nationality is golfer David Park?

13. With which sport do you associate the names Michael Hadschieff and Ye Qiaobo?

14. Who was women's 10,000m champion at the 1994 I.A.A.F. World Cup?

15. For which rugby league club side does Chris Joynt play?

ANSWERS 1. Skiing **2.** Table tennis **3.** Four person Canadian canoe **4.** Neath **5.** Denmark **6.** Rugby union **7.** Robert Robson **8.** Canberra **9.** Sweden **10.** Basketball **11.** Birmingham City **12.** Welsh **13.** Speed skating **14.** Elana Meyer **15.** St. Helens.

POP

1. Which group recorded the album *Aion*?

2. Who had a Top 10 hit in February 2000 with *Adelante*?

3. Which member of The Charlatans was imprisoned after getting mixed up in an armed robbery?

4. Who had a 1990 Top 10 hit single with *Enjoy the Silence*?

5. Which member of The Jam produced the single *Tom Verlaine* by The Family Cat?

6. Which group recorded a soundtrack to the film *The Virgin Suicides*?

7. In which year did Black Box have a No. 1 single with *Ride On Time*?

8. In which city were group Rip, Rig & Panic based?

9. Who recorded the 2000 album *And Then Nothing Turned Itself Inside Out*?

10. Who played drums on Joe Jackson's album *Body and Soul*?

11. Which member of The Farm was killed in a car crash in 1986?

12. In which year did the Mahavishnu Orchestra form?

13. What was the title of Martine McCutcheon's 1999 debut album?

14. What is the name of the dog on wheels on the sleeve of Belle and Sebastian's single *Dog on Wheels*?

15. Which group covered *Everything I Do (I Do It For You)* in 1992, reaching the Top 10?

GEOGRAPHY

1. In which county is St. Albans?

2. What is the capital of the French department of Val d'Oise?

3. What is the county town of the Irish county of Wexford?

4. What is the highest peak of the Rhaetian Alps?

5. On which river is the Illinois port of Peoria?

6. Which is the largest of the Azores group of islands?

7. The Belgian town of Namur lies on a promontory between which two rivers?

8. Helena is the capital of which U.S. state?

9. Mount Vancouver is a mountain on the border between Canada and which U.S. state?

10. On which river is the city of Semipalatinsk in Kazakhstan?

11. What is the capital of the Italian region of Campania?

12. In which South American country is Mount Sorata?

13. Which river separates the Bronx from Manhattan in New York City?

14. On which river is the German town of Esslingen?

15. The Japanese port of Shimonoseki is on which island?

ANSWERS 1. Hertfordshire **2.** Pontoise **3.** Wexford **4.** Piz Bernina **5.** Illinois River **6.** São Miguel **7.** Sambre and Meuse **8.** Montana **9.** Alaska **10.** Irtysh **11.** Naples **12.** Bolivia **13.** Harlem **14.** Neckar **15.** Honshu.

GENERAL KNOWLEDGE

1. Who was a Best Actor Oscar nominee for the 1985 film *Murphy's Romance*?

2. Who wrote the 1916 novel *The Brook Kerith*?

3. Who was 1939 Wimbledon women's singles tennis champion?

4. Which Turkey-born shipowner married Jackie Kennedy in 1968?

5. Who wrote the 1929 novel *The Seven Dials Mystery*?

6. What is the comic alter ego of actor Patrick Fyffe?

7. Who was a Best Actor Oscar winner for the 1944 film *Going My Way*?

8. Who wrote the novel *Life and Loves of a She-Devil*?

9. Who is aunt and guardian of Lydia Languish in the play *The Rivals*?

10. Which 19th-century statesman led the Anti-Corn-Law League with Richard Cobden?

11. Which European country houses the Rhodope Mountains and Balkan Mountains?

12. Who was King of Mercia from 757-796?

13. What novel is the second part of Roddy Doyle's *Barrytown Trilogy*?

14. Who was a Best Actor Oscar nominee for his role as composer Chopin in the film *A Song to Remember*?

15. On which river is the new town of Newtown in central Wales?

ANSWERS 1. James Garner **2.** George Moore **3.** Alice Marble **4.** Aristotle Onassis **5.** Agatha Christie **6.** Hilda Bracket **7.** Bing Crosby **8.** Fay Weldon **9.** Mrs. Malaprop **10.** John Bright **11.** Bulgaria **12.** Offa **13.** The Snapper **14.** Cornel Wilde **15.** River Severn.

ENTERTAINMENT

1. Who played a robot in the 1999 film *Bicentennial Man*?

2. Which playwright scripted the 1966 comedy film *After the Fox*?

3. Who left *The Big Breakfast* as a regular presenter in July 1999?

4. Louise McClatchy and Jai Simeone comprise which comedy duo?

5. What do the main protagonists attempt to build in the 1986 film *Eat the Peach*?

6. Which stand-up made the show *Bring the Pain* for U.S. cable channel H.B.O.?

7. Which comic actor assisted in the 1983 sketch series *Michael Barrymore*?

8. What is Robert Carlyle's character name in the Bond film *The World Is Not Enough*?

9. In which city is the 1986 film *Echo Park* set?

10. Who played an astronaut in the 1999 film *The Astronaut's Wife*?

11. Who directed the 1999 film *The Straight Story*?

12. Who is the male lead in the 1952 swashbuckling film *Against All Flags*?

13. Who is the female star of the 1996 film *Last Dance*?

14. Which actress directed the 1990 film *Impulse* starring Theresa Russell?

15. What is Eddie Murphy's character name in the 1996 film *The Nutty Professor*?

SPORT

1. Who won the women's 100m at the 1999 World Athletics Championships?

2. In cricket, which wicketkeeper made eight catches for Somerset against Combined Universities in their 1982 Benson & Hedges Cup?

3. By what score did England beat the United States at rugby union in August 1999?

4. For which sport is the Espirito Santo Trophy awarded?

5. For which rugby union club side does Will Johnson play?

6. Which Briton won the 1971 British Grand Prix in Formula 1?

7. Which women's golfer won the Compaq Open in August 1999?

8. How many times have Castleford won the rugby league Challenge Cup?

9. Who was women's single-seater winner in luge toboganning at the 1983 World Cup?

10. By what score did Wales beat Canada at rugby union in August 1999?

11. Which horse won the 1979 Grand National?

12. How many golds did Ethiopia win in the 1999 World Athletic Championships?

13. Which athlete was 1993 BBC Sports Personality of the Year?

14. Who was 1980 Olympic women's long jump champion?

15. Bob Howe and Mary Hawton won the 1958 Australian Open mixed doubles tennis title. What nationality were they?

POP

1. Which group recorded the 1990 album *Goodbye Jumbo*?

2. Which group recorded the album *MACHINA/the machines of god*?

3. Which solo artist had a 1999 Top 10 single with *Waiting For Tonight*?

4. Which group recorded the 2000 mini-album *Hotel Baltimore*?

5. Whose debut solo album was *Raw Like Sushi*?

6. Which Goth group recorded the live album *Gotham*?

7. In which year did Faust sign to Virgin Records?

8. From which country do the group Daryll Ann hail?

9. Who co-produced the Tom Waits album *Mule Variations* with the singer?

10. Which heavy metal band recorded the 2000 album Q2k?

11. In which town did the group Meat Beat Manifesto form in 1986?

12. Who had a 1990 hit single with the song *Elephant Stone*?

13. Who had a 1999 Top 10 single with *I Knew I Loved You*?

14. Which member of Nick Cave's backing group leads the combo Dirty Three?

15. On which label did the Waterboys record the album *Room to Roam*?

HISTORY

1. Who succeeded General MacArthur in 1951 as Commander-in-Chief of U.N. forces in Korea?

2. What was Fidel Castro's father's occupation?

3. In which year did Alfred the Great die?

4. In which year did Martin Bormann become chief of staff to Rudolf Hess?

5. In which year was the Challenger space shuttle disaster?

6. With which country did Britain engage in a Cod War in 1958?

7. In which month of 1967 was the Six-day War between Israel and the Arab nations?

8. Who, in 1947, organized the R.P.F. movement in France?

9. In which year did Olof Palme first become Prime Minister of Sweden?

10. Who served as Minister of Housing from 1951-54?

11. The burning of whose house in 1847 in Athens led to Lord Palmerston sending a fleet to Piraeus, Greece in 1850?

12. In which year did Russia's Lunik III first send back pictures of the dark side of the moon?

13. Who was appointed Chancellor of the German Reich in 1930?

14. In which year did poet and soldier Sir Philip Sidney die?

15. In which year of the 1960s was the Sino-Indian War?

GENERAL KNOWLEDGE

1. Which England Test bowler took 7 for 39 against South Africa at Lord's in 1955?

2. Which river of northern England flows to the Irish Sea near Preston?

3. What was the alter ego of John Mannering in a 1960s TV series starring Steve Forrest?

4. What was Bernard Bresslaw's character name in the sitcom *The Army Game*?

5. Which 1993 film by Robert Altman is based on stories by Raymond Carver?

6. Which 1983 film in the *James Bond* series featured Louis Jordan as the villain Kamal?

7. Which English royal house ruled from 1485 to 1603?

8. In which year did U.S. poet Robert Frost die?

9. Which Christmas book by Charles Dickens features the character Toby Veck?

10. Which Eurasian plant is also called clove pink?

11. For which 1946 film was Charles Coburn a Best Supporting Actor Oscar nominee?

12. Which English organist composed the five-part madrigal *Hence Stars*?

13. What is capital and chief port of Mauritius?

14. What is the name of the mouse in George Herriman's *Krazy Kat* cartoon strip?

15. Which actress played Lillie Langtry in the 1975 TV drama *Edward the Seventh*?

ENTERTAINMENT

1. Which comic actor and actress appeared in the BBC TV sitcom *Beggar My Neighbour* as Harry and Lana Butt?

2. Who directed the 1981 film comedy *SOB*?

3. Which comic actress starred in the 1996 film *Eddie*?

4. Who played Sir Percy Blakeney in the 1934 film *The Scarlet Pimpernel*?

5. Who played Tarzan in the 1933 film *Tarzan the Fearless*?

6. Who played Kevin Webster in *Coronation Street*?

7. Who directed the 1998 film *Rounders*?

8. Who starred in the leading role in the 1953 film *The Eddie Cantor Story*?

9. Who directed the 1999 film *Bowfinger*?

10. Which author scripted the 1936 film *San Francisco*?

11. The 1998 film *Palmetto*, starring Woody Harrelson, is based on a novel by which crime writer?

12. From which country do comedy act *The Doug Anthony All Stars* hail?

13. Who directed the 1956 film *The Vagabond King*?

14. Which comedy actress played a psychotherapist in the 1994 sitcom *Downwardly Mobile*?

15. Which artist won Best Single and Best Video awards at the 2000 Brits?

SPORT

1. How many kilometres did cyclist Jules Dubois ride in an 1894 1 hour speed record?

2. For which club side does French rugby union player Abdelatif Benazzi turn out?

3. Dugald McPherson was British Amateur champion in 1928. At which sport?

4. Who did Rangers beat in the 1930 Scottish F.A. Cup Final?

5. How many runs did W. W. Hinds score on his debut Test innings for West Indies against Zimbabwe in 2000?

6. With what sport is Austrian Mathias Zdarsky associated?

7. In which city was Welsh rugby union player Simon Easterby's mother born?

8. What nationality is canoeist Renn Crichlow?

9. For which team is Giancarlo Fisichella driving in the 2000 Formula 1 season?

10. Between 1978-84, how many times did Grete Waitz finish in the first three of the world cross country championships?

11. What nationality is tennis player Andreas Vinciguerra?

12. In which year did Spion Kop win the Epsom Derby?

13. By what score did Dewsbury beat Stanley Rangers in the 2000 Silk Cut Challenge Cup in rugby league?

14. How many golds have China won at the summer Olympics from 1896-1996?

15. Which athlete was 1963 BBC Sports Personality of the Year?

THE CARLING PUB QUIZ BOOK

POP

1. Which rock star authored the 1989 autobiography *Long Time Gone*?

2. Who was drummer with the Boomtown Rats?

3. In which city was singer Lene Lovich born?

4. Which female singer had a 2000 No. 1 with *Born To Make You Happy*?

5. Which group's singles include 2000's *The Facts of Life*?

6. On which studio album by Boston does No. 1 single *Amanda* appear?

7. Which jazz guitarist died in December 1999, aged 74?

8. On which label did Chemical Brothers release their 1999 hit single *Let Forever Be*?

9. Which U.S. group had a 1966 U.S. hit with *The Eggplant That Ate Chicago*?

10. Which girl group recorded the 1999 single *Jesse Hold On*?

11. In which year was *Spirit in the Sky* a No. 1 hit for Norman Greenbaum?

12. Who was guitarist in the group Bow Wow Wow?

13. Which duo formed the group The Lovin' Spoonful in 1965?

14. Whose country albums include 1970's *Okie from Muskogee*?

15. In which U.S. state was singer Sheryl Crow born?

ANSWERS 1. David Crosby **2.** Simon Crowe **3.** Detroit **4.** Britney Spears **5.** Black Box Recorder **6.** Third Stage **7.** Charlie Byrd **8.** Virgin **9.** Dr. West's Medicine Show and Junk Band **10.** B*witched **11.** 1970 **12.** Matthew Ashman **13.** Zal Yanovsky & John Sebastian **14.** Merle Haggard **15.** Missouri.

WORDS

1. Who might wear a rochet?

2. Who would use the technique of effleurage?

3. In zoology, if something is acuadal, what does it lack?

4. What would you have done with a tickey in South Africa until 1961?

5. In which gambling game is the phrase *à cheval* used?

6. What is foxing to a cobbler?

7. What does the prefix agro- denote?

8. Who would perform a *pas seul*?

9. What in India is alap?

10. In Egypt, what would a canopic jar have contained?

11. What does the prefix onto- mean?

12. Where would an ecclesiastic wear a zucchetto?

13. What is homiletics?

14. Louping ill is a disease of which animal?

15. What does the Yiddish phrase *meshuga* mean?

ANSWERS 1. A churchman - it is a surplice **2.** Masseur **3.** A tail **4.** Spent it - it was a coin **5.** Roulette **6.** A piece of leather used to reinforce part of the upper of a shoe **7.** Agriculture, soil or fields **8.** A dancer **9.** Vocal music without words **10.** The entrails of a mummy **11.** Existence or being **12.** On the head **13.** The art of preaching or writing sermons **14.** Sheep **15.** Crazy.

GENERAL KNOWLEDGE

1. Who was scorer of the winning goal for West Bromwich Albion in the 1968 F.A. Cup Final?

2. Which wine bottle holds the equivalent of twenty normal bottles?

3. What is the setting of the TV sitcom *Father Ted*?

4. Who was 1987 Australian Open women's singles tennis champion?

5. Whose volume of poetry, *The Birthday Letters*, won the 1999 Whitbread Book of the Year Award?

6. Who was 1999 U.S. P.G.A. golf champion?

7. Which ancient Egyptian god was ruler of the underworld?

8. Who wrote the play *Steaming* which was filmed in 1985 by Joseph Losey?

9. Mount Smolikas is the highest peak in which mountain range in Greece?

10. In which year was the town of Guernica in North Spain destroyed by German bombers during the Spanish Civil War?

11. What is the name of the U.S. rap group whose albums include *It Takes a Nation of Millions to Hold Us Back*?

12. Who was chancellor of West Germany from 1969-74?

13. Who wrote the 1950 book *I, Robot*?

14. In Greek mythology, which of the three Fates was the spinner of the thread of life?

15. In which year was Irish disc jockey and TV presenter Terry Wogan born?

ENTERTAINMENT

1. Who played Damien Day in the sitcom *Drop the Dead Donkey*?

2. Which pop singer appeared as Micky Shannon in a 2000 episode of the drama series *Heartbeat*?

3. Who did Ian Moor impersonate to win *Stars in Their Eyes* in 1998?

4. Who drove the Ring-a-Ding Convert-a-Car in the cartoon series *Wacky Races*?

5. Which former *EastEnders* star headed the cast in the ITV drama *Hero of the Hour*?

6. Who starred as *Joan of Arc* in a 2000 Luc Besson film?

7. Who played the lead in the film *Whatever Happened to Harold Smith*?

8. What is Charlie's surname in TV's *Ground Force*?

9. Who played an ambitious weathergirl in the 1995 film *To Die For*?

10. In which year was comedian Charlie Drake born?

11. Who starred in the 1928 film *Pandora's Box*?

12. In which year was the pilot for the sitcom *The Dustbinmen* shown?

13. Which actress played Christian Bale's wife in the 1997 film *Metroland*?

14. In which country was the 1971 film *Valdez is Coming* shot?

15. Who played *The President's Analyst* in the 1967 film?

SPORT

1. At what sport was John Shea a 1932 Olympic champion?

2. How many golds did Italy win at the 1999 World Athletics Championships?

3. In which city was the 1977 U.E.F.A. Champion Clubs' Cup Final played?

4. For which sport is the Swaythling Cup competed for?

5. Who was women's 200m champion at the 1985 world indoor athletics championships?

6. Who finished third in the 1999 Belgian Grand Prix in Formula 1?

7. How many matches did Tom Richardson take to grab 1000 first-class wickets from 1892-6?

8. In which city is the headquarters of the Badminton Association of England Ltd.?

9. Which golfer won the 1993 U.S. Women's Open?

10. In cricket, who scored 111 for Glamorgan vs. Northants in the 2nd innings of their 1999 county championship game?

11. In which year was the Trials Riding world championship for motorbikes inaugurated?

12. Who did Stephen Hendry beat in the quarter-finals of the 1999 British Open in snooker?

13. Which team won the 1999/00 Premier League?

14. In which year did Australian tennis player Daphne Akhurst die?

15. What nationality were the 1992 & 1994 Olympic two-man bob champions?

ANSWERS 1. Speed skating 2. One 3. Rome 4. Table tennis 5. Marita Koch 6. Heinz-Harald Frentzen 7. 134 8. Milton Keynes 9. Lauri Merten 10. Steve James 11. 1975 12. Stephen Lee 13. Manchester United 14. 1933 15. Swiss.

POP

1. Who recorded the 1970 country album *Tall Dark Stranger*?

2. In which year did The Who record a concert at Leeds University?

3. In which year did David Bowie release the album *Young Americans*?

4. Which artist produced the single *Stop Your Sobbing* by the Pretenders?

5. Who replaced Carl Wayne in the group The Move?

6. Who had a 2000 Top 10 single with *Because of You*?

7. In which year was Simon Garfunkel's *Bridge Over Troubled Water* LP released?

8. What was the title of Jesus Loves You's first album?

9. On which label did Texas record the hit album *The Hush*?

10. Under what name did Louis Hardin record in the 1960s?

11. Who was lead singer with the group The Lurkers?

12. Which rock musician married Jennie Franks in 1970?

13. Which jazz trumpeter died in October 1999 aged 58?

14. Who recorded the 1999 Top 10 single *Give It To You*?

15. Which singer-songwriter released the 1988 album *Worker's Playtime*?

SCIENCE

1. In which year was Mariner 2 launched by the United States?

2. Which scientist moved to London in 1696 as Warden of the Royal Mint?

3. Which American invented the microprocessor in 1971?

4. In which year did the U.S.S.R. launch the Vega space programme?

5. Bianca is a satellite of which planet?

6. What is the name given to the region of the atmosphere from 12 to 30 miles above the Earth's surface?

7. Which American invented the liquid-crystal display in 1964?

8. What is the atomic number of Thorium?

9. What nationality was physicist Augustin Jean Fresnel?

10. On which island was scientist Robert Hooke born in 1635?

11. Which scientist married research biochemist Dorothy M. Moyle in 1924?

12. Approximately how many miles in diameter is Jupiter's moon Ganymede?

13. What nationality was mathematical physicist J. Willard Gibbs?

14. In which year did scientist and philosopher René Descartes graduate from the University of Poitiers?

15. Where in the U.S. is the headquarters of the National Academy of Sciences?

ANSWERS 1. 1962 2. Isaac Newton 3. Ted Hoff 4. 1984 5. Uranus 6. Ozone layer 7. George Heilmeier 8. 90 9. French 10. Isle of Wight 11. J. T. M. Needham 12. 3160 miles 13. American 14. 1616 15. Washington D.C.

GENERAL KNOWLEDGE

1. Who was winner of the 1999 British Grand Prix in Formula 1 motor racing?

2. Who directed the Best Picture Oscar nominee *The Thin Red Line*?

3. Which golf club hosted the 1999 Qatar Masters which was won by Paul Lawrie?

4. Who was the female star of the film *You've Got Mail*?

5. What was Kirstie Alley's character name in the sitcom *Cheers*?

6. In which year was American silent film producer Hal Roach born?

7. Who was 1999 U.S. Open women's singles tennis champion?

8. Which Brit was Best Supporting Actress Oscar winner in 1999?

9. Who was men's 400m hurdles champion at the 1999 I.A.A.F. World Championships in Seville?

10. Who was elected Labour M.P. for Cardiff West in May 1997?

11. Who succeeded Paddy Ashdown as leader of the Liberal Democrat Party?

12. Who replaced Glenn Hoddle as England football coach?

13. Who was 1999 French Open women's singles tennis champion?

14. Who authored the 1999 children's book *Harry Potter and the Prisoner of Azkaban*?

15. Who is the wife of Prince Edward?

ANSWERS 1. David Coulthard **2.** Terrence Malick **3.** Doha Golf Club **4.** Meg Ryan **5.** Rebecca Howe **6.** 1892 **7.** Serena Williams **8.** Judi Dench **9.** Fabrizio Mori **10.** Rhodri Morgan **11.** Charles Kennedy **12.** Kevin Keegan **13.** Steffi Graf **14.** J.K. Rowling **15.** Sophie Rhys-Jones.

ENTERTAINMENT

1. Who played Dawson in *Dawson's Creek*?

2. Who directed the 1991 film *The People Under the Stairs*?

3. Who played Marmalade Atkins in the children's TV series *Educating Marmalade*?

4. What was comedian Dick Emery's middle name?

5. In which year did Zoë Ball and Kevin first co-host the Radio 1 Breakfast Show on a regular basis?

6. What is the 1993 follow-up to Wim Wenders's film *Wings of Desire*?

7. Which actor played the owner of Empire Industries in the 1984 sitcom *Empire*?

8. Who played Professor X in the 2000 film *The X-Men*?

9. In which year was actor Verne Troyer born?

10. Who did Jacqueline Pirie play in *Emmerdale*?

11. Who did Hervé Villechaize play in the Bond film *The Man with the Golden Gun*?

12. Who won Best Supporting Actress Oscar in 2000 for her role in *Girl, Interrupted*?

13. Who played Fidgit in the film *Time Bandits*?

14. Which actor played Joseph Valachi in the 1972 film *The Valachi Papers*?

15. Which actor played *Pancho Villa* in the 1972 film?

ANSWERS 1. James Van Der Beek **2.** Wes Craven **3.** Charlotte Coleman **4.** Gilbert **5.** 1997 **6.** Faraway, So Close **7.** Patrick Macnee **8.** Patrick Stewart **9.** 1969 **10.** Tina Dingle **11.** Nick-Nack **12.** Angelina Jolie **13.** Kenny Baker **14.** Charles Bronson **15.** Telly Savalas.

SPORT

1. What nationality is golfer Jarrod Moseley?

2. How many winning rides did Fred Archer have in 1877?

3. Who signed Canadian ice hockey player Marc Hussey in August 1999?

4. Who was men's 800m champion at the 1987 world championships?

5. Who was 1974 Australian men's singles tennis champion?

6. Aldo Montano was 1938 men's sabre world champion in fencing. Which country did he represent?

7. What is the nickname of rugby league player Jason Robinson?

8. What time did John Jarvis take to win the 1900 Olympic men's 400m freestyle swimming title?

9. Which UK golfer was runner-up to Greg Norman in the 1980 world matchplay championship?

10. In which year did Paul Laurie first take part in the Ryder Cup?

11. Which snooker player won the Rothman's Grand Prix in 1984?

12. Who did Llanelli play in the quarter-finals of the 2000 Heineken Cup?

13. For which country did Test cricketer Ravi Shastri play?

14. Who is the Australian coach of Salford rugby league side?

15. Who won the Cy Young Award as outstanding pitcher in baseball's American League in 1987?

POP

1. Brett and Rennie Sparks comprise which country duo?

2. From which New Zealand university did Neil Finn get a B.A. degree?

3. In which year did Kenny Rogers have a No. 1 hit single with *Coward of the County*?

4. Who had a 2000 Top 10 single with *(Welcome) to the Dance*?

5. Which group's singles include 2000's *Poodle Rockin'*?

6. Which group recorded the singles *Honey Be Good* and *Crystal Palace*?

7. On which label did Shania Twain record the album *Come On Over*?

8. Which two members of the group Episode 6 joined Deep Purple in 1969?

9. Which group had a 1999 single with *Kiss (When the Sun Don't Shine)*?

10. Which violinist had a 1995 hit single with *Classical Gas*?

11. Which group recorded the 1988 album *Tighten Up Vol. 88*?

12. In which year was singer Luther Vandross born?

13. Who had a 1999 Top 10 single with *Barber's Adagio for Strings*?

14. Which Scottish group's name means *from the womb* in Greek?

15. Which male vocalist had a 1983 hit with *Young Americans Talking*?

PEOPLE

1. In which year did Lord Denis Howell die?

2. What was the middle name of U.S. vice-president John Garner?

3. In which year was actor Sir Ian McKellen born?

4. Who played Billy in the TV comedy show *Ally McBeal*?

5. What nationality was racing cyclist Fausto Coppi?

6. Which former athlete was head of BBC general features from 1969-72?

7. In which U.S. state was ice skater Peggy Fleming born in 1948?

8. In which year was broadcaster Peter Jay born?

9. Which actor starred in the Hollywood film version of Nick Hornby's book *High Fidelity*?

10. Which 50-stone rap artist died in 2000, aged 28?

11. For what was 'Buzz Lightyear' voice artist Tim Allen jailed in 1978?

12. What is Los Angeles cop Marcelo Rodriguez famous for?

13. In which year was composer Andrew Lloyd Webber born?

14. Lucy Hobbs Taylor was the first American woman to receive a degree in which field?

15. Vanessa Bell was elder sister of which writer?

GENERAL KNOWLEDGE

1. In which year was Saint Ignatius Loyola born?

2. What is the name given to a calendar year of 366 days?

3. Which actor voiced the Genie in the 1992 animated film *Aladdin*?

4. Which Italian football team were the winners of the 1999 U.E.F.A. Cup?

5. Which manager of Newcastle United resigned early in the 1999/2000 season?

6. Which actor played Death in the film *Meet Joe Black*?

7. Who wrote the 1999 novel *The Alibi*?

8. Which tennis player knocked Martina Hingis out of the 1999 ladies singles tournament at Wimbledon?

9. Who was author of the 1999 novel *Inconceivable*?

10. Which new minister was put in charge of the Greenwich Dome following the departure of Peter Mandelson?

11. Which comedian starred in the 1999 film *The Debt Collector*?

12. Which celebrity got married in 1999 to DJ Fatboy Slim?

13. Who was winner of the 1999 French Open men's singles tennis championship?

14. Who was men's marathon winner at the 1999 I.A.A.F. World Championships?

15. Which boardgame features two kings, two queens and sixteen pawns?

ANSWERS 1. 1491 **2.** A leap year **3.** Robin Williams **4.** Parma **5.** Ruud Gullit **6.** Brad Pitt **7.** Sandra Brown **8.** Jelena Dokic **9.** Ben Elton **10.** Lord Falconer of Thoroton **11.** Billy Connolly **12.** Zoë Ball **13.** André Agassi **14.** Abel Anton **15.** Chess.

ENTERTAINMENT

1. What is Kim Basinger's profession in the 1987 film *Nadine*?

2. What is the nickname of headmaster Harry Andrews in the 1980s sitcom *A.J. Wentworth, B.A.*?

3. Which actor presented the 2000 Channel Four series *Six Experiments that Changed the World*?

4. Who does Liz Dawn play in *Coronation Street*?

5. Who directed the 1956 film *Trapeze*?

6. Who plays a sideshow ventriloquist in the 1925 film *The Unholy Three*?

7. Who starred as a film producer in the 1991 film *Grand Canyon*?

8. In which city did Placido Domingo make his debut as a baritone?

9. Who directed the 1980 film *Scanners*?

10. Who won Best Director at the 2000 Golden Globes?

11. Who played Holly Goodhead in the Bond film *Moonraker*?

12. Who played Governor Earl Kemp Long in the 1989 film *Blaze*?

13. What is the name of the malfunctioning penguin in the film *Toy Story 2*?

14. In which comedy show do the characters Papa Lazarou and Hilary Briss appear?

15. Who plays W.S. Gilbert in the film *Topsy Turvy*?

ANSWERS 1. Hairdresser **2.** Squid **3.** Ken Campbell **4.** Vera Duckworth **5.** Carol Reed **6.** Lon Chaney **7.** Steve Martin **8.** Mexico City **9.** David Cronenberg **10.** Sam Mendes **11.** Lois Chiles **12.** Paul Newman **13.** Wheezy **14.** The League of Gentlemen **15.** Jim Broadbent.

SPORT

1. For which rugby league side do Mick Withers and Scott Naylor play?

2. Who rode Diesis to victory in the 1982 Dewhurst Stakes?

3. Is cricketer J.J. Bates a right-handed or left-handed bat?

4. Who won the roller hockey title when it was a demonstration sport at the 1992 Olympic Games?

5. At what sport have Emma Carney and Chris McCormack been world champions?

6. What was unusual about the weapon Boris Onischenko used in fencing at the 1972 Olympics?

7. How many golds did Germany get in the 1999 World Athletics Championships?

8. Which Scottish football team entered the 1871/2 F.A. Cup in England?

9. Which ice hockey player is known as the 'Russian Rocket'?

10. Yuriy Sedykh set a world record for hammer throw on 30th August 1986. How far was it?

11. How many Tests did cricketer David Capel play for England?

12. Ron Northcott was winning skip three times at the curling world championships. For which country?

13. In cricket, who scored 265 for Surrey vs. Middlesex in the 1st innings of their 1999 county championship game?

14. In which year was the European Cup-Winners' Cup in men's handball first held?

15. In which year did British tennis player Dora Boothby die?

ANSWERS 1. Bradford Bulls **2.** Lester Piggott **3.** Right-handed **4.** Argentina **5.** Triathlon **6.** It registered hits when no contact had occurred **7.** Four **8.** Queen's Park **9.** Pavel Bure **10.** 86.74m **11.** 15 **12.** Canada **13.** Alistair Brown **14.** 1976 **15.** 1970.

POP

1. Which group recorded the song *I Want a New Drug* on the 1983 album *Sports*?

2. Who had a 1954 No. 1 single with *Finger of Suspicion*?

3. Which group had a 1992 hit with *Who's Gonna Ride Your Wild Horses*?

4. Which group recorded the 1968 album *Cheap Thrills*?

5. In which year was U.S.A. for Africa's *We Are the World* a No. 1 hit?

6. On which label did Vengaboys release the 1999 album *The Party Album!*?

7. Which group had a 1994 Top 40 hit with *Girl You'll Be A Woman Soon*?

8. Which hip-hop group recorded the song *Millie Pulled a Pistol on Santa*?

9. Which male singer had a 1991 hit with *Cold Cold Heart*?

10. Which veteran rock 'n' roller recorded the 1995 album *Young Blood*?

11. Which group had a 1993 Top 10 single with *The Key the Secret*?

12. Which group had a 1999 Top 10 single with *Steal My Sunshine*?

13. Which group had a 1996 hit single with *Pearl's Girl*?

14. Which Scottish group were dropped from an Alice Cooper tour in the early 1980s for reportedly being 'too weird'?

15. On which label did the Undertones record the 1981 hit *Julie Ocean*?

ANSWERS 1. Huey Lewis and the News **2.** Dickie Valentine **3.** U2 **4.** Big Brother & the Holding Company **5.** 1985 **6.** Positiva **7.** Urge Overkill **8.** De La Soul **9.** Midge Ure **10.** Jerry Lee Lewis **11.** Urban Cookie Collective **12.** Len **13.** Underworld **14.** Big Country **15.** Ardeck.

THE CARLING PUB QUIZ BOOK

ART

1. Whose novels include 1996's *Goodbye, Johnny Thunders*?

2. What was the real name of artist Paolo Uccello?

3. In which year did Italian painter Giacomo Balla die?

4. Which painter was the mother of Maurice Utrillo?

5. Who wrote the 1839 novel *Jack Sheppard* about the notorious highwayman?

6. Which South African wrote the 1988 novel *States of Emergency*?

7. In which novel by Thomas Hardy does the character Aeneas Manston appear?

8. In which year did the first of Hugh Lofting's 'Dr. Doolittle' books appear?

9. Which novel by Agatha Christie introduced Hercule Poirot?

10. Which U.S. cartoonist drew *The Yellow Kid*?

11. Who painted 1982's *Nanny, Small Bears, and Bogeyman*?

12. Who painted the work *Lear and Cordelia* in the mid-19th century?

13. In which city did artist Francis Bacon die in 1992?

14. The Tate Gallery houses the painting *Amy Robsart*. Who painted it?

15. Whose novels include *Ladder of Years* and *The Accidental Tourist*?

GENERAL KNOWLEDGE

1. Who was elected Labour Co-operative M.P. for Cardiff South and Penarth in May 1997?

2. Who was elected Israeli prime minister in May 1999?

3. Which comedian won the Perrier Award at the 1999 Edinburgh Festival in his guise as 'The Pub Landlord'?

4. Which island of the Mediterranean is separated from Italy by the Strait of Messina?

5. Who did Monty Woolley play in the 1942 film *The Man Who Came To Dinner*?

6. Which bird makes its first appearance on the seventh day of Christmas in the song *Twelve Days of Christmas*?

7. Who was the director of the 1966 film *The Bible*?

8. What type of creature is a nilgai?

9. In which year did stage and film comedian Charlie Chaplin die?

10. In which year was world light-heavyweight boxing champion Archie Moore born?

11. Who directed the 1940 film *Christmas in July*?

12. In which year was actress Ava Gardner born?

13. By which name is the Eurasian plant cleavers also known?

14. Which 17th century Dutch portrait painter was born Pieter van der Faes?

15. What was the name of the world's security command in children's television puppet show *Captain Scarlet and the Mysterons*?

ENTERTAINMENT

1. What is Roger Moore's profession in the 1985 film *The Naked Face*?

2. What is Russ Abbot's real name?

3. Who plays Mr. Blume in the film *Rushmore*?

4. Which actress played Winnie Purvis in *Emmerdale Farm*?

5. Who won the 1992 Perrier Award at the Edinburgh Festival for Best Newcomer?

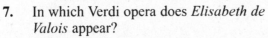

6. Who did Patrick Cargill play in the 1971 film version of *Up Pompeii*?

7. In which Verdi opera does *Elisabeth de Valois* appear?

8. Who directed the 1939 film *Union Pacific*?

9. Who composed the 1832 opera *The Love Potion*?

10. In which Mozart opera does the character Don Alfonso appear?

11. Who directed the 1927 film *The Unknown* starring Lon Chaney?

12. In which Australian city was actor-manager Sydney W. Carroll born?

13. Who stars as a boys' school teacher in the 1971 film *Unman, Wittering and Zigo*?

14. Which American actress stars in Kenneth Branagh's film *Love's Labours Lost*?

15. Who directed the film *Holy Smoke* starring Kate Winslet?

SPORT

1. Who was runner-up in the 1966 Formula 1 world championship?

2. In cricket, who scored 105 for Durham vs. Essex in the 1st innings of their 1999 county championship game?

3. Which club won the Welsh league in rugby union in 1997/8?

4. Which motor racer was 1973 Sports Illustrated Sportsman of the Year?

5. What nationality was WBC super-featherweight boxing champion Cornelius Boza Edwards?

6. In cricket, who scored 201 for Hampshire vs. Sussex in the 2nd innings of their 1999 county championship game?

7. Which U.S. jockey earned over $203m from 1974-96?

8. In cricket, who scored 111 n.o. for Hampshire vs. Sussex in the 2nd innings of their 1999 county championship game?

9. Who were men's team winners in the 1982 World Fresh Water Championships in angling?

10. Which American pair won the 1938 and 1939 Wimbledon women's doubles title?

11. In which city was the 1978 BDO world professional darts championship held?

12. What is the full name of Welsh rugby union player Rupert Moon?

13. Briton Martin Potter was a world professional champion in 1989. At what sport?

14. In which year did VfB Leipzig first win the German League?

15. What nationality is swimmer Brendon Dedekind?

ANSWERS 1. John Surtees **2.** James Daley **3.** Swansea **4.** Jackie Stewart **5.** Ugandan **6.** William Kendall **7.** Chris McCarron **8.** Adrian Aymes **9.** Holland **10.** Alice Marble and Sarah Fabyan **11.** Nottingham **12.** Rupert Henry St. John Barker Moon **13.** Surfing **14.** 1903 **15.** South African.

POP

1. Which singer featured on Y-Tribe's 1999 hit *Enough is Enough*?

2. Gore, Fletcher, Gahan. Which pop group?

3. What was Piero Umiliani's only hit single?

4. On which label did George Michael record his album *Songs from the Last Century*?

5. Which group did Ian Broudie form in 1982?

6. Which group had a 1986 hit with the single *All Fall Down*?

7. In which year did The Tourists have a Top 10 single with *I Only Want to Be With You*?

8. Which female singer had a 1983 Top 10 hit with the song *Move Over Darling*?

9. In which year did Gary Numan first have a hit single with *Cars*?

10. In which year did Elvis Costello have a Top 10 single with *I Can't Stand Up For Falling Down*?

11. Which singer guests on the song *First Man in Space* by the group The All Seeing I?

12. What is the title of George Michael's debut solo L.P.?

13. Who featured on Technotronic's 1990 hit single *Get Up (Before the Night Is Over)*?

14. What is the title of the second album by the group The Fugs?

15. Which ex-soap actress had a 1999 Top 10 single with *I've Got You*?

ANSWERS 1. Elisabeth Troy **2.** Depeche Mode **3.** Mah na mah na **4.** Virgin **5.** Care **6.** Ultravox **7.** 1979 **8.** Tracey Ullman **9.** 1980 **10.** 1979 **11.** Phil Oakey **12.** Faith **13.** Ya kid D **14.** The Fugs Second Album **15.** Martine McCutcheon.

GEOGRAPHY

1. In which ocean are the Schouten Islands?

2. Wensleydale is the valley of which Yorkshire river?

3. What was the capital of the former Russian principality of Muscovy?

4. In which county is Swindon?

5. Which country controlled the port of Muscat from 1650-1741?

6. In which Asian country is the university city of Shiraz?

7. What was the name of Bognor Regis prior to 1929?

8. Chatham, Kent, is near the mouth of which river?

9. On which canal is the German city of Münster?

10. In which U.S. state is Gettysburg?

11. In which African country is the copper mining city of Mufulira?

12. Which channel separates the Isle of Sheppey from the mainland?

13. In which U.S. state is the city of Grand Rapids?

14. In which South American country is the city of Barquisimeto?

15. On which river does the town of Warwick stand?

GENERAL KNOWLEDGE

1. Which horse was the 1964 winner of the Epsom Derby?

2. Which Old Testament prophet annointed the first two kings of the Israelites?

3. In which year was English actor Bernard Lee, known for playing *M* in various *James Bond* films, born?

4. Which actor played Mark Slate in the television series *The Girl from UNCLE*?

5. In which year was the author Henry Miller born?

6. In which musical does the song *The Rain in Spain* appear?

7. Who wrote the children's story *How the Grinch Stole Christmas*?

8. In which year was former director of the F.B.I. J. Edgar Hoover born?

9. Which military officer holds commissioned rank immediately junior to a captain?

10. Who was 1975 Wimbledon men's singles tennis champion?

11. Who is Prince Ramiro's valet in Rossini's opera *La Cenerentola*?

12. Who is the American author of the 1949 book *The Sheltering Sky*?

13. Which volcanic island in Indonesia was partially destroyed by its eruption in 1883?

14. Which American football coach led the Green Bay Packers to victory in the first two Super Bowls?

15. Which 1997 film, directed by Kevin Allen, is set in Swansea?

ENTERTAINMENT

1. For which film was Sean Penn a Best Actor Oscar nominee in 2000?

2. For which film was Janet McTeer a Best Actress Oscar nominee in 2000?

3. In which opera does the character Ellen Orford appear?

4. What is Joanna Lumley's character name in *Absolutely Fabulous*?

5. As what does David Lynch appear in the 1994 vampire movie *Nadja*?

6. Which scientist is the subject of the 1960 film *I Aim at the Stars*?

7. Who directed the 1949 film *Take Me Out to the Ball Game*?

8. Who plays sleuth Philo Vance in the 1929 film *Canary Murder Case*?

9. Who starred in and directed the 1993 film *A Perfect World*?

10. Who plays a con-man in the 1956 film *The Rainmaker*?

11. Who directed the 1991 film *The Fisher King*?

12. Who played chauffeur Thomas in the BBC TV sitcom *Butterflies*?

13. Who plays Brad Pitt's mother in the film *A River Runs Through It*?

14. Who wrote the sitcom *How Do You Want Me*?

15. Who directed the 1992 film thriller *Raising Cain*?

ANSWERS 1. Sweet and Lowdown **2.** Tumbleweeds **3.** Peter Grimes **4.** Patsy Stone **5.** Morgue attendant **6.** Werner Von Braun **7.** Busby Berkeley **8.** William Powell **9.** Clint Eastwood **10.** Burt Lancaster **11.** Terry Gilliam **12.** Michael Ripper **13.** Brenda Blethyn **14.** Simon Nye **15.** Brian De Palma.

SPORT

1. What nationality is skier Christl Cranz?

2. In which Australian city is the Albert Park Formula 1 racetrack?

3. What nationality are canoeists Beniamino Bonomi & Daniele Scarpa?

4. For which team did Formula 1 driver Jenson Button compete in the 2000 Grand Prix season?

5. Which state withdrew from the National Football League in Australian Rules Football in 1977-8?

6. In which sport were Ichiro Ogimura & Yoshio Tomita world champions in 1956?

7. Who rode the 1953 winner of the Oaks, Ambiguity?

8. For which county did cricketer Darren Bicknall make his debut in 1987?

9. How many gold medals have Lithuania won at the summer Olympics from 1896-1996?

10. Who is the mother of athlete Daniela Caines?

11. Michael Staksrud was 1973 world men's speed skating champion. What country does he represent?

12. With which field event do you associate Philippa Roles and Judy Oakes?

13. Who were Everton's three scorers in their 1985 European Cup-Winners' Cup Final win?

14. What nationality is swimmer Lars Frolander?

15. Who was men's 100m champion at the 1977 I.A.A.F. World Cup?

POP

1. Who had a 1985 Top 10 single with *Material Girl*?

2. In which year did the Jesus and Mary Chain release the *Some Candy Talking* E.P.?

3. Which studio album by Fun Boy Three features the song *The Farm Yard Connection*?

4. Who produced the Jam's 1980 single *Goin' Underground*?

5. Who recorded the 1977 album *Bullinamingvase*?

6. Which Australian entertainer recorded the 1965 single *Linda*?

7. Which funk group recorded the 1970 album *Osmium*?

8. On which label did Feeder record the album *Yesterday Went Too Soon*?

9. Which Dutch group recorded the 1978 single *Rock 'N Roll*?

10. Who produced Ian Gomm's 1978 single *Hold On*?

11. Which group recorded the 1985 album *The Clock Comes Down the Stairs*?

12. To which label did Furniture sign in 1986?

13. In which year did Sad Café have a Top 10 single with *Every Day Hurts*?

14. Who recorded the 1982 album *10,9,8,7,6,5,4,3,2,1*?

15. Which duo recorded the album *Freeze Frame*?

HISTORY

1. Who was elected vice-president of the U.S. in 1852 but died six weeks after being sworn in?

2. Who was mayor of West Berlin from 1957-66?

3. In which year was the Philippeville Massacre in Algeria?

4. In which year did Hosni Mubarak become president of Egypt?

5. The War of the Bavarian Succession was fought between which two countries?

6. In which year did Dick Turpin die?

7. Which treaty, signed in 1360, ended the first phase of the Hundred Years' War?

8. In which year did Jacques Chirac first become prime minister of France?

9. In which month of 1981 was Pope John Paul II shot?

10. In which year did the Seven Years War end?

11. In which year of World War II was Coventry Cathedral destroyed?

12. In which year did Cory Aquino become president of the Philippines?

13. In which year was the Battle of Towton in the Wars of the Roses?

14. In which year did Edward Heath become M.P. for Bexley?

15. In which year was English Roman Catholic prelate Reginald Pole born?

GENERAL KNOWLEDGE

1. Who was 1954 winner of the British Open golf tournament?

2. Which actress played Purdey in the television show *The New Avengers*?

3. Who had a 1973 No. 1 single with *Can the Can*?

4. Which Phoenician prince in Greek mythology slew the dragon guarding the spring of Ares?

5. What was the name given to the army established in 1645 during the Civil War by the English parliamentarians?

6. What is the name given to the mass of lymphoid tissue at the back of the throat behind the uvula?

7. In which Italian city is La Scala opera house?

8. What was the former name from 1940-62 for the Russian port of Perm?

9. Who wrote the 1969 play *Breath*?

10. In which year did U.S. aviator and polar explorer Richard Byrd die?

11. In which year did Italian operatic tenor Enrico Caruso die?

12. What is the name of the female reproductive part of a flower?

13. Which genus of woodland plants includes the windflower?

14. Which French novelist authored *François le Champi*?

15. Who were the male and female leads in the 1974 film *The Night Porter*?

ANSWERS 1. Peter Thomson **2.** Joanna Lumley **3.** Suzi Quatro **4.** Cadmus **5.** New Model Army **6.** Adenoids **7.** Milan **8.** Molotov **9.** Samuel Beckett **10.** 1957 **11.** 1921 **12.** Pistil **13.** Anemone **14.** George Sand **15.** Dirk Bogarde and Charlotte Rampling.

ENTERTAINMENT

1. Who directed the 1974 film *The Taking of Pelham One Two Three*?

2. Which comedian stars in the 1972 film *Cancel My Reservation*?

3. Who directed the 1979 film *Cuba* starring Sean Connery?

4. What is the real first name of entertainer Max Bygraves?

5. Who won Best Female Artist at the 1999 European MTV Awards?

6. Which comedienne was born Lynne Shepherd in 1945?

7. Who wrote and directed the film comedy *Fanny and Elvis*?

8. Who plays an orphan in the 1978 film *Candleshoe*?

9. Who plays Christmas Jones in the Bond film *The World is Not Enough*?

10. Which actress plays Annie Spadaro in the sitcom *Caroline in the City*?

11. What is comedian Ali G's version of *Who Wants to be a Millionaire* on *Da Ali G Show*?

12. Which husband and wife team played David and Mary Caxton in the 1958 sitcom *Caxton's Tales*?

13. Who directed the 1999 film *Random Hearts*?

14. Who played Alec Picton-Jones in the sitcom *Hippies*?

15. Who played *Candyman* in the 1992 film?

ANSWERS 1. Joseph Sargent **2.** Bob Hope **3.** Richard Lester **4.** Walter **5.** Britney Spears **6.** Marti Caine **7.** Kay Mellor **8.** Jodie Foster **9.** Denise Richards **10.** Amy Pietz **11.** Who Wants to Win an Ounce **12.** Wilfred and Mabel Pickles **13.** Sydney Pollack **14.** Julian Rhind-Tutt **15.** Tony Todd.

SPORT

1. By what score did Lindsay Davenport beat Martina Hingis in the 2000 Australian Open singles tennis championship final?

2. In which year were Surrey crowned the first official cricket county championship winners?

3. For which NHL side does hockey player Jay Panolfo turn out?

4. What nationality is golfer Colleen Walker?

5. Who was 1954 Sports Illustrated Sportsman of the Year?

6. Which Frenchman won the 1987 Belgian Grand Prix in Formula 1?

7. Who finished second in the men's 100m at the 1999 World Athletics Championships?

8. Who won the Harry Sunderland Trophy in 1980 whilst with Widnes?

9. How many golds did Romania win at the 1999 World Athletics Championships?

10. With what winter sport are Anton Fischer and Jeffrey Jost associated?

11. Which rugby league club signed Keith Senior in September 1999?

12. Which horse won the 1917 Grand National?

13. From which country is runner Maria Mutola?

14. How many Olympic gold medals did Lasse Viren win from 1972-6?

15. Which Swedes won the 1987 Australian Open men's doubles tennis title?

POP

1. Who composed the soundtrack for the 1985 film *Birdy*?

2. On which label was Haircut One Hundred's single *Prime Time* released?

3. Who is credited with vocals on the single *I Don't Want To Live With Monkeys* by the Higsons?

4. How old was Rory Gallagher when he died in 1995?

5. What is the B-side of the Human League's 1978 single *Being Boiled*?

6. Which Richard Thompson song features on the reverse of the single *Peace in Our Time* by The Imposter?

7. Which group's debut album in 1992 was *You, the Night and the Music*?

8. Who wrote the Jam song *Innocent Man*?

9. Who had a 1994 Top 10 single with *Confide in Me*?

10. Who recorded the 1984 album *Medicine Show*?

11. Which Smokey Robinson song did Japan release as a single in 1982?

12. In which year did R & B singer Billy Stewart die?

13. Which Neil Young song did Jason and the Scorchers record on the B-side of the single *White Lies*?

14. Which artist recorded the 1988 album *Born 2B Blue*?

15. Which two singers appear on album sleeves on the cover of Jilted John's single *Jilted John*?

WORDS

1. What is a sticktight - a plant or an insect?

2. How many wings does a triplane have?

3. What on a bat is a patapium?

4. Icterus is another name for what medical condition?

5. On what method of transport would you find a derailleur?

6. What is chayote - a fabric or a fruit?

7. What does a banksman do?

8. What does *feng shui* translate as?

9. Who would use a fifi hook?

10. What type of of creature is a geelbek?

11. What in New Zealand is hokonui?

12. What is a juba - a dance or a tree?

13. What is linsey-woolsey?

14. What is a wickiup?

15. What type of creature is a vervet?

ANSWERS 1. Plant 2. Three 3. A web of skin that functions as a wing 4. Jaundice 5. Bicycle 6. Fruit 7. He signals instructions to a crane-driver 8. Wind water 9. A mountaineer 10. Fish 11. Illicit whisky 12. A dance 13. A thin rough fabric 14. A type of crude shelter 15. A monkey.

GENERAL KNOWLEDGE

1. Which actor played Max in the television series *Hart to Hart*?

2. Who directed the 1955 film *The Long Gray Line*?

3. Which principality in S.W. Europe includes the port La Condamine?

4. Which board game was invited by Alfred M. Butts?

5. Which actress starred in the title role of the 1968 Robert Aldrich film *The Legend of Lylah Clare*?

6. Which German philosopher's works included *The World as Will and Idea*?

7. Ljubljana is capital of which republic in central Europe?

8. Which fish is also called a long-fin tunny?

9. Which genus of plants includes the wood sorrel?

10. What is the basic SI unit of amount of substance?

11. Who was the mother of the English king Richard I?

12. Which comedy actor played Charles Brown in the television sitcom *Sykes*?

13. Which actor played Hoss Cartwright in the television western show *Bonanza*?

14. Which actress played Meg Richardson in the television soap *Crossroads*?

15. Who was the 1987 world Formula 1 motor racing champion?

ANSWERS 1. Lionel Stander **2.** John Ford **3.** Monaco **4.** Scrabble **5.** Kim Novak **6.** Arthur Schopenhauer **7.** Slovenia **8.** Albacore **9.** Oxalis **10.** Mole **11.** Eleanor of Aquitaine **12.** Richard Wattis **13.** Dan Blocker **14.** Noele Gordon **15.** Nelson Piquet.

ENTERTAINMENT

1. Who wrote the 1999 Channel Four drama *Kid in the Corner*?

2. Who played headmaster Richard Nixon in the 1997 sitcom *Chalk*?

3. Who played cyborg T-1000 in the 1991 film *Terminator 2: Judgement Day*?

4. What is Brad Pitt's character name in the film *Fight Club*?

5. Who directed the 1991 film *Jungle Fever*?

6. During the making of which film was Montgomery Clift disfigured in a car crash?

7. Who played Stacey Sutton in the Bond film *A View to a Kill*?

8. Who is the female star of the 1942 film musical *Iceland*?

9. Who directed and starred in the 1969 comedy *Take the Money and Run*?

10. Who directed 1932 film *I Am a Fugitive from a Chain Gang*?

11. Which comedian thinks he has only two weeks to live in the 1939 comedy *Never Say Die*?

12. Who directed the 1967 film *Ulysses*, based on a novel by James Joyce?

13. Who wrote the 1970s sitcom *Alexander the Greatest*?

14. Which author does Ewan McGregor play in the 2000 film *Nora*?

15. In which city is the 1973 film *The Sting* set?

ANSWERS 1. Tony Marchant **2.** John Wells **3.** Robert Patrick **4.** Tyler Durden **5.** Spike Lee **6.** Raintree Country **7.** Tanya Roberts **8.** Sonja Henie **9.** Woody Allen **10.** Mervyn LeRoy **11.** Bob Hope **12.** Joseph Strick **13.** Bernard Kops **14.** James Joyce **15.** Chicago.

SPORT

1. In which year were the Endurance Riding World Championships in equestrianism first held?

2. In which year was boxer Julius Francis born?

3. What country did champion Nordic skier Lyubov Korzyryeva represent?

4. Who was 1924 Olympic women's 200m breaststroke swimming champion?

5. Which Spanish golfer won the 1983 U.S. Masters?

6. By what score did England beat Ireland in the 2000 Six Nations rugby union tournament?

7. In which year did cricketer Timothy Bloomfield make his county debut for Middlesex?

8. How many times did Kapil Dev take 5 or more wickets in an innings in his 131 Tests?

9. Who took 7-73 for Nottinghamshire vs. Somerset at Taunton in 1998?

10. Which baseball player had the best batting average in 1962?

11. Who replaced Robert Howley as Welsh rugby union captain in 2000?

12. Who rode Wolfhound to victory in the 1993 Haydock Park Sprint Cup?

13. In cricket, who scored 117 for Essex vs. Northants in the 1st innings of their 1999 county championship game?

14. In which year was the Tennis & Rackets Association formed?

15. Who knocked Eccles out of the 2000 rugby league Silk Cut Challenge Cup?

ANSWERS 1. 1986 **2.** 1964 **3.** U.S.S.R. **4.** Lucy Morton **5.** Seve Ballesteros **6.** 50-18 **7.** 1997 **8.** 23 **9.** M.N. Bowen **10.** Tommy Davis **11.** David Young **12.** Michael Roberts **13.** Stuart Law **14.** 1907 **15.** Wath Brow.

POP

1. Who recorded the 1999 single *Gin-Soaked Boy*?

2. Who had a 1999 Top 10 single with *Larger Than Life*?

3. Which group recorded the 1988 album *Isn't Anything*?

4. Which punk group recorded the 1990 album *39/Smooth*?

5. Who had a 1990 Top 10 single with *Could Have Told You So*?

6. Which group released the E.P.s *3.99* and *Skrika*?

7. Who had a 1999 Top 10 single with *Sing It Back*?

8. Which group recorded the 1993 album *In Utero*?

9. Which group recorded the 1991 album *Bandwagonesque*?

10. Which blues singer recorded the 1977 album *Let's Make a Deal*?

11. Which Canadian group recorded the 1991 album *0+2=1*?

12. Who produced Heather Nova's 1995 L.P. *Oyster*?

13. Which guitarist joined Green on Red in 1983?

14. Which group's debut L.P. included the tracks *The Dream Police* and *My Love is a Liquid*?

15. What was on the reverse of the 1990 Blur single *She's So High*?

SCIENCE

1. What nationality was pioneer photographer Nadar?

2. Which element did Otto Hahn and Lise Meitner discover in 1918?

3. In which European capital was Jacques Lucien Monod born?

4. Who became Professor of Mathematics at the University of Pisa in 1589?

5. What colour is pitchblende?

6. Of which planet is Desdemona a satellite?

7. What is the name given to the point at which the three phases of water; vapour, liquid and ice, are in equilibrium?

8. Which German physicist discovered the 'uncertainty principle' in quantum theory in 1927?

9. What is the average diameter in miles of Neptune's moon Galatea?

10. What organization in the U.S. is the A.A.A.S.?

11. What does MS-DOS stand for in computing?

12. Which chemical element has the symbol Hs?

13. What nationality was nuclear physicist Horni Bhabha?

14. What is the largest of Neptune's moons?

15. Whose greatest published work was *De Re Metallica*?

ANSWERS 1. French **2.** Proactinium **3.** Paris **4.** Galileo **5.** Black **6.** Uranus **7.** The triple point **8.** Werner Heisenberg **9.** 108 miles **10.** American Association for the Advancement of Science **11.** Microsoft Disk Operating System **12.** Hassium **13.** Indian **14.** Triton **15.** Georgius Agricola.

GENERAL KNOWLEDGE

1. Who was the 1996 world Formula 1 motor racing champion?

2. Which city in Switzerland was headquarters of the League of Nations?

3. Who wrote the 1953 novel *After the Funeral*?

4. Who wrote the 1939 novel *No Orchids for Miss Blandish*?

5. Which 1969 film starring Richard Burton and Rex Harrison was based on a play by Charles Dyer?

6. Who wrote the 1906 novel *The Man of Property*?

7. What is a vaporetto?

8. Who wrote the 1968 novel *Only When I Larf*?

9. On which lake is the Scottish village and fishing port of Ullapool?

10. Which English naval officer was chief minister of Naples from 1779-1806?

11. Who was the 1982 U.S. Open golf champion?

12. Who was the 1994 Commonwealth women's 10,000m champion?

13. Which city in the Netherlands was the residence of Charles II of England during his exile?

14. Which 1960s rock group comprised Eric Clapton, Jack Bruce and Ginger Baker?

15. Matilda Alice Victoria Wood was the real name of which English music-hall entertainer?

ENTERTAINMENT

1. What is the name of Woody's horse in the film *Toy Story 2*?

2. Who plays Alan Turner in *Emmerdale*?

3. Who directed the film *Double Jeopardy*, which stars Ashley Judd?

4. Who was the male lead in the 1988 film *The Unbearable Lightness of Being*?

5. What anniversary did news programme *Newsnight* celebrate in 2000?

6. What is the theme song to the 1955 prison drama film *Unchained*?

7. Which comedienne plays Kirsten in the sitcom *Beast*?

8. Who directed the 1947 film *Unconquered*?

9. In which year did opera singer Stafford Dean make his debut at Glyndebourne?

10. Who stars as film star Nick Lang in the 1991 film *The Hard Way*?

11. Who composed the 1919 opera *Fennimore and Gerda*?

12. Which *Monty Python* member played *Yellowbeard* in a 1983 film?

13. Who directed the 1949 film western *The Walking Hills*?

14. Who won the Best Actor in a Drama award at the 2000 Golden Globes?

15. Who starred as Alex in a 1989 stage production of *A Clockwork Orange*?

ANSWERS 1. Bullseye **2.** Richard Thorp **3.** Bruce Beresford **4.** Daniel Day-Lewis **5.** 20th **6.** Unchained Melody **7.** Doon Mackichan **8.** Cecil B. De Mille **9.** 1964 **10.** Michael J. Fox **11.** Frederick Delius **12.** Graham Chapman **13.** John Sturges **14.** Denzil Washington **15.** Phil Daniels.

SPORT

1. At what sport have Keiji Okada and Yuko Hasama been world champions?

2. Which cricketer was 1975 B.B.C. Sports Personality of the Year?

3. For which two clubs did Scot Jimmy McGrory net 410 league goals from 1922-38?

4. For which Premier League side did veteran goalie Neville Southall appear in the 1999/00 season?

5. Which man set a world record of 10.2 for the 100m on 20th June 1936?

6. Which stadium was built to host the 1908 Olympic Games?

7. Which woman took a hat-trick for Australia against England in a Test match in February 1958?

8. In which city was cricketer James Boiling born?

9. How many gold medals did gymnast Vitaliy Scherbo win at world championships from 1992-5?

10. In which year did U.S. tennis player Dwight Davis die?

11. Which Briton won the 1962 South African Grand Prix in Formula 1?

12. Where were the 1987 World Student games held?

13. Which country did rugby union's British Lions tour in 1997?

14. In which county is the Grand National Archery Society based?

15. Christophe Tiozzo was 1990 WBA super-middleweight champion. Which country did he represent?

POP

1. Who recorded the 1969 album *New York Tendaberry*?

2. In which city was the singer Mary Margaret O'Hara born?

3. Who featured on Another Level's 1999 Top 10 single *Summertime*?

4. Who played bass and later lead guitar in Kevin Ayers's group *The Whole World*?

5. Which member of the KLF recorded the 1986 album *The Man*?

6. Strummer, Kelleher, Timperley, Dudanski. Which 1970s group?

7. On which label did The Only Ones release their eponymous debut L.P.?

8. In which year was Al Green's album *I'm Still In Love With You* released?

9. Which group released the 1990 album *Songs of Praise*?

10. Which vocalist recorded the 1996 album *Anthem of the Sun*?

11. Collins, Kirk, McClymont, Daly. Which Scottish group?

12. Who recorded the 1999 single *Swastika Eyes*?

13. In which year did Orbital form?

14. Which Grant Lee Buffalo member replaced R.E.M. drummer Bill Berry on their 1995 world tour?

15. Which vocalist recorded the 1996 album *Miracle*?

ANSWERS 1. Laura Nyro **2.** Toronto **3.** TQ **4.** Mike Oldfield **5.** Bill Drummond **6.** The 101'ers **7.** CBS **8.** 1972 **9.** African Head Charge **10.** Grateful Dead **11.** Orange Juice **12.** Primal Scream **13.** 1989 **14.** Joey Peters **15.** Bim Sherman.

PEOPLE

1. Which singer wrote the autobiography *Take It Like a Man*?

2. Which U.S. comedian was nicknamed 'Mr. Television'?

3. In which year was ballerina Natalia Bessmertnova born?

4. Which actress played Mrs. Robinson in the play *The Graduate* on stage in the West End in spring 2000?

5. In which country was choreographer Dai Ailian born?

6. *Still Memories* is a book of memoirs published in 2000. Which actor wrote it?

7. In which Welsh city was poet Gillian Clark born?

8. Which trade union leader became General Secretary of the T.G.W.U. in 1945?

9. In which year did film director Akira Kurosawa die?

10. What is the first name of playwright Pam Gems?

11. Eddie Fenech-Adami became prime minister of which country in 1998?

12. What was the original name of singer/actress Julie Andrews?

13. In which year did actor/manager Geoffrey Kendal die?

14. Who founded Dinky Toys in the 1930s?

15. In which year was actor Gérard Départdieu born?

GENERAL KNOWLEDGE

1. In English history, what is the name given to the parliament which sat from 1648-53?

2. About which historical figure was the 1951 film biography *The Lady with the Lamp* starring Anna Neagle?

3. Which English actor was Best Supporting Actor Oscar nominee for the film *Billy Budd*?

4. Who was Best Supporting Actress Oscar winner for the film *Ghost*?

5. Who was a Best Actor Oscar nominee for his role in the film *East of Eden*?

6. In which year was T. S. Eliot's poem *The Waste Land* first published?

7. Who was author of *The Railway Children*?

8. Which opera by Michael Balfe contains the song *I dreamt that I dwelt in marble halls*?

9. Who were the male and female leads in the 1935 film *The Farmer Takes A Wife*?

10. Which 1960s TV drama series starred John Thaw as military policeman Sgt. John Mann?

11. Which city in Florida is the site of Walt Disney World?

12. Which river in New York State is the largest tributary of the Hudson?

13. What is the name of the thick rectangular straw mat used as a standard to measure a Japanese room?

14. Which Australian cricketer took 7 for 38 against India in the Adelaide Test of 1947/48?

15. Which star in the constellation Centaurus is also called Rigil Kentaurus?

ANSWERS 1. The Rump Parliament **2.** Florence Nightingale **3.** Terence Stamp **4.** Whoopi Goldberg **5.** James Dean **6.** 1922 **7.** Edith Nesbit **8.** The Bohemian Girl **9.** Henry Fonda and Janet Gaynor **10.** Redcap **11.** Orlando **12.** Mohawk **13.** Tatami **14.** Ray Lindwall **15.** Alpha Centauri.

ENTERTAINMENT

1. Who directed the film *A Room for Romeo Brass*?

2. Which actress played Elizabeth Corday in the TV drama *E.R.*?

3. What nationality is tenor Gregory Dempsey?

4. Who played a wheelchair-bound criminal in the film *Things to Do in Denver when you're Dead*?

5. Esther Williams later married her leading man from the 1953 film *Dangerous When Wet*. Who was he?

6. In which year was comedian Alexei Sayle born?

7. Who played the wife of Sam Neill in the film *Dead Calm*?

8. Who directed the 1996 film *Girl 6*?

9. Who wrote the 1980s sitcom *The Gaffer*?

10. Who directed the 1959 film *Dangerous Liaisons 1960*?

11. Who replaced Ben Chaplin in the sitcom *Game On*?

12. Who created and starred in the ITV sketch show *Gayle's World*?

13. Who wrote the 1988 sitcom *A Gentleman's Club*?

14. What nationality was Jean De Reszke?

15. Who directed the 1945 war film *A Walk in the Sun*?

SPORT

1. Where were the 1954 Asian Games held?

2. Who was 1990/1 National Hunt champion jockey?

3. What nationality was 1992 Olympic men's singles tennis champion Marc Rosset?

4. Who was women's individual world archery champion in 1971?

5. Who was 1998 women's singles tennis champion at Wimbledon?

6. Who was 1980 Olympic individual show jumping gold winner?

7. What nationality is golfer Jean van de Velde?

8. What nationality is snooker player O. B. Agrawal?

9. Who was the Football Writers' Player of the Year in 1994 in England?

10. For which rugby league side did Paul Wellens play?

11. Marianne Jahn and Erika Hess are champions at what sport?

12. In cricket, where was the 1st Test between Australia and New Zealand played in March 2000?

13. What nationality was canoeist Gert Fredriksson?

14. Who did Warrington beat to reach the semi-finals of the 2000 Challenge Cup in rugby league?

15. Who was 1989 All-England Championships badminton men's singles title winner?

ANSWERS 1. Manila 2. Peter Scudamore 3. Swiss 4. Emma Gapchenko 5. Jana Novotna 6. Jan Kowalczyk 7. French 8. Indian 9. Alan Shearer 10. St. Helens 11. Skiing 12. Auckland 13. Swedish 14. Salford 15. Yang Yang.

POP

1. How old was Roy Orbison when he died?

2. Which duo's songs included *Jesus at MacDonald's* and *Stuffin' Martha's Muffin*?

3. In which state did the Nitty Gritty Dirt band form?

4. Who had a 1999 Top 10 single with *Bug a Boo*?

5. In which year did the group Gorky's Zygotic Mynci form?

6. Who produced the 1996 album *After Murder Park* by The Auteurs?

7. At which music college did Kraftwerk's Ralf Hütter and Florian Schneider meet in 1968?

8. In which country was singer Nick Drake born in 1948?

9. Tomita's album *Snowflakes Are Dancing* features versions of which composer's works?

10. Which singer-songwriter recorded the album *Either/Or*?

11. Which singer had a 1999 Top 10 single with *Better Off Alone*?

12. Which singer recorded the 1976 album *Yes We Have No Mañanas*?

13. Which group's debut single was *Looks Like Chaplin*?

14. Which studio album by Gomez features the songs *We Haven't Turned Around* and *Rhythm & Blues Alibi*?

15. Which Newcastle group's debut chart single was *Stars* in 1995?

ANSWERS 1. 52 **2.** Skid Roper and Mojo Nixon **3.** California **4.** Destiny's Child **5.** 1990 **6.** Steve Albini **7.** Düsseldorf Conservatory **8.** Burma **9.** Debussy **10.** Elliott Smith **11.** Alice Deejay **12.** Kevin Ayers **13.** Stereophonics **14.** Liquid Skin **15.** Dubstar.

ART

1. In which novel by Anthony Trollope, published in 1861, did Griselda Grantly marry Lord Dumbello?

2. Which Irish author wrote *The Third Policeman*?

3. Who painted the portrait *Miss Agnes Mary Alexander*?

4. In which city is Jake Arnott's book *The Long Firm* set?

5. Which pop artist painted 1963's *Vox Box*?

6. Whose book *Miss Wyoming* was published in 2000?

7. Who made the 1957 collage *Hommage à Chrysler Corp.*?

8. Who is the author of the short story collection *Tough, tough toys for tough, tough boys*?

9. Whose sculptures include *Discs in Echelon*?

10. Who is the central character in Samuel Butler's *The Way of All Flesh*?

11. Who authored 1896 novel *Rodney Stone*?

12. Which cartoonist's characters included Krazy Kat and Ignatz Mouse?

13. Who authored the 1936 novel *Antigua, Penny, Puce*?

14. Who painted 1885's *The Potato-Eaters*?

15. Who authored the 1990 story collection *Dirty Faxes*?

ANSWERS 1. Framley Parsonage **2.** Flann O'Brien **3.** James Whistler **4.** London **5.** Joe Tilson **6.** Douglas Coupland **7.** Richard Hamilton **8.** Will Self **9.** Dame Barbara Hepworth **10.** Ernest Pontifex **11.** Arthur Conan Doyle **12.** George Herriman **13.** Robert Graves **14.** Vincent Van Gogh **15.** Andrew Davies.

GENERAL KNOWLEDGE

1. Which blues musician led the band the Mahara Minstrels from 1896-1903?

2. Which seaport lies at the mouth of the Guadalmedina River in southern Spain?

3. Which U.S. showman was also called Buffalo Bill?

4. Which island group in the Arabian Sea were formerly known as the Laccadive, Minicoy and Amindivi Islands?

5. Which industrial city of north-west France is home to the Pasteur Institute?

6. Which soprano was known as 'the Swedish nightingale'?

7. Which province of the Republic of Ireland includes the counties of Carlow and Meath?

8. What was the belated 1978 film follow-up to 1944's *National Velvet*?

9. Which fabled place in South America was sought by Spanish explorers in the 16th Century in a quest for treasure?

10. Who was author of the 1957 novel *Voss*?

11. Which American tenor saxophonist was nicknamed 'Prez'?

12. Which Pontefract-born rugby league player captained Castleford to victory in the 1969 Challenge Cup Final?

13. Who was author of the play *The Broken Pitcher*?

14. Who recorded the 1969 No. 1 record album *Nashville Skyline*?

15. Which Italian poet authored the 1573 pastoral drama *Aminta*?

ENTERTAINMENT

1. Which comedy duo starred in the 1943 film *The Dancing Masters*?

2. Who impersonated Pegy Lee on a 1999 *Stars in Their Eyes* celebrity special?

3. Who played Frank Butcher in the soap *EastEnders*?

4. The 1952 film *I Dream of Jeanie* is a film biography of which composer?

5. Who won the Best Actor Oscar in 2000 for the film *American Beauty*?

6. Who directed and starred in the 1986 film *Ratboy*?

7. Who directed the 1966 film *Faster, Pussycat! Kill! Kill!*?

8. Which *Carry On* actor played Nicholas the Beadle in the 1972 TV comedy drama *Clochemerle*?

9. Who played game show host *Bob Martin* in the ITV comedy drama series?

10. Who played superhero George Sunday in the sitcom *My Hero*?

11. Which actor took over as director when Anthony Mann died during the filming of *A Dandy in Aspic* in 1967?

12. Who directed and starred in the film *The Prince of Tides*?

13. Which pop singer appeared in the 1990 TV film *Les Dogs* for the *Comic Strip* team?

14. Which actress played Rollergirl in the film *Boogie Nights*?

15. Which two members of the *Monty Python* team wrote and appeared in the 1969 sketch show *The Complete and Utter History of Britain*?

SPORT

1. Which two teams contested the 2000 F.A. Cup Final in football?

2. Which jockey rode the 1977 St. Leger on Dunfermline?

3. With which sport is Jan-Ove Waldner associated?

4. Which country were 1986 women's relay world champions in ski orienteering?

5. What nationality is swimmer Yana Klochkova?

6. What time did Chris Witty take to do the 1000m in March 1998 to set a speed skating world record?

7. For which club did cricketer Melvyn Betts make his county debut in 1993?

8. How many minutes of the 1973 U.E.F.A. Cup Final 1st leg at Anfield were played before the game was abandoned?

9. What nationality is golfer Lucas Parsons?

10. Grazyna Rabsztyn was 1977 & 1979 I.A.A.F. World Cup women's 100m hurdles champion. Which country did she represent?

11. Which cricketer scored 5,176 runs in the Benson & Hedges Cup for Essex from 1973-97?

12. What time did Wilson Kipketer run in the 1000m in Stuttgart in February 2000 to set a new world record?

13. Phyllis Preuss and Anne Quast Sander were leading amateur golfers. For which country?

14. Where did snooker plater Marco Fu come from?

15. In which game might the Brighton Bears play the Milton Keynes Royals?

ANSWERS 1. Aston Villa and Chelsea **2.** Willie Carson **3.** Table Tennis **4.** Norway **5.** Ukrainian **6.** 1:14.96 **7.** Durham **8.** 27 minutes **9.** Australian **10.** Poland **11.** Graham Gooch **12.** 2:15.25 **13.** United States **14.** Hong Kong **15.** Basketball.

POP

1. Who recorded the 1995 hit single *Here Comes the Hotstepper*?

2. Which Elton John song features on *The Sounds of Science* by The Beastie Boys?

3. Who recorded the 1983 album *High Land Hard Rain*?

4. On which label did Worlds Apart record the 1994 hit *Could It Be I'm Falling In Love*?

5. Who had a Top 10 hit in November 1999 with *Why*?

6. In which year was Stephen 'Tin Tin' Duffy born?

7. What was the title of Hal Willner's Kurt Weill tribute album?

8. On which label was Roy Wood's 1975 hit *Oh What a Shame*?

9. Which Welsh group recorded the album *Joya Magica*?

10. Who recorded the album *So...How's Your Girl*?

11. Which group had a 1999 Top 10 single with *If Ya Gettin' Down*?

12. Which U.S. group recorded the album *When Your Heartstrings Break*?

13. Which New York-born performer wrote a 1992 album for Vanessa Paradis?

14. Which group's Top 20 hits in the 1990s included *Hot Love Now* and *Caught in my Shadow*?

15. Which country artist had a 1999 hit album with *Still Can't Say Goodbye*?

ANSWERS 1. Ini Kamoze **2.** Benny and the Jets **3.** Aztec Camera **4.** Bell **5.** Glamma Kid **6.** 1961 **7.** Lost in the Stars **8.** Jet **9.** 60Ft Dolls **10.** Handsome Boy Modelling School **11.** Five **12.** Beulah **13.** Lenny Kravitz **14.** Wonder Stuff **15.** Charlie Landsborough.

GEOGRAPHY

1. In which U.S. state is the Brooks Range of mountains?

2. In which European country is the city of Pinsk?

3. On which sea is the Russian resort of Sochi?

4. The Pripet River rises in the Ukraine before flowing east into which river?

5. What was the former name of the Bight of Bonny off the African coast?

6. The cathedral city of Viseu is in which European country?

7. On which river does Quebec stand?

8. In which European country is the town of Bastogne?

9. The island of Tenedos is in which European sea?

10. In which county of the Republic of Ireland is the mountain Croagh Patrick?

11. What is the name of the fortified town at the entrance to Kingston harbour in Jamaica?

12. In which African country is the port of Mostaganem?

13. Which city in Morocco was the capital of Spanish Morocco from 1912-56?

14. In which Asian country is the river Chao Phraya?

15. Mount Fairweather is on the border between British Columbia and which U.S. state?

ANSWERS 1. Alaska **2.** Belarus **3.** Black Sea **4.** Dnieper **5.** Bight of Biafra **6.** Portugal **7.** St. Lawrence **8.** Belgium **9.** Aegean **10.** Mayo **11.** Port Royal **12.** Algeria **13.** Tetuan **14.** Thailand **15.** Alaska.

GENERAL KNOWLEDGE

1. Which industrial town in Lancashire is at the junction of the Manchester Ship Canal and Bridgewater Canal?

2. Who wrote the 1856 volume *The Piazza Tales*?

3. Who wrote the 1953 play *Witness for the Prosecution*?

4. Which U.S. swimmer won seven gold medals at the 1972 Olympic Games?

5. What was the capital of West Germany from 1949-90?

6. On which gulf in Italy is the small resort town and ferry port of Amalfi?

7. Who was a Best Actress Oscar nominee for the 1953 film *Lili*?

8. On which river is the Cumbrian town of Kendal in the Lake District?

9. Who was 1997 British Open golf champion?

10. Who wrote the 1863 novel *Five Weeks in a Balloon*?

11. Who wrote the 1922 novel *Futility*?

12. Which river in Germany flows to the Rhine at Mannheim?

13. Which English scientist was awarded the 1922 Nobel prize for chemistry?

14. Which 1995 sci-fi film featured Natasha Henstridge as creature Sil?

15. Which poet's works included *The Floure of Curtesy*?

ANSWERS 1. Eccles **2.** Herman Melville **3.** Agatha Christie **4.** Mark Spitz **5.** Bonn **6.** Gulf of Sorrento **7.** Leslie Caron **8.** River Kent **9.** Justin Leonard **10.** Jules Verne **11.** William Gerhardie **12.** Neckar **13.** Francis Aston **14.** Species **15.** John Lydgate.

ENTERTAINMENT

1. Which actress voices Jane in the 1999 cartoon film *Tarzan*?

2. Who played Terry Raymond in *EastEnders*?

3. In which Verdi opera does the character Abigaille appear?

4. What nationality is soprano Aïno Ackte?

5. Which French actor starred in the 1958 film *Dangerous Exile*?

6. In which opera by Stravinsky does Baba the Turk appear?

7. Which Australian entertainer presents *Animal Hospital* on TV?

8. Who composed the 1924 opera *The Seal-Woman*?

9. Which married couple starred in the 1962 film *If a Man Answers*?

10. Who composed the 1967 opera *The Bear*?

11. Who directed the 1995 film *Heat*?

12. Which comedy actress played the female lead in the 1990s sitcom *Conjugal Rites*?

13. Who composed the 1864 operetta *La Belle Hélène*?

14. Who played advertising man Bob Slay in the sitcom *Perfect World*?

15. Which comedy writer created the 1989 sitcom *Close to Home* starring Paul Nicholas?

ANSWERS 1. Minnie Driver **2.** Gavin Richards **3.** Nabucco **4.** Finnish **5.** Louis Jordan **6.** The Rake's Progress **7.** Rolf Harris **8.** Sir Granville Bantock **9.** Bobby Darin and Sandra Dee **10.** William Walton **11.** Michael Mann **12.** Gwen Taylor **13.** Offenbach **14.** Paul Kaye **15.** Brian Cooke.

SPORT

1. Who won the Formula 1 Canadian Grand Prix in 1997 & 1998?

2. Which woman's tennis player won the Pan Pacific Open title in Tokyo in February 2000?

3. How many times have Salford won the rugby league Challenge Cup?

4. Who did the U.S. play in the quarter-finals of the 2000 Davis Cup?

5. Which country were men's tenpin bowling doubles world champions in 1926 & 1954?

6. In tennis, which duo won the 2000 Australian Open women's doubles title?

7. Which jockey rode the 1928 & 1929 Cheltenham Gold Cup winners?

8. In which year was boxer Mike Tyson born?

9. Who was 1984 Olympic women's 800m champion?

10. Which country won the 1938 Davis Cup in tennis?

11. Which team beat South Korea 5-0 in Group E of the 1998 football World Cup?

12. What nationality is tennis player Stefan Koubek?

13. Who was 1998 women's 400m individual medley swimming world champion?

14. In which year did Colin Montgomerie first win the Harry Vardon Trophy in golf?

15. Who replaced Brian Lara as West Indies cricket captain in March 2000?

ANSWERS 1. Michael Schumacher **2.** Martina Hingis **3.** One **4.** Czech Republic **5.** Finland **6.** Lisa Raymond & Rennae Stubbs **7.** Dick Rees **8.** 1966 **9.** Doina Melinte **10.** U.S.A. **11.** Holland **12.** Austrian **13.** Chen Yan **14.** 1993 **15.** Jimmy Adams.

POP

1. Which group's debut album was 1990s *Spanking Machine*?

2. What was the first Stevie Wonder song to reach No. 1 in both the U.S. and UK singles charts?

3. Which Birmingham group recorded the album *Seven and the Ragged Tiger*?

4. Which duo recorded the 1993 Top 30 hit *I'm Back For More*?

5. Who recorded the No. 1 album *All the Way...A Decade of Song*?

6. In which country did Bachman-Turner Overdrive form?

7. In which year did the Commodores have a Top 10 single with *Sail On*?

8. Which German group recorded the album *Out of Reach*?

9. In which year did Australian group The Saints split up?

10. Who was the original bass player in the group *Bad Company*?

11. Which group recorded the 1968 U.S. hit *Journey to the Centre of the Mind*?

12. Which act had a 1999 Top 10 single with *Stop the Rock*?

13. Who recorded 2000 Top 10 single *Shalala, Lala*?

14. Which legendary producer recorded the albums *Holiday* and *Hearts* for group America?

15. Which David Bowie song features the lyric "Ain't there one damn song that can make me break down and cry".

HISTORY

1. In which year did Hugh Capet become king of France?
2. In which year was the title Duke of York created for Edmund of Langley?
3. In which year did Helmut Kohl join the Christian Democratic Union?
4. What was the name given to the second of the four North American Wars fought between the British and French between 1689-1763?
5. Which politician was Lord Privy Seal from 1955-59?
6. The Battle of Kulikovo in 1380 was fought on the banks of which Russian river?
7. Who was prime minister during the Battle of Trafalgar in 1805?
8. In which year was the Battle of Brices Cross Roads in the American Civil War?
9. The War of the Polish Succession was terminated by which treaty?
10. Who succeeded Umberto I as king of Italy in 1900?
11. Who assassinated Francis Ferdinand of Austria in 1914?
12. What did prime minister Clement Attlee teach at the L.S.E. from 1913-22?
13. In which country did Hastings Banda practice as a doctor from 1942-53?
14. Which country lost the Battle of Marengo?
15. In which month of 1170 was Thomas à Becket murdered?

ANSWERS **1.** 987 **2.** 1385 **3.** 1947 **4.** Queen Anne's War **5.** R.A.B. Butler **6.** Don **7.** William Pitt the Younger **8.** 1864 **9.** Treaty of Vienna **10.** Victor Emmanuel III **11.** Gavrilo Princip **12.** Social science **13.** England **14.** Austria **15.** December.

GENERAL KNOWLEDGE

1. Who was the female author of the 1975 novel *A Word Child*?

2. What is the capital of Newfoundland?

3. What is the name of the glacier in Switzerland which is the largest in Europe?

4. Who was president of the Central African Republic from 1972-6?

5. In which magical land was the novel *The Lion, the Witch and the Wardrobe* set?

6. Which Australian poet's works include 1896's *While the Billy Boils*?

7. What is the seventh letter in the Greek alphabet?

8. What was the real name of the U.S. outlaw nicknamed Billy the Kid?

9. Who was 1968 and 1972 Olympic women's 200m silver medallist?

10. Which youth in classical mythology was abducted by Zeus and made cupbearer of the gods?

11. What type of creature is an entellus?

12. In which year did English actor and theatre manager Herbert Beerbohm Tree die?

13. Which England Test cricketer took 6 for 77 against West Indies at Port-of-Spain in 1989-90?

14. On which sea is the Turkish port of Trabzon?

15. On whose novel is the 1956 film *A Kiss Before Dying* which starred Robert Wagner based?

ANSWERS 1. Iris Murdoch 2. St. John's 3. Aletsch 4. Jean Bokassa 5. Narnia 6. Henry Lawson 7. Eta 8. William H. Bonney 9. Raelene Boyle 10. Ganymede 11. An Asian monkey 12. 1917 13. Devon Malcolm 14. Black Sea 15. Ira Levin.

ENTERTAINMENT

1. Who directed the 1999 film *Angela's Ashes*

2. In which country is the 1997 film *Dangerous Ground* set?

3. Who played Mandy in the 1999 TV drama series *Real Women*?

4. Who directed the 1999 film *Ravenous*?

5. The 1999 film *Man on the Moon* is about which comedian?

6. Who directed the 1988 film comedy *Illegally Yours*?

7. What was the name of the vicar in the sitcom *Dad's Army*?

8. Who played Karen Ericksson in the 1964 film *Guns at Batasi*?

9. Who directed the film *Fight Club*?

10. Who played the lead in the 1977 biopic *MacArthur*?

11. Who picked up Best Lead Actress in a Drama Emmy in 1999?

12. Who directed the 1948 French film *The Eagle with Two Heads*?

13. Who is the actress wife of producer David E. Kelley?

14. What colour is TV dinosaur *Barney*?

15. Who is creator of the cartoon series *The Simpsons* and *Futurama*?

ANSWERS 1. Alan Parker 2. South Africa 3. Pauline Quirke 4. Antonia Bird 5. Andy Kaufman 6. Peter Bogdanovich 7. Timothy Farthing 8. Mia Farrow 9. David Fincher 10. Gregory Peck 11. Edie Falco 12. Jean Cocteau 13. Michelle Pfeiffer 14. Purple 15. Matt Groening.

SPORT

1. Who was 1955 individual world speedway champion?

2. Which New Zealander was coach of the Ireland rugby union side in the 2000 Six Nations?

3. Against which county side did Clive Lloyd of West Indies score 200 in 120 minutes in August 1976?

4. In which year was athlete Christine Arron born?

5. With which sport are Pete Maravich and Austin Carr associated?

6. In which year was cricketer J .M. M. Averis born?

7. Which English jockey won the 1985 Prix de Diane Hermès?

8. Who was named male athlete of 1999 by the I.A.A.F.?

9. Who coached Oxford to ten wins in the University Boat Race from 1976-85?

10. What nationality is cyclist Bobby Julich?

11. What, in motorcycling, replaced the F.I.M. Coupe d'Endurance in 1980?

12. Marina Doria was women's overall water-skiing world champion in 1957. What nationality was she?

13. Who scored Manchester United's consolation goal in their 1994 League Cup Final defeat?

14. At which sport do Tom Bertram and Danny Hall represent Great Britain?

15. How long did Nadezha Ryashkina take to walk 10,000 metres on 24th July 1990?

POP

1. In which year did guitarist Albert Collins die?

2. The Seventh Earl of Cricklewood was leader of which 1960s group?

3. Which group released the 1968 album *This Was*?

4. What is Public Enemy's Terminator X really called?

5. On which studio album by The Pixies did the song *Hang Wire* feature?

6. Which duo recorded the 1999 album *Nightlife*?

7. Which Beatles song, sung by Elliott Smith, features in the film *American Beauty*?

8. Which group's albums include *Recovering the Satellites*?

9. Which Scottish group's debut single was *You've Got the Power*?

10. Which member of The New York Dolls wrote the song *Lonely Planet Boy*?

11. In which year was singer Tiny Tim born?

12. Which duo recorded the 1999 album *Emoticons*?

13. Which group recorded the 1989 album *United Kingdom*?

14. Andy and Steve Flett are members of which group?

15. Who is the female singer in the group Black Box Recorder?

WORDS

1. What is a hanepoot?

2. What would you do with a rondavel?

3. What in Judaism is a luach?

4. Balata is a material similar to what?

5. A lepton is a monetary unit in which country?

6. What is a calamondin?

7. What would you do with an equali – drive it or play it?

8. A farrow is a litter of what animal?

9. What is a hin?

10. What would you do with a kueh in Malaysia?

11. What in India is a machan?

12. What type of creature is a siaming?

13. How many lines are in a poem called a sixain?

14. In which country would you spend a grosz?

15. Psammite is another word for what type of rock?

THE CARLING PUB QUIZ BOOK

GENERAL KNOWLEDGE

1. What is the name of the large island of the Outer Hebrides in Scotland which lies between North Uist and South Uist?

2. Which ship designed by Isambard Kingdom Brunel laid the Transatlantic telegraph cable in 1865?

3. What is a parang?

4. Which actor's TV roles included Trapper John in *M*A*S*H*?

5. In Arthurian legend who was the foster brother and steward of King Arthur?

6. Which Formula 1 motor racing driver won the 1980 Monaco Grand Prix?

7. Who wrote the 1946 novel *Private Angelo*?

8. Which England Test cricketer scored 364 against Australia at the Oval in 1938?

9. Who wrote the 1887 story *A Study in Scarlet*?

10. Who wrote the 1956 novel *Malone Dies*?

11. Who was 1956 Australian men's singles tennis champion?

12. What is the name of the imprisoned sea-captain in the novel *The Count of Monte Cristo*?

13. Which king of the Huns invaded Gaul in 451 A.D.?

14. Which 1950 film starring Tyrone Power and Orson Welles was based on a novel by Thomas B. Costain?

15. Who was a Best Actor Oscar nominee for the 1970 film *The Great White Hope*?

ANSWERS 1. Benbecula **2.** Great Eastern **3.** A short straight-edged knife **4.** Wayne Rogers **5.** Kay **6.** Carlos Reutemann **7.** Eric Linklater **8.** Len Hutton **9.** Arthur Conan Doyle **10.** Samuel Beckett **11.** Lew Hoad **12.** Edmond Dantes **13.** Attila **14.** The Black Rose **15.** James Earl Jones.

ENTERTAINMENT

1. Where is the 1979 film *Saint Jack* set?

2. Who played Max Gallagher in *Casualty*?

3. Who played Jewel Valentine in the 1999 film *One Night at McCool's*?

4. Who directed the 1967 comedy drama film *I'll Never Forget What's 'is Name*?

5. Who was the female presenter of the ITV sport show *On the Ball*?

6. Who played Lord Cumnor in the 1999 TV adaptation of the novel *Wives and Daughters*?

7. What is Haley Joel Osment's character name in the film *The Sixth Sense*?

8. Who starred in the 1997 film *The Saint*?

9. What is Bruce Willis's job in the 1997 film *The Fifth Element*?

10. What is Caroline Quentin's character name in the drama *Jonathan Creek*?

11. Who played Adam in the TV drama series *Cold Feet*?

12. Who directed the 1984 film *City Heat*?

13. In which year was film director Spike Jonze born?

14. Who played Pippa in the sitcom *One Foot in the Grave*?

15. Who played Napoleon in the 1971 film *Eagle in a Cage*?

ANSWERS 1. Singapore **2.** Robert Gwilym **3.** Liv Tyler **4.** Michael Winner **5.** Gabby Yorath **6.** Ian Carmichael **7.** Cole Sear **8.** Val Kilmer **9.** Cab driver **10.** Maddy Magellan **11.** James Nesbitt **12.** Richard Benjamin **13.** 1969 **14.** Janine Duvitski **15.** Kenneth Haigh.

SPORT

1. In which year was athlete Evelyn Ashford born?

2. Which Frenchman won the 1923 Tour de France?

3. In which year did U.S. tennis player Helen Jacobs die?

4. Fairy Footsteps won the 1981 1000 Guineas. Who was the rider?

5. In which year was athlete Irina Privalova born?

6. How much in dollars did the winner of the 1997 Indianapolis 500 race win?

7. Who replaced Intikhab Alam as Pakistan cricket coach for their Third Test against Sri Lanka in March 2000?

8. Which Frenchman won the single-handed transatlantic yacht race in 1976?

9. Who was the New Zealander coach of Italy's 2000 Six Nations rugby union side?

10. Who was 1972 Olympic welterweight boxing champion?

11. Chris McSorley is coach of which ice hockey team?

12. What was set up as a rival to the NHL in ice hockey from 1972/3-1978/9?

13. Who was replaced by Roger Harper as West Indies cricket coach in February 2000?

14. How many yards gained rushing did Walter Payton achieve in his American Football career from 1975-87?

15. Who partnered Frew McMillan to victory in the 1978 U.S. Open mixed doubles tennis championship?

POP

1. In which year did the group Royal Trux form?
2. Whose debut album is *On How Life Is*?
3. In which year was William 'Bootsy' Collins born?
4. In which year was singer Bobby Gillespie born?
5. Which female singer recorded the 2000 debut album *Kaleidoscope*?
6. On which label did Mary J. Blige record her album *Mary*?
7. In which year did Alan McGee set up Creation Records with a £1,000 bank loan?
8. How did singer Nico die?
9. Which former Thin Lizzy guitarist features on the album *Get Some Go Again* by The Rollins Band?
10. Which group's albums include 1994's *Mars Audiac Quintett*?
11. Which band recorded the 1981 album *I Love Rock 'n' Roll*?
12. Which group recorded the 1999 album *Bon Chic Bon Genre*?
13. Which German group recorded the 1971 album *Dance of the Lemmings*?
14. Who produced Steeleye Span's album *Now We Are Six*?
15. In which year did Edwyn Collins release the album *Gorgeous George*?

SCIENCE

1. In which year did American biochemist Richard W. Holley share the Nobel prize for medicine?

2. Which English scientist was 1st Baron Kelvin?

3. In which year was carbon dating invented?

4. In which century did Japanese scientist Hiraga Gennai live?

5. Which American scientist won the 1968 Nobel prize for physics?

6. What nationality is geologist Elizabeth Truswell?

7. Who invented the maser in 1953?

8. What is the approximate diameter in miles of Saturn's moon Phoebe?

9. Who invented the microwave oven in 1947?

10. In which city was Stephen Hawking born?

11. How many minutes are in a degree in trigonometry?

12. Who invented D.D.T. in 1939?

13. What is the largest moon of Uranus?

14. In which year was cellophane invented?

15. Approximately how many days did the satellite Himalia take to orbit Jupiter?

GENERAL KNOWLEDGE

1. Who was author of the 1973 novel *Saint Jack*?

2. Who was a Best Supporting Actor Oscar nominee for the 1983 film *Cross Creek*?

3. Who was author of the 1973 novel *The Riverside Villas Murder*?

4. What is the capital of Iceland?

5. Spurn Head is a sand spit at the mouth of which estuary in N. England?

6. Which 1965 film by Vincente Minnelli features the song *The Shadow of Your Smile*?

7. What is the name given to the black ball in the game of American pool?

8. Which port in Corsica is the main industrial town of the island?

9. Which artist did the paintings for the 1958 film *The Horse's Mouth*?

10. Who was Best Actress Oscar nominee for the film *Sunset Boulevard*?

11. Who was author of the 1990 novel *Circle of Friends*?

12. Who was Foreign Secretary in the 1935 Stanley Baldwin-led government?

13. Who was author of the 1977 novel *A Morbid Taste for Bones*?

14. What is the capital of Colombia?

15. What is the name given to the scale of temperature in which the boiling point of water is taken as 80°?

ENTERTAINMENT

1. Who played Jules Winnfield in the film *Pulp Fiction*?

2. Who directed the 1999 film *The Haunting*?

3. *I'll See You In My Dreams* is a 1951 film biopic of which songwriter?

4. What is Truman's surname in the film *The Truman Show*?

5. Who directed the 1986 film *Sweet Liberty*?

6. Who directed the 1939 film *Each Dawn I Die*?

7. The film *Payback* starring Mel Gibson is a remake of which earlier 1960s film?

8. Who played Rudyard Kipling in the 1975 film *The Man Who Would Be King*?

9. Which TV show won Best Comedy Series at the 1999 Emmy awards?

10. Which French actress starred in the 1967 film *The Sailor from Gibraltar*?

11. In the 1948 film *Abbott and Costello Meet Frankenstein*, who played Dracula?

12. What is Fred MacMurray's profession in the 1941 film *New York Town*?

13. Which member of *The Fast Show* played a pawnbroker in the 1999 BBC TV dramatisation of *David Copperfield*?

14. Which actor played Jeremy Parsons Q.C. in ITV's *Crown Court*?

15. The 1940 film *Abe Lincoln in Illinois* is based on whose Pulitzer Prize-winning play?

SPORT

1. In which year was the women's World Cup in darts introduced?

2. At what racecourse was the Marstons Midlands Grand National run in March 2000?

3. Which American man broke the 50m freestyle swimming record in 1990 with a time of 21.81 seconds?

4. In which year did 1FC Kaiserslautern first win the German League?

5. Who was on the horse Gloria Victis which fell and was killed at Cheltenham in March 2000?

6. Who was named manager of Hull City in April 2000?

7. Which former St. Helens player is coach of Hull rugby league club?

8. With what sport would you associate Anke Nothnagel & Heike Singer?

9. What nationality is motor racing driver Gaston Mazzacane?

10. Australian Rules Football team Essendon won the 1981 National Football League. Which state are they from?

11. For which rugby union club side did Junior Ton'u play?

12. Which horse won the 1954 Oaks?

13. Who is player-coach with Saracens rugby union team?

14. How many golds have Slovakia won the summer Olympics up to and including 1996?

15. Which Scot won the 1998 Qatar Masters golf tournament?

ANSWERS 1. 1983 **2.** Uttoxeter **3.** Tom Jager **4.** 1951 **5.** Tony McCoy **6.** Brian Little **7.** Shaun McRae **8.** Canoe racing **9.** Argentinian **10.** Victoria **11.** London Irish **12.** Sun Cap **13.** Francois Pienaar **14.** One **15.** Andrew Coltart.

POP

1. Rob Pollard is lead singer with which group?

2. Which country artist recorded the 1981 album *Big City*?

3. Who was lead singer with the group Hatfield and the North?

4. Which husband and wife songwriting team penned *Bye Bye Love*?

5. Which country artist recorded the 1978 covers album *Stardust*?

6. Which duo had a 1985 hit single with *Solid*?

7. What is the title of the 2000 studio album by Violent Femmes?

8. Which studio album by Everything But The Girl includes *Oxford Street* and *Apron Strings*?

9. Who is frontman in the group The Eels?

10. Which Bee Gees song was covered by Richie Havens on the 1970 album *Stonehenge*?

11. Which member of the Swell Maps died in 1997?

12. In which year did Alphaville have a Top 10 single with *Big in Japan*?

13. Who was the original female singer in the band Fairport Convention?

14. Which guitarist recorded the 1980 live album *Stage Struck*?

15. Which guitarist led the group Grin from 1970-3?

ANSWERS 1. Guided By Voices **2.** Merle Haggard **3.** Richard Sinclair **4.** Felice and Boudleaux Bryant **5.** Willie Nelson **6.** Ashford and Simpson **7.** Freak Magnet **8.** Idlewild **9.** E **10.** I Started A Joke **11.** Epic Soundtracks **12.** 1984 **13.** Judy Dyble **14.** Rory Gallagher **15.** Nils Lofgren.

PEOPLE

1. Who resigned in April 1998 as Chief Constable of Grampian, Scotland?

2. Who is the father of singer Madonna's child Lourdes?

3. What is the name of Scary Spice's child by husband Jimmy Gulzar?

4. What did singer Puff Daddy try to smuggle into Britain in November 1999?

5. Who won International Designer at the 1999 Elle Style Awards?

6. *T'rific* is which actor's autobiography?

7. Which entertainer was born in North, South Carolina in the late 1920s?

8. Which rugby union player is nicknamed Campo?

9. In which century did El Cid live?

10. Which U.S. financier, born in 1864, drowned in the Titanic disaster?

11. In which year did actor Robert Donat die?

12. In which year was mountaineer Chris Bonington born?

13. Which Yorkshire-born poet became poet laureate in 1718?

14. In which year was Pakistan politician Benazir Bhutto born?

15. In which century did Ivan the Terrible live?

ANSWERS 1. Ian Oliver. **2.** Carlos Leon. **3.** Phoenix Chi. **4.** A bottle of tomato ketchup. **5.** Stella McCartney. **6.** Mike Reid. **7.** Eartha Kitt. **8.** David Campese. **9.** 11th Century. **10.** John Jacob Astor. **11.** 1958. **12.** 1934. **13.** Laurence Esden. **14.** 1953. **15.** 16th Century.

GENERAL KNOWLEDGE

1. Who wrote the 1917 novel *The Job*?

2. Which Olympic race is run over a distance of 42.195 kilometres?

3. Who was the Best Supporting Actor Oscar nominee for the 1948 film *I Remember Mama*?

4. What is a koto?

5. Who was a Best Actress Oscar nominee for film *Lady Sings the Blues*?

6. Who was U.S. vice president from 1977-81?

7. Who was author of the play *The Duchess of Malfi*?

8. Who is author of the 1987 novel *Chatterton*?

9. In golf, what is the term used to describe a score of two strokes under par for a hole?

10. Who was author of the 1905 novel *Where Angels Fear to Tread*?

11. Which actress starred in 1998 film *The Avengers*?

12. What is the capital and chief port of Senegal?

13. In Greek mythology, who were the parents of Electra?

14. What type of creature is a leguaan?

15. Who was winner, with John Nielsen and Price Cobb, of the 1990 Le Mans 24-hour race?

ANSWERS: 1. Sinclair Lewis **2.** Marathon **3.** Oscar Homolka **4.** Japanese stringed musical instrument **5.** Diana Ross **6.** Walter Mondale **7.** John Webster **8.** Peter Ackroyd **9.** Eagle **10.** E. M. Forster **11.** Uma Thurman **12.** Dakar **13.** Agamemnon and Clytemnestra **14.** Large lizard **15.** Martin Brundle.

ENTERTAINMENT

1. What was the name of Bruce Willis's character name in TV's *Moonlighting*?

2. Which comic actor was the voice of computer SID in the children's TV show *Galloping Galaxies*?

3. Who played writer Christopher Marlowe in the 1978 TV drama *Will Shakespeare*?

4. Who is the father of Senta in Wagner's opera *The Flying Dutchman*?

5. Which comedian played Commissar Solzhenitsyn in the 1982 comedy series *Whoops! Apocalypse*?

6. Which actress and model starred in the 1974 film *W*?

7. Which star of the film *Cabaret* made his debut in the 1952 film *About Face*?

8. Who directed the 1950 film *Wagon Master*?

9. Who produced and starred in the 2000 film *Battlefield Earth*?

10. In which year did comedy show *Whose Line Is It Anyway* first appear on British TV?

11. What is singer Eminem's real name?

12. Who wrote the 1980s TV drama *Widows*?

13. Who played Malachy McCourt in the film *Angela's Ashes*?

14. Which incident in the Second World War is the subject of the 1952 film *Above and Beyond*?

15. What nationality was soprano Gilda Dalla Rizza?

ANSWERS: 1. David Addison **2.** Kenneth Williams **3.** Ian McShane **4.** Daland **5.** Alexei Sayle **6.** Twiggy **7.** Joel Grey **8.** John Ford **9.** John Travolta **10.** 1988 **11.** Marshall Bruce Mathers III **12.** Lynda La Plante **13.** Robert Carlyle **14.** Dropping of the atomic bomb on Hiroshima **15.** Italian.

SPORT

1. At what sport was Rimma Zhukova 1955 world champion?

2. Which Galatasaray player was sent off in the U.E.F.A. Cup Final in May 2000?

3. Which Italian team won the 1961 Fairs Cup in football?

4. In rugby union, who did London Welsh play in the quarter-finals of the Tetley's Bitter Cup in 2000?

5. Who was men's 1500m champion at the 1981 I.A.A.F. World Cup?

6. Who won the men's 100m title at the 1999 World Athletics Championships?

7. How many runs did Devon score vs. Somerset in their NatWest Bank Trophy game in June 1990?

8. In which sport were Shen Jianping & Dai Lili world champions in 1893?

9. In which year was the Solheim Cup in women's golf first played for?

10. How many golds did the Czech Republic win in the 1999 World Athletics Championships?

11. Which Briton won the 1986 Belgian Grand Prix in Formula 1?

12. Which boxer was 1959 Sports Illustrated Sportsman of the Year?

13. Which rugby league club won the championship play-offs in 1908 and 1938?

14. What was the nickname of baseball pitcher Jim Hunter, who died in 1999?

15. Michael Walter was men's single-seater world champion in 1985. At what winter sport?

POP

1. Which song by Tom Waits is covered on the album *Black Music for White People* by Screamin' Jay Hawkins?

2. On which label did Tracy Chapman record the album *Telling Stories*?

3. Which song by the Commodores did Faith No More record as a single in 1993?

4. In which year did Cher have a Top 10 single with *If I Could Turn Back Time*?

5. Which song by the Lovin' Spoonful did Isaac Hayes cover on the 1995 LP *Branded*?

6. In which year was the Blue Nile's LP *Hats* released?

7. Who wrote and performed the song *Things Have Changed* for the film *Wonder Boys*?

8. In which year was Marianne Faithfull born?

9. Which member of the Incredible String Band later became mayoress of Aberystwyth?

10. What was Richard Ashcroft's first solo single after disbanding Verve?

11. Hawkwind named themselves after a story by which author?

12. In which year did Miami Sound Machine have a Top 10 single with *Dr. Beat*?

13. Which singer appeared in the guise of Lieutenant Lush as a backing singer for Bow Wow Wow?

14. Which sisters were vocalists in the group Heart?

15. Which singer recorded the LP *Cowboy Sally's Twilight Laments for Lost Buckaroos*?

THE CARLING PUB QUIZ BOOK

ART

1. Harry and Sally Hardcastle are central characters in which 1933 novel by Walter Greenwood?

2. Who authored the children's book *Eric, or Little by Little*?

3. In which year was Aldous Huxley's *Eyeless in Gaza* first published?

4. In which city was painter Sir Anthony Van Dyck born?

5. Who is the central character in George Orwell's *Keep the Aspidistra Flying*?

6. Who authored the ghost story *An Account of Some Strange Disturbances in Aungier Street*?

7. Who authored the novel *Birdsong* set during World War One?

8. Whose mural for the cafeteria of the Amsterdam city hall was whitewashed over by the city council?

9. Who authored the novel *An Equal Music*?

10. Which Cornish artist's works include a 1782 portrait of Samuel Johnson?

11. Who authored the 2000 novel *White Teeth*?

12. Which English painter's war works include 1917's *Vimy Ridge*?

13. Who authored the 2000 novel *Bad Heir Day*?

14. Which artist created the murals *Wall of the Moon* and *Wall of the Sun* for the UNESCO building in Paris?

15. Which artist was commissioned to paint a portrait of Oliver Cromwell in 1654?

ANSWERS: 1. Love on the Dole **2.** F.W. Farrell **3.** 1936 **4.** Antwerp **5.** Gordon Comstock **6.** J.S. le Fanu **7.** Sebastian Faulks **8.** Karel Appel **9.** Vikram Seth **10.** John Opie **11.** Zadie Smith **12.** Paul Nash **13.** Wendy Holden **14.** Joan Miro **15.** Sir Peter Lely.

GENERAL KNOWLEDGE

1. What was the name of the town in Galilee, north of Nazareth, where Jesus performed his first miracle?

2. Which spice is made from the dried aril round a nutmeg seed?

3. Which British conductor and violinist founded the Academy of St. Martin-in-the-Fields?

4. The 1995 film *Losing Isaiah*, starring Jessica Lange, is based on whose novel?

5. Who wrote the 1929 play *The Apple Cart*?

6. Who was director of the film *Catch-22*?

7. Who was archbishop of Canterbury from 1583-1604?

8. Who was author of the poetry volume *Remembrance of Crimes Past*?

9. What is the name of the large mammal also called a glutton?

10. Who was the 1939 Wimbledon men's singles tennis champion?

11. Which signal flag is displayed by a vessel about to leave port?

12. Which German river flows to the North Sea at Bremerhaven?

13. In which year did American astronomer Carl Sagan die?

14. Who was the 1977 Wimbledon women's singles tennis championship runner-up?

15. Who choreographed the 1951 ballet *Pineapple Poll*?

ANSWERS: 1. Cana **2.** Mace **3.** Neville Marriner **4.** Seth Margolis **5.** George Bernard Shaw **6.** Mike Nichols **7.** John Whitgift **8.** Dannie Abse **9.** Wolverine **10.** Bobby Riggs **11.** Blue Peter **12.** Weser **13.** 1996 **14.** Betty Stove **15.** John Cranko.

ENTERTAINMENT

1. Which comedy actress played Ray Langton's sister Janice in *Coronation Street*?

2. Who directed the 1999 film *The Bone Collector*?

3. Who directed the 1953 film *Niagara*?

4. Which comedy actress played Beatrice in Carla Lane's comedy *Screaming*?

5. Which three directors worked on segments of the 1989 film *New York Stories*?

6. Who played Mike Barratt in the TV drama *Holby City*?

7. What is the profession of Eric Roberts in the 1990 film *The Ambulance*?

8. Who directed and starred in the 1997 film *The Tango Lesson*?

9. Who directed the 1999 film *8mm*?

10. How much was Chris Tucker paid in dollars for the film *Rush Hour*?

11. Who wrote the sitcom *dinnerladies*?

12. In the 1981 film *Americana*, what does David Carradine attempt to rebuild in a rural Kansas town?

13. What is the name of Antony's girlfriend in the TV comedy *The Royle Family*?

14. Which *Monty Python* member played Toad in the 1996 film *The Wind in the Willows*?

15. Who starred as a highway cop in the 1973 film *Electra Glide in Blue*?

ANSWERS: 1. Paula Wilcox 2. Phillip Noyce 3. Henry Hathaway 4. Penelope Wilton 5. Woody Allen, Martin Scorsese and Francis Coppola 6. Clive Mantle 7. Comic-book artist 8. Sally Potter 9. Joel Schumacher 10. $3million 11. Victoria Wood 12. A merry-go-round 13. Emma 14. Terry Jones 15. Robert Blake.

SPORT

1. From which club did ice hockey team Ayr Scottish Eagles sign German Thorsten Apel?

2. Which horse won the 1978 Grand National?

3. In cricket, who scored 125 for Gloucestershire vs. Kent in the 1st innings of their 1999 county championship game?

4. Which team won the 1968 Olympic women's 4 x 100m relay?

5. Who partnered Martina Navratilova to victory in the 1980 Australian Open women's doubles tennis championships?

6. Which rider won the 1993 King George V Gold Cup at the Royal International Horse Show?

7. In basketball, which team ended a 19-game undefeated run by the Los Angeles Lakers in March 2000?

8. Who was 1972 Olympic men's 100m backstroke swimming champion?

9. Which team have won the All-Ireland Championships in Gaelic football most times?

10. For which Welsh rugby union club side does Shane Howarth play?

11. What nationality is skier Carole Merle?

12. Who won the 2000 Australian Formula 1 Grand Prix?

13. Jane Hall was K1 winner at the 1988 Canoe Marathon World Championships. What nationality is she?

14. Who did Featherstone beat in the 2000 Silk Cut Challenge Cup 3rd round in rugby league?

15. Which English pair won the mixed doubles title at the 1968 All-England Championships in badminton?

ANSWERS: 1. Frankfurt Lions **2.** Lucius **3.** Kim Barnett **4.** U.S.A. **5.** Betsy Nagelsen **6.** Nick Skelton **7.** Washington Wizards **8.** Roland Matthes **9.** Kerry **10.** Newport **11.** French **12.** Michael Schumacher **13.** Australian **14.** Wigan St. Patricks **15.** Tony Jordan and Sue Pound.

POP

1. Who is the leader of the group Psychic TV?

2. John Prine's song *In Spite of Ourselves* was written for which movie?

3. Who recorded the 1997 LP *Roll Away the Stone*?

4. What is the title of Lou Reed's 2000 studio album?

5. Phelim Byrne and Donnie Hardwidge comprise which duo?

6. Which member of the Who helped produce the 1968 album *The Crazy World of Arthur Brown*?

7. Who recorded the 1973 album *Back to the World*?

8. Who had a 2000 Top 10 single with *Don't Be Stupid (You Know I Love You)*?

9. Which group had a 1989 Top 10 single with *Sowing the Seeds of Love*?

10. Which mod group's singles included *Shadows and Reflections*?

11. Who, in 1968, released the song *Say It Loud, I'm Black and I'm Proud*?

12. Which indie group's albums included *Truckload of Troubles*?

13. Which solo artist recorded the 1999 album *Rainbow*?

14. In which year was singer Tim Hardin born?

15. Who played harmonica in the original line up of Eddie and the Hot Rods?

GEOGRAPHY

1. Petrified Forest is a national park in which U.S. state?

2. What is the administrative centre of Northumberland?

3. On which Hawaiian island is Pearl Harbor?

4. The Japanese port of Niigata is at the mouth of which river?

5. Tewkesbury is at the confluence of which two rivers?

6. On which lake is the Swiss canton of Unterwalden?

7. In which province is Canada's Lake Mistassini?

8. What was the capital of Selangor state, Malaysia, from 1880-1973?

9. In which European country is Melitopol?

10. Kolar Gold Fields is a city in which Asian country?

11. Macquarie Island lies in which ocean?

12. Lindesnes is a cape at the south tip of which European country?

13. Imphal is the capital of which state of India?

14. On which Scottish loch is Urquhart Castle?

15. On which island of the Philippines is the port of Legaspi?

ANSWERS: 1. Arizona 2. Morpeth 3. Oahu 4. Shinano 5. Severn and Avon 6. Lake Lucerne 7. Quebec 8. Kuala Lumpur 9. Ukraine 10. India 11. Pacific 12. Norway 13. Manipur 14. Loch Ness 15. Luzon.

GENERAL KNOWLEDGE

1. Who was the pope from 1623-44?

2. Which novel by Thomas Hardy features Elfride Swancourt?

3. Which island off the coast of Italy was Napoleon's place of exile from 1814-5?

4. In which year did German architect Johann Neumann die?

5. Who was the 41st president of the U.S.?

6. Who wrote the 1985 play *Biloxi Blues*?

7. Who was author of the story *The Prince and the Pauper*?

8. For which 1966 film was Michael Caine a Best Actor Oscar nominee?

9. Who was the first man to hold the world land and water speed records simultaneously?

10. The island group of the Azores are an autonomous region of which European country?

11. In which year was architect François Mansart born?

12. In which year was the Beethoven opera *Fidelio* first performed?

13. Who was author of the 1967 novel *A New Lease of Death*?

14. In which city is there a mosque known as the Dome of the Rock?

15. Which French heroine was born in Domrémy-la-Pucelle?

ANSWERS: 1. Urban VIII **2.** A Pair of Blue Eyes **3.** Elba **4.** 1753 **5.** George Bush **6.** Neil Simon **7.** Mark Twain **8.** Alfie **9.** Henry Segrave **10.** Portugal **11.** 1598 **12.** 1805 **13.** Ruth Rendell **14.** Jerusalem **15.** Joan of Arc.

ENTERTAINMENT

1. Who does Ray Park play in the film *The Phantom Menace*?

2. Which comedian played Elf in the Christmas 1999 TV drama *The Greatest Store in the World*?

3. Who played Teach in the 1996 film *American Buffalo*?

4. What high school does *Buffy the Vampire Slayer* attend?

5. Who played the lead in the 1996 film *Jane Eyre*?

6. Which comedian starred in the 1967 film *Eight on the Lam*?

7. In which year in the future is the 1984 film *The Terminator* set?

8. Which comedian played coach of a girl's soccer team in the 1992 film *Ladybugs*?

9. In which town was the comedy series *That Peter Kay Thing* set?

10. Who played *Lady Chatterley's Lover* in a 1981 film?

11. What is Ken Stott's character name in the TV series *The Vice*?

12. The 1977 film *The American Friend* is based on which novel by Patricia Highsmith?

13. Who played Bulldog in the sitcom *Frasier*?

14. Which actor starred in *Billy*, the U.S. equivalent of the British sitcom *Billy Liar*?

15. Who played Scrooge in the 1992 film *The Muppet Christmas Carol*?

ANSWERS: 1. Darth Maul **2.** Sean Hughes **3.** Dustin Hoffman **4.** Sunnydale High **5.** Charlotte Gainsbourg **6.** Bob Hope **7.** 2029 **8.** Rodney Dangerfield **9.** Bolton **10.** Nicholas Clay **11.** Pat Chappel **12.** Ripley's Game **13.** Dan Butler **14.** Steve Guttenberg **15.** Michael Caine.

SPORT

1. How many golds did Australia get in the 1999 World Athletic Championships?

2. Who rode the 1987 Ascot Gold Cup winner Paean?

3. Which rider, in August 1999, became the first woman to win the European Championship in show jumping?

4. Which country were 1936 Olympic polo champions?

5. What sport is played by the Houston Rockets and Vancouver Grizzlies?

6. Yasuhiro Yamashita was Olympic men's open judo champion. Which country did he represent?

7. Which team won the 1999 NatWest Trophy Final in cricket?

8. By what aggregate score did Bayern Munich win the 1996 U.E.F.A. Cup in football?

9. Who won the 1999 Belgian Grand Prix in Formula 1?

10. How many Commonwealth gold medals did England's Kathy Cook win from 1978-86?

11. What nationality is tennis player Andreas Vinciguerra's father?

12. In which year did Northamptonshire first take part in the cricket county championship?

13. Which athlete was 1968 BBC Sports Personality of the Year?

14. Which country did Lilia Podkopayeva represent in winning the 1996 Olympic combined exercises event in gymnastics?

15. In cricket, who scored 123 for Gloucestershire vs. Kent in the 1st innings of their 1999 county championship game?

ANSWERS: 1. One 2. Steve Cauthen 3. Alexendre Ledermann 4. Argentina 5. Basketball 6. Japan 7. Gloucestershire 8. 5-1 9. David Coulthard 10. Three 11. Italian 12. 1905 13. David Hemery 14. Ukraine 15. Ian Harvey.

POP

1. In which year did rockabilly artist Charlie Feathers die?

2. Bernard Butler walked out during the recording of which album by Suede?

3. The Fugs were based in which U.S. city?

4. Who had a 2000 No. 1 single with *Bag It Up*?

5. *Saturate Before Using* was the debut album of which singer-songwriter?

6. On which studio album by MC5 does the track *The Human Being Lawnmower* appear?

7. Who had a 1980 Top 10 single with *Games Without Frontiers*?

8. Which Irish singer had a 1996 hit single with *The Voice*?

9. Who recorded the 1979 album *Repeat When Necessary*?

10. Whose third Top 10 single, in 1964, was *Someone, Someone*?

11. In which year did Gene Pitney have a Top 10 single with *24 Hours From Tulsa*?

12. Who had a top 30 single in 1976 with *Let's Make A Baby*?

13. Under what name did Elvis Costello and T-Bone Burnett record the 1985 single *The People's Limousine*?

14. Who had a 1981 chart single with *Help, Get Me Some Help!*?

15. Whose third Top 10 single, in 1964, was *Somewhere*?

HISTORY

1. In which year did King Zog abdicate as Albanian ruler?

2. In which month of 1936 did the Jarrow march begin?

3. Which future king of Belgium did Princess Astrid of Sweden marry in 1926?

4. Which two leaders signed the Atlantic Charter in 1941?

5. In which month of 1948 was the republic of Israel proclaimed?

6. In which year did Italian revolutionary Giuseppe Mazzini die?

7. What was prelate St. Edmund of Abingdon also known as?

8. In which century did Byzantine general Belisarius live?

9. Who was French minister of state for Justice from 1956-7?

10. In which year was Benjamin Franklin elected to the Pennsylvania Assembly?

11. On January 1st of which year did the Czech Republic come into being?

12. Which treaty established the European Court of Justice?

13. Who was elected prime minister of Canada in 1867?

14. Who did Napoleon I marry in 1796?

15. In which year was the Battle of Chickamauga in the American Civil War?

GENERAL KNOWLEDGE

1. Why would a beach be pleased if it had a Golden Starfish?

2. Which actress took over from Brigitte Bardot in 1985 as model for Marianne, the symbol for the French Republic?

3. What is eBay?

4. Which ex-boxer co-presented the TV show *It's A Knockout* with Keith Chegwin in 1999?

5. With which political party is the landlord of the Golden Lion hotel in Ashburton, Devon associated?

6. Against which organization did Dave Morris and Helen Steel defend a libel action for three years in the 1990s?

7. What was 50 Elliscombe Road, Greenwich better known as on TV in 1999?

8. In which part of the body is the fovea centralis?

9. In which Scottish city is the public school of Fettes College?

10. In what month of 1999 was national Breakfast Week?

11. How many of the Ford Ka Black were released in 1999 as a limited edition?

12. Who played Chief Miles O'Brien in the TV show *Star Trek: Deep Space Nine*?

13. Which singer recorded the 1994 album *Grace*?

14. In which year did poet John Dryden die?

15. Which group recorded the 1991 album *Shift-work*?

ENTERTAINMENT

1. Who directed the 1984 film *The Element of Crime*?

2. What is the real name of dog Eddie in the sitcom *Frasier*?

3. Who played Hugo Horton in the sitcom *The Vicar of Dibley*?

4. The 1933 film *Lady for a Day* is an adaptation of which story by Damon Runyon?

5. Who played a housekeeper in the 1980s sitcom *That's My Boy*?

6. What priceless artefact is at the centre of the plot in the 1936 film *Satan Met a Lady*?

7. In which year did *That's Life* first appear on the BBC?

8. In which year was comedian Bill Cosby born?

9. In which year in the future is the 1979 film *Alien* set?

10. Which Oscar-winning Hollywood star played a jet squadron leader in the 1955 film *Tarantula*?

11. Who directed the 1987 film *Angel Heart*?

12. Who is actress wife of playwright David Mamet?

13. Who played Rowley Birkin Q.C. in *The Fast Show*?

14. Who composed the 1882 opera *The Duke of Alba*?

15. Which actor directed the 1983 film *Angelo, My Love*?

SPORT

1. Which Briton won the 1968 German Grand Prix in Formula 1?

2. In which year was the Northern Ireland Athletic Federation founded?

3. How many teams contested the 1987 rugby union World Cup?

4. In which year did German tennis player Cilly Aussem die?

5. In which year was the world outdoor championship in men's bowls instituted?

6. In cricket, who scored 138 n.o. for Somerset vs. Kent in the 1st innings of their 1999 county championship game?

7. Who trained the winner of the Champion Hurdle at Cheltenham from 1985-7?

8. In which year did U.S.A. and Great Britain first contest the Wightman Cup in tennis?

9. Chuhei Nambu won the 1932 Olympic triple jump. Which country did he represent?

10. At what sport have Son Tae-Whan and You Su-mi been world champions?

11. Anja Straub was 1989 épée winner at the fencing world championships. Which country did she represent?

12. In cricket, who scored 113 n.o. for Zimbabwe vs. West Indies in the 1st innings of their 1st Test in Port of Spain in 2000?

13. Who was 1998 men's 400m freestyle swimming world champion?

14. How many dollars did golfer Fred Couples win in taking the 1991 Johnny Walker world championship?

15. What nationality is rugby union referee Paul Honnis?

ANSWERS: 1. Jackie Stewart **2.** 1989 **3.** 16 **4.** 1963 **5.** 1966 **6.** Rob Turner **7.** Nicky Henderson **8.** 1923 **9.** Japan **10.** Taekwondo **11.** Switzerland **12.** Andy Flower **13.** Ian Thorpe **14.** $525,000 **15.** New Zealander.

POP

1. Apart from *24 Hours From Tulsa*, which other hit by Gene Pitney features the number 24?

2. Which studio album by Billy Idol features the songs *Mark of Cain* and *Cradle of Love*?

3. Who features on Scritti Politti's 1991 hit *She's A Woman*?

4. Which female singer's Top 10 hits include 1955's *Prize of Gold*?

5. Which group recorded the 1985 album *The Small Price of a Bicycle*?

6. Which solo singer's 1979 tour was called *The Tour of Life*?

7. Who had a 2000 Top 10 single with *All the Small Things*?

8. In which year did Townes Van Zandt die?

9. In which year was rapper Ice Cube born?

10. On which label was Elastica's debut single *Stutter* recorded?

11. Which guitarist did Eric Clapton replace in The Yardbirds?

12. Who produced the single *Original Sin* by INXS in 1984?

13. What Blur song was adopted by the U.S. National Hockey League as a theme song?

14. Which group recorded 1980's *Work Rest and Play* E.P.?

15. In which year was *Abba: The Album* released?

ANSWERS: 1. 24 Sycamore **2.** Charmed Life **3.** Shabba Ranks **4.** Joan Regan **5.** The Icicle Works **6.** Kate Bush **7.** Blink 182 **8.** 1997 **9.** 1969 **10.** Deceptive **11.** Anthony Topham **12.** Nile Rodgers **13.** Song 2 **14.** Madness **15.** 1978.

WORDS

1. Where would you have worn a heaume in the 12th century and 13th century?

2. A havildar is a noncommissioned officer in which army?

3. What in East Africa is a debe?

4. What is a cudgerie - a type of tree or type of food?

5. What in jewellery is a culet?

6. What in the Middle East is a souk?

7. What type of creature is a squilla?

8. What would you do in Scotland with a broch?

9. What type of creature is a brolga?

10. What is a lucarne?

11. What is gros point?

12. What is a rote - an ancient musical instrument or a Scandinavian poem?

13. What is monarda - a type of plant or a type of body armour?

14. Where on a ship would you find a lasket?

15. A zila is an administrative district in which country?

ANSWERS: 1. The head – it's a helmet **2.** Indian **3.** A tin **4.** A tree **5.** The flat face at the bottom of a gem **6.** An open-air market place **7.** Shrimp **8.** Live in it **9.** Bird **10.** A type of window **11.** A needlepoint stitch **12.** Musical instrument **13.** Plant **14.** The foot of a sail **15.** India.

GENERAL KNOWLEDGE

1. Who wrote the 1928 novel *Beau Ideal*?

2. Which medieval instrument of torture consisted of a hinged case lined with spikes?

3. Which boardgame is associated with Boris Spassky and José Capablanca?

4. Which U.S. blues singer was born Huddie Ledbetter?

5. Which two Radio 1 disc jockeys had a 1976 Top 10 single under the name of Laurie Lingo and the Dipsticks?

6. What is the name given to the dish of toast, covered with ham, eggs and hollandaise sauce?

7. Who wrote the 1855 novel *Israel Potter*?

8. What is the name of the TV dramatist whose works include 1972's *The Stone Tape*?

9. What is the name of the secret intelligence service of Israel?

10. Which ancient country of central Italy was situated between the Rivers Tiber and Arno?

11. Which Hungarian actor was born Laszlo Löwenstein in 1904?

12. Who was the 1996 Wimbledon men's singles tennis champion?

13. Who wrote the 1988 play *Speed-the-Plow*?

14. What is the capital of Russia?

15. With which driver did Henry Liddon win the 1964 Monte Carlo rally?

ANSWERS: 1. P.C. Wren **2.** Iron maiden **3.** Chess **4.** Leadbelly **5.** Paul Burnett and Dave Lee Travis **6.** Eggs Benedict **7.** Herman Melville **8.** Nigel Kneale **9.** Mossad **10.** Etruria **11.** Peter Lorre **12.** Richard Krajicek **13.** David Mamet **14.** Moscow **15.** Paddy Hopkirk.

ENTERTAINMENT

1. Which Lancastrian co-starred with Constance Bennett in the 1946 film *Paris Underground*?

2. Whose last opera as a composer was 1973's *Death in Venice*?

3. What did O.S.I. stand for in the TV show *The Six Million Dollar Man*?

4. Who wrote the 1964 musical play *Maggie May*?

5. Who played a poor naturalist in the 1995 film *Angels and Insects*?

6. Who played Nicola Marlow in the TV drama series *The Singing Detective*?

7. Who directed the 1998 film *Sliding Doors*?

8. Who is female presenter of the Radio 4 show *Desert Island Discs*?

9. Which actor played the lead in the 1944 film version of Eugene O'Neill's play *The Hairy Ape*?

10. Who played Phil in the Radio 4 soap *The Archers*?

11. Haley Joel Osment advertised which organization in his first acting job, aged five?

12. In which year was newsreader Peter Sissons born?

13. In which year did John Barton become associate director of the R.S.C.?

14. In which opera does the character Fenena appear?

15. Which actor played a British diplomat in the 1986 film *Half Moon Street*?

THE CARLING PUB QUIZ BOOK

SPORT

1. In which county of the Republic of Ireland is the Benson & Hedges Irish Masters snooker tournament held?

2. In cricket, who scored 216 n.o. for Sri Lanka vs. Zimbabwe in the 1st innings of their 1st Test in November 1999?

3. For which country did Desmond Haynes play Test cricket?

4. In which year was cricketer Paul Aldred born?

5. Which Spanish team have won the men's European Championship for Clubs in basketball the most times?

6. Which cricketer scored 118 for Pakistan vs. Australia in the 2nd innings of their 2nd Test in November 1999?

7. Which horse won the 1998 Irish 1000 Guineas?

8. What nationality is runner Assefa Mezegebu?

9. On which river was the first Olympic rowing competition held?

10. For which Minor Counties cricket side did Ian Bishop play in 1998?

11. Ricardo Tormo was 1978 world 50cc motorcycling champion. What nationality is he?

12. Which golfer was 1960 Sports Illustrated Sportsman of the Year?

13. Which team beat Liverpool 1-0 to win the 1914 F.A. Cup Final?

14. What nationality is judo player Dmitri Budolin?

15. Christa Vahlensieck set a world record for women's 10,000m on 20th August 1975. What time did she run?

ANSWERS: 1. County Kildare **2.** M.S. Atapattu **3.** West Indies **4.** 1969 **5.** Real Madrid **6.** Inzamam-ul-Haq **7.** Tarascon **8.** Ethiopian **9.** River Seine **10.** Devon **11.** Spanish **12.** Arnold Palmer **13.** Burnley **14.** Estonian **15.** 34:01.4.

POP

1. Who was drummer in the group Iron Butterfly?

2. In which year did Jive Bunny and the Mastermixers get to No. 1 with *Swing the Mood*?

3. Which Scottish band recorded the album *Elephant Shoe*?

4. Who had a 1989 Top 10 single with *If Only I Could*?

5. In which year did the Pretenders have a No. 1 single with *Brass in Pocket*?

6. In which year did Bruce Dickinson join Iron Maiden as lead singer?

7. Which studio album by ABC contains the song *When Smokey Sings*?

8. Whose albums include 1993's *San Francisco Days*?

9. Which female singer recorded the 2000 album *Black Diamond*?

10. Which Beatles song was recorded by Dillard and Clark on the 1968 album *Through the Morning, Through the Night*?

11. Which studio album by Madonna includes the song *Take A Bow*?

12. Clinton are an offshoot of which group?

13. Who had a Top 10 hit single in 1990 with *How Am I Supposed To Live Without You*?

14. Who replaced Mark Evans as bass player with AC/DC?

15. Which guitarist recorded the solo album *Vozero*?

SCIENCE

1. Who, in 1983, was the first non-American to fly on a U.S. spacecraft?

2. Who invented the cash register in 1879?

3. Of which planet is Despina a satellite?

4. In which year was physicist Sir Nevill Mott knighted?

5. Pandora is a small satellite of which planet?

6. Which scientist was Professor of Zoology at the University of Freiburg from 1886-1912?

7. What nationality was 17th-century astronomer Christiaan Huygens?

8. Which London museum houses the Cockcroft-Walton particle accelerator?

9. Which American naturalist wrote the 1931 book *Strange Animals I Have Known*?

10. In which county was the chemist Joseph Priestley born in 1773?

11. Approximately how many days does the moon Dione take to orbit Saturn?

12. Of which planet is Ophelia a small satellite?

13. Which German naturalist authored the 1843 work *Travels in New Zealand*?

14. How many elements constitute the Noble Gases?

15. In which year was Saturn's moon Prometheus discovered?

GENERAL KNOWLEDGE

1. Who played Jesus Christ in the 1977 TV drama *Jesus of Nazareth*?

2. Who was the bank-robber partner of Bonnie Parker?

3. Which creatures would live in a formicary?

4. Who authored the 1934 novel *A Handful of Dust*?

5. Who was the author of the book *The One Hundred and One Dalmatians*?

6. What is the name of the promontory at the west end of the Gower Peninsula?

7. In which year did U.S. humorist Ogden Nash die?

8. Who authored the 1879 play *A Doll's House*?

9. Aquae Sulis was the latin name of which city in S.W. England?

10. Which genus of plants includes the cabbage?

11. In darts what is the name given to the mark on the floor behind which a player must stand to throw?

12. Who authored the story *Bartleby the Scrivener*?

13. Hermosillo is the capital of which state of North West Mexico?

14. The 1996 film *A Time To Kill*, starring Sandra Bullock, is based on a novel by which author?

15. What is the name given to the broad sash worn by Japanese women and children as part of their national costume?

ANSWERS: 1. Robert Powell **2.** Clyde Barrow **3.** Ants **4.** Evelyn Waugh **5.** Dodie Smith **6.** Worms Head **7.** 1971 **8.** Henrik Ibsen **9.** Bath **10.** Brassica **11.** Oche **12.** Herman Melville **13.** Sonora **14.** John Grisham **15.** Obi.

THE CARLING PUB QUIZ BOOK

ENTERTAINMENT

1. What nationality was baritone John Brownlee, who died in 1969?

2. In which year did Kathleen Ferrier, the British contralto, die?

3. How many million dollars did Robert De Niro get for the film *Ronin*?

4. Who played Nigel in the Radio 4 soap *The Archers*?

5. Who is Wotan's favourite daughter in Wagner's opera *Siegfried*?

6. Who played Audrey in the 1983 sitcom *Good Night and God Bless*?

7. In which year did Alan Bates make his London stage debut?

8. In which year did *The Goodies* start on TV?

9. Who played Satan in the 1999 film *Little Nicky*?

10. In which year did English theatre manageress Lilian Baylis die?

11. Who composed the 1844 opera *I Due Foscari*?

12. What was Mr. Rumbold's forename in the sitcom *Grace and Favour*?

13. Who played the gentleman thief *Raffles* in the 1930 film?

14. In which year did John Simpson join the BBC as a news reporter?

15. Who directed the 1938 film *Angels with Dirty Faces*?

THE CARLING PUB QUIZ BOOK

SPORT

1. What nationality was world champion triathlete Kirsten Hanssen?

2. Which Swedish cyclist won the 1976 Olympic individual road race title?

3. Who took over as Australian cricket captain against Sri Lanka in September 1999 when Steve Waugh went off with a broken nose during the game?

4. Which famous New York harness race was won in 1988 by Armbro Goal?

5. In cricket, who hit 115 n.o. for Sussex vs. Somerset in their 1999 C.G.U. National League Game?

6. Which team won the 1978 constructors' championship in Formula 1?

7. Which athlete won bronze in the men's 100m at the 1999 World Athletic Championships?

8. Which country won the 1920 and 1924 Olympic rugby union tournament?

9. Who did London Irish play in their 2000 Tetley's Bitter Cup quarter-final?

10. Kevin Kelley was W.B.C. featherweight boxing champion from 1993-5. Which country did he represent?

11. How many golds did Britain win in the 1999 World Athletics Championships?

12. In horse racing, what was the prize money in dollars to the winner of the Dubai World Cup in 1996?

13. In which year was Irish rugby union captain Keith Wood born?

14. Which college American Football player won the 1968 Heisman Trophy?

15. Which pair won the 1967 Wimbledon mixed doubles tennis title?

POP

1. Which member of the Isley Brothers died in a car accident in the 1950s?

2. In which year was Shelby Lynne born?

3. Which group recorded *The Contino Sessions*?

4. Who had a 1989 Top 10 single with *French Kiss*?

5. In which year did country rocker Johnny Horton die in a car crash?

6. Which single by Adam and the Ants contains the line "Ridicule is nothing to be scared of"?

7. Whose debut album is entitled *My Beautiful Demon*?

8. Who recorded the 1979 hit *I'm in the Mood for Dancing*?

9. Which song has Chrissie Hynde recorded for a proposed tribute album to The Doors?

10. Which actor played guitar on Iggy Pop's song *Hollywood Affair*?

11. Which group recorded the album *Gettin' High On Your Own Supply*?

12. Who was the original keyboard player in the group Magazine?

13. Which poet supported Elvis Costello on his *Armed Forces* tour?

14. In which year did the Buzzcocks make their live debut?

15. Which duo had a 1989 Top 10 single with *Drama!*?

ANSWERS: 1. Vernon **2.** 1968 **3.** Death in Vegas **4.** Lil' Louis **5.** 1960 **6.** Prince Charming **7.** Ben Christophers **8.** The Nolans **9.** Touch Me **10.** Johnny Depp **11.** Apollo Four Forty **12.** Bob Dickinson **13.** John Cooper Clarke **14.** 1976 **15.** Erasure.

PEOPLE

1. What is the name of Vanessa Paradis and Johnny Depp's child, born in May 1999?

2. *Oh What A Circus* is which songwriter's autobiography?

3. Lucy Askew died on 9 December 1997. At what age?

4. In which year did gangster Lucky Luciano die?

5. Who invented the Portakabin?

6. In which year was German general Alfred Jodl executed?

7. In which year was Labour politician Gordon Brown born?

8. In which year did Charles De Gaulle die?

9. In which country was painter Emily Carr born?

10. In which year did Jim Callaghan become prime minister?

11. In which country was writer Charles Bukowski born?

12. In which year were Prince Charles and Lady Diana married?

13. In which year was Yuri Andropov elected Soviet president?

14. In which year was Princess Anne created Princess Royal?

15. What is the name of Noel and Meg Gallagher's child born in January 2000?

ANSWERS: 1. Lily-Rose Melody 2. Tim Rice 3. 114 4. 1962 5. Donald Shepherd 6. 1946 7. 1951 8. 1970 9. Canada 10. 1976 11. Germany 12. 1981 13. 1983 14. 1987 15. Anaïs.

GENERAL KNOWLEDGE

1. What is the capital of Mozambique?

2. Who was the Korean servant of *Goldfinger* in a book by Ian Fleming?

3. Which German novelist won the 1972 Nobel prize for literature?

4. Which 1976 film was based on the play *Journey's End*?

5. What is the state capital of Massachusetts?

6. Between which two rivers did the North American Indian people called the Osage formerly live?

7. Who was English leader of the Kentish rebellion in 1450?

8. Who authored the 1821 novel *Kenilworth*?

9. Which crime writer authored the 1946 novel *The Hollow*?

10. In which opera by Puccini is the aria *Nessun Dorma*?

11. In which year did Swedish painter and etcher Anders Zorn die?

12. What type of method of tranport was a dromond between the 12th century and 15th century?

13. What was the name of the bellows-mender in Shakespeare's *A Midsummer Night's Dream*?

14. Which Indonesian president resigned in May 1998?

15. Who was the French composer of the symphonic sketches entitled *La Mer*?